29.95

OAKLAND COMMUNITY COLLEGE
HIGHLAND LAKES LIBRARY
7350 COOLEY LAKE ROAD
UNION LAKE MICHIGAN 48085

DT 15 .P34 1985
Partitioned Africans :
  ethnic relations across
  Africa's international
HL LRC 12/88 $ 29.9

OAKLAND COMMUNITY COLLEGE
HIGHLAND LAKES LIBRARY
7350 COOLEY LAKE ROAD
UNION LAKE MICHIGAN 48085

12/88

PARTITIONED AFRICANS

PARTITIONED AFRICANS

Ethnic Relations across Africa's International Boundaries 1884–1984

EDITED BY
A.I. ASIWAJU

Professor of History and Dean of the Faculty of Arts University of Lagos

ST. MARTIN'S PRESS, NEW YORK

© 1985, University of Lagos Press
All rights reserved. For information, write:
St. Martin's Press, Inc., 175 Fifth Avenue, New York, NY 10010
Printed in Great Britain
First published in the United States of America in 1985
ISBN 0-312-59753-3

Library of Congress Cataloging in Publication Data

Main entry under title:

Partitioned Africans.

    Bibliography: p.
    Includes index.
    1. Africa--Ethnic relations. 2. Africa--History--
1884-1960. 3. Africa--History--1960-   . I. Asiwaju,
A. I., 1939-   .
DT15.P34 1985   323.1'67   84-18002
ISBN 0-312-59753-3

```
DT 15 .P34 1985
Partitioned Africans :
  ethnic relations across
  Africa's international
HL LRC 12/88            $ 29.9
```

PREFACE AND ACKNOWLEDGMENTS

This book is an attempt to focus on the human factor in Africa's international boundaries which existing studies of those boundaries have tended to ignore. While a great deal is known about the diplomacy, particularly the law and politics, which govern state relations across the boundaries, scholarly literature on the border populations and the social, cultural and economic relations they generate across the frontiers is relatively scanty and uncoordinated. Yet this socio-cultural dimension is an important part of the context in which the laws and politics operate. The socio-cultural situation has also been important as a factor in the various types of clandestine activities across the border, activities which have on occasions posed serious threats to state security and a more or less permanent challenge to the economy.

Part of the assumption in this book is that a large part of the sum total of African boundary problems has defied solution precisely because of the over-concentration of official policy and supportive studies on the diplomatic aspects, while cultural aspects have been neglected. All the studies presented here show with repeated emphasis that the attitude of African states, favouring a policy of absolute boundary maintenance, has been and will remain essentially at variance with the realities of social relations across the boundaries. For example, there is little or no correlation between the protracted Kenya-Tanzania conflict, which has led to the official closure of the border between the two states, and the fact of everyday movement and related routine activities of the pastoral Maasai whose homeland straddles the border. The Kenya-Tanzania position is very easily generalised for other African border situations including that of the Aja- and Yoruba-speaking peoples across the Togo-Benin border, which till recently has been one of the most frequently closed borders in the continent.

The findings of the case studies included in this book and the continent-wide phenomenon they represent challenge yet another established position. The studies demonstrate that the continental unity, which is taking so long to achieve at the level of the Westernised African élites and the modern states they lead, has long been in evidence at the level of the African culture areas, which in every case have retained their coherence and resilience despite their division by the inter-state boundaries and the resulting state formation processes. The culture areas on the ground produce behaviour which suggests an avoidance of the attitude of the Westernised élites who, though determined to maintain rather rigidly the state boundaries which divide the continent into territorial states, desire at the same time the unity of the continent.

Achievement of unity at the grassroots level has been based on the essentially logical rejection of the boundaries as lines of separation and acceptance of them as lines of contact. This is why, despite their general awareness of the location of the boundaries drawn through several ancestral territories, inhabitants of the various culture areas have maintained across the boundaries kinship ties and other sociocultural relations, as well as economic activities. Were they to do otherwise — namely accept and respect the new international boundaries as effective lines of division — they would be embarking on a course of self-liquidation as ethnic units.

In order to survive, politically partitioned African groups, like their counterparts in other parts of the world, were assisted by a well-known capacity which enables borderlands communities to function — in the words of Ellwyn Stoddard, a US-Mexico borderlands scholar — as 'differential converter' systems, translating the political, social and economic institutions and conditions from the fringe of the state on one side of the international boundary to the other side. Such a role makes the borderland a region of overlapping culture in terms not only of the identical nature and character of the local people on each side of the frontierline, but also of the influences of the modern states separated by the boundary. The policy recommendations offered in the last chapter are based on the view of borderlands as regions deserving recognition as special areas of states for developmental purposes.

In 1979, when the idea of this book was first conceived, there was no awareness of plans, later implemented, to organise commemorative conferences and launch special publications in 1984/5 in Bremen (West Germany) and in Leipzig and East Berlin (East Germany) to mark the centenary of the Berlin West African Conference of 1884/5. However, the African village-level perspective on the Partition, which involves tacit rejection of Partition, and which this study of partitioned Africans intends to stress, shows the centenary programmes to be irrelevant to most peoples in the borderlands.

We have attempted an 'Area Study' of African borderlands. The task involves, among other demands, the need for adequate and up-to-date ethnographic surveys of the continent, including the parts that relate to the international boundaries. However, several obstacles are encountered here: an oustandingly difficult one is that arising from the problem of the definition of ethnic groups and 'boundaries' in view of the realities of the inter-group penetrations and the continual expansion (contraction also) of ethnic groups and culture areas, usually through migration and marriage. The resulting

Preface and Acknowledgments

difficulty in discerning 'pure types' in most African culture areas is highlighted in the chapters on Senegambia and the Alur, as well as that on the Chewa and the Ngoni. Together with the other methodological difficulties, further elaborated in Chapter 1 and the preamble to the Checklist (pp. 253-6), this question has ruled out the possibility of providing adequate cartographical illustration for every chapter in the book.

The essential message is not that the notion of boundary is new: man in Africa, as elsewhere, is given to organisation into groups, and the concept of state in Africa is shown, by the several accounts of both the centralised and decentralised categories of state, to be especially ancient. What is in focus is the nation-state-type of political boundary, which contrasts sharply with most of the preceding types on account of its exclusivist attributes. The data presented demonstrate that man's inclination, at any rate in Africa, is for boundaries that join rather than those that divide.

Acknowledgments

The book has been made possible by a grant from the University of Lagos Central Research Committee. This has enabled me to undertake continent-wide research trips for the compilation of the checklist of the partitioned groups (pages 253-9). These travels have also facilitated personal contacts with many of the contributors, whose relevant research orientations would otherwise not have been known. The idea of the book itself was fully developed in the course of a four-month study leave at the Hoover Institution at Stanford in 1979, made possible through a Fulbright Award by the United States Council for the Exchange of Scholars. I wish to express my appreciation to the University of Lagos and the US Council for the Exchange of Scholars for their moral and material assistance.

My gratitude is also due to the national universities, research institutions and Nigerian diplomatic missions in the various African countries visited in the course of the research: namely Senegal, Ivory Coast, Upper Volta, Niger, Mali, Benin and Togo in West Africa; Morocco, Egypt and the Sudan in Arab Africa; Ethiopia and Djibouti in the Horn of Africa; Kenya and Tanzania in East Africa; Zambia, Zimbabwe and Botswana in Southern Africa; and Zaire, Congo, Gabon and Cameroon in Central Africa.

Many individuals — too many to be fully listed — offered encouragement and ideas. These include Michael Crowder, formerly Research Professor at the University of Lagos Centre for Cultural Studies, and Professor J.F. Ade. Ajayi with whom I discussed the initial plan for the book. Professor Roland Oliver of the School of

1. Senegal
2. Gambia
3. Guinea (Bissau)
4. Sierra Leone
5. Liberia
6. Togo
7. Benin
8. Equatorial Guinea
9. People's Republic of the Congo [formerly Congo (Brazzaville)]
10. Cabinda (part of Angola)
11. Lesotho
12. Swaziland
13. Malawi
14. Burundi
15. Rwanda
16. Djibouti

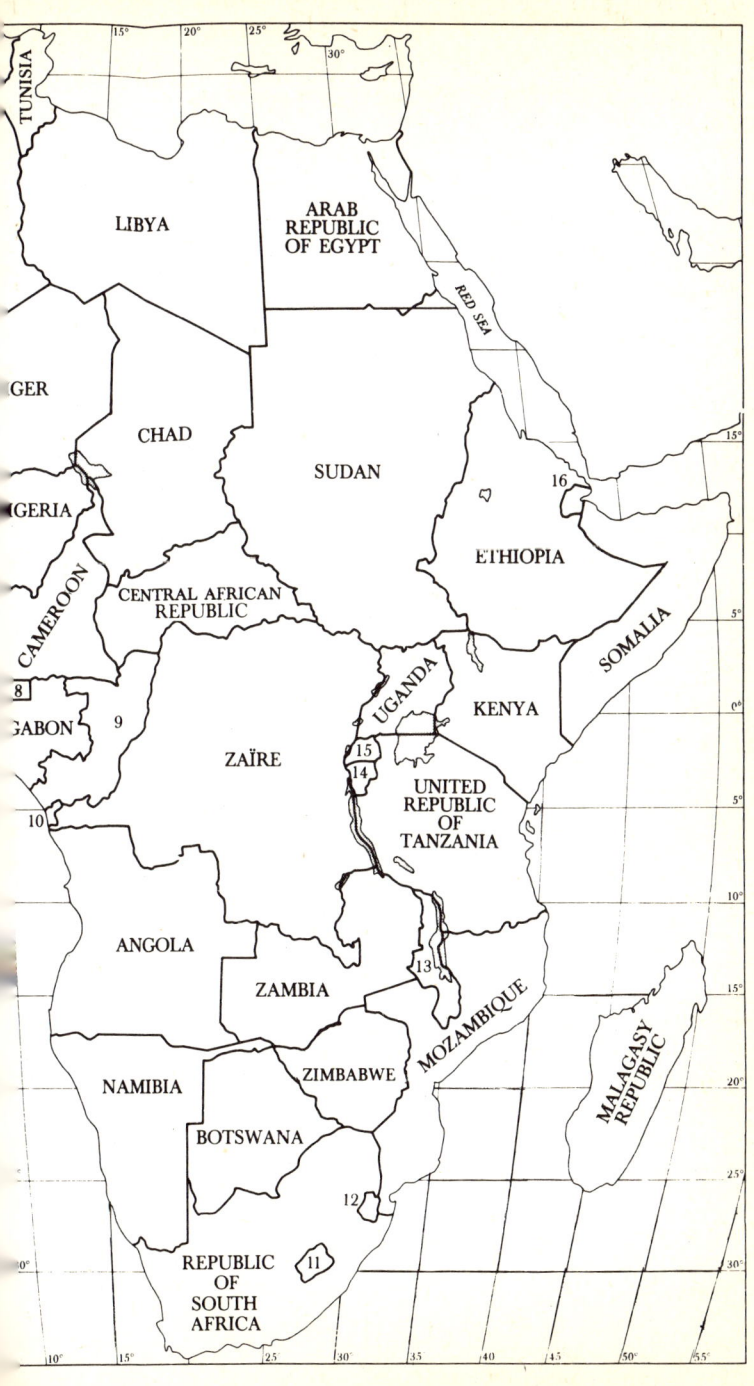

Oriental and African Studies, University of London, and a member of the Minority Rights Group of Britain, first drew my attention to the special feature of mutilated ethnic groups as minority groups; he also pointed out the usefulness of a detailed checklist of the partitioned African culture areas to supplement the case studies. Professor B.A. Ogot of Nairobi and B.I. Obichere of the University of California in Los Angeles, as well as Dr David Laitin of the University of California in San Diego, commented on my initial outline for the project and offered vital bibliographical advice and further introductions.

The special encouragements from within the University of Lagos need to be mentioned. The outstanding names include Professor Akin Adesola, Vice-Chancellor; Professor Michael Durojaiye of our Faculty of Education and formerly Deputy and Acting Vice-Chancellor; Professor N.O. Alao, Dean of Arts throughout the period of the research; Professor I.A. Adalemo of our Department of Geography and current Dean of the Postgraduate School; Professor A. Herbert of our Department of Modern European Languages and Mr S. Tomori of the Department of Economics. Dr Roger Gravil of the Department of History helped with stylistic criticisms. The typists in the History Department typed much of the material.

In the last stage of the preparation of the manuscript, the Director of the Centre for Black and African Arts and Civilization (CBAAC) at the National Theatre in Lagos, Mr Z.S. Ali, was kind enough to allow me the use of the Centre's facilities. Finally, I wish to thank my wife Victoria and my children — Omodele, Olukemi, Omobola and Oluyomi — for having put up with the inconvenience of my frequent absences from home caused by the work.

Needless to say, the book is a co-operative effort of the several experts who have contributed the specific chapters. While I take the responsibility for initiating the project and collating the materials, the merits of the individual contributions must be credited directly to the authors. If the book succeeds in drawing attention to the gap in the existing literature of the persistent problem of Africa's international boundaries, then my own dream will have been to some extent fulfilled.

Imeko, Ogun State, Nigeria A.I. ASIWAJU
June 1984

CONTENTS

Preface and Acknowledgments   *page* v

PART ONE

1. The Conceptual Framework   *A.I. Asiwaju*   1
2. The Making of the Boundaries: Focus on West Africa
   J.D. Hargreaves   19

PART TWO

3. The Mandara astride the Nigeria-Cameroon Boundary
   Bawuro M. Barkindo   29
4. The Kakwa of Uganda and the Sudan: The ethnic factor in national and international politics   *Ade. Adefuye*   51
5. Ethnic Affinity: Partition and political integration in Senegambia   *F.A. Renner*   71
6. Partitioned Alur   *Aidan Southall*   87
7. National Integration, Rural Development and Frontier Communities: The case of the Chewa and the Ngoni astride Zambian boundaries with Malawi and Mozambique   *S.H. Phiri*   105
8. Chiefs and Ethnic Unity in Two Colonial Worlds: The Bakgatla baga Kgafela of the Bechuanaland Protectorate and the Transvaal, 1872–1966
   R.F. Morton   127
9. The Somali Dilemma: Nation in search of a state
   Said S. Samatar   155
10. Partitioned Culture Areas and Smuggling: The Hausa and groundnut trade across the Nigeria-Niger boundary up to the 1970s   *David Collins*   195

PART THREE

11. Partitioned Groups and Inter-State Relations
    Saadia Touval   223
12. The Global Perspective and Border Management Policy Options   *A.I. Asiwaju*   233

Partitioned Culture Areas: A checklist   *A.I. Asiwaju*   252
Select Bibliography   260
Index   267
Notes on the Contributors   274

Part One

1

THE CONCEPTUAL FRAMEWORK

A.I. Asiwaju

Perspective of the study

From the viewpoint of the Western powers concerned and the associated world of Eurocentric scholars and men of affairs, the centenary of the Partition of Africa took place in November 1984. It was in November 1884 that the Berlin West Africa Conference opened;[1] it lasted till February 1885. However, it will be recalled that the Berlin conference, despite its significance for the subsequent history of Africa, was essentially a European affair: there was no African representation, and African concerns were, if they mattered at all, completely marginal to the basic economic, strategic and political interests of the negotiating European powers. Indeed, as we now know, the fact of the Partition was not really made manifest to African peoples and their states and governments until the European powers began the process of conquest (referred to euphemistically in the different colonialist literatures as 'pacification') of the African territories that had been assigned to the respective European nation-states.[2] Against this background, the year 1884 will only be meaningful in terms of a Eurocentric or, analytically, the nation-state structural perspective. In this context the preferred functional approach, which should focus on the localised impact on African peoples, is liable to be neglected.

Our main concern in this book is to emphasise the African perspective of this very important aspect of the continent's history; and here a choice has had to be made between two distinct, though not unrelated, levels of analysis. On the one hand is the perspective of modern African states, which are mostly successors to the colonial entities created in consequence of the European partition. Since the attainment of political independence, there is hardly one of these states which has not had cause to worry about the position of its boundaries *vis-à-vis* its neighbours.[3] The few occasions of actual boundary adjustments — namely those following the referenda organised by the United Nations in Togo in relation to the Gold Coast (later Ghana) in 1956, and in the Cameroons in relation to

Nigeria in 1961; the state merger between Tanganyika and Zanzibar resulting in the present-day United Republic of Tanzania; and the numerous boundary disputes between states, most of which are still to be resolved, point to the conclusion that the Partition of Africa, far from being a closed matter, is an ongoing process the end of which is not in sight. That it is the policy of the Organisation of African Unity (OAU), expressed in one of its maiden resolutions in 1963, that boundaries should be maintained as they were at the independence of member-states, and that the Republic of Somalia and the Kingdom of Morocco have continually objected to this position, makes it clear that the Partition is still far from being settled in such a way as would warrant any celebrations for the centenary.

The other side of the African perspective relates to the attitude in particular African culture areas or ethnic groups which were more immediately affected by the political surgery by being split into two or more colonies and, later, independent African successor-states. While a detailed checklist of the groups is provided as an appendix to this book, we will cite a few examples: the Somali whose essentially continuous culture area was severed into the separate colonies of British Somaliland, French Somaliland, Italian Somaliland, the Northern Frontier District of Kenya and the Ogaadeen province of imperial Ethiopia; the Maasai, cut nearly in half by the Kenya-Tanzania border; the Bakongo across the Gabon-Congo, Congo-Zaire and Zaire-Angola boundaries; the Lunda astride the Zaire-Angola and Zaire-Zambia frontiers; the Zande or the Azande cut by boundaries into different parts in the Sudan, Chad, the Central African Republic and Zaire; the Yoruba and the Aja, each divided between Nigeria, Benin (formerly Dahomey) and Togo; the Gourma truncated into parts located in Upper Volta, Togo and Benin; the Wolof and the Serers of Senegal and the Gambia; the Soninke and the Tukulor across the Senegal-Mauritania boundary; the Tubu mutilated by the Libya-Chad and Chad-Niger borders; the Nubians across the Egypt-Sudan boundary; the Tswana on both sides of the Botswana-South Africa boundary and the cattle-keeping Ova Herero as well as the game-seeking Khoisan Basarwa (the so-called 'Bushmen') astride the Botswana-Namibia border.

In these specifically divided African culture areas, the boundaries have been drawn across well-established lines of communication including, in every case, a dormant or active sense of community based on traditions concerning common ancestry, usually very strong kinship ties, shared socio-political institutions and economic resources, common customs and practices, and sometimes acceptance of a common political control. In many instances, such as the

Uganda-Sudan frontier through the Kakwa territory, the boundaries have separated communities of worshippers from age-old sacred groves and shrines. In other instances, well exemplified by the Somali, the water resources in a predominantly pastoral and nomadic culture area were located in one state while the pastures were in another.

Apart from the division which arises routinely from the mere location of boundaries, partitioned groups were further pulled apart in consequence of the opposing integrative processes set in motion by the different states. Such processes have tended to make the divided groups look in different political, economic and social directions. This has generally been the effect on the partitioned culture areas of the distinct policies which the various states pursue in matters of trade and currency, transport and communication, politics and administration, ideology and education.[4] Different symbols of formal status, above all citizenship, are imposed on the same people.

At local levels, a manifestation of the effort to emphasise separatism has been the systematic application of different cover-names for the same peoples to distinguish between those on different sides of particular inter-state boundaries. This phenomenon often dates back to the establishment of the boundaries themselves. It is especially manifest in regions like West Africa where the two sides of a boundary might fall respectively under the control of different colonial powers, each imposing its own metropolitan culture and particularly its language and orthographic tradition.

Thus for the people who were called the Yoruba in British Nigeria, the name in French Dahomey (now Benin) is 'Nago', which sometimes assumes the characteristic masculine and feminine forms of 'Nagots' and 'Nagottes'.[5] Other examples, again in relation to Nigeria, are the Gude, the Higis and the Matakam who on the Cameroonian side of the common border in the area of the ancient state of Mandara came to be called respectively the 'Djimi', the 'Kapsiki' and the 'Wula'.[6] Other examples include the Kpelle and the Loma in Liberia, referred to respectively as the 'Guerzé' and the 'Toma' in French Guinea;[7] the Baydyaranke in French Guinea or Guinea-Conakry, called the 'Bambaraca' in Portuguese Guinea or Guinea-Bissau;[8] the Fulani in the former British colonies of Nigeria and Sierra Leone, whose kinsmen in the adjacent former French colonies of Niger, Mali and Guinea are often referred to as the 'Peuls'; and the Tubu in French Niger, called the 'Goranes' in Chad.

Despite all these divisive influences, partitioned Africans have nevertheless tended in their normal activities to ignore the boundaries as dividing lines and to carry on social relations across them more or less as in the days before the Partition. The studies of cross-border trade and migrations, which have been undertaken especially in the West African sub-region, show that these activities are on a considerable scale.[9] Judged, therefore, from the viewpoint of border society life in many parts of Africa, the Partition can hardly be said to have taken place.

The purpose of this book is to emphasise the second or village level of the African perspective on the Partition. It is a study of the European partition and the resultant international boundaries as they have affected the borderland areas. The project was originally conceived as an extension of pioneering published researches on the history of Western Yoruba groups split by the Nigeria-Benin (Dahomey) boundary and of the Akan and related groups astride the Gold Coast (Ghana) boundaries with Ivory Coast and Upper Volta.[10] Although these works were primarily comparative case-studies of French and British colonial administrations in West African frontier zones, the materials and analyses also illuminate what A. Pallinder-Law, referring to the Western Yoruba case, appropriately referred to as 'the impact on a culturally relatively coherent area of an international boundary drawn through it'.[11]

This is to be expected in view of boundaries being essentially legal limits for the areas of jurisdiction of distinct political regimes and their respective administrations. Any systematic comparison of the impact of the administrations in the borderlands must therefore subsume the assessment of the impact of the boundaries. The general impression gathered from West African research, especially in relation to the Western Yoruba as a case of partitioned African culture areas, has highlighted the need for a continent-wide survey which will allow for generalisations to be made applying to Africa as a whole.

Objectives

The micro or grass-roots level of analysis has been dictated by two related considerations, namely (1) the need to fill gaps in relevant scholarly literature and (2) the hope that the new insights gained will lead to a reappraisal of the human cost of political divisions generally and the need, in Africa, for a more imaginative policy formulation.

As regards the gaps in existing literature, these are of two types: on political partition generally, and on African partition and the resultant boundary problems in particular. As for the first type, it is necessary to distinguish between the level of partition dealt with in this book and that treated in most existing works on partition.[12]

The latter are works, mostly by experts in international relations and comparative politics, dealing with the relatively spectacular cases of partition. These are imposed, typically, by the United States and the Soviet Union as protagonists in the Cold War between East and West. Examples include Poland, Germany, Korea, China (in relation to Taiwan), Vietnam, Palestine, and Mongolia. Or they deal with the nationalist-oriented divisions in Cyprus, Ireland and (actual and potential) on the Indian sub-continent.

Typical works include that edited by Gregory Henderson, Richard Lebron and John Stoessinger, entitled *Divided Nations in a Divided World* (Mackay, New York, 1974), and R.E. Johnston's *The Politics of Division, Partition and Unification* (Praeger, New York, 1976). A pioneering title covering the same subject is the special issue of the *Journal of International Affairs* (vol. XVIII, no. 3, 1964), entitled 'The Politics of Partition'.

The essays in the present volume differ from these older works not only in terms of the empirical data used but also in the overall conceptual framework. In the existing works, the characteristic definition of partition is that offered by the editor of the special issue of the *Journal of International Affairs* cited above. He defines it as the action of dividing an area forming a single governmental unit into two or more areas under separate authorities.[13] N.J.G. Pound has observed that partition should then be seen as meaning one of two things: it may mean either 'the division of a state so that it loses its identity or even disappears from the political map' or 'the creation of two or more states within a territory which had previously been subjected to only one'.[14] Johnston contributes to this same definition, which is also assumed by Henderson *et al.*, by making partition a political and legal division into two or more politically bounded territories of people who, before that division, showed strong evidence of organisation as a 'sovereign state' or an 'integrated system'.

While this definition has gained currency in the existing literature on the subject, it obviously does not apply to the cases covered in the present work. For whereas the basic factor in the cases covered by the works cited above is that the units subjected to partition were previously established states, the units of analysis in *Partitioned Africans* are mostly culture areas which were not necessarily organised into distinct sovereign states before partition. Thus while in the one situation it is states that have been politically divided into two or more new states; in the second the concern is with culturally coherent territories where peoples of definite cultural identities have had to be split into two or more units, each fraction being placed in the area of jurisdiction of a distinct state which functions to integrate such a part of a pre-existing culture area into a new socio-economic system removed from the original cultural whole. So whereas the older studies emphasise the politics of partition by focussing on the use of state power at both national and international levels to maintain, contain or reverse the division, the essays in this book are designed to stress the human factor by examining the behavior of ethnic groups in situations of partition.

Existing studies of political partition and resultant boundary problems have almost always been approached as studies in international relations in which the border populations are of marginal interest, if of interest at all. For example, it is rare to find studies of European boundaries where the focus has been on the implications for such partitioned culture areas as the French split across the boundaries of France with Belgium and Switzerland or the Germans severed into fractions located in the Federal Republic of Germany, the German Democratic Republic, Austria, Poland and Switzerland.[15] This is true even of studies such as those compiled and edited by Astrid Suhrke and Lela Garner Noble in *Ethnic Conflict in International Relations* (New York, 1977) where, despite the cross-border location of the cases selected, the emphasis is still on the political factor, specifically the interaction between domestic and external politics. Nowhere in the book is there any sustained or systematic discussion of how human problems, including the question of social relations and maintenance of group identity, are managed by the ethnic groups in question in the situation of partition and the conditions of conflict described.

The distinction we have drawn between older studies focussing on divided countries (be these nations or states) and the present work where the stress is on partitioned culture areas or ethnic groups is analytically useful and important. However, we do not suggest that the two are mutually exclusive. The situations categorised as state, nation and ethnicity are, in real life, extremely close to one another. This is especially true of the defining characteristics of ethnic groups such as we have adopted for the present study and those of nationalities. Many sociologists dealing with the micro level have tried to distinguish between ethnic groups and nations as states in terms of the criterion of 'self-determination' or 'aspiration to total autonomy' for the group[16] (usually attributed to states rather than ethnic groups); however, a real problem is encountered in the face of arguments such as those advanced by a host of scholars, including Clifford Geertz and Harold Isaac, that ethnic groups, even when not nations, are potential and often very strong 'candidates for nationhood' by reason of the basic properties which they share with nationalities.[17] Kurdish nationalism and irredentism since the war of 1914–18 is a case in point.[18]

This line of argument is amply supported by the prevailing attitude in Russian ethnography, exemplified in an essay by V. Bromley. Here the term '*ethnos*' or ethnicity is taken as a synonym for the generic term 'people' and understood to refer not just to the comparatively small and technologically backward communities which have commanded the attention of most Western anthropologists. '*Ethnos*' is also the reference to 'peoples' such as the French, the English and the Germans with millions of members living in nation-states of high sophistication.[19] A final illustration of the link between studies of 'state' and those focussing on 'people' is provided in Suhrke and Noble, where the studies demonstrate that at least in politics the developments at the level of 'people' can hardly be pursued to the exclusion of interest at the level of 'state'. Quite apart from the question of ethnic conflicts, the very fact of location astride the boundary between two distinct states and the existence of social relations across that boundary between members of partitioned groups lays the groups open to the suspicion of those two states. We should return to this point in the discussion of the policy implications of the studies in the present volume.

With regard to Africa, the gaps in existing literature, some of which we attempt here to bridge, are easier to show. In his most perceptive and stimulating comparative study of international boundaries, published in 1940, Whittemore Boggs, a geographer in the US State Department, correctly observed in a section entitled 'Effects of African Boundaries upon Native Peoples':

If we inquire how the international boundaries function in Africa, ... the influence of the frontiers upon the indigenous peoples and their response to the placing of boundaries through their ancestral territories deserve primary consideration. Little that bears directly upon the subject has been published; available material is widely scattered ....[20]

More than forty years later, the position remains practically the same. 'Little' that has so far been published 'bears directly upon the subject' in so far as this refers to the effects of the boundaries at grassroot level on 'the indigenous peoples' in the border areas who, like their counterparts in Europe and elsewhere, have been 'affected to an exceptional degree'. It also remains a fact that materials such as are now available are not only few but 'widely scattered'.[21] The extent to which Africans in strictly partitioned situations have continued to be neglected in an admittedly increasing body of literature on African boundaries is expressed in the collaborative work *African Boundary Problems* published by the Scandinavian Institute of African Studies in 1969, which still ranks 'the problems of border populations'[22] as second in the list of priorities for further research.

Four works on African international boundaries published since 1969 seem of sufficient importance to merit attention. These are J.C. Anene, *The International Boundaries of Nigeria, 1885–1960: The Framework of an Emergent African Nation,* (Longman, 1970); J.R.V. Prescott, *The Evolution of Nigeria's International and Regional Boundaries, 1861–1971* (Vancouver, 1971); A.C. McEwen, *International Boundaries of East Africa* (Oxford, 1971); and Saadia Touval, *The Boundary Politics of Independent Africa* (Harvard University Press, 1972). These four books are of interest not only because all of them fail to make the partitioned Africans their focus, but also because of the way they represent the main scholarly interests and perspectives that have dominated African boundary studies hitherto. In a brief review of the contents and general orientations, we hope to point to the gaps in the literature which it is our present purpose to fill.

Let us look first at the inadequacy of attention paid to partitioned Africans. In spite of the tribute of Professor J.F. Ade. Ajayi that Anene's work was concerned not just with 'the foreign acts of partition, but with the impact of colonial boundaries on the people in whose history the acts of partition were a major intervention',[23] the actual focus of the book is on the politics of the partition, on the interaction of European diplomacy and contemporary local African political situations, and the way this affected the evolution of the boundaries, rather than on the peoples through whose territories the lines were drawn (and, in some cases, redrawn) during the period 1885–1960. Nowhere in this otherwise fascinating study does the reader encounter a sustained or systematic discussion of the impact of the boundaries and of the indigenous peoples' modes of response to them. What is specifically argued throughout is the rationale for the various European powers in deciding to put the boundaries where they were, and how nothing really different could have happened in view of the essentially fluid socio-political situations prevailing in the localities where the boundaries were located.

Except for the expected difference in orientation, as between a historian and a geographer, which was shown in the obviously superior narrative skill of Anene and in Prescott's greater emphasis on the spatial aspects (witness, for example, Prescott's preoccupation with concepts like 'allocation', 'delimitation' and 'demarcation' of the boundaries), and his inclusion of a discussion of the regional boundaries, the two books overlap not only in the source materials used but also in their general historical orientation. Both concentrate more on the relevant European diplomatic archives and perceive the local African scene largely through the available anthropological data and the published local histories. Local archives and especially oral historical evidence, which would have had to be tapped if the target of research had been the local African peoples, were largely neglected. The two researchers obviously undertook fieldwork in the boundary areas. Although Prescott would appear to have outdone Anene in this, the concern was more for the geographical aspects — the course of the boundaries and boundary markers than for the human histories and cultures directly affected. Even if the two authors had wished to tap the local resources for their analyses, the sheer size of the area and the multiplicity and diversity of the local languages would have baffled them; neither, as far as is known, spoke as his mother-tongue a local language from along the various Nigerian boundaries.[24]

Nevertheless, just how distinct a different research orientation can be is indicated in what sounds clearly like a digression of Prescott's which took place in Ketu the renowned ancient Yoruba city in the present-day Republic of Benin (formerly Dahomey). In an informal interview with Prescott, the only one of its kind which the present writer can find in his book, the Alaketu (King) of Ketu is reported to have said: 'We regard the boundary as separating the English and the French not the Yoruba.'[25] This statement is identical with that credited to a Maasai warrior protesting against the 1898 Anglo-German Boundary Commission carrying out the demarcation of the Laitokitok section of the present-day Kenya-Tanzania boundary; the commissioners, he said, 'were labouring under a misapprehension, as the land belonged, not to the European, but to his own tribe . . . .'[26] These two declarations, made independently by spokesmen of widely different African cultures separated by thousands of miles and over sixty years, indicate a fundamental unity of view and opinion of partitioned African groups. In Ketu area, as elsewhere in Africa, the statement summarised the *modus operandi* for a cultural or ethnic cohesion across and in spite of the boundary throughout the colonial period and beyond.[27]

McEwen's and Touval's works may equally be criticised on the basis of the lack of emphasis on African border populations. Both deal specifically with border disputes. However, while McEwen's study is designed to help a better understanding of the issues of international law involved, Touval discusses and analyses the political dimension of the problem. Although African societies and communities on the ground receive some consideration, the real terms of reference are the states. A comparison of the attitudes in these two books with those in the works reviewed above shows clearly that the diplomatic historian and most political geographers are not too different from the academic lawyer and political scientist in their common disregard for, and marginalisation of, the partitioned Africans. McEwen puts the case of international law very bluntly:

> The legal status of African communities, as traditionally defined in the writings of classical Western jurists, has been that of mere *objects* of international law whose disposition was controllable only by recognized states that alone constituted true international *subjects*. Nor did it appear to matter whether or not the communities succeeded in ousting the control of the foreign state by force, for this was not regarded as a conquest in the international legal sense.[28]

A similar lack of concern or sympathy for local African peoples is shown by Saadia Touval who suggests, largely out of ignorance of the dynamics of history in the various African localities at the time of the partition, that rather than continue to hold them as victims of a historical circumstance, "it would be more accurate to describe African societies as naive."[29] The fact is that these two studies are designed to examine not the problems of local African peoples but relations between states.

This failure so far to focus on the border populations and in so doing to assess the human factor in the African experience of political partition can therefore be explained first and foremost in terms of the obsession of the academic disciplines hitherto connected with boundary studies. International law, international relations, political geography and diplomatic history are all, by definition, studies of states and not of ethnicities or peoples. This has influenced the type of data so far used; and it is significant that, until very recently when research such as that which has resulted in the present volume began to be pursued, scholars engaged in African boundary studies invariably confined themselves to diplomatic archives either of the former colonial powers or of the African successor-states and to the documentation centres of relevant international organisations. The need for a balance between traditional desk research and intensive field investigation, both of which have been emphasised as components in the methodology for the essays in this book, was neglected.

Secondly, there is the confining effect of the boundaries themselves on scholarly interests and pursuits, for just as the boundaries set the limits of the areas of jurisdiction of particular states, the exercise of authority by the states effectively restricted most human activities, including intellectual pursuits, within the boundaries. One terrible effect of colonial partition on Africans has been the establishment of different colonial educational systems and the introduction of official language barriers and a general cultural alienation of the Western-educated Africans one from another even in areas along state boundaries where the educated élites on both sides have the shared background of a common African culture.[30] One manifestation of this alienation was the colonialisation and eventual nationalisation of African intellectual efforts. Consequently researches, especially in the relevant fields of the humanities and the social sciences, which should naturally extend across state boundaries, are generally terminated near or at the borders. This remarkable weakening of scholarly interests in cross-border researches then came to form part of the larger issue of a general neglect of African borderlands by the secular authorities. Thus, exactly as roads and other developmental projects usually peter out as one approaches the boundaries from the centres of intensive acculturation within individual states, so also does the interest of the scholar and the researcher.

Policy implications

The implications for policy raised by the studies presented arise from the location of the selected ethnic groups close to and across boundaries separating two or more distinct states. There are both national and international levels to consider. Within each of the individual states in which a given fraction of a partitioned group is located, there is need for an alternative developmental strategy to achieve a greater measure of integration of the border community than is in evidence. All the cases suggest that border areas and populations are more neglected than those removed from the borders. In almost every African state, border areas are treated as fringe or marginal areas of the state's territory: all the modernisation processes, so much in evidence in the core areas of the states, dwindle as they approach the boundaries. This is probably due to strategic considerations and the urban rather than rural bias of developments.

In many cases, government authorities within states do not know precisely where their states' boundaries are located. It is common knowledge, for example, that most of Africa's 103 international boundaries, amounting to a total length of about 50,000 miles and ranging from the short Nigeria-Chad border of approximately 50 miles to the Zaire-Angola and the Sudan-Ethiopia borders of 1,485 and 1,460 miles respectively, are undemarcated and unpatrolled.[31] Not only has this been so since the conventional definition of the boundaries but, in the opinion of at least one African expert, this position should be maintained by African states in view of the enormous financial costs that would otherwise be involved and the need to avoid the likely negative reactions not only among the states themselves but also among the partitioned ethnic groups in the border areas, most of whom are nomads and pastoralists well-known for their fierce character.[32] The result all over Africa has been an enormous movement of men and material across the boundaries which, as Collins' fascinating study of the Nigeria-Niger case has shown, have invariably functioned less as 'barriers' than as 'conduits' between the states on either side.[33] As the essays suggest, border regions in Africa have always evolved as special areas of socio-political ambivalence, where the loyalty of the local peoples to either of the states sharing the particular culture areas has not been, and never could have been, very strong. Rather than develop a strong sense of attachment to either of the states separated by the boundary, African border populations have at best evolved attitudes and characteristics suggesting a preference for some measure of binationality or dual citizenship.

At the level of the relations between states on either side of a boundary which divides ethnic groups, the presence of portions of the same people in the respective states and the fact of intra-group relations across the particular boundaries cannot but be expected to exercise an important influence. This point is easily illustrated by the significance accorded in existing literature on African boundary conflicts to the factor of partitioned groups or 'population overhang' in disputed areas. While a recent empirical and comparative analysis of this question by J.B. Boyd, Jr, has argued convincingly that the explanatory power of this factor has been much smaller than the existing works have tended to ascribe to it,[34] the fact of partition of single culture areas and the resultant presence of the same people on both sides of inter-state boundaries offer African politicans the opportunity from time to time and from place to place to use this as a pretext for disputes which are often begun and pursued for other more tangible reasons.[35]

But whether as pretexts or real causes of boundary disputes, border populations and the relations they generate across the boundaries have functioned as catalysts and compelling influences on the quality of communication between the respective political regimes and administrations existing on both sides of the boundaries. This point has been especially significant in West Africa where rival and essentially parallel administrations of contiguous French and British colonies are known to have been obliged to open up communication with one another.[36]

There are, therefore, two broad policy questions. The first is how best to resolve the conflict between the attitudes of partitioned groups which tend to ignore the boundaries and the states which are preoccupied with ensuring full effectiveness of the boundaries as lines of demarcation between separate areas of jurisdiction. Second and related to the first is the question as to how states' responsibilities regarding boundary maintenance can best be pursued with the minimum strain on the communities located along the boundaries. As is suggested in the case studies, the most desirable solution is for the African international community, like their counterparts elsewhere in the world,[37] to be persuaded to view with favour efforts at reducing boundary function in the continent. In other words, African states must consider themselves to have now reached the stage at which the Eurocentric and generally outmoded notion of sovereignty, which at their inception led the independent states to insist dogmatically on maintaining their territorial boundaries, should be seriously questioned.

While the need for this has already been recognised, as the history and activities of several multinational and bilateral organisations operating in Africa has shown,[38] the usual economic arguments must be broadened by studies to show that the human cost incidental to the alternative policy of absolute boundary maintenance can also be reduced. Policy should be directed to achieve a harmony between the interests of partitioned groups whose members have to cross the boundaries and the states who exercise control over cross-border movements. One important policy recommendation, offered with specific reference to the Somali case but equally applicable elsewhere, is that special governmental arrangements should be evolved at the local level to accommodate the idiosyncracies of the border societies. Where, as in the Somali case, the groups show strong feelings of solidarity, they should be organised into distinct local governments with capacities to relate across the given borders. In this way the boundaries can be maintained and promoted as lines of mutual contact rather than of exclusion.

The Case Studies

This book aims at a continental coverage and has been made to rest, as much as possible, on carefully selected cases intended to reflect Africa's extremely diverse situations. There have been three main types of level of diversity to be balanced: (1) the main types of political regime or administrative tradition prevailing along Africa's numerous boundaries; (2) the variety of African cultures and culture areas that have been partitioned; and (3) the main geographical regions.

These three bases are not mutually exclusive; and so it has been possible to select cases where more than one of the three criteria are combined. For example, the Hausa and the Mandara cases can be seen as representative of situations, mostly in West Africa, where distinct colonial administrations operated in a parallel fashion along particular inter-state boundaries. This explains the comparability of the findings in the Nigeria-Niger and the Nigeria-Cameroon cases. On the same score, not only is it valid to consider the Somali as typifying the situation in the Horn of Africa; the case can also be viewed as representative of reactions in nomadic and pastoral culture areas, including those of the West African Fulani, the Saharan-Sahelian Tuaregs, the Maasai of the Kenya-Tanzania border region, and the Ova Herero across the Botswana-Namibia boundary. As for a balance among the regions, West Africa has been focussed in the Mandara, Hausa and Senegambia cases; East and Central Africa in the cases of the Kakwa, the Chewa and the Ngoni; Southern Africa through the Bakgatla baga Kgafela; while the Somali case adequately reflects the situation in the Horn.

As in all works based on the type of assumptions made here, problems of explanations and analysis arise, typically: Why are there differences in the articulation of dissatisfaction although most of the case studies demonstrate the validity of Tolstoy's observation, noted by Gregory Henderson, that 'every divided country or partitioned people is unhappy'?[37] Why are the Somali the only partitioned group in Africa among whom reactions have taken the form of an active nationalist movement? Why have the Ewe of Togo and Ghana failed to organise themselves in the same way despite repeated expressions of their spokesmen in favour of re-unification for reasons similar to those used by the Somali? What explains the relative inarticulacy of the Yoruba and the Gourmantche who, like the Somali, were split among more than two distinct states? Why are the Sahrawi — the common name assumed by the peoples of the ex-Spanish colony of the Western Sahara now claimed by Morocco — organised into a nationalist movement under the Polisario banner in a manner similar to the Somali case, despite the fact of their ethnic diversity? Why the differences in basic similarities and the similarities in basic differences? What continental pattern has emerged for Africa and what are the implications for the wider world of divided peoples? What are the conditions, if any, which convert cases of inarticulacy to actively organised forms, and vice versa?

These questions are of both theoretical and practical interest; and it was largely to provide some meaningful discussion of the issues raised that the present studies were commissioned. Authors of case studies were, from the start, given uniform guidelines as to the type

The Conceptual Framework

of issues to be investigated and the sources of information to be tapped. The details of the themes covered include

(1) a discussion of the pre-partition situation to show the degree of pre-colonial cultural and historical unity;
(2) a brief history of the partition;
(3) effects of the boundary upon the African group(s) concerned. The discussion here is designed to cover such issues as (*a*) the general character of government policies on both sides of the boundary during and since the colonial period; (*b*) cross-border trade; (*c*) cross-border migrations and the patterns of border population and settlement; (*d*) minority problems including incidents of irredentism, if any; (*e*) a general discussion of the impact of the boundary on the affected African cultures; (*f*) the effects of the relations prevailing between the metropolitan European cultures concerned and the effects of the contact between those cultures and the particular African cultures on the ground; and (*g*) policy recommendations.
(4) the methodology advised was to use primary sources, preferably the relevant local archives supplemented by oral evidence obtained directly from partitioned peoples themselves.

This guideline is not a straitjacket. While all contributors were selected on evidence of direct research experience in their various subjects, the specialisations and disciplinary backgrounds vary and are accommodated. Thus, while all contributors have addressed the issues contained in the third guideline, the emphasis has varied according to the specific aspects of border society life on which the different authors have focussed in their researches. All the case studies touch on the various aspects of the local peoples' responses to partition, but emphasis and the types of categorisation have differed. Thus while some notes on smuggling or cross-border trade are included in the studies of Mandara and the Bakgatla ba Kgafela, the special emphasis in each of these is on the primordial pull exercised by cultural or group awareness. On the other hand, the central concerns in the cases of the Chewa and the Ngoni and the Hausa are with the specifically economic dimensions, despite reference to chieftaincy institutions. Likewise, the Somali case is a contribution to the knowledge of the subject as it relates to the more specifically political area. The Kakwa case study focusses on the significance for international relations.

The book has three parts. Following the first, introductory part are the six case studies which make up Part II. Chapter 9, based on Hausa data, provides the bridge between these pure case studies and the last two chapters which are devoted to the discussion of policy questions. The checklist and select bibliography are designed not only to highlight the continental and global dimensions of the subject and to supplement the case studies, but also to suggest directions for further research.

It is easy to notice the near-absence of concern for theory. The descriptions suggest the stress that is intended to be placed on the plain facts of the situation. A good part of the research task in the field is still concerned with the collection and collation of the primary data. Further research, which the present efforts are hoped to generate, should lead ultimately to a state of more rigorous analysis and of confident generalisation and theorisation.

NOTES

1. For a study of the Conference, see S.E. Crowe, *The Berlin West African Conference, 1884–1885* (London, 1942). A well-articulated proposal for a commemorative programme in 1984 was that of *Archiv* in West Germany (*West Africa* of 20 Dec. 1982, 28 Feb. 1983 and 29 Aug. 1983).
2. Of the studies of the European conquest, mention can be made of Michael Crowder (ed.), *The West African Resistance* (London, 1971) and A.S. Kanya-Forstner, *The Conquest of Western Sudan: A study in military imperialism* (London, 1969).
3. Samples of work done on this subject include Saadia Touval, *The Boundary Politics of Independent Africa* (Harvard University Press, 1972); C.G. Widstrand (ed.), *African Boundary Problems* (Uppsala, 1964); and A. Ajala, *Pan-Africanism* (New York, 1974).
4. For a case study of the differential impact, see A.I. Asiwaju, *Western Yorubaland Under European Rule, 1889–1945: A comparative analysis of French and British colonialism* (Longman, 1976).
5. Other related examples in the Yoruba culture area included "Shabe" in British Nigerian documentation and 'Savé' in the French Dahomeyan for the Yoruba sub-group normally referred to as the 'Sabe'; and 'Ohori' in British Nigeria and 'Hollidje' or 'Hollidge' in French Dahomey for another Yoruba sub-group who call themselves 'Ije' (see 'Notes on Names' in Asiwaju, *op. cit.*).
6. These details are contained in B. Barkindo's study of the Mandara in this volume (pp. 29–49).
7. I owe the information on Liberia-Guinea (Conakry) to Professor James Gibbs of Stanford whose anthropological research has focussed on the Kpelle of Liberia.
8. See Ibrahima Diallo, 'Border Migrations: A Survey of the Senegambian Rural Areas 1970–1971' (Dakar; IDEP 1972), p. 16.
9. For studies of cross-border trade, see A. Modjannagni, 'Quelques aspects historiques, économiques et politiques de la Frontière Nigéria-Dahomey, *Etudes Dahoméennes*, (NS) 1, 1963-4, pp. 17–59; J.D. Collins, 'The Clandestine Movement of Groundnut Across the Niger-Nigeria Boundary', *Canadian Journal of African Studies*,10, 2, 1976, pp. 254–78; O.J.P. Igue, *Le commerce de contrebande et les problèmes monétaires en Afrique Occidentale* (Cotonou: Centre de Formation Administrative et de Perfectionnement, 1977), p. 56. On cross-border migrations, see Asiwaju, 'Migration as revolt: the example of the Ivory Coast and the Upper Volta before 1945', *Journal of African History*, IVII, 4, 1976, pp. 557–91. and I. Diallo, *op. cit.*

The Conceptual Framework   17

10. See Asiwaju, *Western Yorubaland, op cit.*, and his 'Migration as Revolt', *op. cit.*
11. See A. Pallinder-Law's review in *Journal of African History*, XVIII, 3, 1977, p. 463.
12. Although internal administrative boundaries like those in Nigeria and Uganda are known to have partitioned culture areas and historical states with political consequences similar to those produced by the inter-state or international boundaries, they are analytically excluded from this book. But for a case study of each internal boundaries, readers can see O. Adejuigbe, *Boundary Problems in Western Nigeria* (Ife, 1977), and the review of it by A.I. Asiwaju in *Africa* (London: I.A.I.), 48, 2, 1978, pp. 194–5.
13. See the Editor's foreword in the special issue *Journal of International Affairs*, XVII, 3, 1964, p. vii.
14. N.J.G. Pound, 'History and Geography: a perspective on partition', *Journal of International Affairs*, XVIII, 3, 1964, p. 162.
15. For a strong confirmation of this observation, see J.W. House, 'The Franco-Italian Boundary in the Alpes Maritimes', *Translations of the Institute of British Geographers*, 26, 1959, pp. 107–31, one of the demonstrably few efforts to fill this very important gap in knowledge. House significantly states: 'Studies of the broad effects of boundary change upon the economics of the States concerned are more numerous than those of localised results in the economy and social life of frontier communities' (p. 107). Writing in 1965, J.R.V. Prescott, in his short but extremely useful book *The Geography of Frontiers and Boundaries* (London, 1965), was still of the view that 'Few workers have selected this subject [the study of border landscapes] as the focus of their study.'
16. Crawford Young, cited in A. Suhrke and L.G. Noble (eds), Ethnic Conflict in *International Relations* (New York: Praeger, 1977), p. 4.
17. Clifford Geertz and Harold Isaac cited in Suhrke and Noble (eds), *Ethnic Conflict*, op, cit., p. 4.
18. See George S. Harris, 'The Kurdish Conflict in Iraq' in Suhrke and Noble (eds), *op. cit.*, pp. 68–92.
19. V. Bromley, 'On the Typology of Ethnic Communities' in R.E. Holleman and S.A. Arutiunov (eds), *Perspectives on Ethnicity* (Paris, 1978), p. 15.
20. S. W. Boggs, *International Boundaries: A Study of Boundary Functions and Problems* (New York: Columbia University Press, 1940), p. 169.
21. These include Asiwaju, *Western Yorubaland, op. cit.*, which remains the only full-scale case study so far; Mondjannagni, *op. cit.*; L.R. Mills, 'An Analysis of the Geographical Effects of the Dahomey-Nigeria Boundary' (unpubl. Ph.D. thesis, Durham, England, 1970); D.J. Thom, 'The Niger-Nigeria Border-lands' (unpubl. Ph.D. thesis, Michigan State University, 1970), also his 'The Niger-Nigeria Boundary 1890–1906: A Study of Ethnic Frontiers and a Colonial Boundary' (Athens; Ohio University Centre for International Studies, 1975); J.D. Collins, Government and Groundnut Marketing in Rural Hausa Niger' (unpubl. Ph.D. thesis, S.A.I.S., John Hopkins University, 1974), also his 'Clandestine Movement of Groundnut across the Niger-Nigeria Boundary', *op. cit.*, pp. 25–278. The present effort is to pool these materials together in a handy form.
22. C.G. Widstrand (ed.), *African Boundary Problems* (Uppsala, 1964), p. 180.
23. Anene, *op. cit.*, p. x.
24. Anene's claims (p. xvii) on the use of 'oral tradition' are not quite borne out by the book.
25. Prescott, *op. cit.*, p. 103.
26. McEwen, *op. cit.*, p. 148.
27. For details see Asiwaju, 'The Alaketu of Ketu and the Onimeko of Meko: The Changing Status of Two Yoruba Rulers Under French and British Colonialism

and Independence', a chapter in Crowder and Ikime (eds) *West African Chiefs* (University of Ife Press, 1970) and the Appendix to this book.
28. McEwen, p. 16. A monumental addition to works on the legal perspective is Ian Brownlie, *African Boundaries: A legal and diplomatic encyclopaedia* (London; C. Hurst, 1980).
29. Touval, *op. cit.*, p. 4. The analysis by Anene and, in a smaller area, by Asiwaju (*Western Yorubaland*, Chs. 1 and 2), of the historical situations in what became the boundary areas of modern Nigeria cannot lead one to accede to the judgement of Africans as 'naive'.
30. For the Yoruba case, see Asiwaju, *Western Yorubaland*, ch. 10.
31. These details are contained in Boggs, *op. cit.*, pp. 213–15; R. Hodgson and E. Storeman, *The Changing Map of Africa* (London, 1968), p. 63, cited in B.A. El-Gaali, 'Boundaries in Africa: A Case Study of the Diplomatic Evolution and Legal Aspects of the International Boundaries of the Sudan, With Special Emphasis on the Boundary with Egypt' (unpubl. Ph.D. thesis, University of London, 1975), p. 29.
32. El-Gaali, *op. cit.*, p. 33, Dr El-Gaali is currently the Director of the Dept. of International Boundaries, Ministry of Interior, Khartoum, Sudan.
33. Collins, *op. cit.*,
34. J.B. Boyd. Jr, 'African Boundary Conflict: an empirical study', *African Studies Review*, XXII, 3, 1979, pp. 1–14.
35. Depending on particular cases, Boyd lists these other factors: the degree of domestic ethnic homogeneity, the salience of ethnicity domestic politics, general domestic unrest, élite or leadership instability, and resultant personality and/or ideological conflicts, and the gap between a country's size and the dimension of influence wielded or intended to be wielded (Boyd, p. 3).
36. Asiwaju, *Western Yorubaland, op. cit.*, ch. 6; Asiwaju, 'Migration as Revolt', *op. cit.*, and Asiwaju, 'Socio-Economic Integration of the Western African Sub-region in Historical Context: Focus on the European Colonial Period', *Bulletin de l'IFAN*, Dakar, T. 40, série B, 1978, pp. 160–78.
37. For notes on boundary regimes and effects on border population outside Africa, see Boggs, *op. cit.*, pp. 96–133, on aspects of the European Boundaries. What Boggs suggested for Europe in the late 1930s has been fulfilled especially in the 1970s and 1980s by the inauguration of trans-border associations and cooperations in Europe through the instrumentality of the Council of Europe.
38. The Mano River Union is a customs union between Sierra Leone and Liberia; the Lake Chad Commission is an organisation in which all the states bordering on the Lake Chad — Nigeria, Chad, Niger and Cameroon — are represented; the Senegambian Liaison Office, located in Banjul, was jointly set up by the Gambia and Senegal to look after interests common to the two geographically and ethnographically interlocking states.
39. Henderson *et al.* (eds), *Divided Nations in a Divided World, op. cit.*

2
THE MAKING OF THE BOUNDARIES
FOCUS ON WEST AFRICA[1]
J.D. Hargreaves

Explanations of historical development can be broadly classified in three groups: the determinist, the conspiratorial and the accidental (or, more vulgarly, the 'cock-up') theories. So many African boundaries appear arbitrary and irrational that it seems impossible to explain their demarcation (as distinct from the wider historical context of the European partition) by any determinist hypothesis. Conspiracy theories are more tempting; surely only positive malevolence can explain some of those geometrical constructions through the centres of living communities. But to what end? Explanation seems difficult without ample recourse to H.A.L. Fisher's formula of 'the contingent and the unforeseen'. Yet study of the records usually reveals a certain short-term rationality within the narrow horizons of the respective European negotiators; it was the accidental convergence of these, with the ensuing conflicts and compromises, which determined the final outcome. The roads along which accidents take place have usually been constructed with some purpose; and the aim of this essay is to sketch the changing historical context within which those durable boundaries were provisionally fixed. It will involve one more look at the behaviour of the fighting elephants, though it will suggest that their behaviour was not unaffected by events in the grass beneath their feet.[2]

During most of the nineteenth century Europeans were able to pursue their purposes in tropical Africa — usually as traders or as missionaries — without needing, or desiring, to make major encroachments on the territorial sovereignty of African states. The object of 'free-trade imperialism' was to extend the area open to European activity, rather than to establish national reservations; most of the small coastal colonies originated as leases held at the pleasure of an African landlord. What the Europeans needed, said Guizot in 1843, were 'strong and secure maritime stations .... to support our commerce'[3]: this coincided with the perception of African rulers like Al Haj 'Umar that 'the whites are only traders'. In Senegambia, one area where inland penetration seemed feasible, the Vienna settlement of 1815 confirmed a *de facto* partition of waterways, not land; the French controlled access from the ocean to the

Senegal river, the British held a dominant position in the Gambia, the Portuguese were left a consolation prize in the Rio Grande. Inter-European conflicts did occur but to the chagrin of the home governments, which assumed there was plenty of room for all. 'Friendly European nations ought to avoid *elbowing* each other ... in such countries as Africa,' wrote a British official in 1866.[4]

By that date, it is true, elbowing was becoming more frequent: British and French officials were claiming incompatible rights by virtue of treaties with African rulers, or of their own military and naval action. Sometimes (for example during Faidherbe's governorship in Senegal, 1854–61 and 1863–5) this can be attributed to imperialistic ambition — the conscious desire to assert power, or to promote specific economic interests. More often, the immediate cause was the need of governors of the small coastal colonies, obliged as they were to finance their own administration out of local revenue, to collect customs duties on European trade. Although initially their right to do this usually rested on treaties, wittingly or unwittingly signed by African rulers, this form of indirect taxation was not welcomed by those engaged in commerce (of whatever nationality, European or African); not surprisingly, the establishment of a customs house was commonly followed by a displacement of trade to coasts where taxes were payable only to the African ruler. Thus, when heavy liquor and tobacco duties were imposed at Lagos in 1863, French and Brazilian importers switched much of their business to Porto Novo, where a fierce Anglo-French struggle for power began.

This particular local confrontation was in many ways typical of a new phase in international rivalry on the West African coast, not least because African rulers joined in to exploit the situation to their own short-term advantage. Although French and British objections were initially confined to the shores of the coastal lagoon, the line along which they finally partitioned south-west Yorubaland in 1889 largely reflected the territorial and dynastic objective of King Tofa.[5] During the 1860s, '70s and '80s the British, French, and later German governments, without any initial intention to extend their colonial empires over African populations, repeatedly claimed fiscal sovereignty over strips of coast. By 1884 this coastal 'scramble' had extended to Eastern and South-Western Africa, and the Berlin Conference was convened to bring a little order into the inter-European rivalries which had been engendered. Henri Brunschwig emphasises that even now European statesmen did not intend to partition Africa into colonial dependencies; 'they were not talking of partitioning Africa but rather of ensuring the continuation of the traditional free-trading system on its coasts and its great rivers.'[6] Only in

The Making of the Boundaries: West Africa

a few exceptional areas, such as the Senegal valley and the southern Gold Coast, could one talk of colonial administration in 1884.

The following year however saw wide extension of 'jurisdictional imperialism' through the elastic device of the Protectorate.[7] This nebulous legal concept acquired a new popularity because it seemed to offer a method of asserting rights which other European governments could recognise without extending the protector's administrative obligations in the countries which were being exploited commercially. The early partition treaties were essentially allocations of fiscal resources, and of responsibility for maritime police; their negotiators were not envisaging problems of administering the African interior. Nevertheless colonial governors were increasingly led to expand their political power, not only through economic pressure and patriotic fervour, but to support the interests of African collaborators on whose consent the fiction of Protectorate depended.

It emerged that the territories within which Africans pursued their interests rarely corresponded to the allocated spheres of European influence. Thus an agreement of 1882 concerning the Northern Rivers of Sierra Leone (which were also the *Rivières du Sud* of Senegal) allocated the basin of the Mellacouric to France, that of the Scarcies to Britain; this bisected not only Samu chiefdom, but the commercial, religious and political unities of a wider historical arena within what has been called 'the Sierra Leone-Guinea system'.[8] (This was not exactly a 'culture area', since Susus, Temnes and Limbas spoke different languages and were bound together by conflicts as much as by communities of interest.) Had the European negotiators been able to envisage the future problems of government in their region, they might have sought some wider arrangement, which could have done less violence to African trade-routes, and enabled them to evolve more coherent policies towards their African neighbours; but by the time the disadvantages of the line became apparent, interests and attitudes had hardened and any substantial revision of what had been agreed proved beyond the range of European statecraft.

The Anglo-French 'Arrangement' of 10 August 1889 marked a reluctant recognition that the old system of free trade imperialism in West Africa would have to be replaced by one involving fixed colonial boundaries. Recognising 'the practical impossibility of putting timely and adequate checks upon the acquisitive energies of officers employed in remote and unexplored countries',[9] British and French diplomatists sat down in Paris to draw lines which would keep them apart in four areas of colonial conflict. From purely metropolitan viewpoints, it did not matter greatly where the boundaries were set, although the French were anxious to exclude all

British influence from the upper basin of the Niger while the British (apart from their important interests in Nigeria, which they believed to be already secure) wanted to place a substantial territorial buffer around Freetown harbour. The more progressive imperialists, like Augustus Hemming of the Colonial Office, favoured a comprehensive partition, following the 10th parallel from the mouth of the river Pongos to 4° West and thence going directly north-east to a place called Burrum on the Niger, with British settlements on the Gambia exchanged against the French outposts in Dahomey and the Ivory Coast. Such a crude carve-up would have greatly reduced the number of African peoples doomed to partition; ironically it was British ministers' fears that one African community, the Creoles of Banjul, might create political difficulties which preserved the identity of British Gambia, and ensured the eventual fragmentation of colonial West Africa.

Failing such a simple and radical allocation of responsibilities, it was necessary to draw many boundaries. An Anglo-French Commission of diplomatists and colonial experts was formed for this purpose, but the limits of its expertise soon became evident. Lord Salisbury sardonically explained how, in the cause of international peace,

We have been engaged in drawing lines upon maps where no white man's feet have ever trod; we have been giving away mountains and rivers and lakes to each other, only hindered by the small impediment that we never knew exactly where the mountains and rivers and lakes were.[10]

Although geographers were available to advise, European knowledge of the physical, let alone the human, geography of Africa was still rudimentary. Although a famous epigram defines geography as being about maps rather than chaps, its value is always defined by the knowledge of the chaps who draw the maps. In 1889 the French geographical expert, a Foreign Ministry official called Desbuissons, relied on a map drawn up five years earlier by Captain P.L. Monteil to define a line which seemed to meet the objective of excluding Britain from the upper Niger basin. Later, on comparing the location of Timbo as fixed by other travellers, he concluded that this line had had a precisely contrary effect.[11] Fortunately, the British were prepared to agree to an alteration; but this only made Desbuissons more determined to uphold his own interpretation of such questions as the route traversed by E.W. Blyden in 1872, which had somehow become one of the criteria for defining the boundary under that 1889 Arrangement. The British however had their own experts, officers of the War Office Military Intelligence, who remained equally confident in their own back-room topography.[12]

Faced with this combination of ignorance and intransigence among the colonial experts, diplomatists whose concern was with the wider relationships of European nations groped for some criterion which, in each individual case, would point to an unambiguous line of partition. Although it may seem that this could have been best provided by following existing African boundaries, well-defined territorial sovereignty had not become a general rule in Africa, as it had in Europe. The experts of the British Military Intelligence Department crudely simplified this problem of assigning firm boundaries to mobile populations, and in multi-ethnic areas:

The tribes themselves have as a rule no idea of territorial limits, their locations are constantly changing, and there often exist small tribes between the large ones which owe allegiance sometimes to the one and sometimes to the other.[13]

Rather than attempting to follow the boundaries of states whose rulers might not be able to describe them accurately, the French preferred to allocate territory along some natural feature like a watershed.[14] But often even topographical features could not be identified on the ground in the form envisaged; the classic case was the Rio del Rey, accepted as the Nigeria-Cameroon boundary in an Anglo-German agreement, which proved to be an estuary receiving several small streams.[15] The safest way to avoid ambiguity and consequent conflict might thus be to use lines of latitude and longitude, which ought to prove capable of objective survey; 'it is a question if a wrong line is not better than no line.' Provided that the Demarcation Commissioners charged with applying diplomatic texts to African terrain were authorized to recommend minor deviations to accord with 'ethnological divisions', it seemed that no great difficulty should arise.

This expectation proved unduly sanguine. The arduous task of trekking through the tropical bush to lay down boundary markers by agreement with a foreign colleague usually fell to ambitious young patriots, often military officers with some knowledge of surveying, who might regard it as their duty not merely to define their national claims, but to extend them as far as was conceivably compatible with the agreements they were supposed to be executing. One way of doing this was to uphold such territorial claims by Africans as coincided with the interests of the power in question. Captain Lang, appointed to demarcate the western frontier of the Gold Coast in 1892, espoused the claims of the Appolonians and other Akans who had for years been moving westwards, while his French colleague Captain Binger defended the territorial integrity of Kinjabo, Indenie, and other states of the lower Comoe and Bia valleys whose rulers had accepted treaties with France.[16] Meanwhile in the Sierra Leone-Guinea Boundary Commission Captain Lamadon, hoping to consolidate African opposition to Samori, was maintaining close relations with Karimu, whose political influence remained strong in the British sphere in the Scarcies valley, while his British colleague Captain Kenny relied on the advice of Alimami Sattan Lahai, one of the Temne chiefs most involved in the politics of the area claimed by France. European intervention was not the sole or even the principal cause of these African conflicts, and there was no possible frontier which could have kept the antagonists apart; but the proceedings of Lamadon and Kenny seem to have inflamed relations between Temne and Susu, as well as between French and British.[17]

Hence, although the Boundary Commissions established to apply the 1889 Agreement to Lagos and Senegambia were able to fix boundaries of some sort, the attempts to do the same with Sierra Leone and the Gold Coast actually made things worse. The diplomatists could only return to their inadequate maps, and try to devise less ambiguous instructions. 'Far away from an African sun and its notoriously irritating influences, unexposed to the narrowing advice of naturally jealous local authorities, one might arrive at a solution which now seems hopeless.' Unfortunately the conciliatory disposition of this particular diplomatist went far beyond what his colleagues in temperate London would accept.[18] And during the mid-1890s the freedom of detached negotiators to accept rational compromises was complicated by the intensification of European — particularly, Franco-British — colonial rivalries.

The years between 1894 and 1898 marked the high-point of popular colonialism in Europe, and pressure-groups in France and Britain competed in demanding strong action to protect supposed national interests on the Niger and the Nile. In this climate diplomatists concerned to avoid international conflict could not give much weight to the complaints of Africans, or even of colonial Governors, about the deficiencies of colonial boundaries. When in May 1894 the energetic new Governor of Sierra Leone proposed a revised boundary with Guinea, affecting the section already agreed as well as that still under discussion, which would pay greater attention to African political alignments and trade routes and respect the integrity of Samu and Luawa chiefdoms, officials recoiled from the thought of further protracted negotiations. Secretary Ripon wrote:

I sympathize strongly with Col. Cardew's desire not to divide the territories of Native Chiefs. It is a wretched system, unjust to the chiefs and their people, and a fruitful source of disputes and trouble to the dividing Powers.

But of course we cannot now deal with these matters as if the negotiations were to be entered upon for the first time.[19]

In fact, diplomatists under pressure were even then drawing new border-lines just as arbitrary as the old.

Most African boundaries still reflect the arbitrary compromises of the two decades when the chauvinistic forces of the European nation-state were most closely focussed upon colonial rivalry. Exceptionally, subsequent diplomacy might secure some minor adjustments. In 1904 a particularly tortuous piece of political geometry redefined the Anglo-French frontier in Sokoto so as to facilitate the movement of caravans with Niger.[20] Seven years later an adjustment of the Anglo-Liberian border partly restored the unity of Luawa chiefdom—a rare example of an African ruler, Fabunde, being able to influence a boundary change.[21] But in general, the early provisional frontier settlements endured.

Thus study of European archives supports an accidental rather than a conspiratorial theory of the marking of African boundaries. The only logic which can be discerned in the record is that untidy form of historical rationality which derives from the interaction of conflicting interests and objectives. Primarily, of course, this meant the interests of certain European nation-states which had temporarily become dedicated to territorial empire in Africa; but sometimes African rulers were able to play minor roles in settling actual boundaries. The populations of the frontier areas were envisaged, if at all, only as dim and inarticulate presences in the background — which did not mean that they were unable to influence the manner in which the imposed boundaries subsequently operated.

African experience in this respect, however, represents only an extreme example of contemporary international practice. Until the Paris Peace Conference of 1919 attempted to apply Wilsonian principles of self-determination, with no great success, European boundaries too were commonly settled by interacting ambitions of remote potentates. The partitions and repartitions of Poland, the drawing of the Franco-German frontier through Lorraine in 1871, the tripartite division imposed on the 'Big Bulgaria' of 1878, gave no more weight than African boundary agreements to the wishes and interests of the populations involved.[22] In both continents, the inhabitants of the grass had to learn to endure the trampling of contending elephants — and to cope with other predators as well.

This essay has been deliberately focussed upon the West African region, with which the author's studies have been primarily concerned. Some of the features described clearly affected boundaries elsewhere in Africa — the predominant imperatives of European 'national interests', the high degree of geographical ignorance on the part of negotiators and their consequent desire to avoid ambiguity by defining lines capable of objective survey, the growing tendency of the 1890s for European politicians to identify African territory with national 'prestige'.

However, Afro-European relations on the West Coast had distinctive historical characteristics which may limit continent-wide generalisations. To start with, the longer period of contact meant that African rulers in general played more active and more sophisticated roles in pre-partition politics than in much of Eastern and Southern Africa — the obvious exceptions being Ethiopia, Buganda and Lesotho. The activities of Egypt and Zanzibar present further complications. Secondly, the larger number of European leases, settlements, colonies and related claims on the West African coast before 1800 meant that there were more frontiers to settle, some enclosing very small territories indeed. Finally, because the Foreign Office, not the Colonial Office, was responsible for British interests in Eastern Africa while Germany had no independent Colonial Office until 1907, diplomatic negotiations were usually conducted by a single government department. This made the process of delimitation much simpler than in the West African Joint Commissions, where the British and French delegations had to reconcile the conflicting priorities of Foreign and Colonial Office — of diplomacy and colonial administration. But by and large, the 'accidental hypothesis' seems likely to hold up on a continental basis.

NOTES

1. The essay is based on research for my *Prelude to the Partition of West Africa* (1963) and *West Africa Partitioned* (Vol. I, 1974; Vols II and III, forthcoming; hereafter *WAP*) and further references may be found in those works.
2. This metaphor is based on the Igbo proverb which states that when two elephants fight, it is the grass beneath the two that suffer. Here the elephants are the partitioning European powers, and the grass the defenceless Africans, especially those in the area through which negotiated boundaries were drawn.
3. Speech by Guizot, 31 March 1843, quoted B. Schnapper, *La Politique et le Commerce français dans le Golfe de Guinée de 1838 à 1871* (Paris, 1961), p. 13.
4. CO.267/287. Minute by T.F. Elliot, 14 Nov., on Blackall, 72, 11 Oct. 1866.
5. See N.S. Senkomago, 'The Kingdom of Porto Novo, with special reference to its external relations, 1862–1908', unpubl. Ph.D. thesis, University of Aberdeen, 1976.
6. H. Brunschwig, *Le Partage de l'Afrique noire* (Paris, 1971), p. 51.
7. See W. Ross Johnston, *Sovereignty and Protection: a Study of British Jurisdictional Imperialism in the later Nineteenth Century* (Durham, NC, 1973).
8. A.M. Howard, 'The relevance of spatial analysis for African economic history: the Sierra Leone-Guinea system', *Journal of African History*, XVII, 1976, pp. 365–85.

The Making of the Boundaries: West Africa 27

9. Salisbury Papers (Christ Church, Oxford) A57, Lytton to Salisbury, 12 Dec. 1888. For the context of this negotiation, WAP, pp. 230–46.
10. Speech by Salisbury, 6 Aug. 1890, *The Times,* 7 Aug.
11. Archives Etrangères, Paris (AE), Mémoires et Documents, Afrique 129, Note sur la Délimitation entre les Possessions françaises et britanniques . . . 1890.
12. For this controversy, see CO.267/399, F.O. to C.O., 16 Nov. 1892; also the correspondence with W.O. in CO.267/397.
13. FO.84/1899, Memo by Lake and Darwin (M.I.D.) 16 July 1889.
14. AE. Afrique 129, Note, 13 Jan. 1891.
15. See J.C. Anene, *The International Boundaries of Nigeria* (Longman, 1970), Chap. 3.
16. Archives Nationales, Section d'Outre-mer, Paris. Côte d'Ivoire III/S. Binger's report on Boundary Commission, esp. fo. 8.
17. Kenny's report of 24 May 1892 in CO.879/35, C.P. African 422, No. 81; Lamadon's is in AE Afrique 130. I hope to treat this question more fully in Vol. II of *WAP*.
18. CO.879/35. C.P. African 422, No. 88, Phipps to Differin, 30 May 1892; cf CO.267/399 Minute by Hemming on F.O. to C.O. 16 Nov. 1892 and on Phipps to Anderson, Phe 15 Nov.
19. CO.267/409. Minute by Ripon, 27 June, in Cardew to Ripon, Conf. 38. 23 May 1894.
20. Anglo-French Convention of 8 April 1904, *British Documents on the Origins of the War,* II, pp. 381–2.
21. M. McCall, 'Kai Lundu's Luawa and British rule', unpubl. D.Phil. thesis, University of York, 1974, ch. IV; A.J.G. Wyse, 'The Sierra Leone/Liberian boundary: A case of frontier imperialism', *Odu,* n.s. 15, 1977, pp. 5–18.
22. This global perspective is elaborated in Chapter 12 below.

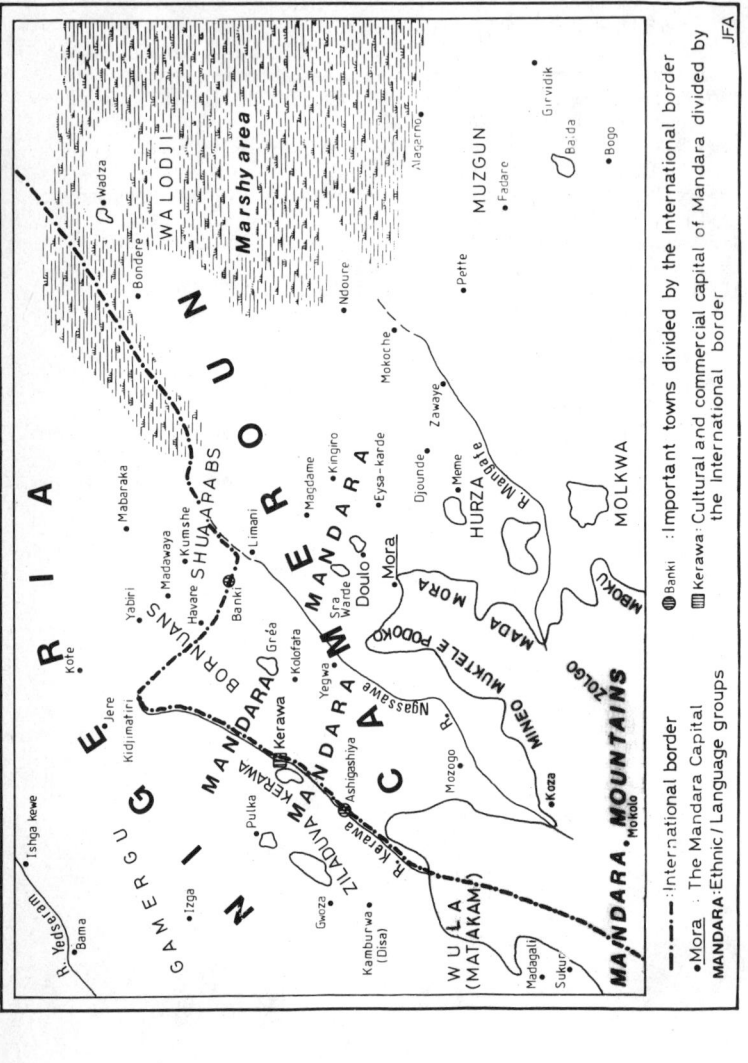

Part Two

3

THE MANDARA ASTRIDE THE NIGERIA-CAMEROON BOUNDARY

Bawuro M. Barkindo

Introduction

After the defeat of Germany in the 1914–18 war, German Cameroon* was divided between France and Britain to be ruled first as Mandates of the League of Nations and after 1946 as Trusteeship Territories of the United Nations. As far as the two powers were concerned, these were colonies; there was little attempt to deal with them in any other way. While French Cameroon was retained as a distinct colony, British Cameroon was split into two, the north administered as part of Northern Nigeria and the south as part of Southern Nigeria. The discussion in this paper is mainly confined to the northern part of British Cameroon.

Scholars who have undertaken the study of the divided peoples in the area tend to lay more emphasis on Adamawa and Borno than upon Mandara.[1] This essay does not question the significance of the partitioning of these two states but suggests that such studies have resulted in an imbalance in the overall picture. Certainly the greater part of pre-colonial Adamawa, one of the most extensive Emirates of the Sokoto Caliphate, is still to be found in the Cameroon Republic. Most of the dependencies of the pre-colonial Borno empire, one of the oldest states in the area, are now found in Cameroon, Chad and Niger. The argument is that each fraction of the divided larger states appeared to have been big enough to stand on its own and so there were fewer problems with minorities on the different sides of the border.

For the smaller states and peoples, splitting them into two different countries meant not only additional minority problems but greater administrative problems. This is because often, for easier

---

* In historical literature, this word is found spelt in the French way (Cameroun), the German way (Kamerun) and the English way (Cameroon or Cameroons). For simplicity the English way is used in this article, singular and without the definite article.

administration, they were joined with other peoples — often their former rivals — to constitute new administrative units. There was then an attempt to impose new rulers. All this increased tension and conflict. Mandara is a good example of a smaller state which was divided — in this case between Nigeria and Cameroon.

Mandara Sultanate before the partition[2]

Mandara — or, in its local form, Wandala — is a multiple reference to the land, the people, their language and their state. It is an area encompassing both plains and hills situated south of Lake Chad. The greater part of Mandara now forms part of the Republic of Cameroon while the remainder is in Nigeria. It was founded in the early fifteenth century by the coming together of various Chadic-speaking peoples who gradually moved their settlements southwards to avoid pressures from the then recently established Saifawa state of Borno. By the sixteenth century, it was well established; in fact, its capital Kerawa was important enough to be noted in early European records as a centre from where iron was being distributed to other places in the Lake Chad region.[3]

In the seventeenth century, the political capital was transferred southwards to Doulo for strategic and political reasons. Kerawa still remained the commercial and cultural capital. Mandara soon began to expand and dominate its smaller neighbours partly by military but more effectively by religious and economic means. The ruler, the *Tlikse*, was the most important ritual figure of the area, the commerce of which the Mandara traders dominated. The principal export was iron obtained in the mountains. This was worked into household and farm implements, weapons and ornaments. Some of it was also worked into rods or balls (*shabu*) chiefly for export and as a medium of exchange. The surplus iron found its way to Kerawa through the agency of Mandara traders. Other items exported from Mandara included slaves and ivory, which were obtained from the Musgun, and the famous Mandara horse, the *Barb*, a cross-breed between the Musgun pony and the North African horse. There were also copper and brass ornaments which were distributed throughout the region by traders.

In exchange for its exports the state received brass and copper scrap, breeding horses and other products of North Africa and Borno. The chief gateway for Mandara trade was Borno, but by the eighteenth century Bagirmi had also become important.

By the end of the eighteenth century, Mandara had become a dominant political, economic and cultural power in the area from the southern marches of Borno in the north up to Lake Lere in the

Mundang territory in the south, from the Massa-Musgun area in the east to the Gamergu territory along the Yedseram valley in the west. Even beyond this area it was the dominant cultural centre for places a few days journey from the Benue in the south. Its economic influence in this region continued up to the beginning of colonialism while traces of its cultural dominance can still be found. This development became more noticeable from the beginning of the eighteenth century when Mandara accepted Islam,[4] from which followed further territorial expansion and changes in the traditional political system. When Mandara defeated the invading forces of Borno around 1781, it had reached the zenith of its development and its fame.

The beginning of the nineteenth century, however, saw Mandara at the nadir of its fortunes when the *Jihad* of Modibbo Adama and the creation of the Emirate of Fombina (Adamawa) detached much of its territory and forced the Sultan to seek the aid of Borno.[5] Although Mandara could re-conquer little of this territory, the state survived, and by the middle of the century it had made a substantial economic recovery despite the menace of Borno and the Fulbe (Fulani) Emirate of Fombina. It managed to recapture most of the markets and trade routes which had been lost to the Fulbe.

Towards the end of the nineteenth century Mandara took the offensive and tried to recapture those territories lost to Fombina; and it was making some progress when Rabeh bin Fadlallah appeared on the scene. After defeating and occupying metropolitan Borno around 1893, Rabeh sent his forces which defeated those of Mandara and devastated Doulo the capital around 1895. From that time Doulo's role as the capital was taken over by Mora. Although Rabeh sent his troops to attack the state several times, it was one of the few powers in the area that continued to resist him up to the end of his occupation of the area. By the time he was killed in 1900 the European colonial powers had already arrived.

The colonial scramble and Mandara

Before the European colonial scramble for Africa very few European travellers had visited Mandara. Its first European visitor appears to have been Major Dixon Denham in 1823.[6] This was the time when the state was making every effort to defeat the Fulbe and dislodge them from its territory. The Borno-Arab military expedition which Denham accompanied to Mandara was not a slave-marauding party as popularly believed,[7] but Borno's contribution to the attempt by Mandara to deal with the Fulbe, who were then the enemies of both countries.[8] The joint Borno-Arab-Mandara forces were, however, defeated by the Fulbe. Most of those who read Denham's journal in Europe seem to have concluded that after this defeat Mandara was almost swallowed by the emerging power of the Fulbe.[9]

This wrong assumption re-echoed in the writings of Heinrich Barth who visited the area in the years 1849–55. Barth, who did not actually visit Mandara, dismissed its Sultan as the 'petty chief of Mandara whose ancestors had once completely defeated a countless host of Bornu people',[10] but who at the time 'inhabit the small Alpine country, which in consequence of Captain Denham's adventurous journey has become known to Europeans under the form of Mandara.'[11] Barth did not hide his desire for the eventual colonisation of the area and concluded that it was the Fulbe who could pose problems to the Europeans rather than smaller states like Mandara. Even if the Europeans were to succeed in colonising the area, Barth's advice was that they should rule through the Fulbe. After his visit to Yola he wrote:

The Fulbe are continually advancing, as they have not to do with one strong enemy, but with a number of small tribes without any bond of union. It remains to be seen whether it be their destiny to colonize this fine country themselves, or in the course of time to be disturbed by the intrusion of Europeans. It is difficult to decide how a Christian government is to deal with these countries, where none but Muhammadans maintain any sort of government. It cannot be denied that they alone have succeeded in giving to distant regions a certain bond of unity, and making the land more accessible to trade and intercourse.[12]

Barth discovered that Yola was the capital of an extensive Emirate which was potentially rich in agricultural and forest resources and products. It was also strategically situated for tapping the trade of Fombina through the excellent trade routes and especially through the River Benue and its tributaries. In fact when he arrived on the Benue, Barth prophesied that 'along this natural high road European influence and commerce will penetrate into the very heart of the continent.'[13]

The writings of Barth almost became the theoretical justification for European colonisation in the area.[14] Colonial agents and adventurers all seemed to have worked towards the implementation of his ideas. For example, Robert Flegel, the German colonial adventurer who did all he could to win Adamawa (Fombina) for Germany, agreed with Barth on the importance of the Benue, not only because of transport but also because along the banks of the river 'the whole country is densely populated not with naked pagans, but with Mohammedan tribes, who have a passion for voluminous wrappings, people who take 14 yards of cloth to make a pair of trousers and quite as many for a turban.'[15] Barth's views about using the Fulbe to rule the area was later accepted by no less a person than Sir Frederick (later Lord) Lugard, the chief architect of Indirect Rule in Nigeria, when he said:

> I believe myself that the future of the virile races of the protectorate lies largely in the ... Fulani [Fulbe]. Their ceremonial ... their mode of life and habits of thoughts, appeal more to the native populations than the prosaic business-like habits of the Anglo-Saxon can do.[16]

When the Europeans set out to partition the area, they were primarily concerned with the acquisition of territories for profitable economic exploitation, and therefore they wanted extensive territories endowed with human and natural resources. They also wanted to control well-known trade routes which they could use or on which they could establish posts in order to collect customs duties and regulate trade for their own benefit. Equally important, the Europeans wanted to control the waterways through which the country could be more easily penetrated.

Through the writings of Barth and other nineteenth- and early twentieth-century travellers Adamawa seemed the El Dorado for European colonialism. This was why there was a race to Adamawa by the three European powers Britain, France and Germany.[17] Mandara was relegated to the background during these early stages of colonialism because, following Barth, the Europeans wrongly thought that it was an inconsequential mountain state. It was only much later that they came to realise that it was a kingdom embracing an area of plains dotted with hills inhabited mostly by non-Muslim peoples who they thought had never been organised. It was also much later that they came to realise that Kerawa, the commercial capital of Mandara, was among the most important trade centres in the region.

The first partitions and German rule, 1886–1914

The turn of the century brought the partition of the whole area of the Chad and Benue basins among the British, French and German powers. Although in the official records only the names of Borno and Adamawa featured regularly, this was also the area in which the Mandara state was located. The Anglo-German agreements of 1886 and 1893 partitioned Adamawa into British and German spheres of influence, and the Anglo-French Agreements of 1890 divided Borno into British and French spheres while recognising that Germany too had a share in the spoils of the dismembered ancient state.[18] The fate of the smaller states and peoples was not discussed. However, according to the maps of the Anglo-German Agreements of 1893, metropolitan Mandara fell within the area of German sphere of influence.

Before the European powers could effectively occupy the area between Lake Chad and the Mandara mountains, it had been conquered and occupied by Rabeh bin Fadlallah. Each of the powers reacted differently to this military adventurer in order to protect its own interest. The French suggested to the Germans that their joint forces should simultaneously attack him and thereafter divide his territories between them.[19] The Germans refused such a venture since it would have benefited the French more than themselves.[20] By the earlier conventions most of the area occupied by Rabeh belonged to the German sphere of influence, and the Germans were in favour of developing friendship with him in order to prevent his venturing further southwards into their territory.[21] Meanwhile they hoped to develop Garua which, they envisaged, would in time replace Yola — which was under the British influence — as the political and economic headquarters of Adamawa. The Germans were also more in favour of turning the trade of Adamawa away from Yola towards the Cameroon coast.[22] The British for their part were using the threat of Rabeh to Adamawa to obtain concessions from Emir Zubairu of Yola.[23] Finally the French engaged Rabeh on their own and after several engagements killed him in 1900. But the fact was that most of the key battles were fought in the area of German influence.[24]

With the defeat of Rabeh the colonial race in the area was resumed with all vigour. On 5 February 1901 a large body of French troops left Ubangi ostensibly on its way to Lake Chad to deal with Rabeh's son Fadlallah. According to the rumour carried by the *Africa Times*, the official object of France was to garrison Bagirmi and Wadai which had fallen to it under the Anglo-French convention of 1899.[25] France, continued the paper, also intended to undertake a military conquest of the whole area over which Rabeh exercised his influence.[26] Although, this may not have been correct, the fact that they still had not taken possession of the area should have worried the Germans. A few months later, on 2 September 1901, the British forces stormed and captured Yola.[27]

Alarmed, Germany decided to demonstrate its military strength not only to the Africans but also to the other European powers in the area. In October 1901, the greatest military expedition in the history of the German conquest of Cameroon left Duala for the hinterland. It was commanded by no less a person than Oberstleutnant von Pavel, the Commander of the German imperial troops in Cameroon. It literally fought its way from the coast to Lake Chad and the area was formally occupied. On 18 April 1902, Pavel arrived in Mora, the new Mandara capital, where Sultan Umar was ordered to swear allegiance to the German Emperor.[28] We can only speculate as to the Sultan's feelings at the arrival of this alien force. His neighbours had, in various ways, been made aware of the European interventions. Mandara had been excluded from these earlier warning signs.

In 1903–4 the frontier from Yola to Lake Chad was surveyed and protocols were signed, and in 1912–13 the border between British Nigeria and the German Cameroon was finalised. Most of metropolitan Mandara fell under German rule.

Germany, like Britain, adopted the method of Indirect Rule in the predominantly Muslim north of her territory, and — also like Britain — picked on the Fulbe and the Kanuri rulers as her agents. Therefore, throughout the German period in the area, the authority of the Sultan of Mandara was continuously undermined in favour of his Fulbe neighbours. For example, during his tour of the area in 1905, Hauptmann Zimmermann, the *Resident*, wanted to transfer the district of Disa to the Fulbe district of Madagali, although Disa people objected and told him that they had belonged to Mandara from time immemorial and would like to remain so.[29] In the Gwozo area he arbitarily transferred Gwozo, Lufua and all other areas further south to Madagali despite clear evidence that the whole area belonged to Mandara.[30]

Encouraged by the attitude of the German administration, the Fulbe of Madagali and Maroua simultaneously moved into the Mandara Sultanate and occupied some of its villages.[31] Despite complaints to the German administration by the Sultan of Mandara, and although the new border worked out in 1907 showed that the Fulbe were illegally occupying the territory of Mandara, the Fulbe refused to leave.[32] When *Resident* Stieber finally ejected them by force, he was seriously reprimanded by Governor Seitz.[33]

In 1905, Hamman Yaji, the ruler of Madagali, sought permission to subdue the inhabitants of Miltu and incorporate them into his district.[34] Not only was he allowed to do so, but the *Resident* also supplied him with government troops to help him in his conquests.[35] On the other hand, when the Goshe who resided not far from Mora, the Mandara capital, rebelled and refused to pay taxes, the *Resident* was told to steer clear of what was presented as a conflict between Muslims and non-Muslims.[36] In fact when Sultan Umar appeared to be still powerful in his domain, he was deposed by the German authorities in 1911 and replaced by his son Bukar Afadi who was considered more malleable.

On the whole, throughout the duration of German rule, while the

Fulbe rulers were allowed and even encouraged to consolidate their power, these efforts undermined the authority of the Sultan of Mandara even in the area over which he had personal rule.

Impact of the First World War

During the First World War, German Cameroon became a bitter battlefield of the European powers, each supported by battalions of well-trained African soldiers led by seasoned European officers. Mora was one of the chief theatres of the so-called Cameroon campaigns.

On the 13 August 1913, Hauptmann von Crailsheim, the *Resident* of German Adamawa, informed the ruler of Garua that Britain and Germany might soon be fighting one another; the war, however, would probably be confined to Europe where the Emperor would surely win since he had more soldiers. Should the war take place also in Africa, the Germans would like the Fulbe of German Adamawa to help them in the fight. The ruler was promised that if his people would co-operate with the Germans he would receive the Emirship of Yola which they hoped to capture.[37]

On 29 August, the British forces from Yola attacked Garua but were repulsed with heavy losses. There followed an intensive military build-up at Garua since it was considered the most precious German possession in northern Cameroon. After the Germans were defeated and forced to evacuate Duala by a joint British and French attack, the First Company was ordered to rush to the defence of Garua, and arrived there on 16 September. Five days later a 3.7 cm. revolving cannon and other sophisticated weapons arrived in Garua from the south, and finally, towards the end of October, the newly-created 12 Company also arrived.

All these efforts failed to prevent its fall. By the beginning of June 1915, the British and French forces had converged there and after a few bloody engagements the town capitulated to the Allied forces on 10 June 1915. A British officer who took part in its final capture noted:

The moral effect of the fall of Garua on the native mind cannot be over-estimated and it is likely to do a great deal to finish the operations in the south Camerouns as the natives now realise that we are going to have the Camerouns and the Germans are not going to have Nigeria.[38]

Certainly the fall of Garua speeded the collapse of German Adamawa, for by 27 June Ngaundere had fallen, followed a few days later by Gashaka. When Maroua fell soon afterwards, a plan for a general withdrawal of the German troops towards the Adamawa plateau was abandoned, for German Adamawa was by then as good as lost.

The war in Mandara was totally different from that in Adamawa to the south. On the same day that von Crailsheim was informing the ruler of Garua about the war, Hauptmann von Raben, the *Resident* of the area of Lake Chad province, was ordering the mobilisation of his troops at Mora and their evacuation to the Mora mountains where he determined to resist the British and the French.[39] On 19 August 1914, the British forces crossed the border into Mandara from the west, followed a week later by the French forces which crossed over from Fort-Lamy (now N'Djamena). After overrunning the border posts, the Allied Forces converged on Mora where they blockaded the German troops from 27 August 1914 to 18 February 1916, when they finally capitulated.

There were many bloody engagements and, unlike the Adamawa campaign, the war took a great toll of the Mandara people. The mountain peoples, among whom the two opposing sides finally settled, were daily harassed by both the Germans and the Allied forces either on suspicion of aiding the enemy or in order to loot foodstuffs. The plains farmers also suffered greatly, their crops were forcibly harvested and domestic animals confiscated by the soldiers of both sides. At one time when a German patrol entered Mora town, it discovered that the German station had been destroyed and looted by the Allied forces. The patrol decided to vent its anger on the Sultan of Mandara whom they suspected of supporting the Allied forces. They burnt his palace to ashes. Yet as soon as the British forces were in control of most of the Sultanate in 1915, they deposed the unfortunate Sultan whom they accused of working for the Germans!

With the capitulation of the Germans in Mora on 18 February 1916, the conquest of Cameroon was complete and Germany was dispossessed of the territory in the same way as she was of her other African colonies in the course of the war.

The Mandate and the final partition, 1919–1922

After the defeat of Germany, Mandara, together with the rest of Cameroon, became a booty to be divided among the victors. At the Versailles Conference in 1919, Germany renounced in favour of the principal Allied and associated powers all her rights over her overseas possessions including Cameroon. On 10 July, the Anglo-French Declaration announced the partition of the Cameroon, although it was only in 1922 that the final British and French Mandates over it came into being.

Our sources tend to show that this Mandate failed to do justice to Borno and Adamawa since the former glories of the two states were never restored.[40] Borno was said to have been dispossessed of its former dependencies which were now found in Cameroon, Chad and Niger, while metropolitan Borno itself remained in Nigeria. Two-thirds of the area that had once been Adamawa was still separated from the Emir of Yola; while Yola remained in Nigeria, her traditional dependencies were retained in French Cameroon. It is reported that when the Emir realised this, he declared with bitterness that the 'Europeans had cut off the body and left him with only the head of his Kingdom'.[41]

But on the whole it would appear that both Borno and Adamawa, within the colonial structure, gained by this final border delimitation. Metropolitan Borno, which had been separated into British and German Borno, was now re-united under British administration. In addition, as we shall see, Borno gained some areas of Mandara which she never controlled. In Adamawa, the northern and southern parts of the mandated territory, comprising a third of the area of the province, 40 per cent of its population and three-quarters of its wealth, were added to the jurisdiction of the Emir of Adamawa — under the cloak of the Mandate.

Mandara and other smaller states and peoples were the principal victims of the new dispensation. People who belonged to the same cultural groups or societies were indiscriminately separated and usually given different names in order to justify their separation. The new border, for example, separated the Gude people into two, and to justify that action those on the French side were called Djimi. The Higis, who were separated from their kinsmen now in Nigeria, were named Kapsiki and those Matakam now found on the Anglophone side were named Wula to differentiate them from their kinsmen in French Cameroon.[42] In Mandara proper there was an attempt in the initial stages to sort out Mandara and Borno so that all the former would remain in French territory,[43] since Kerawa was to be in French Cameroon. Even if this had been followed, Mandara would still have lost some of its territory since the majority of the inhabitants of its northern districts were Bornoans and Shuwa Arabs. But in the final analysis no one paid any attention to a true sorting out of the populations since Kerawa town itself was divided into two with one part in French Cameroon and the other part in British Nigeria.

A border 87 km. long, separated the newly-created Mora division of French Cameroon from British Cameroon.[44] It was simply a superimposed boundary. There were feeble attempts to follow natural features like mountains or rivers when these appeared convenient and acceptable to the two principal powers; but generally no one seemed to care if the border affected former cultural or political units.

From Mogode in the south up to Kidjimatiri in the north the border followed the Mandara mountains then, towards the north, the River Kerawa. This meant that two former districts of Mandara, Doure and Disa, were completely cut off and located in Nigeria. In addition, the River Kerawa ran through the middle of the district of Kerawa, Ashigashiya and Gwozo which meant that about half of these districts were separated from Mandara. Kerawa town, as we have already noted, was (and still is) the principal commercial and cultural centre of Mandara. It was also the capital of a large and prosperous district containing about 8,000 people at the time of partition. Next to Kerawa, Ashigashiya was also an important town that was cut in two by the partition. It was mostly out of the Kerawa and Ashigashiya districts that the Gwozo division in Nigeria was created.

From Kidjimatiri in the north-west to Limani in the north-east the border was mostly indeterminate, being marked either by single trees or by foot-paths. For example, the village units of Banki and Amchide were both partitioned into two, and the border was a foot-path traversing them. This section of the border was the one largely populated by Bornoans. After a large part had been apportioned to Nigeria, the remaining two districts of Kolofate and Limani were still mostly populated by them. Thus, instead of 'sorting out' the Bornoans, the new border simply complicated matters by separating into two distinct countries related Bornoans who had been in Mandara for centuries.

Further east of Limani, in the Walodji area, the Shuwa Arabs who originally belonged to Mandara were also separated. The district of Kumshe was amputated and assigned to Nigeria.

Effects of the new frontier

As we might expect, many problems arose from the arbitrary separation of a once-united people. Many Mandara who found themselves separated from the main Sultanate resisted the arbitrary separation. The District Head of Disa considered himself a descendant of one of the three brothers who, in the traditions of origin, were credited with the foundation of the Mandara state.[45] He was one of the most important functionaries at the court of the Sultan of Mandara and when informed that he was to answer to the Shehu of Dikwa instead of the Sultan, the *Tlikamburwa* (the official title of the ruler of Disa) immediately abandoned his post on the British side and migrated to Mandara. He would rather be a commoner there than a ruler elsewhere. He was soon followed by a majority of his people, and very soon after the new border amputated Disa, the former ancient walled town situated in very fertile country was deserted; it is still in ruins.[46]

After parts of Mandara had been transferred to Nigeria, an attempt was made by the British authorities to replace the former rulers of the area by appointees of Kanuri, Fulbe or some other origins. For example, a younger brother of the Shehu of Dikwa was appointed District Head of Ashigashiya (after Ashigashiya, Kerawa and some hill areas were constituted into a single district). But in 1927, he had to be removed after some eighteen months in office since he was found 'unsuited to the work of this District which presents many difficult and peculiar administrative problems'.[47] His successor, a former messenger of the Divisional Officer, was removed soon after in 1929 for the same reasons. He in turn was succeeded by Kachalla Ali, a Sara (from Chad) who, as the administrators discovered, 'has no hereditary connection with the hills but has been closely associated with them since they were first brought under British administration.'[48]

A similar set of events occured in other units. The District Head of Gwozo was Yerima Jato, a Fulani and a brother of Hamman Yaji the ruler of Madagali.[49] For long the people objected to this alien domination and it needed a great amount of force for a simple order to be obeyed. Some fifteen years after the demarcation exercise, a British District Officer reported

I should add that although it is theoretically objectionable to have alien Village Heads and District Heads, I do not see what else could have been done at the time when the administration began. I should urge caution in making any drastic alteration.[50]

In fact, for many of these people on the British Nigerian side of the border who had formerly belonged to Mandara, only men with titles like *Shetima*, *Mala*, *Zaka* and *Tlupwe* were seen as legitimate functionaries, and then only if the titles had been bestowed by the Sultan of Mandara.[51] So there were many Village Heads and other functionaries who crossed the border to buy titles from the Sultan. Thus, although politically separated from his people the Sultan, physically located in Cameroon, still wielded influence in the Nigerian area, and has continued to do so.

The French, however, did not favour the strong influence of the Sultan even in his own domain. We have seen that during the war Sultan Bukar Afadi was deposed by the British forces; his father Umar, earlier deposed by the Germans, was brought back and reinstated. In 1922, when the French found him 'un-cooperative', Sultan Umar was deposed a second time and another of his sons, Amada, was appointed his successor.[52] The latter however was only allowed to rule for some two years before being in turn deposed in 1924.[53]

Determined to do away with the ruling dynasty, the French appointed Kola Adama who had no connection with the ruling house. The new Sultan was given every encouragement by the French to destroy not only the ruling house but all those dignitaries who supported it. On his recommendation some high dignitaries like Tligrea Mustapha, Tlikire Limani and Shetima Hamidu were removed and imprisoned on trivial or trumped-up charges.[54] He seems to have wished to destroy all the potential successors in the ruling house. In September 1924, a British official touring in Mubi reported:

The son of the late Chief of Mandara arrived in this Division. He stated that his father had recently died and been succeeded by a slave and that he fled across the bordeer to avoid the unpleasant custom practised by successful aspirants to the Mandara chieftaincy — cutting off ears to prevent future succession.[55]

Kola Adama died in 1926 to the disappointment of the French. When the people of Mandara were approached about a new ruler, they insisted not only that the royal dynasty be re-established but that they still regarded Sultan Bukar Afadi, deposed in 1915, as the legitimate Sultan. The French accepted this with reluctance. However, the old Sultan was not allowed to die in office, and was deposed again in 1942.[56] Only from this time was there some stability in Mandara, but by then the Sultan's powers had been heavily eroded.

The two administrations had different systems of taxation. In 1949, the taxation in the British Kerawa was: for Muslims, 7s. 9d. per adult male, 7s. per adult female and 3s. per head of cattle. In addition, the rulers received 'Zakat' on animals and an additional 1s. per household during *Maulud* (birthday of the Prophet) celebrations. For non-Muslims it was 5s. per household and 1s. 6d. per head of cattle.[57] In French Mandara, there was a great variation, but on the whole the taxes were higher. In the Limani district in the same period every household paid an equivalent of 10s. while about 2s. 6d. was received on every head of cattle. In the Boundaeri district every adult both male and female paid 8s. 9d., while 3s. was received on every head of cattle.[58] In addition, every adult had to pay a special annual tax to be permitted to carry on his or her legitimate trade.[59] Among non-Muslims, underage children and recently dead members of the household were often assessed and payments were forced out of their relations.⁶⁰

These different systems of taxation led to frequent crossings of the border whenever a taxation exercise was taking place. Many families of the non-Islamic Mandara used to cross over into Nigeria to work as hired labourers in order to go home and pay their taxes. On the Nigerian side many Muslim Mandara used to cross into French Cameroon to escape paying taxes. But since since their names were already on the register this usually meant additional problems for relatives left behind since they either had to pay or had their property confiscated.

Mandara, like most smaller border areas, was generally neglected when facilities such as schools, wells or medical clinics were being established. Although a formal school was opened in 1924 at Dikwa on the Nigerian side of the border, it was only some three years later that it started offering junior elementary classes to children drawn from all over the division. For senior primary education, children had to go to the senior primary school at Maiduguri. Very few children from the British Mandara benefitted from the Dikwa and Maiduguri schools. For the Muslim parents, the schools were situated so far from home that few agreed to send their children there. No one cared to explain to the non-Muslim Mandara the benefit of European education, and hence they mistrusted the whole business. In 1929, a small elementary school was opened in Gwozo which was meant to serve the Mandated area to which Mandara was attached.[61] But it all failed, since some five years later the school had to be transferred to Hambagda, a non-Muslim area near the hills because 'The disturbing element crept in when ... it was observed that the hill boys were coming under the predominating Moslem influence of Gwozo.'[62] The story on the French side of the border was even worse. For a long time the only school in the area was the one at Garua, a place almost twice as far from Dikwa as from Mora. Both administrations discouraged the activity of missionaries in the area.

There was an attempt by both authorities to replace the Mandara language as the lingua franca of the area. Certainly, there was a feeble attempt by the British authorities to use Mandara as a language of instruction in the junior classes of the Gwozo school (1929–34),[63] but this was given up when the school was transferred to Hambagda. From that time there was a concerted effort to replace Mandara by either Kanuri or Fulfulde. On the French side there was a similar effort to replace all indigenous languages with French as the first language and Fulfulde as the second language. As it turned out, however, the Mandara on both sides of the border resisted this attempt to relegate their language to the background. Mandara is still spoken on both sides of the border, but with some differences arising from the impact of French on one side and of English on the other.

The towns of Kerawa, Ashigashiya, Bakarise and Gakara refused to see themselves as divided between the British and the French. People still attended each other's markets and ceremonies to mark births and deaths. By 1940, there were still about forty families in the town of British Kerawa who gained their livelihood through farms which were on the French side of the border.[64] Equally, the divided Bornoans and Shuwa Arabs had more in common with each other than with groups more distantly related to them in the Dikwa Division with whom they were now linked administratively.

But gradually, as the people came to accept the division, border incidents especially over farmlands became a regular feature of the area. In the Kerawa and Ashigashiya areas, as we pointed out, the River Kerawa was the frontier; but by 1945 the river had so altered its course that, except where it divided actual towns and villages, it had changed the border, agreed in the Anglo-French convention of 1920.[65] Now there were various clashes and disputes about farmlands especially among the Matakam and their Wula kinsmen or between Gude and the Djimi — people formerly united but now differentiated by the border.

Another problem which faced both administrations was the steady increase in crime in the border areas. A murderer or robber would simply walk a few kilometres across the border and be among his kith and kin who would give him all the protection he needed. Goods stolen in one section were quickly carried over the border to be disposed of. Very soon after the border exercise, smuggling and the buying of smuggled or stolen goods became very profitable trades. In 1929, a census showed that there was a great depopulation in the border region of British Borno (to which British Mandara was attached); one of the reasons was said to be an increase in crime since the new border came into being. At Abba Abunari, a village of Konduga bordering on Mandara, it was found that there were a number of professional criminals of various ethnic identities including the Shuwa Arabs, Kanuri, Hausa and Mandara.[66] They organised thefts, robberies and smuggling.

This made life insecure for the ordinary citizens, many of whom migrated. The approach of the British authorities to the problem did not help to solve it. Not only were the border villages indiscriminately raided by the agents of the local authority, but fines were regularly levied on the Village Heads as a result of robberies and thefts committed near their villages. In 1929, many of the

Village Heads in Konduga and Ashigashiya threatened to migrate into French Mandara if the unfair raids and fines were not stopped.[67]

For a long time the only answer of both the French and the British authorities to the border problems was high-handedness. Some fifteen years after the delimitation, a British Divisional Officer in the area noted:

> Murder, slave-dealing, highway robbery and all kinds of lawlessness were rife, and it was decided to post a permanent military detachment at Bama, to prevent things going from bad to worse and to obviate the necessity for punitive measures on a large scale at a future date. An administrative officer was attached to this detachment of troops.[68]

The answer of the French authorities was similar.[69] Military posts were established at Mokolo and Mora, and the local administrators were usually military men. Periodic raids were carried out by the opposing military posts right across the border, which often resulted in mini-military confrontations between the two administrations.

Only from about 1940 did the local administrative officers on the opposing sides begin to realise that the border areas could not be effectively ruled except through the co-operation of both administrations. And it was from this time that efforts were made to understand some of the problems of the divided peoples. In 1942 Bradshaw, a British administrative officer in the area, travelled to French Cameroon where he conferred with Lauverge, the sub-divisional chief officer of Mokolo, on many aspects concerning the uneasy border.[70] In January 1945, the *Sous-Préfet* of Mora and the Divisional Officer of Bama met on the Mandara border, each accompanied by a host of local functionaries.[71] At the meeting many complaints were heard from both sides and efforts were made to deal with some of them. The meeting also retraced the 1920 border which, as we noted, was out of place in many areas. In addition, there was an attempt to soften the rigid laws at the borders to ensure easier flow of peoples who refused to be separated. People who had farms across the border were also allowed to retain them, and arrangements were made to see that no impediments should arise in future. In August 1947 a similar meeting was held to see how the arrangements of 1945 were working.[72] Both parties were satisfied and from this time there were regular meetings of the local administrators of both countries to review their co-operation in practice.

Despite that attempt to show concern for the area, it was still comparatively neglected. British Mandara was still included among the 'unsettled Districts', which meant no person could enter except indigenes of the district, public officers and persons holding a licence to do so or permitted by a general authority granted by the Governor or his representative. The reason for this restriction was claimed to be 'that some of the inhabitants are still prone to inter-village affrays in the dry season and violent impulses in the excitement of personal disputes'.[73] British Cameroon experienced two internationally supervised plebiscites in 1959 and 1961 to determine its political future, in particular to decide whether the people would remain in Nigeria or be re-united with Cameroon. It is interesting to note that Bama Division, to which Nigerian Mandara was attached, voted overwhelmingly in support of re-unification with Cameroon. It was only the votes of other parts of North Cameroon which prevented the re-unification. The Mandara attitude at the polls was predictably determined by the desire to re-unite with the vast majority of their kinsmen who had been placed on the French side of the border. The Nigerian Mandara voting pattern is comparable to that of the Ewe of the Gold Coast who, at a similar plebiscite in 1956, voted to re-unite with their kinsmen in French Togo.

Conclusion

The Anglo-French Declaration of 1920 brought the final partition of the Sultanate of Mandara and some of its neighbouring peoples who had been part of a wider political and cultural complex. This brought many problems both to the people concerned and to the administrations in Nigeria and the Cameroon. The greater part of Mandara was found in French Cameroon where the political capital and the Sultan were and still are to be found. But the French colonial regime did not favour a strong indigenous ruler, nor did it take kindly to the retention of several local languages and traditions in its area of administration. The influence of Mandara traditional authority was continually being undermined; the Sultans were accused of incompetence or embezzlement of funds, and were publicly rebuked and deposed. At one time, there was even an attempt to replace the ruling dynasty. In addition, there was an attempt to replace the Mandara language by French and, failing that, by Fulfulde (the Fulani language) as the lingua franca of the area.

On the British side, there was an attempt to appoint new rulers in the Mandara area. There was also an attempt to replace the language by either Kanuri or Fulfulde as the lingua franca although, as we have seen, there was an ambivalent attitude when a further attempt was made to prevent the non-Muslims 'from falling under the influence of the Muslims'.

Both administrations refused to encourage the establishment of Christian missions in the area, and for a long time the two governments denied schools and medical services to the area. There were attempts to divide the people physically; homogeneous groups found themselves divided and given different names, and generally there was an attempt to prevent the free movement of the people across the border.

The people resisted these restrictions. They still attended each other's markets and associated culturally; the Sultan in the French territory continued to be regarded by his people under the British jurisdiction as the fountain of all traditional authority and genuine chieftaincy titles. Nevertheless, the division has had its effect: the different administrative systems, monetary systems and economic values, and different educational systems and official languages have all left their distinctive impact on the people of Mandara.

The most serious problem arising from the division was the increase in crime and disputes across the border. The fact that the border often divided people of the same family and settlements made it difficult to check crime or control smuggling, which soon became a highly profitable business in the area. Law enforcement agencies on both sides of the border often faced the problem of identifying offenders who were usually protected by their relations on the other side.

What the two governments in Nigeria and the Republic of Cameroon need to do now is attempt a true understanding of the history of all peoples in the border areas. Educational and cultural exchanges between the communities on both sides and joint developments should be encouraged.

Above all, we should explore the areas which unite us as Africans, and one of the best ways of achieving this must be to study and encourage cultural links across political boundaries — which should be emphasised as points of contact and not of separation. The case of the Mandara appears typical of the several cases of ethnographical and cultural links between Nigeria and the Republic of Cameroon. The potential of these links as a major factor in binational relations between Nigeria and Cameroon has yet to be fully realised and explored.

NOTES

Acknowledgment. My profound thanks to my colleagues Isa A. Abba, with whom I discussed various issues in the paper, and John Lavers, who kindly read the article in draft and gave me useful suggestions for its improvement.

1. See for example J.C. Anene, *The International Boundaries of Nigeria 1885–1960* (Longman, 1970); C. Weladji, 'The Cameroun-Nigeria Border' in *ABBIA*, nos

27–28, June 1974; A.H.M. Kirk-Greene, 'Barth's Journey to Adamawa' in H. Schiffers (ed.), *Heinrich Barth. Ein Forscher in Afrika*, Wiesbaden, 1967.
2. For more details on the history of Mandara see B.M. Barkindo, 'Origins and History of the Sultanate of Mandara to 1902', unpubl. Ph.D. thesis, Ahmadu Bello University, 1980.
3. G.L. Anania, *La Universal Fabrico de Mondo, Overos Cosmographia*, Naples, 1573, 1576; Venice, 1582, 1596, pp. 323–52.
4. For the introduction and impact of Islam on the Sultanate of Mandara see B.M. Barkindo, 'Islam in Mandara, its introduction and impact on the state and the people', *Kano Studies*, 1, 4, 1979.
5. For the effects of the Fombina Jihad on Mandara see B.M. Barkindo, 'Mandara-Fombina relations in the pre-colonial period', *Kano Studies*, 2, 1, 1980.
6. D. Denham, *Narratives of Travels and Discoveries in Northern and Central Africa in the Years 1822, 1823 and 1824....*, London, 1826.
7. See for example Colonel Warrington's letter to Denham, Tripoli, 13 July, 1823, Public Records Office, London, C.O. 2:13, part I, *Mission to the Interior of Africa*, 1821–6, I.
8. See note 5 above.
9. After this battle, news soon spread that the Muslim Fulbe had won a major victory against a large Borno-Mandara force which included Arabs and Christians armed with guns. See Clapperton's concersation with Sultan Mohammed Bello of Sokoto in Denham, *Narratives of Travels*, II, p. 83.
10. H. Barth, *Travels and Discoveries in North and Central Africa...... in the Years 1849–1855* (London, 1857; centenary edn 1966), p. 343 (all references are from the 1966 edn).
11. H. Barth, *Collection of Vocabularies of Central African Languages* (London, 1862; 1971), I, p. ccxxix.
12. Barth, *Travels and Discoveries*, II, p. 196.
13. *Ibid.*, p. 168.
14. For further discussions on this see G. Launicke, 'Zur Einschatzung des deutschen Afrikareisenden Heinrich Barth', Karl-Marx-Universität, Leipzig, unpublished, 1966; A.H.M. Kirk-Greene, 'Barth's Journey to Adamawa', *op. cit.*
15. *Africa Times*, 27 Oct. 1885.
16. Annual Report for Nigeria, 1902, cited in Kirk-Greene, 'Barth's Journey to Adamawa', p. 24.
17. H. Stoecker *et al.*, 'Die Eroberung des Nordostens' in H. Stoecker (ed.) *Kamerun unter deutscher Kolonialherrschaft*, Berlin, 1968, II, pp. 55–9.
18. For more information on the details of the partition of Borno and Adamawa, see C. Herstslet, *The Map of Africa by Treaty*, III, 1894, 1967; Anene, *The International Boundaries of Nigeria*; Weladji, 'The Cameroun-Nigeria Border'.
19. Herr Munster, German Ambassador in France, to Prince von Hohenlohe, the German Chancellor, 26 Nov. 1898, in Reichkolonialamt (RKA), Potsdam, GDR, File no. 3301, *Die Benue-Expedition*.
20. See Oppenheim's Report to von Bucka, Director, German Colonial Department, Berlin, 12 Dec. 1901, in RKA 3301.
21. Dominik's Report, Garua, 26 July 1901, in RKA 3306, *Expedition des oberleutnants Dominik nach Garua*, Report of Governor Puttkamer, Buea, 25 Dec. 1901, in RKA 3303 *Die Benue-Expedition*.
22. Ibid.
23. See for example 'Translation of Autograph letter from Zubairu Emir of Yola', dated 20 Feb. 1893, Public Records Office, London; F.O. File 27, no. 3160, *France (Africa) various*.
24. W.K.R. Hallam, *The Life and Times of Rabih*, Ilfracombe, Devon, 1977, p. 269.

25. *Africa Times* (London), 5 February 1901.
26. *Ibid.*
27. For more details see Sa'ad Abubakar, *The Lamibe of Fombina*, Ahmadu Bello University/Oxford University Press, 1977, pp. 145–6; M.Z. Njeuma, *Fulani Hegemony in Yola (old Adamawa) 1809–1902*, Yaounde, 1978, pp. 222–38.
28. Report of Commandant Pavel, August 1902, in RKA 3350 *Expedition des Kais. Schutz*, pp. 197–207.
29. Report of Hauptmann Zimmermann, *Resident* of German Adamawa, Garua, 1906, in RKA 4229, II, p. 15.
30. *Ibid.*
31. Report of Hauptmann Stieber, *Resident* of the Areas of Lake Chad Province, Kussiri, 28 June 1906, in RKA 4230, III, p. 28.
32. *Ibid.*, pp. 30–3.
33. Governor Seitz to Hauptmann Stieber, Buea, 31 December 1908, in RKA 4230, pp. 36–8.
34. Report of Zimmermann in RKA 4230.
35. *Ibid.*
36. Governor Seitz to Stieber in RKA 4230.
37. Report on the war situation in Adamawa Duala, 19 Sept. 1914, RKA 3922, *Der Krieg in Kamerun*, 1914/18, I, p. 196.
38. 'The Cameroun Campaigns' in *West Africa World*, 13, 1915.
39. The war in Mandara has been reconstructed from the following sources: oral evidence collected by the author in Mandara in 1972, 1979 and 1980; F. Damis, *Auf dem Moraberge* (Berlin, 1930); J. Ferrandi, *Conquête du Cameroun-Nord 1914–15* (Paris, 1928); H. Georges, *The Great War in West Africa* (London, 1930); K. Strumpell, *Blätter aus der Geschichte der Schutztruppe für Kamerun* (Berlin, 1921).
40. See for example Kirk-Greene, 'Barth's Journey to Adamawa', pp. 196–7.
41. A.H.M. Kirk-Greene, *Adamawa Past and Present* (Oxford 1958), pp. 67–8.
42. Oral traditions on both sides of the border.
43. 'Partition of the Cameroun 1919–30', II, in National Archives, Kaduna (NAK).
44. My profound gratitude to all my informants and guides who accompanied me to the various points of the frontier.
45. Kamburwa-Disa traditions, Gwozo, April 1978.
46. *Ibid.*
47. British Cameroons, Report by H.B.M.'s Government to the Council of the League of Nations on the administration of the Mandate (London, 1928), p. 15.
48. 'Madagali District organisation in connection with Borno Province', Yola prof. File no. 2301, p. 1, in NAK.
49. *Ibid.*, p. 2.
50. *Ibid.*, pp. 3–4.
51. M. Lembezat, 'Tournée dans la subdivision de Mora, Mars-Avrie 1947', p. 60 in Archives coloniales Francaise (ACF), Mora; M. Flouries, 'Rapport sur les groupes ethniques du Caméroun qui se retrouvent en zone britannique', March 1949, p. 11, in ACE Mora.
52. Sultan Bichair Umar of Mandara, April 1979. See also E. Mohammadou, *Le royaume du Wandala ou Mandara* (Bamenda, 1975), p. 39.
53. *Ibid.*
54. Oral traditions, Kerawa, Doulo and Meme, April 1979.
55. 'Recurrent Reports: Northern Districts', September 1924, File B 2.F. in NAK.
56. Mohammadou, *Le royaume du Wandala*, pp. 40–1.
57. Fouries, Rapport, 1949, pp. 16–17.

58. *Ibid.* It must be noted that the two administrations followed different monetary systems.
59. Oral traditions, Kerawa, Mora, Mokolo, 1972, 1979.
60. Oral traditions, Mora, Mokolo, 1979.
61. *British Cameroun* . . . Report for the year 1929, p. 83.
62. *Ibid.* Report for the year 1934, p. 81.
63. 'Examinations in the Mandara language', Maiprof, File 1861/s in NAK.
64. Fouries, Rapport, 1949, p. 11.
65. 'Rencontre avec M. Le District Officer de Bama', January 1945, in ACF Mora.
66. J.D. Harford, 'Konduga District Special Report', 1929, p. 2, Malprof. File Acc 2362, D. 1. Vol. 4, in NAK.
67. Capt. Peter, 'Report on Kanduga District General', 1929, Maiprof. File No. AC 956 in NAK.
68. 'Madagali District in conjunction with Borno Province', p. 4, in NAK.
69. Lembezat, Rapport, 1947, p. 67.
70. 'Anglo-French Relations: visit exchanged between French and British administrators' officers', 1942, Yola prof. File 6493 in NAK.
71. 'Recontre avec M. Le District Officer Bama', Jan. 1945 in ACE.
72. Report of the Touring Officer of Northern Area of Adamawa, 27 Aug. 1947, Yola prof. File c.493 in NAK.
73. *Ibid.*

4

THE KAKWA OF UGANDA AND THE SUDAN
THE ETHNIC FACTOR IN NATIONAL AND INTERNATIONAL POLITICS

Ade. Adefuye

Introduction

The Kakwa at present inhabit the West Nile district in north-western Uganda and the Yei district of the Southern Sudan. A number of them can also be found along the Uganda border with Zaire. Their geographical location across the frontiers of three independent African states had tended to make them play important roles in the pattern of post-independence politics in these countries. As Uganda, the Sudan and Zaire came to grapple with the problems of nation-building, the Kakwa became an important element in their internal politics, later assuming international dimensions, thus giving the Kakwa a political importance disproportionate to their number.

Our purpose here is to attempt a brief historical survey of the Kakwa using them as a case study of the factors which determined the boundaries of African states as imposed by the colonial authorities, and the reaction of Africans to such delimitations. With particular reference to the Southern Sudanese boundary, they are presented as a case study of similarly partitioned African culture areas including the Azande and the Moru across the frontier with Zaire; the Acholi, the Toposa and the Dongatona across the border with Uganda; and the Turkana and Donyiro astride the boundary with Kenya. The study will focus on how the Kakwa, because of their membership of two sovereign states, Uganda and the Sudan, influenced internal politics and dictated the changing nature of the relationship between the two countries.

The pre-partition situation

The Kakwa belong to one of the three major linguistic groups in East and Central Africa which, for want of a better definition, are called Nilo-Hamites.[1] The two others are the Nilotes and the Bantu. The expression Nilo-Hamites is commonly used to refer to the peoples of the South-eastern Sudan, North-western Uganda, Western

Kenya and Northern Tanzania who, while being basically of Nilotic stock, show a few traces of Hamitic influence. The Kakwa are a part of the northern group of Nilo-Hamites which includes among others the Bari, the Kuka and the Lotuko. Their relatively low population density and apparent backwardness in Western educational terms, coupled with the political instability which has engulfed the Ugandan borders with the Sudan and Zaire since 1960, accounts for the paucity of information on their early history.[2]

The basis for the classification of the Kakwa and others as Nilo-Hamites is linguistic. Historically, the relations among the Nilo-Hamites are uncertain for nothing is known of their origin beyond the vague traditions of coming from the east or north. Like the Bari, many of the Kakwa claim to have come from the east, possibly from the direction of Ethiopia, after travelling along the Kiya and Kaiya valleys in the Sudan. They later settled in parts of the present-day Sudan, Uganda and Zaire after intermingling with various groups such as the Madi, the Bari and the Lotuko.[3]

The Kakwa's indigenous political system features the organisation of the community in independent groups or clans under clan heads who used to (and still do) exercise political as well as judicial powers. Within each clan there is a council of elders presided over by the head who adjudicates on all civil cases. In the past, compensation was payable for assault, but murder was an offence which could only be settled by killing in retaliation. In a case of accidental injury, the individual who caused it was to offer to help the injured to recover. Farming used to be and still remains the basis of the economy. The Kakwa grow maize, millet, potatoes and cassava. They tend some cattle but not on the same scale as the Nilotes who, by virtue of their location along the Nile basin, have greater access to pasture.

As with most other African societies, the factors of history and environment had largely dictated the nature of the Kakwa economy as well as their social and religious institutions. These in turn affected the nature of their reaction to such events as the coming of the European, the imposition of colonial rule and their role in the post-independence politics of the countries in which they found themselves. It was the nature of the terrain, for instance, which conditioned the attachment to farming. This in turn explains the importance attached to the institution of rainmaking. The rainmakers, called *Bura* (singular *Buaso*), bless the crops and perform important rituals and sacrifices. Although they are not the rulers, the society accords them a great deal of respect because they are a kind of link with the ancestors through whom they were believed to have received their powers.[4]

The ancestor cult is an important element in the Kakwa traditional religious system, which is centred around the belief in a supreme deity referred to as 'Nguleso'. Kakwa ancestors are believed to be the intermediaries between Nguleso and the living whose requests to Nguleso are usually presented by the rainmakers after the performance of certain rituals. It is Nguleso who, through the ancestors, brings good health or sickness, joy or misfortune depending on how it feels the entire society or particular individuals are abiding by its wishes. Whenever sickness or misfortune befalls an individual, a rainmaker is consulted to find out the reason and what should be done to appease the ancestors. The rainmakers also produce the 'Water of Yakan'.[5] This is a liquid mixed with a drug obtained from a plant called *Kumiojo*, and after the mixing the rainmakers appeal to Nguleso through the ancestors for blessing in order to make it effective. The Water is believed to confer immunity from death or disease, and in the colonial period it was believed to offer protection against arrest by the police. Its users felt themselves sufficiently equipped to disobey government orders including the obligation to pay taxes. It was believed that once the Water of Yakan was sprinkled all over the body, bullets would turn to water if and when fired.

On the question of colonial boundaries, the belief in the efficacy of the Water of Yakan strengthened the resistance of the Kakwa against attempts by the colonial governments to separate them from their kinsmen by means of barriers. Attempts to create boundaries between the Sudan and Uganda and restrict movements across the frontiers was resisted by the Kakwa, who always felt the need to visit the graves of their ancestors and consult with relations who were located on the other side of the British-imposed boundary. In flouting the British order restricting movement among the various Kakwa groups, the Water of Yakan was a source of encouragement, because all that the Kakwa felt he needed to do was to sprinkle the water over his body and he would either not be detected or, if shot at by the police, would not be injured. In actual fact the colonial government at that time was itself facing a manpower problem and was thus not in a good position to effect the order restricting movement. To an average Kakwa, however, it was the Water of Yakan that was protecting them and making it possible for them to cross the forbidden frontier without harm.

The Kakwa contact with the outside world did not begin with the British attempt to divide them into two distinct political entities. It was Khedive Muhammad Ali of Egypt who, in an effort to consolidate his position at home by strengthening the dwindling resources of the Egyptian treasury, sponsored an expedition to the

Sudan in 1841.[6] Captain Salim, who commanded the expedition, sailed as far south as Gondokoro and was able to collect some quantities of gold and ivory as well as discover strategic spots that became useful when the Sudan came to be occupied. Muhammad Ali's efforts were improved upon by his successors, notably Khedives Said and Ismail, the latter of whom sent Samuel Baker, Richard Gordon and Emin Pasha to the Sudan asking them to establish a formal Egyptian protectorate over the area. Between 1864 and 1878, these European agents of the Egyptian Khedive actually reached the southern extremity of the present-day Sudan and the northern part of Uganda including the Kakwa territory, and declared an Egyptian protectorate over what they termed the Equatorial Province.

The way in which these officials carried out their assignments in the territory gave rise to a series of grievances including charges of corruption, maladministration, and deliberate victimisation of the affected people. By 1880, when the reckless financial policy of Khedive Ismail had brought about his abdication from the throne of Egypt, anti-Egyptian sentiment was given expression in the outbreak of the Mahdist revolt, an essentially religious movement with economic and political overtones. The success of the movement and the evacuation of the Egyptian governor Emin Pasha from the territory put a rather decisive end to Egypt's authority over the area. It was left to the British to wage a war against the Mahdists at Omdurman in 1898,[7] after which they established what was known as an Anglo-Egyptian Condominium over the Sudan. But the exact southern boundary of the Condominium area was not fixed, probably because both the Sudan and the territory immediately to the south, namely the Ugandan kingdoms of Buganda and Bunyoro, were then under British influence. Politically the exact boundary between the two administrative units was of no immediate concern to the British. It is against this background that one must seek to understand the series of debates which took place as to where the Kakwa should be placed when it became necessary to define the boundary between Uganda and the Sudan.

Uganda boundaries

One of the major problems confronting newly-independent African states is that of unity. The majority of them, having inherited their frontiers from the former colonial masters, do not embrace one people with a common culture, language and history. The late nineteenth-century European scramble for Africa and subsequent partition left many of the African successor-states a heritage of artificially contrived borderlines, with each state having a multitude of ethnic and linguistic groups within its territory, some of which are separated from their kith and kin by the international frontiers. Although the Organisation of African Unity (OAU) had advocated the retention of frontiers as inherited from the colonial masters, there have been irredentist claims by groups whose traditional frontiers seem to have been violated by the imposed boundaries. The East African example shows clearly that what each of the various colonial powers was primarily interested in at the time of boundary negotiations was grabbing as much African territory for itself as possible. They were not concerned with the consequences of disrupting ethnic groups or undermining the indigenous social, religious, or political order.[8] The boundaries, including those of Uganda, were defined mostly through routine diplomatic negotiations and were only later defined by special boundary commissions. The knowledge of the nature of the populations, and of the traditions of mobility in affected areas, were of marginal consideration at the time the boundaries were made. All that interested the colonial officials was how they could acquire the economically rich areas and how British public opinion in Uganda could best be satisfied. The memorandum drawn up by Governor Hesketh Bell of Uganda on the delimitation as it affects the salt lake at Katwe clearly illustrates the factors which influenced the British attitude towards Uganda's frontiers.

The possession of Katwe salt lake is of great importance to His Majesty's Government. Its loss would be felt throughout the length and breadth of the Southern portion of the Uganda Protectorate and would injure British prestige. It supplies the treaty kingdoms of Buganda, Ankole and Toro with salt. The possession of Mount Stanley is more desirable for sentimental reasons than for any others. It is of no practical value.[9]

Three points stand out clearly from these quotations. H.M. Stanley had explored the area with financial support from Britain, and the mountain named after him should therefore be included in the British sphere. Here the explorers' and colonial interests converged. The second point is the idea of prestige, although in this case the salt lake was also a financial asset to the area mentioned by Bell. Thirdly Governor Bell was concerned about criticism from the British public at home and in Uganda. It is important to note that nowhere did he indicate in his memorandum a glimmer of concern about the people for whom this boundary would provide a new barrier.

The British adopted the same attitude to the question of Uganda's border with the Sudan, which provides a classic example of an artificial boundary designed to consolidate a colonial sphere of influence without the least regard for the affected population. The debate as to which of the British-administered territories, Uganda or the Sudan, the Kakwa should have as their home went on over a period of forty years. The Colonial Office favoured the idea that the former Equatorial Province should be retained within one colonial territory, preferably the Sudan.

The reluctance to have the Kakwa in Uganda stemmed from the fact that the Middle Nile Valley region, which includes present-day Northern Uganda and the Southern Sudan and in particular the Kakwa homeland, was affected by the sleeping sickness which not only stunted and killed cattle, but also caused an epidemic among humans and depopulated the areas affected. The disease was caused by the tse-tse fly which is found mainly in the present-day Southern Sudan.[10] The disease proved particularly infectious and the British thought that the best way to limit its destructive effect was to restrict its carriers (men and cattle) to where the disease originated, namely the Sudan. The other peoples and places to which the disease might spread could then be protected. By 1911 the Palwo of Northern Bunyoro had felt the impact of the epidemic and the entire population of one of the two counties (Kihukya) had to be evicted to the neighbouring Kibanda county.[11]

It was at this period that the Governor of Uganda, J.J. Fallers, having dealt with the Palwo victims of the epidemic, proposed that a 5-mile-wide strip of land between the Sudan and Uganda Kakwa should be cleared of people. This was to be policed to stop illegal movement across the border. When the proposal was eventually implemented and the Kakwa were driven into the remaining territories on either side of the Ugandan and Sudanese borders, the problem arose as to how to provide them with enough land on which to subsist because the neighbouring peoples would not share what they had with them. This problem of overpopulation coupled with that of insufficient personnel to police the no man's land eventually made the scheme ineffective.

The Provincial Commissioner of Uganda's Northern region, commenting on the border problem, observed that the no-man's-land would not prevent illicit intercourse so long as the boundary divided the Kakwa of Kajo Kajo in Sudan from their friends and relations in Uganda.[12] Those Kakwas who were pushed into the Sudan were the principal culprits in violating the sleeping sickness regulations in the area. When the no-man's-land scheme failed, a number of orders-in-council were enacted (one of them in 1914) shifting the

Sudan-Uganda boundary. But each time this was done — with the object of preventing the spread of sleeping sickness—the frontier divided the Kakwa. Particularly abhorrent to the Kakwa was the attempt to separate some of them from the ancestral graves and the shrine of their supreme deity Nguleso, all of which were located in Uganda's West Nile District a few miles from the village of Koboko. According to Kakwa folklore, it was Nguleso who threw a man down from heaven; he happened to be the first Kakwa king, who taught the people agriculture. Kakwa ancestors of the first generation are believed to have been buried around Koboko and it is believed that the spirits of the ancestors can send sickness or any other misfortune should they be neglected. The sanctuary around Koboko was also the location of the greatest concentration of Kakwa rainmakers who, as has already been noted, are important for diagnosing cases of misfortune and offer sacrifices to appease Nguleso. It is also the rainmakers who make the famous Water of Yakan. Thus the belief in the effectiveness of the Water of Yakan, coupled with the need to continue offering sacrifices to Nguleso, made it impossible for the Kakwa to comply with the order restricting movement between the Southern Sudan and Northern Uganda. Besides, it was an established custom of the Kakwa farming population to practise shifting cultivation, moving north and south of the proposed frontier.

The colonial government's explanation of the need to restrict movement across the border in order to contain the sleeping sickness epidemic made no impressions on the Kakwa, since they believed that the epidemic had spread because some of them had incurred the wrath of Nguleso by obeying the orders restricting them to the Sudan and in the process had failed to offer sacrifices to him when due. For the Kakwa in the Sudan, the solution to the sleeping sickness problem was in crossing the border and appeasing Nguleso. Moreover as news about the spread of the epidemic in the Sudan reached the Kakwa in Uganda, they felt the need to visit the sick and bereaved relations. The arrest and detention of a few of them was seen as an act of annoyance on the part of Nguleso because they had waited so long to cross the border to perform the necessary ritual and not as a proof of the Water of Yakan's ineffectiveness.

Because the order restricting Kakwa movement was so difficult to enforce, the issue of the Uganda-Sudan border was finally regarded as intractable and in 1936 the colonial government more or less reconciled itself to the impossibility of separating the Kakwa, arguing that 'the troubles of boundaries cutting across tribes is not unusual and that with time the co-operation of the respective administrations would produce a tolerable solution'.[13] This was why a part of Kigezi was given to the Belgians while its bulk is in Uganda. Rwanda also had a section of its territory severed and joined to Uganda, while the Digo and Maasai are divided by the Kenya-Tanzania border. The Tanzania-Zambia border also bisects the Makonde and the Yao while the Alur are divided between what was the Belgian Congo (Zaire) and Uganda.

The case of the Kakwa clearly illustrates the conflict between the inter-colonial state boundaries and the pre-colonial state frontiers. The fact is that in the consolidation of boundaries for colonial jurisdiction, sociological factors were ignored, with the effect that in the post-independence period this issue affected politics within African states and also dictated the pattern of relations between the states. According to McEwen,[14] the British order-in-council of 1914 was made the basis of negotiations between the authorities in the Sudan and Uganda before Uganda's independence. The agreed boundary, however, still left part of the Kakwa in Northern Uganda and part in the Southern Sudan. The no-man's-land scheme had to be abandoned because grass grew over the area, which was eventually inhabited by the Kakwa.

The presence of a branch of the Kakwa in the Sudan was an important factor in the country's internal politics in that they teamed up with other ethnic groups in the South to present a common Black African front against the Arab North centred on the capital Khartoum. At the same time, their presence in Uganda affected that country's initial attitude to the problem of the Southern Sudan, and when a Kakwa in the person of Idi Amin Dada became a principal figure in Uganda's leadership crisis, the political support which he received from the Southern Sudan, which has been widely acknowledged, was a factor which helped sustain him in power for so long. The fluid nature of the Sudan-Uganda boundary, determined largely by the situation on both sides of peoples with a common cultural identity, has come to affect the relations between the two countries.

At independence both countries faced the problems of building distinct nation-states out of diverse ethnic and religious groups. That of the Sudan was the more apparent, in that there was a clear division between the Arabs of the North and the Africans of the South, including the Kakwa. In Uganda, the conflict was initially between the Nilotes and the Bantu, and later between the Nilotes and the Nilo-Hamites. In this situation, which Ali Mazrui described as one of 'amorphous national identity and imminent political violence', it follows, as Mazrui further argued, that 'the quarrels of one country spilled over into another and transnational interpenetration became facilitated by international cleavages.'[15]

It was the Sudan's internal crisis that first became a serious issue with the emergence in 1955 of a guerrilla movement, referred to as the Anya-Nya, aimed at pressing for the rights of the non-Arabised peoples in the South. The crisis in Uganda did not become a serious issue until Obote's attack on the Kabaka of Buganda's palace in 1966. The presence and the involvement of the Kakwa in the conflicts of both countries were such that in the first six years of Uganda's independence, a Uganda factor was never absent in the Sudanese civil war. But by 1971, when the Kakwa Idi Amin seized power from Milton Obote, it became clear that a Sudanese factor also existed in Uganda's power struggles.

The Sudanese civil war and the Kakwa factor

The origin of the Sudanese civil war can be traced to the events which followed the successful British attack on the Madhist state in 1898 and the establishment of a Condominium over the Sudan. According to Russell and McCall,[16] the British policy in the Sudan had been to develop the three Southern provinces of Upper Nile, Bahr Al Ghazal and Equatoria along distinctively African lines to the exclusion of the Islamic and Arab influences from the North. However, by 1946 the British reversed this policy as a result of strong pressure from Western-educated Northerners in Khartoum for independence for the whole of the Sudan, and pressure from Egypt not to separate the South from the North in the hope that one day the whole country might be united with Egypt. It should be pointed out that in the course of the abandonment of the Southern Sudanese policy, no Southerner was consulted by the Khartoum government.

When this fact was pointed out to the British officials, a conference was convened in Juba in 1947 to discuss the issue of the relationship of the South and the North. However, it was attended by relatively inexperienced Southern politicians who were hurriedly hand-picked a few days before the conference. At that conference, the British Civil Secretary made it clear that the separation of the South from the North was no longer practicable, and although many of the Southerners spoke against the idea of one legislative assembly for the two sections of the Sudan, the British officials went on to record that the Southerners and Northerners had agreed to unite. Future negotiations for independence were carried on by the Northerners without due reference to the Southerners under the pretext that, since the South had been united with the North in 1947 and the Southerners had not developed enough to have political organisations, their interest could be represented by the Northerners. This was precisely what happened in the Anglo-Egyptian agreement of 1952.

By 1954 the seeming unwillingness of the government to give special attention to the South had increased the fears and suspicions of Southerners with regard to an independent Sudan. In August 1955 the Southern corps of the army mutinied and before it was put down it had grown into a popular uprising in which 261 Northerners living in the South were killed. Before Southern legislators could support the motion for independence of the Sudan, they got included in the motion a clause stating that their claim for a federal system of government would be given full consideration in the forthcoming constituent assembly. At independence in 1956, the South was given only three seats on the 46-man constitution committee, and the federation idea made no headway. Mahgoub, the chairman of the committee, announced that the Southern claim for federation could not work in the country. The idea of federation was permanently dropped in 1958 when Prime Minister Abdallah Kali handed over power to the army.

Southerners then gave up hope of achieving their aim by constitutional means and started fighting in the bush. The Anya-Nya guerrilla movement emerged, and all the Southern exile groups agreed to unite under General Lagu to prosecute a war against the Khartoum government. One important aspect of the military confrontation between the Southern Sudanese and Khartoum is that the Anya-Nya army which emerged was patterned upon the army of the Madhia in that it was initially recruited along ethnic lines with accepted military leaders for each group in the Southern Sudan. Thus within the Anya-Nya, there was a Lotuko regiment and one each for the Bari, Madi, Kuku and Kakwa. All these groups, however, fused under one leadership, and as the war progressed the ethnic origins of the army members were submerged under the overall desire to establish the rights of the Southern peoples in an independent Sudan.

It was while this war was raging that Apolo Milton Obote emerged in 1962 as the first Prime Minister and later the executive President of the Republic of Uganda, with Idi Amin, a Kakwa from the ancestrally influential village of Koboko, as one of his two most senior army officers. By 1964, Amin had virtually become the head of the Ugandan army. As a Black African, Obote could not help being persuaded by the arguments of the Southern Sudanese for the support of fellow Africans in the struggle against the Khartoum government. Statistics were published showing discrimination against Southerners in recruitment to the police, civil service and secondary education. In addition, the Southern Sudanese made it clear that most of the problems connected with the dispute between the North and the South in the Sudan had an underlying racial basis and that the expressed policy of the North seemed to be to 'assimilate' the Southerners in a bid to replace the various indigenous cultures by a single Islamic and Arabised one.[17]

Obote's first action was to provide facilities for a meeting of the various black Sudanese political organisations aimed at working out strategies for the evolution of a common front. In November 1964, he allowed the first general convention of the Sudan African National Union to meet in Kampala.[18] Aggrey Jaden was elected president, and it was decided that the newly-elected officers should begin making arrangements for the party to move inside the Southern Sudan. This was done in 1965 and the implementation was carried out with the active assistance of the Ugandan government under the supervision of Idi Amin. Between 1965 and 1969, Obote vacillated between working towards a peaceful settlement and supporting the blacks in the Sudanese conflict. While taking part in many peace moves, he secretly provided military and logistic assistance to the Southern Sudanese at the same time, perhaps in the belief that the resistance of the Southerners would compel the Khartoum government to seek a peaceful solution to the conflict.

Apart from the ethnic factor, there were some external pressures on Uganda to aid the Southern Sudanese. When Obote emerged as the first leader of independent Uganda, he like other African leaders sought external assistance to improve his country's economy and build her defence. He found ready assistance from the Israelis, who realised that the Arabs were a power in the Organisation of African Unity (OAU) and so decided to improve relations with as many Black African countries as possible and establish embassies in order to prevent them from gravitating towards the Arabs in the Middle East conflict.[19] Uganda provided a special attraction to the Israelis in that it bordered on the Sudan where black Africans had been fighting against the Arabs because, among other things, the Arab-dominated central government wanted to unite the entire country with Egypt. The Israelis therefore decided to back the Southern Sudanese as a means of stabbing the Arabs in the back, prolonging the war in the Sudan, and preventing any possibility of this merger with Egypt or active support for it. This required the support of Uganda, which could be used as a base for military and material aid to the Southern Sudanese.

This partly explains the very cordial diplomatic relations between Uganda and Israel during the early period of Obote's regime; the Israelis pumped in military and financial assistance; and it was they who built the radar at Uganda's international airport at Entebbe, equipped and trained the air force and gave generous loans to develop the country's agriculture. Thus the Israelis' strategic interest came to combine rather harmoniously with Obote's emotional attachment to the cause of his fellow Africans and Idi Amin's feeling of solidarity with his kinsmen to ensure Uganda's sympathy and active support for the Southern Sudanese between 1963 and 1969. David Martin reports that on several occasions in those years Israeli officers were seen inside the Southern Sudan with the Anya-Nya, and air drops of equipment were made regularly by Israeli planes flying into the Southern Sudan across Ethiopia and Uganda. Thirty of the Anya-Nya guerrilla leaders were trained in Israel and sent back to the Sudan through Uganda. A quantity of the equipment which Israel captured from the Arabs in the six-day war in 1967 was delivered to the Anya-Nya through Uganda. General Lagu, head of the Anya-Nya, was several times seen in Uganda holding discussions with Idi Amin who co-ordinated the Israeli military assistance to the Southern Sudanese, most of which was sent in through Uganda.[20]

The assumption of authority by General Nimeiry in the Sudan in May 1969 subtly altered the delicate balance of power between the Sudan and Uganda. The preceding two years had seen a gradual rift develop between Obote and the Western powers. After his attack on the Kabaka and the declaration of Uganda as a republic, Obote proceeded to pursue revolutionary economic and political policies which were obviously distasteful to the Western powers and earned Obote serious criticism in their press. His 'common man's charter' and 'move to the left' were criticised as unrealistic and out of tune with Uganda's history. Despite this, Obote and the Israelis continued to tolerate each other until 1969 when Nimeiry on assuming power not only identified himself with the 'progressive' African bloc but also promised to find a lasting political solution to the problem of the Southern Sudan. Moreover, it seemed to have dawned on Obote that his revolutionary policies were at odds with his continued economic and military link with Israel. By 1969, he took actions which indicated his preparedness to cut the link. Early in 1970 the Uganda cabinet security committee had been asking questions about the activities of Colonel Barlev, the Israeli security adviser in the country, and it was later decided that all foreign military advisers should leave before the end of the year. The Israeli ambassador, Mr Ofri, complained at the decision of the committee as well as the fact that it had been indicated that Israeli training of the police special force would be terminated in 1971. Ofri also complained at Uganda having sent her ambassador in Cairo to the United Nations where he had voted for what Israel regarded as a pro-Arab resolution.[21]

With regard to Israeli activities in the Southern Sudan, Obote made it clear that he no longer needed them, partly because of the trust he reposed in Nimeiry as a fellow African revolutionary. In 1969 Rolf Steiner, a West German mercenary who had been fighting on the side of the secessionists during the Nigerian civil war then still in progress, arrived in Uganda preparatory to joining the Anya-Nya. Obote captured him and handed him over to Nimeiry.[22] A month before Steiner's arrest, the chief of Israel's Central Intelligence Organisation, General Zamir, sought refuelling rights in Uganda for their arms ferry to the Anya-Nya, but received a blunt refusal from Obote. Akena Adoko, Obote's cousin and head of the General Service department, was approached but said he could do nothing.

The Israelis then went to Amin who, because of his close ethnic ties with the Southern Sudanese, responded more positively. He was subsequently in the Southern Sudan with the Israeli officers. Despite Obote's disapproval, Amin ordered officers in charge of army units near the Sudan border to allow supplies which included weapons and food to go from Uganda to the Anya-Nya, and there were cases when medicines bought with Ugandan funds for their own armed forces were diverted on Amin's orders to the Southern Sudanese. Amin made many trips to the Southern Sudanese secessionist fighters inside the Sudan and occasionally met the Anya-Nya leaders in Uganda's West Nile district.[23] If the African in Obote enabled him to entrust Nimeiry with the task of meeting the demands of the Blacks in the Sudan, the Kakwa in Amin felt that mere promises of a solution and identification with the cause of the OAU were not enough justification for the denial of military and logistic support for the Southern Sudanese in their war against Khartoum.

The rift between Amin and Obote had started and Obote began to groom Brigadier Okoya as a replacement for Amin. Rumours of Amin's involvement in gold and ivory smuggling across the border with Zaire, coupled with his alleged involvement in the murder of Brigadier and Mrs Okoya, completed Obote's disenchantment. The near-open disagreement between Amin and Obote made Uganda's political atmosphere highly charged on the eve of Obote's departure to Singapore in January 1971 to attend the Commonwealth prime ministers' conference, where the issue of Britain's alleged intention to supply military equipment to South Africa was discussed.

Power struggle in Uganda

The Israelis and the Southern Sudanese were not happy at Obote's change of attitude to the Sudan question. As mentioned earlier, Israel's support for the Southern Sudanese was part of its Middle East strategy. When Obote voted for a pro-Arab resolution at the United Nations the Israelis began to think of what could be done to stop him. They probably thought of using Amin. They were equally disappointed by Obote on behalf of the Southern Sudanese, but were apparently consoled by the fact that the Southerners' kinsman, Amin, was still on their side. Thus when Amin and Obote began to drift apart, the Israelis in co-operation with the Southern Sudanese began to prepare Amin for an eventual showdown with Obote. Israeli military intelligence helped him to arrange a series of clandestine meetings with the Anya-Nya and Kakwa elements in the Uganda army shortly before and after Obote's departure for the conference in Singapore.

It was while Obote was attending that conference that Amin staged a successful *coup* against his regime, thereby emerging as Uganda's head of government. Since the *coup*, Obote's supporters have insisted that the critical factor which tipped the balance against them was the involvement of at least 500 Southern Sudanese Anya-Nya guerrillas, some of whom had been transported from the Southern Sudan (in lorries supplied by a company owned by Felix Onama, at one time Uganda's Interior Minister) to Bombo where Amin met them and discussed details of the *coup*. Amin later posted a number of his Kakwa officers to the critical Malire Mechanised Batallion and sent others whose loyalty to him he doubted off on leave as soon as Obote left for Singapore. The details of how the *coup* was executed need not detain us here. What is important is the fact that on 25 January 1971 Idi Amin, a Kakwa, seized power in Uganda with the active assistance of his Anya-Nya brothers who, apart from the ethnic factor, also felt the need to repay him for his earlier support across the borders and so secure Uganda's government support in their struggle against Khartoum. The Israelis were quite happy about the *coup* and some insisted that it was they who drove the armoured vehicles which played so prominent a part in the *coup* and manned the radio stations when news of the take-over was announced. If the Israelis supplied the technology and intelligence, it was the Kakwa and the Anya-Nya movement in the Southern Sudan who supplied the manpower.

The Sudanese factor in Uganda's power struggles did not end with Amin's assumption of power. It was also instrumental in helping him to consolidate his hotly disputed authority. Apparently acting on the advice of the Israelis, whose country was the first to which Amin paid a state visit, Amin embarked on a massive reorganisation of the Uganda army during which fellow Kakwas in Uganda and some Anya-Nya guerrillas were placed in sensitive positions. Obote's immediate reaction on hearing the news of his overthrow was to plan for a military showdown with Amin and regain power. General Nimeiry of the Sudan rightly felt that the Amin regime in Uganda would mean an escalation of the conflict in the South and he decided to give all possible assistance to Obote. He allowed Obote to establish a training camp at Owiny-ki-bul, a former Anya-Nya administrative centre, which had been captured and garrisoned by the Sudanese troops. It was about 10 miles inside the Sudan from the Ugandan border, and Nimeiry ensured that over 200 Sudanese soldiers would provide a perimeter guard for Obote.[24] Messages were then sent to loyal members of Obote's Uganda People Congress (UPC) asking them to report at the camp.

Amin and his Anya-Nya allies were aware of what was going on at the camp, and on 14 April 1971, 617 of Obote's UPC supporters who in response to a recruitment call were going to Owiny-ki-bul, were captured by the Southern Sudanese after crossing the Aswa river into the Sudan. They were handed over to Amin's troops and slaughtered near Palabek.[25] In August of that year, a Ugandan reconnaissance plane, piloted by an Israeli officer with Amin and some Anya-Nya leaders as passengers, flew low over the camp at Owiny-ki-bul. The plane, whose radio was monitored at the camp, had to take hurried evasive action because of heavy ground fire.[26] Twice in January 1972 Anya-Nya guerrillas, supported by Amin's troops, attacked Obote's camp, but on both occasions the Sudanese troops repulsed the attack.

The following month, attempts which had been going on behind the scenes to end the sixteen-year-old Sudanese civil war, which had cost an estimated 500,000 lives, suddenly bore fruit. Representatives of the Khartoum government and the Anya-Nya met secretly in Addis Ababa with observers from the World Council of Churches and African Churches. With surprisingly little difficulty, a peace settlement was reached. The Anya-Nya, who a year earlier had backed their kinsman Amin in ousting Obote from power, no longer required the sympathy of the government in Kampala, but nonetheless they still wanted their kinsman to succeed as head of state in Uganda. At the same time, the peace settlement imposed new pressures on General Nimeiry. He needed the co-operation of the Anya-Nya to seal the peace.

The Anya-Nya knew about Obote's men at Owiny-ki-bul, and certainly, once the settlement was ratified, they would not have tolerated the Southern Sudan being used as a springboard to overthrow Amin, their kinsman in Kampala. Obote, who had been warned in December 1971 by the Khartoum government that he might have to move should the peace efforts succeed, was asked to move his forces out in May 1972. His UPC supporters moved through Mongalla and later Port Sudan before sailing down the Red Sea and on to Tanzania. The peace settlement of 1972 ended Obote's harassment of Amin from the Sudanese border, thus leaving the exiled Ugandan leader with Tanzania as his only base from which to attack Amin.

The extent of the fluidity of the boundary between Uganda and Sudan, particularly during the Sudanese civil war and the period of Amin's rule in Uganda before the peace settlement of 1972, can be seen in the statistics of refugees released by the United Nations High Commission for Refugees. Of an estimated 200,000 refugees outside the Sudan 70,000 were said to be in Uganda.[27] 'For reasons of contiguity', said J.D. Denoon, 'Uganda was the first resort to most of the refugees.'[28] Not all the Sudanese refugees left Uganda after the peace settlement, which merely provided some of them with an opportunity to render their military services elsewhere. Amin needed them, for by 1972 rumours of attempted *coups* against him were rife. From the 500 Sudanese soldiers which Amin recruited for his *coup* against Obote, the number rose to 1,000 in 1972, and by 1973 there were at least 3,000 of them in the Uganda army. Obote's attempts to unseat Amin in 1972 and 1973 were followed by Amin's execution of military officers whose loyalty he had cause to doubt whether or not there was evidence of their complicity in the *coup* attempts.

These men were replaced by Southern Sudanese. By late 1973 it was reported that of the twenty-four top military positions in Uganda, only three were held by persons who were neither Southern Sudanese nor Kakwa in origin.[29] When Amin's position became more precarious following his rift with the Western world — which began with his break in diplomatic relations with Israel and the expulsion of the Asians — he came to rely ever more heavily on the Southern Sudanese to retain his hold on Uganda. It is on record that when he was eventually overthrown, the invading force of the Uganda National Liberation Front (UNLF), assisted by the national army of Tanzania, came not from the direction of the Sudan but from Tanzania, and that Amin made his escape through the Sudan. It is indeed a fitting testimony to the resilience of Amin's excellent relationship with the Southern Sudanese that since his overthrow, the only major threat to the new government has come from the Southern Sudan.

Conclusion

An effort has been made to show that the British attempt to partition the Kakwa between Uganda and the Sudan did not affect the people's feeling of brotherhood towards one another. The Kakwa of the Sudan and Uganda showed clearly the artificial nature of the colonial boundaries inherited by the independent African countries. Whether in the Anya-Nya or in Amin's struggles, the Kakwa still regarded themselves as one and worked together. There is abundant evidence that Amin, even as late as 1972, exhibited characteristics similar to those of the typical Kakwa with their strong belief in the supernatural. Amin often claimed to be acting on the instructions of his witch doctors and from messages he received in dreams. It was in one of his dreams that he claimed to have received a message urging him to declare an economic war by expelling the Asians. A wealthy Zambian, Dr Francis Ngombe, claims that just before Amin seized power, he predicted the overthrow of Dr Obote. After the coup, Dr Ngombe became Amin's personal soothsayer and prophet. A Ghananian mystic who claimed he could raise people from the dead was flown to Uganda and Amin subsequently claimed to have talked with a man who had been resurrected.

Although some of Amin's demonstrations of belief in witchcraft were interpreted as evidence of his eccentricity, what is often not realised is the fact of his complete commitment to Kakwa culture including the belief in the efficacy of customary rituals and sacrifices. His village, Koboko, was close to the grove of Nguleso, the Kakwa supreme god, and he saw the protection of fellow-Kakwa, whether in Uganda or the Sudan, as his primary responsibility. In addition, he felt that it was his right to call on them for aid when he needed it. There is no denying that Amin's disagreement with Obote's change of policy over the Southern Sudan was one of the reasons for his falling out of favour with Obote and which compelled him to move against his former master with the active assistance of his Kakwa kinsmen. The Southern Sudanese in turn helped Amin even when it appeared that the tide had turned against him. It is therefore clear that in spite of their location in Uganda and Sudan, the Kakwa retained their ethnic identity in utter disregard for the boundary imposed by the colonial authorities.

NOTES

1. See G.W.B. Huntingford, 'The Northern Nilo-Hamites', *Ethnographic Survey of Africa: East Central Africa*, Part VI (London: International African Institute, 1953), pp. 53–6. Of recent years African scholars have been showing resentment at the use of the concept 'Nilo-Hamites' because of its seemingly racist connotation. They have been trying to adopt the use of a substitute word 'Sudanic' to describe the people concerned. See J.B. Webster, *Uganda before 1900* (Nairobi: East African Publishing House, forthcoming).
2. The Kakwa number about 50,000 in Uganda, but this writer did not come across a single Kakwa throughout his two years' stay in Makerere University. Ever since 1955 up till early 1972, civil war had been raging in the Sudan.
3. Huntingford, *op. cit.*
4. *Ibid.* and C.G. Seligman, *Pagan Tribes of the Nilotic Sudan* (London, 1932), pp. 296–8.
5. *Ibid.*
6. For details see R. Gray, *History of the Southern Sudan* (London: Oxford University Press, 1961).
7. See P.M. Holt, *A Modern History of the Sudan* (London: Weidenfeld and Nicolson, 1961), pp. 77–108.
8. See A.C. McEwen, *International Boundaries of East Africa* (Oxford University Press, 1971).
9. T.B. Kabwegyere, *Uganda: The politics of state formation* (Nairobi: East African Literature Bureau, 1971), p. 58.
10. For details of the origin and impact of the sleeping sickness epidemic on Uganda, see H.G. Soff, 'A History of Sleeping Sickness in Uganda: Administrative response 1900–1970' (unpubl. Ph.D. thesis, University of Syracuse, 1971).
11. For the effects of the sleeping sickness on the Palwo, see Ade. Adefuye, *A History of the Palwo*, ch. 5 (Enugu: Nok Publishers, in press).
12. Kabwegyere, *op. cit.*, p. 60
13. See L.F. Nalder, *A Tribal Survey of Mongalla Province* (Oxford University Press, 1937).
14. McEwen, *op. cit.*, p. 258.
15. Ali Mazrui, *Soldiers and Kinsmen in Uganda: The Making of a Military Ethnocracy* (Sage Publications, 1975), p. 121.
16. For details see Peter Russell and Storrs McCall, 'Can Secession be Justified? The Case of the Southern Sudan' in Dunstan Wai (ed.), *The Southern Sudan: The problems of national integration* (London: Frank Cass, 1973), pp. 83–122. Other chapters in the book treat the origin and nature of the Sudanese conflict.
17. For an example of the propaganda of the Southern Sudanese, see the speech of Aggrey Jaden, President of the Sudan African National Union, at the inauguration of the Union in Kampala in 1964 in which he said: 'The Sudan falls sharply into two distinct areas both in geographical area, ethnic groups and cultural systems. There is nothing in common between the various sections of the community, no body of shared beliefs, no identity of interests, no local signs of unity and above all, the Sudan has failed to compose a single community.'
18. For details see Russell and McCall, *op. cit.*
19. For details of Israeli activities in Africa see Abel Jacob, 'Israel's Military aid to Africa', *Journal of Modern African Studies*, 9, 2, 1971. See also Ade. Adefuye, 'Israel and Nigeria', *International Studies*, Oct.–Dec., 1979.
20. See David Martin, *General Amin* (London, 1978), pp. 181–4. See also *Newsweek*, 10 May 1971.
21. Martin, *op. cit.*

22. *Ibid.*, p. 51.
23. *Ibid.*, p. 196.
24. *Ibid.*, p. 197.
25. *Ibid.*, p. 191.
26. See Edgar O'Ballance, *The Secret War in the Sudan* (London: Faber and Faber. 1977), p. 146.
27. J.D. Denoon, 'The Education of Southern Sudanese Refugees' in Dunstan Wai (ed.), *The Southern Sudan, op. cit.*, pp. 137-45.
28. See table showing origin of the commanding officers of the Uganda army, David Martin, *op. cit.*, Appendix.

5

ETHNIC AFFINITY, PARTITION AND POLITICAL INTEGRATION IN SENEGAMBIA

F.A. Renner

Cette image [i.e. the metaphorical image of a big brother sitting a little sister on his lap] affective et assurante à la fois résume éloquemment les destins mêlés des deux pays. L'histoire, la géographie, la culture y ont issu, depuis des siècles, des liens immémoriaux. Si la colonisation européenne les a artificiellement séparés, les interêts vitaux de leurs peuples ont créé, entre eux, une interdépendance à l'épreuve du temps. Pour cette raison, le Sénégal, que des liens juridiques particuliers lient de surcroit à la Gambie, se devait de voler au secours de la Gambie — parce que la stabilité et la démocratie de la Gambie sont aussi la paix et la stabilité du Sénégal.

— Bara Diop, *Le Soleil*, 9 February 1982

Introduction

Undoubtedly the Senegambian Confederation, which came into effect on 1 February 1982, has raised the question, repeatedly posed since the 1960s, as to why such a positive move has not been made before and has only come about as a result of a historical accident. Given the relatively fragile economies of Senegal and the Gambia, the fact that the two states constitute a complementary geographical sub-region, and above all the cultural and historical ties binding the constituent ethnic groups across the common boundaries, it would appear that the basic elements for close co-operation — if not of outright union — are present, despite the differential impact of European colonialism.

Yet the history of the search for a viable and mutually acceptable partnership between Senegal and the Gambia has hitherto proved to be singularly fraught with difficulties, setbacks and frustrations.[2] It is significant that even now the political arrangement agreed upon is that of a confederation, and not a federation or a union.

While some attempts have been made to highlight factors which have tended to militate against political integration between Senegal and the Gambia, the arguments have concentrated almost exclusively on the effects of the differing colonial experience, especially as manifested in the cultural attitudes of the ruling élite. While the factor of differential colonial experience is crucial in any discussion of political union in Senegambia,[3] the emphasis placed on it minimises and even eclipses the pre-colonial forces which had precluded the emergence of an all-embracing macro-state despite the natural links among its diverse constituent ethnic groups. By discussing the pre-colonial situation, we shall seek to place the factor of differential colonial impact in proper perspective. It will be inferred that in Senegambia, as elsewhere, cultural similarities and relationships do not necessarily constitute a sure base for political integration.

Centripetal and centrifugal forces in Senegambia from early times to the 1880s

As well as being a geographical region which facilitated the movement of men, animals and goods, the Senegambian savannah belt was also one which encouraged the intermingling of people speaking various languages. One major advantage of this latter development is that most Senegambians became bi- or multilingual. The main languages spoken — Mandinka, Wolof, Serer and Pular — have striking similarities which suggest contact among their speakers sometime in the past. It has been suggested that the phenomenon of multilingualism could be attributed to the activities of the itinerant traders, Muslim clerics and empire builders who hailed from empires like ancient Ghana, Mali, Futa Jallon, Futa Bundu, Kaarta and Ja.[4] Moreover, despite the rigid system of social stratification among the various ethnic groups including the Wolof, Mandinka, Serer, Tuculor and Fulbe, avenues have been open for cross-ethnic associations. Examples of these were the age-grade societies which brought youths together during the period of ritual seclusion at puberty, irrespective of ethnicity and social status. It was also possible for inter-ethnic marriages to take place as long as the parties involved were of the same social standing. In fact, according to some sources, there has been so much intermingling of ethnicities that in Senegambia it is almost impossible to find a pure ethnic type.[5] There is also the practice among parents of naming their children after their chosen heroes such as Muslim clerics or famous rulers who might belong to other ethnic groups. Thus it is seldom easy to tell a person's ethnic origin from his name. There exist jokes and good-natured bantering between some ethnic groups like the Jolas and Serers, Fulbe and Serer, and Serer and Wolofs, which indicate that the groups are sufficiently familiar with one another.

Traditionally, all Senegambians have been *Soninke* or *tyeddo* (adherents of traditional religion). They worshipped at each other's shrines, which they visited especially to seek panaceas for their worldly afflictions. When Islam was introduced into the region after the eighth century, Muslim converts too congregated in *morikundas* or *zawiyas* where they kept in touch with fellow-Muslims all over Senegambia. When, in the course of time, tension mounted and devotees of traditional religions were pitted against Muslims, people of different ethnic groups went to the aid of their co-religionists. Thus in the seventeenth century, Wolof Muslims fought on the side of Moors from the area of present-day Mauritania to topple their own non-Muslim rulers in Waalo.[6] Similarly, Fulbe Muslims from Futa Jallon went to the aid of their Mandinka co-religionists of Kaabu in the nineteenth century.[7] Muslim leaders like Al Hajj Umar Taal, Fode Sillah, Fode Kaba Dumbuya and Maba Diakhu were able to recruit their clientele and fighting forces from a medley of ethnic groups.

There have also existed from time immemorial marked similarities in the social customs of the various ethnic groups in Senegambia. For instance, Senegambians share identical value systems which emphasise such commonly accepted norms as integrity and *noblesse oblige* (*gor*), self-respect (*njom*), politeness (*kersa*), empathy (*yermande*), a predisposition to accommodate strangers (*teranga*), and being one's brother's keeper (*ndimbalante*). These values are further reinforced and perpetuated in the extended family, kinship or clan organisation referred to as *ker* among the Wolof, *kabilo* by the Mandinka and *Galle* by the Pular-speaking people. Migrant labourers (*tilibonkas* or *navétanes*) and itinerant Muslim traders or clerics had little difficulty in settling down temporarily or permanently in most areas of Senegambia.

Commercial interdependence was also a hallmark of the region. The hinterland peoples of Bure, Bambuk, the Futas and Kaarta were dependent on the salted and dried seafood like fish, cockles and oysters that were obtainable from the coastal areas. The coastal people, in turn, needed the iron, gold, locally woven cloth and kolanuts which came from the interior. The *juula*,[8] who acted as agents between the two areas, travelled to the weekly *lumus* or market days that were held at various centres located on the river Gambia and parts of Senegal. The *juula* network itself was an example of the harmonious association of traders of different ethnic groups, many of whom were multilingual and conversant with one another's customs. European traders and government officials in the pre-colonial and early colonial era discovered to their cost that *juula* solidarity was a formidable factor that could not be ignored. Any threat directed against a *juula*, whatever his ethnicity, was collectively fended off by the entire *juula* network.[9]

People also tended to settle in areas they found economically, agriculturally or commerically viable rather than where members of their own ethnic group lived. Thus, it was common in pre-colonial times to find several ethnic communities juxtaposed, under one dominant ethnic group. This was true of all the empires and states that have arisen in Senegambia. If any ethnic group felt threatened by the activities of the rulers or their agents, or if natural disasters struck (e.g. floods or droughts), they generally migrated to other places often to give their allegiance to another potentate who would guarantee them safety or a more viable living.

At the same time, Senegambia before 1880 was characterised by a series of socio-political tensions, conflicts and crises. The unfavourable physical conditions which affected the area fairly regularly, especially floods and drought, were at the heart of the problems of survival in the area, and led to the high incidence of wars of politico-economic origin that have plagued the region over the centuries. These wars were based on competition for such scarce resources as arable or pastoral land, as well as for the control of flourishing trading centres and trade routes. In the battles for survival much enmity was generated among the ethnic groups in the region which has persisted and still sours relations between them. It was most probably for this reason that no Senegambian empire ever emerged. Social breaches could be healed, but crises over land and livelihood proved far less manageable.

Religion was another divisive factor in Senegambia. Ethnic groups, members of the same clan and even members of the same family were split into potentially antagonistic groups of Muslims and non-Muslims. Non-Muslims have been forced to flee from Islamic nomocracies for fear of being victimised by uncompromising Muslims. Others, like *Jakhanke* pacifist Muslims, have fled their areas of provenance on account of their eschewing violence and their desire to extend Islam by peaceful means.

The Atlantic slave trade compounded the differences between Senegambians. Those from the coastal areas have always regarded the hinterland peoples as inferior, and so had little compunction over enslaving and selling them. As the ruler of Futa Bundu confessed to a Wesleyan missionary, some of the religious wars were also opportunities for procuring slaves.[10]

The colonial presence in the coastal areas from the seventeenth century was to emphasise factors of divergence at the expense of those favouring convergence. In the first place, the name Senegambia adopted by the British and French for the dependency they created in the eighteenth and nineteenth centuries evoked different points of reference in the minds of the colonial powers. By extension, the various ethnic groups who came under their sway and socialisation processes inherited the prejudices of the particular European culture to which they were subjected.[11] When, in the period of the Scramble for Africa in the 1880s and 1890s, the hinterland areas of Senegal and the Gambia fell after a series of protracted wars to the British and French,[12] the colonial powers sought to perpetuate the anglophone/francophone dichotomy in Senegambia by the policies they pursued.

Differing colonial policies and the parallel socialisation process

Partition in Senegambia meant, in effect, a drastic breaking-up of the lands of pre-existing states and the reorganisation of the various parts into new administrative units—Provinces in the Gambia and Cantons (now *Arrondissements*) in Senegal—carved out by the British and French. For example, the former territory of the Wolof-Serer state of Saloum in Pakala-Mandach was split into British and French sections, the French naming their own area the Canton of Sine-Saloum (the present-day *Arrondissement* of Sine-Saloum), while the British integrated their section partly into what came to be called North Bank Province and partly into McCarthy Island Province.[13] Fogni and Kabada on the south bank of the Gambia came in for similar treatment. The upshot of these administrative restructurings was that the British colony of the Gambia came to look like the filling of a sandwich, with the colony of Senegal forming its upper and lower crusts. Senegal itself became truncated, and could only be linked by traversing the Gambia or by using the much lengthier overland route. The partition was undertaken without any consideration for cultural ties, economic viability or regional coherence.

The British and French proceeded to institute and maintain distinctions between British Gambia and French Senegal. To this end, the socialisation process, begun in the nineteenth century, was continued in the twentieth. Basically, the aims of the two colonising powers were identical — the exploitation of the human and material resources of their respective dependencies. But the methods they employed were distinct enough, particularly in terms of the type of Protectorate administrative policies they pursued. Although both the French and the British claimed to rule through African agents, the *chefs* and *seyfos*, it was British officials like Major Macklin and Governor Cameron who took pains to identify the ancient ruling families and select local rulers from among them. In contrast to the

French, who regarded their African agents as mere tools chosen to serve French interests, *seyfos* in the Gambia were allowed a fair amount of officially sanctioned initiative in formulating or carrying out policy at the local level. They were allowed to retain part of the taxes they collected for the purposes of defraying the expenses they incurred in the course of their work. They had their own policemen, locally known as 'badge messengers', and from 1944 the *seyfos* met annually with the British Commissioners assigned to their Provinces to give account of their stewardship and bring specific issues to the notice of the colonial government.[14] In fact, these *seyfos* were perceived by the local people as far more powerful than the pre-colonial rulers of Senegambia.[15] Most significantly, they held their own courts.

The situation in the French colony of Senegal was strikingly different. The *chefs* were utilised essentially as salaried officials who executed the will of the French colonial administration. The *chefs* were important only in so far as they put at the service of the French *Commandant de Cercle* their complete loyalty and energies, knowledge of the country and the genuine influence which they might exert over their people.[16] They did not have to belong to the traditional ruling families to be appointed *chefs*.

The differences in the status and privileges of African rulers in the two territories were to continue into the post-colonial period; and it has been correctly observed that the reluctance of Gambia to join Senegal in a political union all along had been partly due to the fear of the Gambian *seyfos* that they would lose their prestige and privileges.

Economically, the two colonies became differentiated into the franc and sterling zones. The taxation systems of the colonial powers also differed. Whereas the British collected taxes on adult persons and properties including huts and farms, the French imposed a capitation tax of 15 francs flat rate on all persons above the age of ten.

There were also differences in the political obligation expected of Senegalese and Gambians. The British did not conscript Gambians into their territorial army, but the French did so during and between the two World Wars. The large-scale protest migrations from the French to the British sides of the common borders, occasioned by this difference in policy, have been sufficiently documented not to warrant any further discussion here.[17]

Officially, the Senegambians were socialised into anglophones and francophones. Related to this change was the introduction of different educational systems. One important effect of this is the use of parallel orthographies for indigenous names. Names rendered as

Ndiaye and Mbaye among the Wolofs in Senegal, for example, become Njie and Mbye among their Gambian kinsmen. Similarly Serer names like Diouf and Faye came to be spelt Joof and Fye in the Gambia. Other examples include Fulbe/Tuculor names such as Diallo, Dia and Thiam in Senegal, anglicised as Jallow, Jah and Cham in the Gambia; Mandinka names like Ly and Diaouara in Senegal were spelt Leigh and Jawara in the Gambia; Jola names like Badiani and Diame in Senegal became Badjan and Jammeh in the Gambia. Similar effects on place-names have produced significant consequences for cartographic representations on maps of the different sides of the inter-colonial (today international) boundaries.

The educational policies of the colonial powers widened the gap between Senegalese and Gambians still further. The curricula were geared towards examinations monitored and held respectively in Britain and France. It was not surprising that the élite groups from these two systems became progressively alienated from one another. In the first place, the medium of instruction was in the different European languages, English in Gambia and French in Senegal. Whereas no value was attached to the use of the indigenous Senegambian languages, great dividends could and were obtained from Western education. Jobs and social status came to depend on the level of the new education to which individuals could aspire. Certificates, degrees and related credentials from Britain and France came to be the coveted goals in the Gambia and Senegal.[18]

Examples from such élite groups included Blaise Diagne, Lamin Gueye, and Leopold Senghor in Senegal; and Sheikh Omar Faye, Sir Samuel Forster, and Bishop J.C. Fye of the Gambia. These élites were initially drawn mainly from Bathurst (now Banjul) in the Gambia and the Four Communes of Senegal (Dakar, Goree, St Louis and Rufisque). As among the Senegalese vis-à-vis France, Gambians developed the habit of sending their children to Britain where they embraced such British customs as tea-drinking, the playing of cricket, membership of the Boy Scouts and Girl Guides, and so on. The Gambian and Senegalese élites mingled with their European colleagues and developed attachments to important personalities in Britain and France respectively. The British Royal Family evoked a special fondness among the Gambian peoples, and in turn the British felt affection for their 'loyal little colony'. This was similar to the affinity that developed between the French and the citizens of the Four Communes of Senegal.

Hence it is little wonder that there have been no irredentist moves among any ethnic group either in Senegal or the Gambia, as has happened say among the Ewe or Somali. On the contrary, the phenomenon of parallel socialisation of the two élite groups has meant that Senegalese had more in common with other francophone areas than with their Gambian neighbours and *vice versa*.

Restrictions were also placed on the movement of people across the border. The French in Senegal kept strict guard over the border areas to screen human and material movements, and insisted on their subjects having identity cards, and on foreign (Gambian) subjects producing their passports at border crossing points. Thus divisions were inaugurated and maintained in virtually all spheres of life which kept the sundered peoples from coming together politically, economically and socially. But how did the people thus alienated from one another react to these developments?

The Senegambian responses

Among the divided peoples, it was mainly the assimilated élites in the colony areas who were affected by the colonial boundaries. The majority of the Senegambians living in the rural areas acted very much as if the frontierlines did not exist. Socially, the precolonial intercourse which had operated from time immemorial continued unchecked and even unnoticed. Intermarriage continued between Senegalese in the Sine-Saloum district and Gambians in Upper Saloum, a largely Wolof-Serer and Tuculor area, and between Sénégal Orientale and the Upper River Province of the Gambia.[19]

In many areas there were divided villages with a part on either side of the border; in some cases the two parts bore, and still bear, identical names. There was a Baro Kunda in Gambia directly opposite Baro Kunda in Senegal in the Sénégal Orientale/Upper River Province area. Other examples can be found in the Jola and Fulbe regions on the south bank of the Gambia and in the French province of Casamance. In all these areas people continued to cross the border to visit their Islamic or traditional co-religionists and to worship at common shrines.[20] Among the Muslims, this was a common occurrence, particularly on important days of the Islamic calendar. Events like *Tobaski* or the *Magal* of the Mourides, for instance, took many Gambian Muslims into Senegal.

The British tended to accept these border migrations as inevitable, but the French were generally averse to them. A case in point was the arrest and deportation of Sheikh Anta in April 1931 by the French authorities, allegedly for visiting the Gambia without a passport.[21] The question raised in the Gambian newspaper which reported the incident was why the British did not arrest him for violating their immigration regulations. It was suspected that the

French reaction stemmed from the fear that the wealthy Muslim leader, who had a following of about 6,000, was planning to move over to the British side.

Despite the tight rein kept on movements, the local people still managed to move from one colony to the other. When in 1925 Nakolang Koma, *seyfo* of Upper Niani in the British McCarthy Island Province, fell foul of the British authorities, he opted to settle on the French side.[22] Similarly, the villagers of Panchang, Bati Ndar, Hoofa, Mbuntum, Keur Sait Gueye, Leboh, Bulgoh and Keur Sama ka decided to transfer to Senegal because their *seyfo* in Upper Saloum, Omar Ceesay, was making life untenable for them.[23] Conversely, during and between the two World Wars, many Senegalese fled to the Gambia to avoid French conscription, as we have already seen, and were given shelter in the Gambia. Some of these defectors boldly claimed that they were British and were even prepared to swear an oath to that effect on the Koran![24]

The weekly *lumus* continued to be held at their respective locations. Despite the fact that the 5-franc pieces introduced by French merchants into Senegambia in the 1840s had been banned from circulation in the Gambian areas in 1921, this French unit of currency continued to be popular as a unit of exchange up till the 1940s.[25] In fact people use the denomination for reckoning purposes to this day. It was also reported that clandestine markets known locally as *marché golo* (monkey markets), where contraband goods were bought and sold, flourished at most border towns and villages. A veteran Gambian smuggler displayed scars inflicted by the bayonet of a French border patrolman, thus testifying to the brutality with which customs officials treated those caught smuggling.[26]

Despite such ruthless vigilance and penalties meted out to smugglers, the act was rife. In Saloum and Maka Colobane in Senegal (and certainly in other parts of Senegambia too) informants referred to the large profits to be gained from smuggling. Diallo identified some of the commodities sold through this underground source. Those coming from the Gambia into Senegal included imported clothing from Nigeria locally referred to as 'Lagos', printed cotton from Ghana, fish, salt, kolanuts and pharmaceutical products, also from Nigeria; and electronic equipment, liquor, tobacco, petroleum products, sporting cartridges and hurricane lamps from Britain. From Senegal into the Gambia came cigarettes, French wines, agricultural implements and fertilisers.[27]

In addition, groundnut harvests were smuggled into either colony depending on the attractions of the prevailing price. Like their counterparts in other parts of Africa, especially the groundnut farmers in the Niger-Nigeria borderlands, farmers tended to take their crops across the border if they could thereby sell them more profitably. What often determined their preferences were first a higher price, secondly an early buying season, and thirdly the availability of cheap consumer goods. From 1955 to 1967, when the French were subsidising Senegalese groundnuts, it was the British in the Gambia who suffered from the loss of groundnut harvests as many of their subjects sold their groundnut crops in Senegal. But from 1967, Senegal has been faced with a serious drain on its groundnut harvests. This is because the Gambian market has offered higher prices, immediate cash payments and cheaper consumer goods.

It is not surprising that from 1967 relations between Senegal and the Gambia have been strained over the smuggling issue. Throughout the post-colonial period, the Senegalese government has harboured a deep-seated fear that their country's economy was being sabotaged by the Gambia's liberal fiscal policy. A major crisis was precipitated in 1969 when the Senegalese Finance Minister, Jean Collin, announced that the smuggling issue was 'an act of economic aggression' perpetrated by Gambians, and that it ought to be resisted as such since it constituted a 'moral peril' to the Senegalese state.[28] This vehement outburst was followed by the incursion of Senegalese army units into Gambian territory where suspected smugglers were manhandled. The Gambia appealed to the United Nations against such a violation of its territorial integrity. The Senegalese were embarrassed by this step and the matter was eventually settled by diplomacy. However, subsequent border incidents in 1973 and 1974 showed that the Gambia was still considered a threat to Senegal's economic stability.

In cases where villagers felt their livelihood to be at stake, Senegalese and Gambians tended to emphasise their separateness from their kinsmen across the border. Thus, for example, the Mbyes on the Gambian side were reluctant to share their wells with their Senegalese relations, and squabbling over access to these wells continues to this day.[29] In some cases British authorities were given undivided support in enforcing regulations concerning the sealing of the border during periods of epidemics.[30]

But perhaps most of the problems between Senegal and the Gambia stem from the basic uncertainty over the real position of the boundary and the related confusion over the political and legal status of border towns. In a notorious incident the headman and yard-owners of the town of Chargi were arrested for failure to pay tax to the French in Senegal. It took a Commission of Enquiry to ascertain that Chargi was incontestably British, and the taxes collected by the French were duly returned.[31] The Senegalese government in post-colonial times too has found it difficult to demarcate and maintain its frontiers with the Gambia. As mentioned earlier, in 1971 and 1973–4 a series of border incidents involving loss of life drove wedges between the two countries and inspired resentment among Gambians towards Senegalese gendarmes.

Present realities and policy

Although both Senegal and the Gambia face similar economic disadvantage, the size of the Gambia and the ability of its civil servants to keep the country solvent have meant that, despite predictions to the contrary, it has survived a long period of nationhood. In Senegal, on the other hand, problems connected with the co-operative societies which control the most important sector of the economy are compounded by other factors which militate against the country's economic viability: a rapid rise in population and consequent over-crowding on the land, leading to over-cultivation and soil exhaustion, which have stimulated massive rural-urban migration and in turn urban unemployment. To these difficulties must be added the problem posed by a drought which began in 1973 and lasted throughout the 1970s, impelling people to abandon their farms or shift from groundnut to subsistence farming. Moreover, the low prices offered in the world market for raw materials have been devastating for the Senegalese economy. Although the economic situation in both Senegal and the Gambia has been affected by a disastrous fall in groundnut production since the 1970s, the future of Senegal seems bleaker in view of its greater overheads.

Relative to the Gambia at least, Senegal is a budding industrialised state which is finding it hard to take off with the economic constraints in the country. The consumption habits of the élite are extravagant and the cost of living in Senegal is prohibitive, and much higher than that in the Gambia. Senegalese continue to migrate to the Gambia in search of temporary or permanent homes despite attempts by their government to provide new homes for many of them in Eastern Senegal.[33]

In spite of all this, cultural links have continued to exert great influence on development in Senegal and the Gambia. Much cordiality remains among ethnic groups despite the phenomenon of parallel socialisation and politicisation. For example, it was reported in a Gambian newspaper that the Senegalese soldiers who were deployed to police Banjul following the *coup* attempt in 1981 came armed with addresses of relatives in the Gambia, and when they were off duty they searched for their kinsmen, hoping to renew old ties.[34] Both Sir Dawda Jawara of the Gambia and former President Senghor of Senegal have suggested that it is in the cultural field that the concept of Senegambia would be easiest to realise and make acceptable in both countries.[35] The eagerness with which Gambians have taken up learning to speak French and Senegalese to learn English in recent times testifies to this. Yet the obstacles which have always hindered the progress of a political union still have to be surmounted.

In order to make the Senegambian Confederation a reality and avoid the pitfalls and mistakes encountered by earlier abortive attempts at inter-state union in Africa such as the Ghana-Guinea-Mali, Senegal-Mali and East African Federation schemes,[36] a drastic reorientation is called for in the minds of those in charge of policy in Senegal and the Gambia. Above all, note must be taken of the statement of President Abdou Diouf of Senegal in reference to the Senegambian Confederation: 'Mettons entre parenthèses ce qui nous sépare et co-opérons en tous autres domaines, ce qui nous aide à rapprocher nos points de vue.'[37]

The barriers between the Senegalese and Gambians are primarily the official languages of French and English. For some time, if not in perpetuity, bilingualism should be the recommended line of action. It would be impractical to cut off either Senegal from its francophone connections or the Gambia from its anglophone ones. This is mostly because it is within such contexts or cultural blocs that invaluable help was rendered to these two countries during and since their years of struggle to attain nationhood.

The second major area of separation is related to the legal, administrative and local government systems which have been in existence for so long that their dismantling would cause more problems than their continuance as they are. Trans-border cooperation between local governments should, however, be encouraged. The adoption of a common national anthem and flag for the confederal states may be considered an appropriate bridge-building exercise.

The third and perhaps most crucial problem relates to the operation of parallel economic systems including the issue of different currencies. This calls for measures to harmonise the economic and planning policies of the Senegambian states. While the two states are already pursuing this objective within the wider context of the Economic Community of West African States (ECOWAS), there is need for an acceleration of steps to bring about in Senegambia the customs union ultimately being aimed at by ECOWAS. Tariffs in the Gambia may have to be raised to the same level as those that operate in Senegal but the Gambia would need to be compensated.

The execution of the low-cost housing scheme of the Gambian government could be specially grant-aided and assisted in other ways by Senegal as the latter had a more established experience in such a project. This should satisfy the need for sacrifice on both sides.

In the final analysis, the challenge posed by the Senegambian Confederation lies in the achievement of unity in diversity. To gain this objective, policy-makers in the two countries ought to be guided less by their inherited mutual antipathy and distrust and more by logical and fruitful preoccupations with strengthening their historical links. The behaviour of the westernised élites and the states they have come to dominate as rulers and administrators should be guided more by the customary Senegambian inter-group feeling inspired by *yermande* (empathy) than the outmoded European diplomacy based on the principle of national self-interest.

NOTES

The preparation of this paper has benefited from specific archival research in Banjul and Dakar as well as field investigation along the borders, undertaken in January–February 1982 in the course of a month's research assistantship to the Editor of this volume. The financial support was in the form of a research grant from the University of Lagos, and this is gratefully acknowledged.

1. After the abortive *coup* attempt of 30 July 1981 which exposed the Achilles heel of the Gambia — the lack of an adequate defence force — the President, Sir Dauda Jawara, broached the question of political integration with Senegal in the form of a Confederation — an idea which he had hitherto treated with circumspection. See for example J.H. Proctor, 'The Gambia's Relations with Senegal: The Search for Partnership', *Journal of Commonwealth Political Studies*, V, 2, July 1967, pp. 148–9.
2. See Proctor, *op. cit.* Also H. Hughes, 'Senegambia revisited, or changing Gambian perspectives of integration with Senegal' in R.C. Bridges (ed.), *Senegambia* (Proceedings of a colloquium at the University of Aberdeen, 1974).
3. For a discussion of the term Senegambia and the areas to which it applied see A. Mboge, 'Senegambia as a historical region' in R.C. Bridges, *op. cit.*, pp. 35–9.
4. See for example H. Houis, 'Mouvements historiques . . . .', *L'Homme*, I (1961), pp. 72–92, and P. Diagne, 'La Mandingophonie comme facteur d'unification . . . .', Manding Conference, London, 1972.
5. Alhaji Momodu Sowe, Gangi, Upper Saloum, McCarthy Island Division, interviewed 6 February 1982. See also I. Diallo, *Border Migrations: A survey of the Senegambian rural areas, 1970–1971* (Dakar: IDEP, 1972) p. 126.
6. B. Barry, *Le Royaume du Waalo* (Paris, 1972).
7. G. Innes, *Kaabu and Fulladu* (London, 1976).
8. *Juula* was the generic name in Mandinka for the itinerant traders of Senegambia. See P.D. Curtin, 'The Western Juula', and R. Launey, 'Clans and Castes', both papers read at Manding Conference, University of London, 1972.
9. For a useful illustration see D. Grant, *The Fortunate Slave* (London 1968), pp. 189–90.

10. MMS 293. Fox to MMS. 25.2 1839 Fox to MMS.
11. For details see J.D. Hargreaves, *France and West Africa* (London, 1969) and J.M. Gray, *A History of the Gambia* (London, 1969). Also H. Hardy, *La Mise en Valeur du Sénégal de 1817–1870* (Paris, 1921); H.O. Idowu, 'Assimilation in 19th century Senegal', *BIFAN*, XXX, 4, 1968; F. Mahoney, 'African leadership in 19th-century Gambia', *Tarikh*, II, 2, 1968. Also Interview with S. Goddard.
12. See B.O. Oloruntimehin, 'The Western Sudan and the coming of the French 1800–1893' in J.F.A. Ajayi and M. Crowder (eds), *History of West Africa*, II, pp. 344–79. S.C. Ukpabi, 'The Gambia expedition of 1901', *BIFAN*, XXX, B, 1971, pp. 285–98. Also A.J. Mboge, 'The States of the Gambia Valley and their neighbours, with special reference to the impact of British and French Policies, 1876–1899' (draft Ph.D. thesis).
13. G.P.R.O. 62/13 Short History of Upper Saloum.
14. *Ibid*. Also 77/5 Historical Reports on Central Baddibu; also extracts in Lord Hailey's questionnaire concerning Native Administration in Africa, 9/103 and 104.
15. For details of pre-colonial governments see J. Suret-Canale, 'The Western Atlantic Coast 1600–1800' in Ajayi and Crowder, *op. cit.*, pp. 287–340.
16. J.D. Hargreaves, *France and West Africa*, pp. 210–13.
17. See A.I. Asiwaju, 'Migrations as Revolt: The Example of the Ivory Coast and the Upper Volta Before 1945', *Journal of African History*, XVII, 4, 1976, pp. 577–94, and his 'Migrations as Expression of Revolt: The Example of French West Africa Up to 1945', *Tarikh*, 5, 3, 1977; G.P.R.O. 3/26 minute paper by Colonial Secretary dated 9 Dec. 1916. Also in the same folio Hopkinson to Colonial Secretary, 15 March 1918, and paper on Immigrations of Natives from French territory, esp. 12 Nov. 1916, Hopkinson to Colonial Secretary.
18. See M. Crowder, 'What is wrong with the Gambia?', *New Commonwealth*, XXX, 12, 1955, pp. 282–5, and G.W. Johnson, *The Emergence of Black Politics in Senegal* (Stanford, 1971). For a similar trend elsewhere see A.I. Asiwaju, 'Formal Education in Western Yorubaland, 1889–1960: A Comparison of the French and British Colonial Systems', *Comparative Education Review*, 19, 3, 1975, pp. 434–50.
19. I. Diallo, *op. cit.*, pp. 127–8. Interview with Alhaji Momodu Sowe, Sait N. Ceesay, Alhaji Mattau, and Fafa Turay, all residents of Saloum district in McCarthy Island Division, 6 Feb. 1982.
20. *Ibid*.
21. *Gambia Outlook and Senegambian Reporter*, 11 April 1931.
22. G.P.R.O. 58/6 Annual Reports on McCarthy Island Province 1922–1932 Report of 1925 by Major R.W. Macklin, 30 March 1925. Also ANS 1 F 2, 24 September 1924, Governor-General of Senegal to Governor of Gambia.
23. G.P.R.O. 62/13 Commissioner M.I.P. to Colonial Secretary, April 1924, reporting complaints made to him by Modi and Molima Ceesay of Bati Hai.
24. G.P.R.O. 75/19, Governor of St Louis to Governor of Gambia, 20 March 1940.
25. G.P.R.O. 75/5 C/M.I.P. to Colonial Secretary, 10 Jan. 1940.
26. Interview, 6 February 1982. We have refrained from recording the biodata of this interviewee for obvious reasons.
27. I. Diallo, *op. cit.*, pp. 14–98, 110–13.
28. *West Africa*, 12 April 1969, p. 403.
29. Interview, Alhaji Momodu Sowe, 6 Feb. 1982.
30. *Ibid*.
31. See ANS I F I, Incident de Chargi, 1923–4. Also G.P.R.O. 3/71 C/S.B.P. to Colonial Secretary, letters 1924–5.
32. See D. Cruise O'Brien, 'Co-operators and bureaucrats: class formation in a Senegalese peasant society', *Africa*, 41, 4, 1971 pp. 263–73.

33. I. Diallo, *op. cit.*
34. *Gambia News Bulletin*, 119, 4 November 1981, entitled 'The exemplary action of the Senegalese soldiers in the Gambia'.
35. See Carew Treffgarne, 'Senegambia: Possibilities for closer co-operation in the field of Education' in R.C. Bridges, *op. cit.*
36. See for example Victor T. Le Vine, 'The Politics of Partition in Africa: The Cameroons and the Myth of Unification', *Journal of International Affairs*,. XVIII, 2, 1964. Also J.H. Proctor, 'Efforts to federate East Africa', *Political Quarterly*, 37, 1, 1966, pp. 46–69.
37. *Le Soleil*, Special Issue, Jan. 1982, 'L'An I du Président', p. 28.

6
PARTITIONED ALUR
Aidan Southall

Introduction

To grasp the significance of the colonial partition of Alurland it is necessary to understand who and what the Alur were and how they came to be so. I have elaborated the background to this in my book *Alur Society*[1] more fully than is possible here, and have examined special aspects of it in a number of articles; the significance of oral tradition,[2] rank and stratification,[3] incorporation of other ethnic groups,[4] spirit mediumship cults,[5] and the contrast between British and Belgian colonial administration of the Alur.[6] After thirty years of reflection I feel able to attempt a more succinct outline of these matters.

The Alur were a composite people, emergent over three or four centuries from the fusion and incorporation of diverse migratory movements of peoples of different languages and cultures. It is always a temptation to tell the story from the point of view of the dominant groups, because they tell it most forcefully and clearly, making it appear simpler than it actually was. The temptation must be resisted, yet there is little alternative to making the dominant groups the skeleton to which the multifarious other groups were attached. The ancestors of Alur rulers were part of the long-term movement of Nilotic Lwo-speaking peoples from the Sudan southwards into what is now Uganda and Kenya. They took part in founding the powerful Bito dynasty of Bunyoro, which took over from the previous Cwezi realm, but they also peopled Acoliland with numerous small chiefdoms. This shows that the Lwo could operate a relatively centralised state such as Bunyoro-Kitara, although in this case they became Bantu-speakers in the process; or they could live in acephalous segmentary lineage societies, like the Kenya Luo, or in small polities focused on hereditary leaders, like the Acoli. These variations depended on different ecological, economic and political influences and opportunities, just as the Nilotes of the Sudan lived in different types of acephalous segmentary lineage societies in the case of the Jieng and Nath, or focused on a ritually centralised divine kingship in the case of the Colo (Shilluk).[7]

In this perspective it is most reasonable to suppose that the first Lwo groups to reach Alurland were organised in segmentary lineages, probably on a very small scale, but also focused on certain ritual leaders of special influence. Some of them reached the valley of the Albert Nile from what is now Acoliland, and some crossed the Nile to the west and moved gradually up into the fertile highlands of the Nile-Congo watershed. Others came back again from Bunyoro, down the Nile from Lake Albert northwards, or crossed Lake Albert from Bunyoro to occupy the shores and mountains on the western side.

Probably some of them were absorbed by peoples of different language and culture and were lost to history, though some, like the Mambisa, retained the memory of such an absorption.[8] But most of them seem to have succeeded in imposing themselves on other peoples in positions of special privilege and respect, if not of political dominance. For the country into which they moved was not empty, though most of it was sparsely occupied. Most important, there were the Sudanic-speaking Madi in the north, some Bantu groups on the Nile and round Lake Albert, the Sudanic Okebo and Lendu on the west and south, with other Bantu groups such as Babira and Banyali further south-west.

The early Lwo leaders must have claimed special ritual powers, to make rain and ensure fertility for women and men, animals and crops, and to control witchcraft.[9] They also brought with them cattle and possibly improved strains of millet and beans. At least they were usually successful in attracting the other groups they met to concede some kind of ritual superiority, which provided the basis for an increase in the scale of social organisation somewhat above the level previously achieved by these acephalous peoples, and hence to a gradual process of incorporation, assimilation and fusion, out of which new polities eventually emerged, which usually retained their Lwo identity, but with a modified culture.

How far the increase in scale and in political specialisation proceeded must have depended largely on ecological opportunities. The largest polities, both in numbers and in territory, emerged in the highlands west of the Nile and Lake Albert, which must have offered the advantages of relatively sparsely occupied land of high fertility and good rainfall. There was a great increase of population, and some rulers managed to develop larger polities of the type which I have called the segmentary state.[10]

The increase in territorial size and organisational complexity seems to have approximately paralleled the growth of population and expansion of its area of occupation. That is to say, as population grew, new lineages were formed. Some remained within the enlarged polity, some hived off into partial independence, with effective day-to-day autonomy, while continuing to recognise and support the ritual suzerainty of the original leader.[11] Others eventually broke off entirely to form new polities on the pattern of the old. This usually led to a situation in which the new polity claimed complete independence, or even tried to assert superiority by twisting the oral tradition, while the old polity continued to insist on an overall ritual suzerainty which it probably could not implement, except perhaps on very rare occasions of general crisis or high ceremony.

On the shores of Lake Albert and the Albert Nile most polities remained small. For all of them the fishery resources were important, but the mountains leave hardly any land for cultivation near the shores of the lake, and the valley of the Albert Nile has very low rainfall and poor soil. Another factor, perhaps, was that the people of the Lake Albert shore were rather overawed by the powerful Bunyoro state just on the other side. It was Ragem at the northern end of Alur settlement on the Nile, furthest away from Bunyoro, which succeeded in creating a somewhat larger and more powerful polity. But even this may only have been a recent development, in some way related to Emin Pasha's presence there at Wadelay in the 1880s.[12] In Emin's time the Alur chiefs on the west of Lake Albert were afraid of Kabarega's raids, but by this time Kabarega had access to firearms, which gave him an unfair advantage.

If we consider Alur ethnicity from the internal point of view, a reasonably clearcut territory would have been defined on the basis of those who said 'we are Alur', although it would have had very fuzzy boundaries and many of those making this claim would have had no knowledge of one another's existence. An external definition by objective criteria of language, cultural behaviour and social organisation would not have been very different.

Alur cultural unity

To discuss Alur cultural unity is to discuss the problem of ethnicity in Africa. When writing about the Alur in 1952 I was still using the concept of tribe, knowing no better. But in fact it was the Alur themselves, as I learned the nature of their culture from them, who first taught me the absurdity of the concept of tribe, so that I abandoned it once having thought through what I had learned, and having acquired enough self-confidence to disavow a concept which most of my colleagues were still using (and still are).[13]

I described the Alur political system as a series of partly overlapping and interlocking segmentary states.[14] In pre-colonial times the Alur did not achieve political unity or succeed in organising a unitary, centralised state. Thus it is necessary to ask first who the Alur are and were, and how they came to be so identified. The first written reference to the Alur known to me is on Emin Pasha's map drawn by Ravenstein,[15] for Emin Pasha's famous camp at Wadelai was in Alurland. Wadelai is a corruption of *Wo'Lei*, 'the son of Lei', Lei being the local Alur chief. The map shows 'Lur' as stretching from just south of Msongua (Musongwa) on the west shore of Lake Albert to just north of Wadelai on the west bank of the Albert Nile. In between Musongwa and Wadelai, there are marked successively: Songa, Ang'al, Jabakot, Mahagi, Tunguru, Boki, Okello, Fanyamori, Fanegoro, Faroketo, Fabongo, Koche, Gehm. These are all more or less recognisable versions of the names of chiefs, chiefdoms or localities.

Mounteney-Jephson, who actually 'rescued' Emin Pasha on behalf of Henry Stanley, shows similar places sometimes under alternative names.[16] In his diary he says: 'The people all round Wadelai belong to the Loor race — Loor is pronounced very long. On the opposite side of the river between it and the hills is still the Loor race but beyond the hills are the Shulis.'[17] He is quite right about pronouncing Loor long, but on his map he had written 'Alur or Luri'. This mention of Alur on the east bank of the Nile with the 'Shulis' beyond the hills is quite fascinating, because it proves that the Alur were correct in claiming the east bank of the Nile as theirs. They were deprived of it by the creation of the sleeping sickness reserve in 1906 and subsequently of the Murchison (now Kabarega) National Park.

During these five decades the Uganda Administration came to regard the Nile itself as the eastern boundary of Alurland, so it seemed quite natural that the Acoli claimed the east bank as theirs when there was talk of re-opening it for some cultivation and settlement. It has always been a sore point with the Alur (called Junam in Uganda) and still is, because those living on the banks of the river had evolved a viable exploitation of their ecological niche, whereby they could rest the rather infertile land adequately by using each bank in turn as well as fishing and hunting the river in between. Deprived of one bank, they were left with too little farming land within easy reach of the river, and there was a dearth of water inland.

The 'Shulis' mentioned by Mounteney-Jephson were, of course, the Acoli. My guess is that Sudanese interpreters for Emin, Jephson, Casati, Baker and other early foreigners passing through heard the Acoli speak and recognised the similarity of their language to that of the Shilluk, which is properly called Colo. Probably, in being mangled from mouth to mouth by speakers of different languages, Colo became Shuli and eventually Acoli.

It is supremely ironical that the first Alur recorded should have been those of the Nile Valley, for under the Uganda colonial administration they came to be known not as Alur, but as Junam, 'People of the River', and differentiated themselves more and more from the rest of the Alur, claiming to be a separate 'tribe' and succeeding in getting themselves enumerated as such in the Uganda census.

I do not know exactly how the Alur came to be so called, and found no clear view or consensus on the matter among themselves. The name 'Aluru' occasionally figures in Alur dynastic genealogies, but it is without content or meaning, and no myths or events or specific groups are attached to it, so that possibly it is the product of recent speculation since the writing of genealogies began to be influential. Aluro occurs as the name of a section of the Luo (Jur) near Wau in the Southern Sudan, as a river in Anuakland and even as a chiefdom of western Lugbara.[18] When I was living in the highlands to the west of the Nile, the Alur living there used to refer to going to the lowlands towards the Nile as 'going to Alur'. It seems likely that the name became generalised under the colonial system when it became convenient and necessary to designate larger population groups for administrative purposes. As soon as Europeans came into continuous contact with the Alur, it became fairly easy to define their boundaries. The boundary was least meaningful culturally on the east where the neighbouring Acoli were almost identical in language, both being Western Nilotic speakers of Lwo, but here the Nile provided a clear boundary once the Alur were deprived of the east bank. Further south, Lake Albert separated them from the Bantu Nyoro. On the north the Sudanic-speaking Madi and Lugbara were quite distinct in language, though there was some cultural interpenetration. On the west the Sudanic Okebo and Lendu were similarly distinct in language, but the Alur were in a continuous process of expanding and incorporating them. On the south the Alur were equally distinct linguistically from neighbouring Bantu peoples such as the Babira and Banyali, but here again there was an indeterminate zone of interpenetration.

The Mambisa in the south-west all spoke Lendu but claimed that their chiefs were of Alur origin, which their genealogies seemed to confirm. It would be futile and meaningless to ask whether they are Lendu or Alur. They are Mambisa. Similarly the rest of the Alur thought of themselves mainly as members of a particular chiefdom or cluster of chiefdoms, rather than of any larger ethnic grouping, for the latter had no real importance in their everyday lives.

It is not easy to convey a precise and accurate understanding of the degree of Alur cultural unity. It must be considered both objectively and subjectively. Politically speaking, the Alur were never united, never claimed to be and never acted as such. Ritually, there was some claim, plausible but hard to substantiate, to levels of integration wider than the individual polities, usually following segmentary state lines, the most notable case being that of Ukuru, which claimed all the segments of the Atyak clan,[19] revered the great shrines of Kalowang, Rateng' and Rukidi,[29] and either sent representatives there or were represented by the chiefs of Ukuru or their emissaries. If it is hard to prove that such joint worship ever actually occurred, yet nonetheless the idea is definitely there. The ecological shrine of Riba above Lake Albert[21] was venerated from Ukuru to Mukambo and Jukoth, almost the whole length (if not breadth) of Alurland. The shrine of Puvungu, which according to tradition marked the separation between ancestors of Alur, Acoli and Bunyoro rulers, was widely known and respected, but in fact the Alur Ang'al and Juganda of the Ucibu group, as well as Jukoth and Mukambo, did not share this particular tradition.[22] As unifying factors, these were somewhat like the Olympic Games, or the Delphic Oracle, which provided an occasional ritual expression of unity for most but not all Greeks.

Linguistically, the different local variations of Alur speech were all mutually intelligible, except to the Mambisa and Gungu or Hema who spoke Lendu,[23] but mutual intelligibility would also have spread through Junam to include many Acoli groups also. The term Acoli did not exist in pre-colonial times and it would have been hard to define an objective boundary between today's Acoli and the Alur.

There was certainly a general sense of common ancestry, common history and common process among most of the Alur, granting the fact that the specific traditions of the Atyak, the Ucibu and of many of the lowland groups differed and that the ancestry of the population as a whole went back to the ethnically diverse roots of Lwo, Madi, Okebo, Lendu and other groups incorporated and assimilated under Lwo domination.

Any objective criteria (of language, cultural practices, political organisation or type of economy) which might be used to give a definition to Alur unity would in fact negate it by including others as well, such as the Acoli and Palwo. Any narrower definition which excluded these latter would also exclude other groups normally considered Alur.

It seems then that the Alur who were cut in two by the Anglo-Belgian frontier were not at the time a united people, or a people more than vaguely conscious of the nature and limits of their own existence. The eastern, western, northern and southern margins of Alurland knew little of one another and were not in any direct contact. The colonial frontier did cut in two speakers of a recognisably single language, bearing an essentially similar culture, though with considerable regional variation, but it can hardly be said to have cut a single people in two, for that people was not organised as such or conscious of itself. The frontier therefore divided something that was perhaps in process of becoming. This does not mean that the Alur did not lose thereby, for if they had all found themselves in Uganda, or all in the Belgian Congo, they would no doubt have won extra benefits by carrying much more weight in one country than the severed halves could in either.

The Anglo-Belgian partition

The history of the colonial partition of Alurland was a very complicated one. When Emin Pasha was forced south to Wadelai by the Mahdi's conquest of the Sudan, he found himself in the Lado District of the Egyptian Province of Equatoria whose Governor he was. The Lado District had been founded by General Gordon in 1874 but its limits remained undefined. When Emin and his forces left Wadelai in the late 1880s, Alurland remained in no-man's-land as far as the encroaching colonial powers were concerned. But as Britain had unofficially arranged for Egypt's annexation of the Sudan, and taken upon herself the task of reconquering the Sudan from the Mahdi in Egypt's name at a time when she was exercising a *de facto* Protectorate over Egypt, it was obviously Britain which had the largest potential interest and practical claim in Lado, but one she was not particularly anxious to implement at the time. So Lado, vaguely including Alurland, was nominally transferred to King Leopold II's Congo Free State in 1893. There was one Belgian officer in Mahagi but no established administration.

Meanwhile the Protectorate of Uganda was being established and British influence was spreading, with the assistance of the Baganda and with their joint conquest of Kabarega of Bunyoro, until it obviously reached the east bank of the Albert Nile. At the same time the northern part of Lado District was being administered under the reconstituted Anglo-Egyptian Sudan. So Alurland was being encroached upon by these three colonial entities: the Sudan, Uganda, and the Belgian Congo reconstituted after the scandals of the Congo Free State. In 1910 the country to the west of Lake Albert, nominally claimed by Uganda, was ceded to the Belgian Congo, but the country north of Mahagi and west of the Albert Nile remained nominally under the Sudan until 1914, when it was transferred to Uganda, so that the whole of Alurland now fell into either Uganda or the Belgian Congo, the Anglo-Belgian boundary being defined as the Nile-Congo watershed, with the line from it to Lake Albert near Mahagi remaining to be surveyed.

Between 1911 and 1914 the Belgian forces established control over their part of Alurland. Chief Ujuru of Panduru and Chief Keta of Ang'al both fought against the Belgians but were subdued. Chiefs Songe of Jukoth and Uma of Mukambo also submitted. Many chiefs fled into the bush and those of Panyimur and Paidha crossed into Uganda. The rival influence of the Congo and Uganda on the Albert Nile inflamed a succession dispute in Ragem, the most powerful Alur chiefdom there, so that two battling brothers, Owiny and Ong'wech, were supported against each other by the British and the Belgians respectively. When in 1914 the Belgians transferred their rights on the west bank to the British, the Uganda Administration was left to settle the dispute by installing its favourite, Owiny, as chief of Ragem and taking Ong'wech to assist it in establishing administration over the neighbouring chiefless Lugbara. When the West Nile District headquarters was established at Arua in Lugbaraland, Ong'wech was made chief of the town and when he was retired due to old age his son succeeded him there.

I have recorded many views and opinions about the colonial conquest of old Alur, some of them old enough to have already entered public life at the time of the events in question. But from such recollections forty or fifty years later it is obviously impossible to be sure what the Alur really thought at the time and, besides, it was impossible for anyone, Alur or European, at that time to comprehend the long-term significance of what was happening before their eyes.

The characteristic view of the Ukuru Alur in Uganda was that as they themselves (the Lwo) had exercised dominance over people of other ethnic groups for centuries, so now the British had come to exercise it over them. They were not severely oppressed or interfered with. Their chiefs claim to have *helped* the British, providing them with food supplies, porters and men to guard and guide them. They probably did, and it is not surprising that British official reports put less emphasis on this aspect of the matter than the Alur do.[24] The main problem of British Alurland was its remoteness. Little economic development had taken place in the first thirty years till the end of World War II, but there were markets, schools, dispensaries and churches, though by no means enough for all, and most people except old women and very old men had begun to wear some kind of European clothing. Payment of taxation in cash had been imposed, which led to a large migration of Alur men, and later women also, to grow cotton in Buganda.

Chief Amula of Ukuru was potentially the most influential of all Alur chiefs, since Ukuru was the largest chiefdom and had many chieflets derived from it, but Amula had recently succeeded his father, Alworung'a, who had been defeated and killed by Chief Ujuru of Panduru, now in the Congo. The chiefs of Ukuru and Panduru were of common agnatic descent but had been bitter enemies for several generations. Now they found themselves on opposite sides of the new international frontier. Amula did not attempt to fight the British, perhaps because his realm had scarcely recovered from his father's defeat, perhaps because he knew that Ujuru of Panduru and Keta of Ang'al had already been beaten by the Belgians and was sophisticated enough to realise that armed resistance was useless. Chief Amula received the British District Commissioner peacefully and was made a colonial county chief. But three years later he was deposed in favour of his son Jalaure, under suspicion of harbouring guns, failing to recruit for the war with sufficient enthusiasm and sympathising with the Allah Water Cult, which was a remote offshoot of the Mahdist influence in the Sudan. As with the Maji Maji Rebellion in Tanganyika, its devotees distributed holy water believed to confer immunity from firearms (cf. page 53 above). It never took serious root in Alurland.

At such a juncture, the people of Ukuru cannot have been too displeased with the fact that a new frontier had been imposed which effectively prevented Panduru from attacking them again. But on the other hand, if the frontier had not been there they would certainly have devoted their energies to building up their strength to invade Panduru and revenge themselves in the future. In any case it was quite impossible as yet for them to realise the momentous long-term implications of the new dispensation of *Pax Britannica* which had been imposed upon them—a somewhat ironical *Pax*, since no sooner had it been imposed than the Alur chiefs were asked to devote themselves enthusiastically to recruiting their men for the British forces to fight the First World War against the Germans in Tanganyika (then German East Africa) where heavy loss of life occurred.

British and Belgian administrations compared

There were some differences between the respective impacts of the British and Belgian colonial conquests. The Belgians had to conduct an extensive military campaign to subdue the Alur, whereas the Uganda Alur accepted British overlordship and colonial administration largely with resignation and grudging co-operation, without any serious fighting. How far this was due to the example of the Belgian military subjugation of Alur chiefs which had already occurred, or to a difference in approach on the part of the British virtually imposed upon them by their almost total lack of military force apart from what they managed to improvise on the spot, is a matter of emphasis, for both factors were present. The British had succeeded in establishing a peaceful settlement on the warring brothers Owiny and Ong'wech without military action. But they had already waged a long and extensive war against King Kabarega of Bunyoro, with massive support from Buganda, which culminated in Kabarega's defeat, capture and exile, a devastating lesson which was certainly not lost on neighbouring Alur chiefs, for whom he had been the greatest power in the world they had hitherto known.

The former Alur chiefs, or suitable members of their families, were used to build up the new colonial administration on both sides, with amalgamation of traditional units to make a more consistent three-tiered system of chiefs, subchiefs and headmen. The Uganda Alur were divided into only three administrative chiefdoms (counties), each with a population much larger than that of the corresponding units (*chefferies*) on the Belgian side, which were consequently more numerous (some seven or eight) and approximated very closely to the traditional chiefdoms. Yet the Belgian Alur chiefs were deliberately built up into much more powerful (and potentially oppressive) figures in relation to their subordinate chiefs than were their Ugandan counterparts. They had higher salaries and larger police forces.

Every Alur family on the Belgian side was compelled to produce a specific amount of basic crops. There was no comparable system in Uganda, although before World War II the attempt was made to get the Alur to grow Arabica coffee and they were punished for letting coffee gardens grow weedy. The experiment failed and was abandoned; then more than twenty years later, when Uganda had become independent, the Alur began to grow coffee in large quantities and with enthusiasm.

The Alur were even more distant from the main centres of development in the Congo (Zaire) than in Uganda. Many went to work in the Kilo Moto gold mines which dotted a large area to the west and south-west of Congo Alurland, but large numbers crossed into Uganda to join the Uganda Alur in going to grow cotton in Buganda or find other jobs in the vicinity of Kampala.

The Belgian Congo colonial system was always perceived by the Alur as more oppressive in its administrative methods, its labour requirements and its economic system. Belgian administrators were carried by palanquin in the mountains west of Lake Albert, requiring large numbers of men to be on standby. Such a system was not practised in Uganda.

The sense of greater oppression in the Congo, coupled with more attractive economic opportunities in Uganda, tended to cause a flow of population from Congo to Uganda Alurland and beyond into the rest of Uganda, although Uganda Alurland was more densely populated already. The systematic subjugation of the Alur had begun on the Congo side three years earlier than in Uganda and there were mass flights into Uganda periodically all through the 1910s and 1920s. After 1930 the flights ended but Congo Alur went on going to work in Uganda. In 1947 the Belgians were still very sensitive about losing population to Uganda, and felt that the Ukuru chiefship in Uganda was something of a magnet for all the Alur.

When the period of chaos began in Zaire after 1960, there was yet another incentive for Alur movement into Uganda. By 1970 things were calmer on the Zaire side, and in 1971 and 1972, when many Uganda Alur were killed during the army disturbances under Idi Amin, there might for the first time have been some incentive for Uganda Alur to take refuge in Zaire. But this does not seem to have occurred on any significant scale. The transport system of Zaire was so bad by this time that much of the coffee grown by Zaire Alur had no outlet that side and was sold to Uganda Alur at half price. Even when Amin's Uganda was at its lowest ebb, the profitable route for black market coffee smuggling was eastwards through Uganda and out into Kenya, not westwards into Zaire.

As in all of Uganda, a comprehensive, democratically elected system of local government, with considerable powers and resources at its disposal, was built up during the 1950s for the West Nile District, of which the Alur formed part. There was no comparable development on the Belgian side.

The corollary of the increased popular participation implied and required by the new local government system was that each ethnic group in Uganda began to demand the counterpart of a *Kabaka*. The *Kabaka*, or King of Buganda, symbolised all the advantages which the Baganda had enjoyed, at the expense of other ethnic groups, under British rule. It was perhaps a case of mistaking form for substance, reminiscent of sympathetic magic, but it was the best that they could do in the circumstances. For a bizarre period of a few years, every district in Uganda had its ceremonial head, fabricated by district leaders as best they might, if none existed already. In West Nile District the Alur and Lugbara were the main ethnic power groups. The Okebo and Lendu minorities could be ignored. The Madi were bracketed with their Lugbara 'cousins' of similar speech. The Kakwa of the remote north-west corner were ignored, to burst into the limelight ten years later with Idi Amin's claim to be one of them. The ceremonial Head of West Nile District had the new title of *Agofe-Obimo*. Neither term had ever been used for leaders before, but *agofe* in Lugbara and *obimo* in Alur did convey the sense of leadership. It was an unblushingly deliberate hybrid. The first occupant, who held the office for a number of years until he became senile, was Jalusiga, the chief of Ukuru. The Alur felt vindicated. A Lugbara government chief succeeded him briefly, but the whole fragile fantasy was soon swept away by the realities of the power struggle after independence.

The episode illustrates the dilemma of the Alur as an ethnic group. Not only were they divided between Uganda and Zaire, but within Uganda they were part of a multi-ethnic district which they could not securely dominate, for they were a numerical minority. Should their strategy be to dominate the District, as briefly attempted in merely symbolic fashion through the *Agofe-Obimo*? Or should they go all out for a District of their own, which they had for many years demanded without success? Ironically, it was after the terror of Idi Amin had diverted and sidetracked the previous ethnic ambitions, when everyone was more concerned with personal survival than ethnic advancement, that Idi Amin's arbitrary, but possibly sensible, decision to increase the number of Districts, split up the previous 'tribal' Districts of Ankole, Toro, Lang'o, Busoga, Karamoja and the rest, as well as breaking up the Province of Buganda, and the Alur found themselves united in a single District, when it had ceased to be of any significance. The District was called Nebbi, after the small township which was made its headquarters. It gave little satisfaction to most of the Alur, for it was outside the core area of Ukuru, which was politically dominant, and also outside Junam, which had come to form a new sub-ethnic group with its own claims. Nebbi District satisfied no-one, while formally meeting the demand which Alur had pressed for many decades.

The impact of partition on Alurland

How then can one assess the impact of the frontier on the divided Alur and arrive at guidelines for avoiding or dealing with such problems? At the start of writing this account I expected to document the iniquities of such cultural partition, and still think it iniquitous that culturally homogeneous units should be politically cut to pieces by outside powers without consultation of the people concerned. In an ideal world such events should not occur. But in the less than ideal world we live in one is forced to recognise that partition does sometimes bring certain advantages as well as hardships.

Unquestionably, none of the Alur wished to lose their political independence and to be subjected to European colonial rule, but it is doubtful whether they resented or suffered from it at the time any more acutely because it was also accompanied by partition. As they had never been politically united, they could not miss a unity they had never had. The frontier was often a nuisance, but it was hardly ever truly closed. The Alur passed to and fro with relative ease regularly attending markets on either side. When times were bad on one side, there was some chance of escaping and taking refuge with relatives or friends on the other. Differential economic policies and prices enabled large profits to be made by smuggling— or at least small profits by quite large numbers of people.

Not only had the Alur not been united, but some of the most prominent groups on either side had actually been at enmity with one another. Despite Belgian sensitivity on the matter, there has never been any significant pan-Alur or Greater Alurland irredentist movement and it does not seem particularly likely that there ever will be. Nevertheless, had all the Alur been on one side of the frontier, they would by now be a population group of nearly half a million, able to exercise far more significant influence on policy in the country to which they belonged than they can either in Zaire or in Uganda. This is important, for some of the most intractable problems derive from the large numbers of the separate ethnic groups of which most African countries are composed. Partition has greatly exacerbated this. For better or worse, many African countries have been dominated by the influence of their larger ethnic groups, or by the struggles between them, while the smaller ones get neglected. The popular stereotype, even among Africans, is of a Nigeria consisting largely of Hausa, Igbo and Yoruba, of a Kenya dominated by rivalry between Kikuyu and Luo, of Uganda plagued by the problem of the Baganda, and so on.

Given the understandable attitudes of the OAU and of African heads of state, it is unlikely that much can be done in the near future to reunite partitioned Africans. But it is fairly clear under what circumstances partition causes the greatest frustration to the people involved and leads to the most severe political problems. It is when a partitioned people has a fairly clear awareness of itself as an ethnic and cultural entity, and when at the same time one large section of it has a firm base in a particular national state. This was the case with Somalia which, apart from the Arab states of the north, was unusual in Africa in achieving independence as a nation with a single relatively homogeneous ethnic group. With this strong base it was bound to aim at unifying and strengthening itself by the addition of those outside. The Galla of Ethiopia, though like the Somali they had a large section cut off in Kenya, have not constituted such a problem because, despite their very large numbers, Ethiopia is not primarily a Galla state and therefore does not inevitably arouse Galla nationalism as Somalia did in the case of the Somali. Nor have the Hausa in Nigeria and Niger, or the Yoruba in Nigeria and Benin (Dahomey), constituted a serious problem, because in both cases they had already before the colonial era belonged to their own politically separate city states, despite their general sense of cultural unity. The Yao, Makua and Makonde astride the borders between Tanzania, Mozambique and Malawi have not caused serious problems because, like the Alur, they did not have strongly unified politicial organisations as separate peoples. The Fulani, who stretch all the way through Senegal, Mali, Guinea, Upper Volta, Nigeria, Niger, Cameroon and the Central African Republic, have never, perhaps understandably, pressed for unity as a nation.

Many African peoples were cut in two, or three, by different boundaries of the same colonial power, as in the case of the Samia, divided between Uganda and Kenya, or the Kakwa between Uganda and the Sudan (and also Zaire), or the Mandingo between Guinea and French Sudan (Mali), but in a host of other cases the partition was between different colonial powers with different languages, as in the case of the Alur subjected both to the English-speaking British and the French- and Flemish-speaking Belgians. Consequently, Alur were taught in French on one side of the border and in English on the other. They faced the Christian missions of the fundamentalist Protestant, Anglo-American, Africa Inland Mission and the Italian Roman Catholic Verona Fathers in Uganda, and in the Congo the French and Belgian White Fathers and again the Africa Inland Mission. This not only entailed different languages of higher instruction, but rival orthographies of their own language. A vexatious partition of language, intellect and comprehension was thus added to the political division. A hopeful sign in 1972 was that a group of European missionaries and of Alur from both Catholic and Protestant missions and from both sides of the Uganda-Zaire border were meeting amicably to discuss a common orthography for a new translation of the Bible. One of the severest penalties of partition is that the divided Alur do not provide a large enough market on either side of the border for large-scale economic publishing in their own tongue, nor is their language properly recognised in radio and television programmes of either state.

Generalisation for Africa

The colonial powers balkanised Africa with vexatious boundaries cutting through ethnic unities, yet at the same time state organisation was imposed in a more centralised form than had been present over most of the continent before. But even larger political economies are required if the struggle for economic independence in most parts of Africa is to have any chance of success. If larger states, or federated associations of states, could be achieved, the damage of ethnic partition would be to that extent lessened. If such a prospect is too utopian for the moment, the best that can be hoped for is that the existing boundaries should be as flexible as possible, so that the inconvenience and cultural impoverishment caused by partition can be minimised.[25] Recent events offer little encouragement in this respect, for as long as African economies are dragged down into recession and unemployment by the capitalist world system which dominates them, so long will African states be tempted to expel foreign nationals when it suits them, however close the ethnic ties those 'foreigners' share with their own citizens.[26]

The cutting up of African societies and cultures by imperialist aggression, and by the colonial process which still continues in its latest form today, within the neo-colonial new nations of Africa, raises many burning questions which are far from any solution. We may deplore the political aggression and economic exploitation which occurred, but if we ask what alternative futures were there for African peoples in a world where capitalist economic power supports military aggression and political domination, the answer is far from clear. However deplorable the acts of the past, history cannot be reversed and the more important question is how the cultural fragmentation which Africa has suffered can be overcome in order to create a stronger cultural basis of solidarity and creativity for economic growth, social equality and political autonomy. There is at present a potential conflict between the desire to restore or maintain the cultural solidarities which were broken by colonialism and the need for African states to maintain their integrity against the divisive tendencies which cultural solidarities running across their borders could encourage.

Recognising the short-run wisdom of the OAU in seeking to preserve all existing colonially derived boundaries against a host of secessionist tendencies which could destroy them all, it can hardly be denied that the creation of larger economic and even political unities would assist Africa in the North-South struggle against the present stranglehold of the industrial capitalist powers. The general poverty of African nations and their dependence on outside resources makes them at present inevitably dependent in many other respects also. Among Third World nations only China has succeeded in winning essential economic and political independence, and this is due not only to the strength of its culture and institutions but to its large size and its possession of most of the natural resources required for industrial development.

Africa cannot hope to achieve such autonomy unless it is able to create from within itself equally large and potentially self-sufficient units. At present such a goal seems discouragingly remote and it is in no way helped by the insertion of superpower rivalry and conflict into all major African issues. The African nations face enormous difficulties in any effort to create more viable and potentially self-sufficient political and economic entities, not only from the rivalry of superpowers more concerned to win natural resources or political support for themselves than to strengthen African economic self-sufficiency, but also from the vested interests of their own élites, which have become strongly entrenched in two short decades of political independence. Nonetheless, we should never lose sight of the fact that if Africa is ever to recover from the wounds inflicted by colonialism in carving to pieces its cultural solidarities, it can never be by a return to the basis of these solidarities as they were, but only by creating still larger national entities within which subcultural units may have greater freedom.

The colonial powers endeavoured to create larger units for their own interests in French West Africa, French Equatorial Africa, the East African Community and the Central African Federation. None of these could survive the divisive tendencies which the colonial powers themselves had fostered in the basic colonial units which they created. But until Africans themselves can achieve larger and more self-sufficient entities they will never escape from the economic stranglehold of the older-established capitalist powers, and from the weakness and cultural improverishment of their divided and partitioned condition which helps to perpetuate this stranglehold.

NOTES

1. A. Southall, *Alur Society: A Study in Processes and Types of Domination*, Cambridge and Oxford University Presses, 1956; 2nd edn 1969.
2. A. Southall, 'Alur Tradition and Its Historical Significance', *Uganda Journal*, XVIII, 2, Kampala, 1954.
3. A. Southall, 'Rank and Stratification Among the Alur and Other Nilotic Peoples' in L. Plotnicov and A. Tuden (eds), *Social Stratification in Africa* (New York: Free Press, 1970).
4. A. Southall, 'Incorporation Among the Alur' in John Middleton and Ronald Cohen (eds), *From Tribe to Nation in Africa* (Scranton, NJ: Chandler, 1970).
5. A. Southall, 'Spirit Mediumship Cults Among the Alur', John Bealtie and John Middleton (eds), *Spirit Mediumship and Society in Africa* (London, 1969).
6. A. Southall, 'Belgian and British Administration in Alurland', *Zaire*, VIII, 5, May 1954.
7. A. Southall, 'Nuer and Dinka are people: Ecology, Ethnicity and Logical Possibility', *Man*, 11, 4, 1976.
8. Southall, *Alur Society, op. cit.*, pp. 220–4.
9. M. Godelier, 'Infrastructure, Societies and History', *Current Anthropology*, 19, 3, 1978, pp. 763–71.
10. A. Southall, 'A Critique of the Typology of States and Political Systems' in Michael Banton (ed.), *Political Systems and the Distribution of Power* (London, 1965); 'A Note on State Organisation: Segmentary States in Africa and Medieval Europe' in Sylvia Thrupp (ed.), *Early Medieval Society*, 1967.
11. Southall, *Alur Society, op. cit.*, pp. 181–205.
12. *Ibid.*, pp. 280–1.
13. A. Southall, 'The Illusion of Tribe', *Journal of Asian and African Studies*, 5, 1 and 2, 1970.
14. Southall, *Alur Society, op. cit.*, pp. 243–9.
15. G.A. Schweinfurth *et al.* (eds), *Emin Pasha in Central Africa*, 1888.
16. A.J. Mounteney Jephson, *Emin Pasha and the Rebellion at the Equator*, New York, 1890.
17. D. Middleton (ed.), *The Diary of A.J. Mounteney Jephson*, Cambridge University Press, 1969.
18. Southall, *Alur Society, op. cit.*, p. 235.
19. *Ibid.*, p. 349.
20. *Ibid.*, pp. 372–3.
21. *Ibid.*, pp. 370–1.
22. *Ibid.*, pp. 349–50.
23. *Ibid.*, and maps 16–17.
24. *Ibid.*, pp. 283–5.
25. This point is taken up in a more elaborate discussion in the last chapter (pp. 243–8 ff.).
26. This observation was recorded months before the expulsion of 'Illegal Aliens' from Nigeria in February 1983.

7

NATIONAL INTEGRATION, RURAL DEVELOPMENT AND FRONTIER COMMUNITIES

THE CASE OF THE CHEWA AND THE NGONI ASTRIDE ZAMBIAN BOUNDARIES WITH MALAWI AND MOZAMBIQUE

S.H. Phiri

In most parts of Africa and elsewhere in the world where the modern state is a multi-ethnic structure, its function as an instrument for socio-political integration is invariably hampered by several factors, not least the centrifugal behaviour of constituent ethnic groups or nationalities. Although this problem has been focussed by several studies of state and nation in Africa,[1] its peculiar manifestation in frontier zones has not been subjected to a systematic inquiry.

The division of ethnic groups whose culture areas lay in the region through which the state boundaries were drawn creates the situation which compels subsequent cross-border social relations among members. Under such conditions, ethnic loyalty as an obstacle to the achievement of modern state formation and its integrative functions assumes an international posture that makes it distinct from the similar loyalty expressed by groups whose areas are contained entirely within the defined boundaries of the particular states.[2] This problem is especially manifest in situations like that in Zambia where the state's rural development programme is naturally directed to include frontier zones which, as elsewhere in the continent, are often neglected rural landscape. The problem posed by trans-frontier ethnic loyalty in such a situation lies in the fact that services provided at the expense of a state for its own share of partitioned ethnic groups are often made inadequate by the inevitable infiltration of kinsmen from adjacent states whose governments have not contributed to their cost.

While the focus of this paper is specifically on the Chewa and the Ngoni astride the Zambia-Malawi and Zambia-Mozambique boundaries, the findings and resultant policy implications apply generally to most other parts of Africa including the other international boundaries of Zambia not specifically discussed.[3] The comparability with other African situations is especially strong when we consider the contradiction between, on the one hand, the state formation and the nationalism which evolve within the prescribed boundaries of the post-colonial states and, on the other, the cross-border ethnic or cultural preservation and linkages which tend to confound the demarcating purpose of the boundaries. We draw attention here to the implications of this contradiction for the rural development policy of the Zambia Government as it concerns the land and peoples in the frontier zones.

As with studies of cross-border trade on a number of West African international (formerly inter-colonial) boundaries,[4] the paper demonstrates that the socio-economic space generated by the boundaries spreads far on either side of the political lines themselves. For example, whereas in the case under review the boundaries, in theory, delimit the areas of jurisdiction of Zambia *vis-à-vis* the two neighbouring states of Malawi and Mozambique, the medical, educational and agricultural services provided by the Government for the Ngoni and Chewa settlements located on the Zambian side of the boundaries have been made inadequate largely as a result of the use made of them by kinsmen crossing the boundaries from Malawi and Mozambique.

There is also the problem of clandestine cross-border movements and activities, including especially the smuggling of goods and the immigration of unauthorised aliens, including political refugees and, on occasions, criminals seeking refuge and obtaining sanctuary from the laws of neighbouring states. All of these take place under the general cover provided by the identical cultural environment prevailing on either side of the prescribed boundaries. This situation, which can be easily generalised for most frontier zones in Africa, suggests the need for a special kind of arrangement which will allow for international co-operation at the local level.

The Chewa and the Ngoni before partition

The pre-partition history of the Chewa and the Ngoni is not only that of two contrasting African cultures and traditions; it also concerns one of the best known cases of inter-group relations in the continent before the imposition of European colonial rule.

The Chewa and the Ngoni speak two distinct languages. While the Chewa hold to traditions which originated in the Katanga region of Zaire (formerly the Belgian Congo) to the west, a major component of the pride of the Ngoni as a people is derived from their claims to be descended from the Zulus in the south. In their respective styles of social and political organisation also, the Chewa and the Ngoni present a contrast, the Chewa being a matrilineal society with a matrilocal residential practice while the Ngoni are adamantly patrilineal and patrilocal. Similarly contrastive are the decentralised, familially conceived and essentially agrarian kingship of the Chewa and the extremely centralised, highly hierarchised and militarily disposed territorial state of the Ngoni. Finally, in terms of precedence, the Chewa are known to have settled and dominated the region under study for centuries before the arrival of the Ngoni conquerors in 1870. It was the Ngoni arrival and their expansionist wars which came to determine the hostility of the Chewa and related peoples such as the Nsenga, the Cipeta, the Nyanja, the Mg'anja, the Zimba and the Mbo whom the Ngoni fought and incorporated into their two or three newly-established centralised states.

But distinct as the two peoples were and still largely are, the political interaction of the nineteenth century laid the foundation of enduring social relations which were already producing some measure of cultural fusion between them at the time of the Anglo-Portuguese partition in 1891. Evidence of such a cultural fusion includes the marriage of Chewa women to Ngoni men, and the resultant infiltration into Ngoni society of Chewa cultural traits including language, music and religious and para-religious institutions including spirit mediums and the initiation rites for girls. Indeed, the fact that the Ngoni had to recruit most of their wives from the culturally matrilineal and matrilocal Chewa has inevitably meant a dominant influence of Chewa mothers on the new generation of the Ngoni issuing from these marriages.

The drawing of political boundaries for three distinct colonies — two British and one Portuguese — across this region has therefore led to the splitting into three of the Chewa and the Ngoni. The boundaries also aborted the process of cultural fusion to the limited extent to which it had taken place by the time the differential colonial regimes were imposed — by breaking it into three.

The Chewa

To appreciate the impact of the boundaries of the three European colonies on the Chewa and the Ngoni fully, it is imperative to assess the spatial spread of the two peoples before European partition and the eventual establishment of the three colonial regimes concerned. We begin with the Chewa who preceded the Ngoni in the region.

Among the Chewa, as among other peoples, the nature and character of human settlement and the territorial spread of such a settlement are essentially aspects of political history. Generally, the process of state formation among the Chewa would appear to have fitted into a scheme that suggests that the historical development of pre-colonial African states took them through the four successive phases of kinship polity, chiefdom, kingdom and empire, each succeeding stage in the line of evolution being marked by an increase in both the territorial size and diversity of the constituent populations.

In the Chewa case, this process is held to begin at the point in time when a kinship group moved into an area which appeared uninhabited by any other people. The entrenchment of the group provided the evidence for its claim to be the original owner of the settlement and its immediate neighbourhood. This meant that all adult members of the kinship group could be allocated plots of land around the settlement. If an individual family were for various reason — in particular succession disputes — to be forced out of such a settlement, it would lose its right to cultivate the lands, which because of the withdrawal reverted to the ownership of the community. On the other hand, should other Chewa or non-Chewa kinship groups from elsewhere wish to move into the same locality as the original settlement, such newcomers would seek the permission of the village headman or the *Mfumu ya mudzi*.

The initial expansion of the village into a chiefdom was usually attributed to such arrivals of other Chewa or non-Chewa groups. Expansion also took place when segmentation had not resulted from secession or other adverse political considerations. Where segmentation was related to non-political considerations such as shortage of cultivable land around the original settlement, kinship groups moving away might still regard the original settlement as the centre for the resolution of disputes occuring in the new settlements. In this case, the headman of the original village became the *Mfumu ya ndoko* or the chief for the group of related settlements which together had come to constitute the chiefdom. The initially peaceful expansion might come to involve the systematic use of political sanctions, including warfare. When this happened, the chiefdom would evolve into a kingdom where the *Mfumu ya ndoko* of the chiefdom also evolved into the status of *Mfumu ya dziko*. The kingdom became an empire when it came to incorporate not just the same ethnic group but other distinct cultures or ethnic groups as well.

Although the Chewa state was prone to a continuous process of segmentation, stability at the various levels of political integration mentioned could be achieved through the application of several devices, including the charisma of the ruler and his customary monopoly with respect to access to the *azimu* or the ancestral spirit mediums, considered the most crucial of the power resources. Nevertheless, the decentralised nature of political organisation created a multiplicity of identically structured states and a lack of a common political front, a situation that spelt disaster for the Chewa when confronted with external invaders of which the Ngoni were the most important before the era of European partition.

The oral traditions of the generality of the Chewa point to claims that the people's ancestors, or at any rate the ancestors of their rulers, arrived in the area of present-day Malawi in the thirteenth century. The original settlement was on the south-western shores of Lake Malawi. Soon after their arrival in the area between Lake Malawi and Luangwa River, a group led by one Kalonga founded the first Chewa kingdom. In due course, the Kalonga kingdom extended its political influence over a large section of the Chewa as well as over other ethnic groups and states such as the Nyanja, Mg'anja, Zimba, Mbo, Nsenga and Cipeta. The incorporation of the other groups into the Kalonga kingdom led to the emergence of the Kalonga empire (known also as the Malawi empire) situated mostly in the central and southern parts of the present-day Republic of Malawi. The Kalonga or the first Malawi empire eventually gave way to the Undi or the second Malawi empire founded by Kalonga's nephew, Undi Phiri, *ca*. 1650. The new Malawi empire had its capital in Mano, which is inside the present-day Republic of Mozambique.

As Langworthy has suggested, the Malawi empire — whether that founded by Kalonga or that of Undi Phiri — operated essentially as a federation of Chewa kingdoms, each constituent kingdom enjoying much local autonomy.[5] Although the Undi state managed to survive until the mid-nineteenth century, the decline of the empire was already in evidence by the 1750s. Among the factors leading to its final collapse were a general lack of capacity for concerted political action, the Portuguese intrusion resulting in the establishment of the notorious *Prazo* system, the export slave trade, and finally the Ngoni invasion. As Isaacman has observed, it was on the ruins of the Undi empire that the founders of the Makanga kingdom erected their state, which by 1900 had fallen under the regime of a *Prazo* estate controlled by the Portuguese Pereira family.[6]

The Ngoni

Unlike the Chewa who, due to a decentralised political system and an essentially agrarian economy, were territorially more widespread, the Ngoni had been a mobile warrior nation before they conquered the Chewa and settled in their midst in 1870. It is not intended here to repeat the political history of the Ngoni; Read (1936), Barnes (1954), Hanna (1956), Gann (1964), Omer-Cooper (1966) and Rau (1974) have provided a cumulative literature on the Ngoni in general and Mpezeni in particular.[7]

We however will seek to sketch the spatial implications of the socio-political organisation in order to explain how, in consequence of the European partition of 1891, the Ngoni came to be divided into four distinct colonial territories with the largest concentration in the districts of Mzimba, Dowa, Fort Manning, Dedza and Ncheu in the central and southern parts of present-day Malawi (the British colony at first referred to as the British Central African Protectorate and later as Nyasaland) and the contiguous districts of Fort Jameson and Lundazi in present-day Zambia (formerly Northern Rhodesia) and the rest in the former Portuguese colony of Mozambique and the originally German colony of Tanganyika, later a British mandate and now the mainland area of the present-day Republic of Tanzania.[8]

Despite these four contemporary divisions, especially the first three (i.e. Zambia, Malawi and Mozambique) on which this paper focusses, the Ngoni before the European colonial partition constituted a distinct culture area. Although the people had been organised into three principal kingdoms of Mpezeni, Mwambera and Gomani, each named after its founding paramount ruler, there was, as there still is, a unity of language, patrilineal social customs, a strongly centralised and hierarchised style of socio-political organisation, and a cherished tradition of common Zulu ancestry and militarism. The Ngoni at the time of their arrival in the region were obviously inferior in number to the Chewa and related peoples whom they met on the spot. However, through the use of superior weapons (the Ngoni spear and shield compared to the Chewa bows and arrows) and military tactics, the Ngoni succeeded in conquering a good number of the pre-established communities.

Through a vigorous socialisation process, the Ngoni also succeeded to some extent in integrating non-Ngoni peoples who came within the orbit of the new states. This process made possible the emergence of what Margaret Read has appropriately described as a society or state made up of 'a compound of the Ngoni ruling aristocracy and the conquered indigenous people', all held together by the conscious entrenchment of such basic Ngoni socio-political institutions as the centralised chieftaincy, military training, systematised law courts, recognised ranks in society, patrilineal succession and inheritance, and the use, at least among the ruling class, of a language that was foreign to the generality of surrounding indigenous peoples.[9]

But to discuss the implications or consequences for the present border cultural landscape, it is essential to appreciate the incompleteness of the assimilation process set in motion by the Ngoni following their wars of conquest and resultant efforts to create their new states. To start with, the military conquest of 1870 led to the defeat of only a part and not all of the pre-existing states and communities. Alan, for example, has suggested that on their arrival, the Ngoni succeeded only in occupying an area estimated at 3,367 square kilometres or about 22 per cent of the total habitable area within Fort Jameson District.[10]

As for the Chewa, of the chiefdoms that had been actually defeated only Mkanda stood out as a clear case of a conquered state. Indeed, the Ngoni states were generally noted for having been created in an area that had been part of Mkanda's kingdom. The other Chewa chiefdoms such as those of Mafuta, Chanje, Chikuwe and Chinunda, which fell under Ngoni control, submitted before they were actually defeated; and they were left more or less intact, subject to payment of prescribed tributes. While Chewa chiefdoms, which came within the orbit of the new Ngoni state, were those in the periphery of the Undi empire, the headquarters of the empire at Mano and such constituent chiefdoms of Mlolo, Mwangala, Pembanoyo, Zingalume, Kawaza, Kathumba and Mbang'ombe successfully resisted the Ngoni invasion and were thus regarded by the Ngoni as enemies. In explanation of the failure of the Ngoni to defeat Chewa chiefdoms such as those of Undi, Nwangala and Kathimba, Skeva Mwale has explained as follows:

> [The first reason was that] these chiefs sought refuge in the hills from where the use of poisoned arrows was an effective defence weapon. Secondly, the Ngoni army never carried food. They got their food from the villages that they attacked as they went along. People could tell by the sign of smoke that the Ngoni were within the neighbourhood and so they fled to the hills where they hid their food . . . . By constantly being on the look out and by moving villages nearer hills away from the Ngoni state people were able to resist Ngoni aggression.[11]

This uncompleted nature of the Ngoni conquest and efforts at socio-political integration suggest the real framework within which one should discuss the political, social and economic relations between the Ngoni and other ethnic groups, especially the Chewa. Most writers have emphasised the process in which alien ethnicities were incorporated into the Ngoni state through the household system. Available evidence, however, suggests that incorporation into Ngoni state and culture was successful only when the Ngoni were on the move and not when they had settled within the region under discussion. As Mizeke Msoni suggested:

> On the move it was possible to make *magwala* [aliens] Ngoni since the Ngoni did not stay in one place. It was therefore difficult for the newly incorporated groups to re-trace the way to their original homes where in most cases the whole community had been wiped out by the Ngoni *impis*. But in this area [Fort Jameson], where the Ngoni were surrounded by the Chewa, it was always possible for new captives to trace their way back to their original homes.[12]

This situation, rather than allowing the Ngoni to assimilate or absorb the Chewa, facilitated instead the process for the cultural assimilation of the Ngoni by the Chewa. Thus, while the Ngoni remained politically dominant in the area, social and economic dependence on the Chewa had allowed for a situation in which the latter came to exercise far greater cultural and economic dominance over the Ngoni than is generally appreciated. There were two main reasons for this. First was the dominance of the Chewa culture in the neighbourhood. As long as the Ngoni remained settled within this region, surrounded by the Chewa and other ethnic groups on which they had to rely for their socio-economic needs including as a source for their wives, a situation developed in which the non-Ngoni peoples began to diffuse their cultural traits among the Ngoni. Apart from the evidence of research, the personal experience of the present writer, who has lived in both the Ngoni (mother's and wife's villages) and Chewa (father's village) areas, has led to the direct observation that in almost all Ngoni chiefdoms *nyau* (Chewa cultural dances) are performed with greater regularity than *ingoma* (the Ngoni dance). On the other hand, *ingoma* has failed to penetrate into Chewa areas.

Furthermore, within the Ngoni area there are also spirit mediums generally known as *ziwanda* (spirits). People are possessed with the *ziwanda* of the Bisa, of the Chewa, and of the Azungu (Europeans). There are no *ziwanda* of the Ngoni although some Ngoni men and women can be possessed by the *ziwanda* from other ethnic groups.

Secondly, the fact that the Ngoni state relied partly on external sources for its food supplies created circumstances whereby the leadership was forced to ease political tensions with surrounding polities and thereby facilitated movements out of the Ngoni state for food procurement. This softening of attitude by the leadership suited the matrilineal groups like the Chewa, who came into the Ngoni state as refugees. The result was a remarkable degree of steady movement of the refugees in the Ngoni states to and from their areas of origin. Mizeke Msoni says:

> In times of famine, it was common for some of the Ngoni whose mothers were got from Nsenga (Petauke) to travel there in search of food among their kinsmen.[13]

While, because of their military prowess, the Ngoni exercised political dominance over some Chewa groups, the fact that more Ngoni men intermarried with Chewa and Nsenga women also meant that their offspring were reared by mothers who spoke different languages and whose cultural base was different from the Ngoni culture. Thus, although the Ngoni are patrilineal, the effect of marrying into matrilineal groups exerted a weakening influence on their socio-political institutions to the extent that even the Ngoni language, as it was spoken before the crossing of the Zambesi, became extinct among the Ngoni of Mpezeni. It is from this dimension that we can visualise a situation in which the Chewa/Ngoni relations were not likely to have been as hostile as they are often portrayed.

In view of the political, social and economic relations which the Ngoni established with the surrounding Chewa and other ethnic groups, the frontiers between the Ngoni states and other ethnic polities could be said to have fallen within the category which is classified in political geography as 'frontiers of inclusion'. The superimposition of the boundaries of the three distinct European colonies later transformed into the independent states of Zambia, Malawi and Mozambique has meant a division not only of distinct Chewa and Ngoni cultures but also of the third cultural formulation that was developing as a result of the gradual fusion taking place between the two up till that time. The implications of the location of the Chewa and Ngoni communities across the inter-state boundaries for national integration and the border development policy of the Zambia Government are the focus of the rest of our discussion.

Partition of the Chewa and the Ngoni

The partition of the Chewa and the Ngoni took place largely in consequence of the creation of the British Central African Protectorate (BCAP), now Malawi, and the resultant boundary agreements of 1891. These agreements defined the boundaries between the British and the Germans, separating the BCAP from German Tanganyika (now mainland Tanzania); between the British and the Portuguese, separating the BCAP from Mozambique; and between the British

Foreign Office, which was charged with the affairs of the Protectorate, and the British South African Company (BSAC), whose area of influence included North-East Rhodesia (NER), i.e. the area of present-day Zambia. This boundary arrangement had the effect of splitting up the indigenous polities. While, the boundary between the BCAP and NER split Mpezeni's Ngoni state into two unequal parts with two-thirds in NER and the remaining third in BCAP, the BCAP-Mozambique line split the Chewa into three parts between BCAP, NER and Mozambique.

As elsewhere in Africa, boundary agreements between occupying. European powers merely marked the beginning of the actual process for the establishment of colonial rule. This process, often deceptively described in colonialist literature as 'pacification', normally involved direct or indirect use of force on the part of the European colonial power concerned and armed responses from the peoples and communities over whom control was imposed. In the area under consideration the obviously outstanding case of 'pacification' was Sir Harry Johnston's expedition against Mpezeni's Ngoni state in January 1898.[14] This resulted in the establishment of British rule over the Ngoni in the area of the present-day Republics of Zambia and Malawi.

Significantly, the success of the British expedition was determined not only by the superior fire-arms and military tactics of the invading army; it was also strongly influenced by the predictable support of the Chewa who saw in the British military intervention a means for their liberation from Ngoni imperialism. Thus, as Margaret Read correctly noted, while the Ngoni say 'the European spoiled our country', the Chewa say 'the Europeans saved us.'[15] Accordingly, while British rule was imposed on the Ngoni in consequence of outright conquest, the generality of the Chewa came under British rule on the basis of protectorate treaties.

The impact of the boundaries

If the purpose of boundaries is to set the exact limits of the area of jurisdiction of a modern state, the fact of the superimposition on pre-existing indigenous groups and states generally occasions a situation of contradiction. For while the modern state seeks to contain itself within the new boundaries to the exclusion of interests outside its territorial framework, the reaction in terms of relations within and between indigenous groups on which the new state boundaries have been imposed is to ignore the boundary or accept it more as a line of inclusion than one of separation or exclusion. This is especially true of situations like that considered in this paper where the boundaries of the modern state divide homogenous culture areas. In such circumstances, realities of intra-group relations across the new state boundaries run contrary to the attitude of the state which seeks tacitly to maintain the boundaries as lines of separation from the neighbouring state.

The impossibility of maintaining boundaries of exclusion in the area under study had been in evidence even before the imposition of European colonial states. We have already referred to the manner in which the boundaries set by the territorially structured Ngoni state were systematically violated by their predominantly Chewa and Nsenga subject-populations whose lineage-biased culture and decentralised political organisation generally compelled movements in and out of the set boundaries of the new centralised state system of the Ngoni. The Ngoni themselves later joined the Chewa in the attitude of opposition to the principle of set boundaries once such boundaries were seen to have been externally imposed and to break up the pre-established Ngoni cultural and political unity.

In the colonial era, the first major event that set in motion a large-scale movement of people across the boundaries of the three colonial territories under discussion was the British expedition against the Ngoni in 1898. As with the French conquest of Dahomey in 1892, which caused the exodus of liberated Yoruba and Mahin slaves whom the ancient Fon state had held in subjection,[16] the defeat of the Ngoni generated huge population movements within NER and between NER and the BCAP as a result of the widespread desertion of the defeated state by non-Ngoni men and women whom the Ngoni had incorporated into their state. Much of this movement took the form of a return of the people to their original matrilineal and matrilocal groups and an intensified reversion to the pre-Ngoni socio-political institutions and customs.

In the course of the colonial period, cross-border migrations continued quite steadily largely because of the contrasts in the policies pursued by the three neighbouring colonial administrations of the British and the Portuguese. In such circumstances, the existence of the boundaries and the presence on both sides of people sharing not only the same culture but often even the same family ties increased the possibilities for the local people to cross the borders in a conscious search for refuge from laws and regulations considered too harsh to be tolerated in one or the other of the colonial states. There was, for example, a parallel to the general pattern of protest migrations from French to British colonies in West Africa[17] in the size and persistence of a similar mode of migrations from border communities on the Mozambican side to the NER and BCAP sides of the boundaries out of consideration for the relatively relaxed policies of the

British by comparison with the Portuguese on matters such as taxation and forced labour.

Sometimes the different attitudes of the border populations were in direct response to the administrative style or method in use. The British 'Indirect Rule' has, for example, been found to be a major cause of the increased migrations from Mozambique into the BCAP and NER. As a political strategy, that policy was of course a design to divide and rule Africans. In the British colonies themselves, it was a target for popular criticism on account of its in-built hypocrisy. The indigenous chiefs were presented as leaders of their people, when in fact they were isolated from their communities and used more effectively as agents of the European administration.

While all these criticisms of British Indirect Rule are borne out by evidence, the adoption of this policy left much room for a contrast with Portuguese policy and practice. For whereas the Portuguese exercised direct political control over the Chewa chiefs on the Mozambican side of the boundary, the British in Northern Rhodesia (i.e. the new territory resulting from the amalgamation of NER and North-Western Rhodesia in 1911, the same year as the BCAP was renamed Nyasaland) made use of the Chewa Native Authority. Outwardly, therefore, the Chewa chiefs in Northern Rhodesia appeared to have more power and political influence in their relationship with the European administration than their kinsmen in Mozambique. To make good this higher prestige of the Northern Rhodesian Chewa chiefs, those of them along the border exploited the Indirect Rule policy to attract and admit into their areas an increasing number of immigrants from Mozambique, much as traditional Hausa rulers on the Nigerian side of the border[18] with French Niger and the Yoruba rulers on the British side of the Nigeria-Dahomey boundary[19] were encouraged to pull Hausa and Yoruba from across the boundaries into British Nigeria. In Northern Rhodesia this practice continued up till the time of the liberation war in Mozambique.

Oral historical accounts among the Chewa of Northern Rhodesia/Zambia and Nyasaland/Malawi suggest that the use of the inter-colonial boundaries as sanctuary was not limited to that between Northern Rhodesia and Mozambique. The inter-colonial boundary between the British-ruled territories was also seen more as a line of contact than of separation for the Chewa. For example, when tax collection was in progress in the one colony, persons who could not or would not pay simply crossed over and stayed with kinsmen on the other side of the border, returning after the tax collectors had left. In other words, the Chewa and the Ngoni along this boundary, like their counterparts along the boundary with Mozambique, exploited the existence of the boundary to evade civil obligations on the side where they normally resided and, in the process, reaffirm and reinforce intra-group solidarity.

Cross-border movements since Independence

The question of differential policy by the three distinct governments and the related issue of political, social and economic strains and stresses on the local people, including those along the boundaries, did not cease with the formal termination of colonial rule. For this reason, the tradition of cross-border migratory flow has continued in the post-colonial period.

For example, the independence of Malawi in 1963 and of Zambia in 1964 brought about three major waves of cross-border migrations with considerable consequences for social, political and economic developments in Zambia. The first, which has continued up to this day, comprises members of the Watch Tower Bible and Tract Society (WTBTS), a fanatical Christian sect proscribed in Malawi. Mostly Chewa and Ngoni, they have moved into Zambia and settled among their kinsmen. The second major wave came about in the mid-1960s when the Front for the Liberation of Mozambique (Frelimo) began waging the liberation war against the Portuguese. This again brought refugees into Zambia; but the Ngoni and Chewa among them stayed with relatives rather than in the officially established refugee camps. Lastly, there has been a steady movement of some Zambians in the border areas into Mozambique in search of cultivable land.

All these movements tend to demonstrate that, irrespective of the modern state to which they belong, people along the international boundaries under discussion are bound together by community feeling. They 'belong' to neither one state nor the other, but they 'belong' to themselves. The spate of smuggling across international boundaries within this region clearly demonstrates that the type of economy prevailing within this frontier zone disobeys the national laws of all the three countries concerned.

Both the internal and external policies of Zambia, Malawi and Mozambique differ significantly in character from one state to another despite superficial similarities. There are, for example, substantial differences in their political history and power structures in spite of the common label 'Republic', identical claims to the status of a one-party state, and similar antecedents as European settler colonies. For example, the fact that all three are one-party states would outwardly suggest that political opposition is non-existent. In reality, however, it is clear that except in Mozambique, where

Frelimo was the dominant party at the time of independence in 1975, political opposition was suppressed in Malawi by a Presidential decree while in Zambia political opposition was outlawed through the guided constitutional amendments of 1972. In Malawi, the suppression of opposition signalled the emergence of a dictatorial regime. This in turn has generated a high rate of political exile and of activity among exiled groups which have been organised to engineer the overthrow of President Banda's regime. Since some of these exile groups are allegedly based in neighbouring independent states such as Tanzania, Mozambique and Zambia, the relations between Malawi and her neighbours have been less than cordial. This uneasy political relationship has been exacerbated by the fact that President Banda has not renounced the territorial claims which were made publicly *vis-à-vis* Tanzania, Zambia and Mozambique. Thus, for example, while Zambia and Malawi officially regard each other as friendly nations, in practice the local situation, especially along their common boundary, has not been so friendly. For example, the following report appeared in the *Times of Zambia* in 1977:

> The Ministry of Home Affairs is to investigate reports that Zambians living along the Malawi border are being harassed by that country's police.
> The Ministry's acting permanent secretary, Mr Evans Simukulwa, said in Lusaka yesterday that he would instruct the Chief Immigration Officer to investigate allegations by the Member of Parliament for Muyombe (Northern Province), Mr Sully Mugala. He said Zambians were being detained and imprisoned each time they entered Malawi to visit relatives.[20]

Another bone of contention between the Malawi and Zambian governments has been the latter's willingness to offer shelter to political refugees, notably members of the Watch Tower Bible and Tract Society (WTBTS), who have been 'persecuted' in Malawi for their refusal to salute the country's national flag or sing the national anthem. Because some WTBTS members who are Chewa or Ngoni have settled permanently among their kinsmen in Zambia, Zambia has been accused of harbouring criminals and subversive elements from Malawi.

The political relationship between Malawi and Mozambique could at best be described as cool. The second-in-command at Kaswende Frelimo Camp in Mozambique, Comrade Mandevu, said the following to me:

> Frelimo will never forgive President Kamuzu Banda of Malawi because he is a *kapirikoni* [traitor]. During the freedom struggle against Portuguese colonial forces President Banda's soldiers used to capture Frelimo comrades and hand them to the Portuguese colonialists at Lourenco Marques [now Maputo] where most were hanged, and in exchange for this Kamuzu

was apparently offered the whole of northern Mozambique starting from the Zambesi River.[21]

Malawi was one of the few African states that were not invited for Mozambique's Independence celebrations. Furthermore, there is the fact that the Socialist Organization for the Liberation of Malawi, which has committed itself to toppling President Banda's regime through the use of arms, is based in Mozambique. This sufficiently reflects the attitudes of these two countries towards each other.

One other important factor which differentiates Malawi from her neighbours and indeed all independent African states is that it is the only such state that has established full diplomatic relations with the South African racist regime. Thus it appears that for Malawi there are political considerations that outweigh close ties with her neighbours.

However, while Zambia and Mozambique may not wish to associate with Malawi politically, the Chewa and Ngoni within this border region appear to be concerned primarily with their own cultural ties and socio-economic interests. For example, it was reported in the *Times of Zambia*:

> Many Zambians and Malawians have been arrested by immigration officials in the Eastern Province in connection with smuggling, the member of the Central Committee for the province, Mr Mungoni Liso, said yesterday. He said the immigration department in the province had stepped up its fight against smuggling following reports that the crime was prevalent in the area....
> Mr Liso could not reveal the method the immigration officers were using to detect smugglers. But he said that it was wrong to think that only foreigners were involved in smuggling. 'There are also some Zambians who are involved in the crime. We have caught many red-handed.'[22]

While smuggling should not be condoned, it does appear that, given the ethnic or cultural considerations especially among the Chewa who are also matrilocal, the international boundary has created a peculiar situation. For example, when a Chewa man from either Mozambique or Malawi marries a Chewa woman from Zambia, he is required by customary law to take residence in Zambia. Thus in recent years, due to shortages of some basic consumer items which have been experienced throughout Zambia as a result of the border closure to Zimbabwe during the liberation war in the latter country, quite a large number of 'foreign' husbands have tended to cross the international boundaries to their countries of origin to procure certain consumer items such as soap or sugar. Often on their return journey to Zambia some of these 'foreign' husbands have been arrested for smuggling. The same situation applied to Zambian husbands residing in Malawi. The bewilderment of the frontier communities in this situation has been well put by Labison Banda:

> All the Chewa in Malawi, Mozambique and Zambia are one and in fact the politicians say that Zambians, Malawians and Mozambicans are one. So why is it that when we visit our relatives living in the neighbouring countries we got arrested?[23]

In fact, before the date of Labison Banda's statement, there had been calls for strong cross-border ties by the Zambian Prime Minister, Mr Elijah Mudenda who, according to the *Zambia Daily Mail*,

> called upon Zambians and Mozambicans living around the border to continue strengthening the bonds of friendship between UNIP and Frelimo. Addressing Party and Government Officials at Freira Boma, Mr Mudenda, who is on a 4-day tour of the district and Lusaka Rural, said before Mozambique became independent, people of Freira sacrificed and faced hardships at the hands of the Portugues in support of their Frelimo brothers and sisters who were fighting for their freedom.[24]

In any case, while it is declared government policy in Zambia to support liberation movements, in border areas people took risks and accommodated the refugees who crossed the international boundary mainly on a kinship and ethnic basis. This does not, however, suggest that refugees of other ethnic groups were not welcome. The point to emphasise here is that people living within the Zambia/Malawi/Mozambique border area are bound together by ethnic and cultural links. These considerations are sometimes missed by politicians when they make speeches in connection with aliens within their countries.

For example, the following report also appeared in the *Zambia Daily Mail*:

> Central Committee Member for the Eastern Province, Mr Liso, has ordered a census to determine the number of alien Africans who have settled in the province illegally. The provincial Party chief said this . . . when asked to comment on the influx of Malawi Watch Tower Sect members in the Chipata district. He said that when the census has been completed all aliens without work permits would be deported to their countries of origin.
>
> Mr Liso said the problem of Malawians seeking employment was not a new one. Many Malawians are employed on farms especially in the Sinde-Misale district.[25]

From what has been said so far, it is clear that ethnic or customary laws are not compatible with national laws as they contradict each other. In any case, customary laws are pragmatic since they facilitate the continuation of stronger border links. On the other hand, strict application of national citizenship and immigration regulations would essentially entail that all border residents should have passes to enable them to cross the international boundary. Yet the requirement of an official pass for border residents to cross international boundaries would appear impracticable. For example, between Chadiza and Katete Districts, where the Zambia/Mozambique border runs for almost 200 km., there are only two official border posts, at Kaswende and Mlolo. Similarly, the boundary between Zambia and Malawi is approximately 400 km. long and has only two border posts, at Mwami and Mtocha. Given these circumstances, it would appear that quite a number of people accused of smuggling may not really have been professional smugglers but people caught in the juxtaposition of two distinct traditions along the boundary, namely the tradition of flexibility and mobility guaranteed by customary relations and the Western nation-state boundary tradition of inflexibility and rigidity.

Policy advice

Given the resilience of the trans-frontier loyalty of the Chewa and the Ngoni, it is clear that the right strategy for the management of the border populations and the development of the essentially rural border regions is one which is expressed in the customary rather than the European type of international relations. Rural development among the Chewa and the Ngoni of Zambia is best achieved through the co-operation of the Malawi and Mozambique Governments, which have under their jurisdiction their respective shares of the Chewa and Ngoni ancestral territories and populations. To make the need for this type of inter-governmental co-operation unequivocally clear, it will be necessary to cite specific examples of situations which demonstrate that the peoples living along the international boundaries concerned are crying out for joint rural development planning.

Almost all the government and missionary schools located in the Zambia/Malawi border zone (on the Zambian side) have among their enrolled pupils some who have at least one Malawian parent. I was told by Mr Mudanda, the headmaster of Chiwe Upper Primary School in Lundazi District:

We have pupils in this school who reside in Malawi but attend school here in Zambia. It is, however, extremely difficult to distinguish pupils who are Zambians from those who are not. This is mainly due to the fact that inter-marriages between Zambians and Malawians have been taking place since before the boundary was established. This means that any child born in Malawi who has family links across the border here in Zambia is eligible for enrolment. You cannot turn away such a child from attending school here in Zambia, more especially if the child stays with Zambian relatives.[26]

An earlier investigation at the Sinde-Misale Estate School revealed that out of a possible enrolment of 200 pupils there were at least forty who were from Malawi and were classified by the Immigration Department as shown in the accompanying table.

MALAWIAN PUPILS AT SINDE-MISALE PRIMARY SCHOOL, ZAMBIA

	Sex	Place of birth	Year of entry	Parents' residence
Boys	32			
Girls	8			
Mchinji		26		
Lilongwe		7		
Blantyre		3		
Mangoche		1		
Dedza		1		
Ncheu		1		
Salima		1		
1961			1	
1964			2	
1965			6	
1966			2	
1967			4	
1968			7	
1969			13	
1970			5	
Malawi				12
Zambia				28

Source: Immigration and Naturalization File No. 1mm 9/70 ZNA, Chipata.

It is noteworthy that twenty-six of the forty Malawian pupils were born within the Mchinji District, which actually lies on the Zambia/Malawi boundary, and seven were born in Lilongwe District, the next district to Mchinji. The rest of the pupils came from widely scattered districts in Malawi. The figures appear to confirm that there is considerable interaction among the people residing within this particular border area. It should be noted too that as many as twenty-eight pupils had their parents residing in Zambia, and since

Sinde-Misale is a settlement scheme run by the Tobacco Board of Zambia, it is likely that the parents crossed into Zambia for essentially economic reasons.

At Mtole Primary School (Katete, Zambia), which is about 2 km. from the Zambia/Mozambique boundary, Mr Kapala Phiri, the head teacher, had the following to say:

> This school is attended by both Zambian and Mozambican pupils. There is no way I can truthfully distinguish between them. To begin with, there is the question of intermarriages across the international boundary between Zambians and Mozambicans, and therefore, for schooling purposes, the issue of such marriages adopt Zambian citizenship. Second, some of the Mozambicans who came as refugees decided to stay on in Zambia and were granted permission to stay here by Chief Kathumba [the District Head] hence children of such people have access to this school.
>
> Third, some Zambians have crossed and settled in Mozambique in search of good soil but they still send their children to this school, so it is not easy to tell who is who in terms of nationality. I just have to accept all the pupils who come to this school.[27]

The second area where joint rural development planning can be instituted is the provision of health facilities. An interview with Mr Daka, a medical assistant at Mwami Mission hospital on the Zambia/Malawi border, revealed that almost 25 per cent of patients treated at Mwami were Malawians.[28] This is because on the Malawi side of the boundary people have to pay for all medical services while in Zambia they are provided at government expense. This implies that while the Zambian Ministry of Health specifically allocates money to be spent on the treatment of Zambians, in practice 25 per cent of it is spent on Malawians whose government contributes nothing. Similarly, a visit to Nyanje Mission Hospital (Petauke, Zambia)[29] revealed that substantial numbers of Mozambicans cross the border into Zambia for medical treatment since there are no hospitals on the Mozambican side.

Given that migration within ethnic polities does not take into account the 'exclusion dimension' of the international boundary, in the sense that some Zambians have migrated to settle either in Malawi or in Mozambique and vice versa, it also appears that joint agricultural extension services would be beneficial to all inhabitants of border areas. For example, Mr Yesani Phiri, a relatively prosperous Mozambican farmer, said the following:

> I purchase hybrid maize seed and chemical fertilisers from the Dangwa Producers Co-operative Society in Zambia because it is the nearest to me. I sell all my maize to the same Co-operative for the same reason. Otherwise, I would have to go to Tete which is a three-day round trip from here on a bicycle. On a bicycle I can only manage to carry two bags of fertiliser

and only half a bag of maize. So you can see it is not feasible for me to obtain my agricultural requirements here in Mozambique. All farmers around here depend on Zambian agricultural services.³⁰

Admittedly, while the provision for joint socio-economic services may sound unacceptable due to national interests that may be put in jeopardy, the three practical examples cited above suggest that in one way or another national interests can be heavily outweighed by local ones. The challenge for policy in this situation is in how best to harmonise those two sets of interests.

NOTES

This contribution is distilled from the author's Ph.D. dissertation, 'Some Aspects of Spatial Interaction and Reaction to Governmental Policies in a Border Area: A study in the historical and political geography of rural development in the Zambia-Malawi and Zambia-Mozambique frontiers, 1870–1979' (University of Liverpool, 1980).

1. J. Middleton, *From Tribe To Nation*, and I. Wallerstein, 'Ethnicity and National Integration in West Africa', *Cahiers d'Etudes Africaines*, 3, Oct. 1960, pp. 129–39.
2. For a more general treatment of this subject as it relates to international relations in Africa, see Professor Saadia Touval's contribution to this book, pp. 223–32.
3. The findings and observations apply, for example, to the Zambia-Zaire border (see Musumbachime's Ph.D thesis listed in the Select Bibliography).
4. The West African case studies include J.D. Collins, 'The Clandestine Movement of Groundnuts Across the Niger-Nigeria Boundary', *Canadian Journal of African Studies*, 10, 2, 1976, pp. 259–78; O.J.P. Igue, 'Un Aspect des Echanges entre le Dahomey et le Nigéria: Le Commerce du Cacao', *Bulletin de l'IFAN*, Dakar, series B; and L.R. Mills, 'The Evolution of a Frontier Zone and Border Landscape Along the Dahomey-Nigeria Boundary', *Journal of Tropical Geography*, 36, June 1973, pp. 42–9.
5. J.W. Langworthy, 'Pre-Colonial Kingdoms and Tribal Migrations, A.D. 1500–1900', in D.H. Davies (ed.), *Zambia in Maps*, London, 1971.
6. A.F. Isaacman, *Mozambique: The Africanisation of a European Institution: The Zambesi Prazo, 1750–1902* (Madison, Wis., 1972).
7. M. Read, 'Tradition and Prestige Among the Ngoni', *Africa*, ix, 4, Oct. 1936, pp. 453–84; J.A. Barnes, *Politics in a Changing Society* (Oxford University Press, 1954); A.J. Hanna, *The Beginnings of Nyasaland and North-Eastern Rhodesia, 1859–1895* (Oxford University Press, 1956); L. Gann, *A History of Northern Rhodesia* (London: Chatto & Windus, 1964); J.D. Omer-Cooper, *The Zulu Aftermath* (Longman, 1966); and W.E. Rau, 'Mpezeni's Ngoni of Eastern Zambia, 1870–1920' (unpubl. Ph.D. thesis, University of California, Los Angeles, 1974).
8. Read, *op. cit.*, p. 453.
9. *Ibid.*, pp. 459–63.
10. W. Allan, *Studies in African Land Use in Northern Rhodesia* (Oxford University Press, 1949), p. 72.
11. Interview, Skeva Kwale, 22 Jan. 1977.
12. Interview, Mizeke D. Msoni, 18 Jan. 1977.
13. *Ibid.*
14. *Cf.* Roland Oliver, *Sir Harry Johnston and the Scramble for Africa* (London, 1957).

15. Read, *op. cit.*, p. 470.
16. A.I. Asiwaju, *Western Yorubaland Under European Rule, 1889–1945: A comparative analysis of French and British colonialism*, Longman, 1976, p. 50.
17. For a study of these protest migrations see A.I. Asiwaju, 'Migrations as Revolt: The Example of the Ivory Coast and Upper Volta Before 1945', *Journal of African History*, xvii, 2, 1976.
18. Derrick Thom, 'The Niger-Nigeria Borderlands: A politico-geographical analysis of boundary influence upon the Hausa', unpubl. Ph.D. thesis, Michigan State University, 1970.
19. A.I. Asiwaju, *Western Yorubaland, op. cit.*, ch. 4.
20. *Times of Zambia*, 26 Nov. 1976.
21. Interview, Mandevu, Frelimo commander, 3 Feb. 1977.
22. *Times of Zambia*, 26 Nov. 1976.
23. Interview, Labison Banda, 7 May 1977.
24. *Zambia Daily Mail*, 8 Nov. 1976.
25. *Zambia Daily Mail*, 26 Feb. 1977.
26. Interview, Mr. Mudanda, 16 Oct. 1976.
27. Interview, Kapala Phiri, 3 Feb. 1977.
28. Interview, Mr Daka, 15 Mar. 1977.
29. Interview, admissions clerk, 6 Feb. 1977.
30. Interview, Yesani Phiri, 3 Feb. 1977.

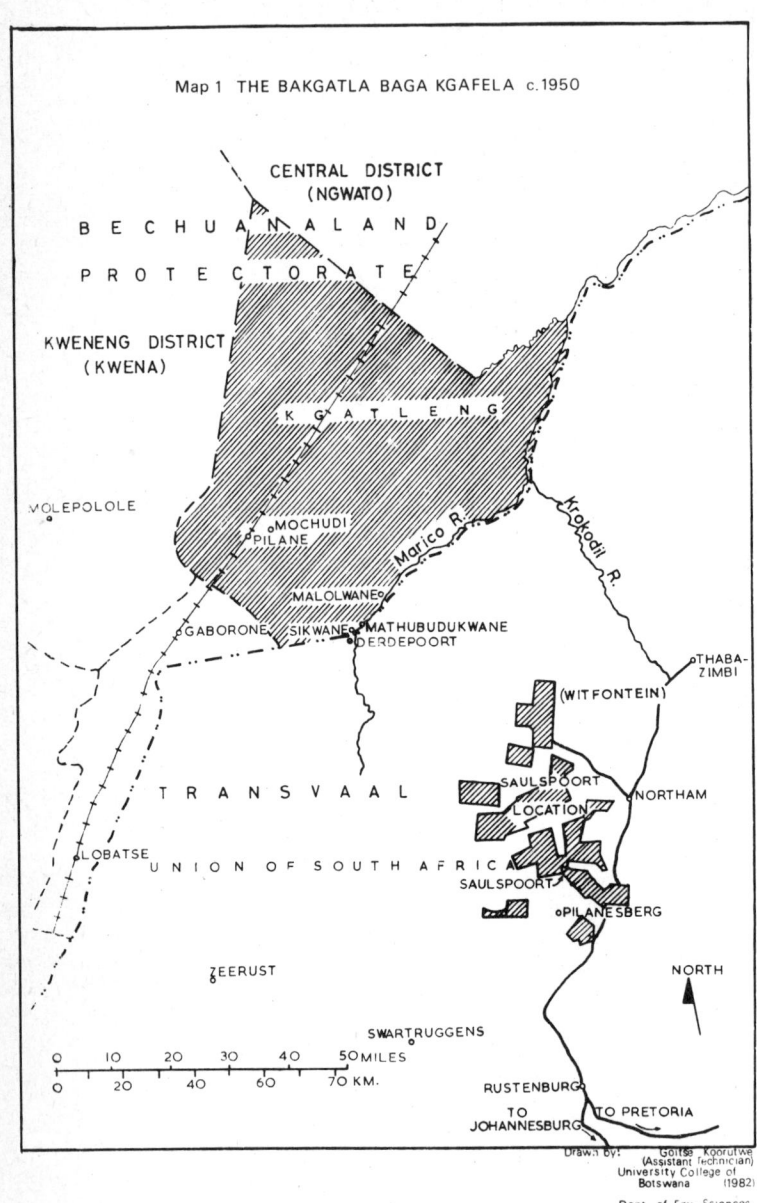

Map 1 THE BAKGATLA BAGA KGAFELA c.1950

8
CHIEFS AND ETHNIC UNITY IN TWO COLONIAL WORLDS
THE BAKGATLA BAGA KGAFELA OF THE BECHUANALAND PROTECTORATE AND THE TRANSVAAL, 1872–1966

R.F. Morton

Introduction

Between 1872 and Botswana's independence, the Bakgatla baga Kgafela, who occupied areas in the Bechuanaland Protectorate* and the Transvaal, remained an ethnic unit under the leadership of a single line of chiefs.[1] The colonial border reduced the authority of the *kgosi* (pl., *dikgosi*, king/chief) in the Protectorate over his Kgatla subjects in the Transvaal, but there a deputised and junior chieftaincy operated with his approval and subject to his appointment. Until the Nationalist Party victory in South Africa in 1948, the political structure was accepted by the Protectorate High Commissioner and the Union of South Africa's Minister of Native Affairs. However, during the reign of Molefi (1929–37, 1945–58), the exercise of many chiefly prerogatives in the Transvaal lapsed at a time when the Deputy Chief there was beginning to feel the growing strength of Afrikaner political power. After 1948, when the Bantustan policies emerged, the Deputy Chief became instrumental in the success of apartheid and, to preserve his position, had to exercise authority in his own name. On account of strong kinship interconnections, however, the Kgatla on both sides of the border endured as a unit in spite of the political divisions emerging, and the *kgosi* of the Protectorate survived as the Kgatla's symbol of common origin and culture and as their most vocal spokesman against apartheid itself.

Throughout the period, the Kgatla occupied two areas separated by territory as well as by the international border. In the Protectorate, the Kgatla Reserve, demarcated in 1899, was bounded on the west by the Kwena Reserve, on the north by the Ngwato Reserve, and from east to south mainly by the Marico River, which after

---

* 'Bechuanaland' became the present-day Republic of Botswana.

1885 formed one segment of the boundary between the Protectorate and the Transvaal.[2] The seat of the *kgosi* of the Protectorate Kgatla was, as it remains, in Mochudi. Consisting of roughly 9,000 square km., the Reserve was by far the larger of the two areas of Kgatla settlement.[3] In the Transvaal, the Kgatla of Pilansberg District occupied 400 square km. of tribally-owned farmland which they had purchased, farm by farm, from their Afrikaner neighbours. Altogether, the Transvaal Kgatla areas consisted of thirty-three farms, not all of them contiguous.[4] Many of these farms are situated on land that was occupied by the Kgatla in the early nineteenth century and before. The most important farm in this respect is Saulspoort 269, on which is located the *kgosing* ward at Moruleng. Adjacent to the Kgatla were farms in the Pilansberg and Rustenburg Districts owned mostly by other African groups, including the Fokeng, Tlhako, Tlokwa and Po, all of whom acquired their land in a fashion similar to the Kgatla. Among Africans in these two districts, the Kgatla were the most numerous and owned the most land. Between the Transvaal Kgatla areas and the Marico River, covering a distance of 55 km., stood a wide belt of farmland occupied by Afrikaners, who since their arrival in the 1830s had reserved the use of this excellent cattle-rearing area largely for themselves. Thus, before being partitioned by colonial boundaries, the Kgatla of the Protectorate were separated physically from their Transvaal brethren by an area of white colonial settlement.

The pre-partition situation

Long before the Afrikaners arrived, the Kgatla (baga Kgafela) had emerged as one of the more important kingdoms in the Transvaal.[5] As with other Sotho-Tswana kingdoms, large and small, the Kgatla were made up of groups, or wards of varying origin, who accepted the authority of the leading members of the senior line in the royal (*kgosing*) ward. In the case of the Kgatla baga Kgafela, the *kgosi* was the senior-ranking male in the patriline of Kgafela, the seventeenth century founder of the kingdom. The Kgafela line was rooted in the original Kgatla lineage which after the fifteenth century had divided gradually into several lines, the most senior being the Kgatla baga Mosetlha.[6] Though junior to the Mosetlha, the Kgafela line proved the more prosperous. Formed in the late seventeenth and early eighteenth centuries as a Mosetlha offshoot, the Kgafela Kgatla attached to their authority a number of conquered and refugee Sotho-Tswana wards, and by 1800 controlled most of the triangle formed by the Krokodil, Marico and Eland's Rivers, roughly 6,000 square km. in area.[7] Legassick suggests that the Kgatla and other prominent Sotho-Tswana of the Transvaal, such as the Kwena, Pedi, Rolong and Hurutshe, emerged at this time because they controlled portions of the routes along which ivory and other game trophies were traded in the direction of the coast.[8] Yet Kgatla traditions of their *dikgosi* make no mention of trade. The motivating concern then and in later centuries, for royal and commoner alike, was the acquisition of cattle and the water and pasturage to sustain them.[9] The Kgafela Kgatla, who organised young men into pan-ward regiments, were successful in gaining both. In their years of ward growth and territorial expansion, the Kgafela Kgatla, too, were blessed by relative calm within the royal family, which averted major splits during times of succession.

The Kgatla kingdom was organised according to patrilineal principles at all levels.[10] In this and other Sotho-Tswana kingdoms, a man's social status, property and office were inherited according to his rank among agnates. The eldest son of a *kgosi*'s great wife (often, but not always, the first married) was first in the line of succession, and his eldest son, should the father predecease him, was usually selected regent for the *kgosi*-designate in his minority. The *kgosi* was the head of the royal ward (*kgosing*), and non-royal wards were administered by the heads of the principal commoner ward lineages. Ward headmen (*dikgosana*, sing. *kgosana*) succeeded to office according to the principles described above. Every family within each ward, royal or commoner, was governed in the same way. In the case of polygamous homes, each wife established her portion of the homestead (*lapa*), and she and her sons received recognition, cattle and other property according to their rank determined respectively by order of marriage and birth. Thus the eldest son of the first wife usually received his deceased father's estate; each son received, according to rank, a portion of the estate given to the mother's *lapa* before the father died.

All persons lived in homesteads in their respective wards, often grouped with other wards into sections. Though built semi-permanently in the form of thatched mud rondavels with courtyards enclosed by mud walls, homesteads were vacated seasonally by some or all members. Men and boys spent months away with their cattle along the Marico and Krokodil rivers at posts assigned by the *kgosi*, and women cultivated plots of land at varying distances from the ward. Every decade or so, when water, wood and soil resources had been depleted, the Kgatla also abandoned their villages and moved elsewhere. Every *kgosi* shifted his capital at least once and seldom chose a site previously occupied. When relocating, however, the *kgosi* remained close to the northern range of the Pilansberg mountains, which stood between the Kgatla and their Tswana neighbours, friendly and hostile, to the south and south-west. Around 1820 the Kgatla consisted of approximately twenty-three wards, grouped into five sections, each separated from the others by a few kilometres at most.[11] The capital, the *kgosing* ward and section, was then located at Mabule, 7 km. north-west of present-day Saulspoort and on the plain north of the Pilansberg mountains. In all, the Kgatla totalled probably no more than 4,000–5,000 persons.[12]

Between 1820 and 1869, when the Kgatla divided into two territorially distinct groups, hardships caused by internal conflict and colonial intruders threatened to destroy their kingdom.[13] In the 1820s they began to fragment and scatter because of the violence and cruelty inflicted by their own tyrant, Motlotle (*d.* 1823), the passing Sebetwane Fokeng (1823) and, from 1825 to 1837, the migrating military state of Mzilikazi's Ndebele. After the Ndebele were dislodged and driven north by Potgieter's commando, the Kgatla regrouped in the north-western Pilansberg and there regained a semblance of unity under their new *kgosi*, Pilane. But the Voortrekkers, who had displaced the Ndebele as the reigning power in the Transvaal and indirectly occasioned the restoration of the Kgatla, easily overpowered resisting groups indigenous to the Western Transvaal, occupied large tracts of land, and extracted labour from the Kgatla and others. After the establishment of the South African Republic in 1851, the Pretoria *volksraad* helped to enforce what had become common Afrikaner practice. Consigned to a humiliating and heavy form of subservience, Pilane and his successor son, Kgamanyane, attempted to reduce the weight of Pretoria's hand by providing military service in Afrikaner campaigns against the Laka in 1854 and Sotho in 1865, and by complying generally with Afrikaner demands for farm hands and herders. For twenty years, Kgamanyane's policy seems to have worked, and in 1864 he moved some of his people off Afrikaner farms and on to a large tract of land he had obtained from an Afrikaner farmer at Saulspoort for — as a local missionary noted — a steep sum.[14] Afrikaner requirements for Kgatla labour continued, nevertheless, even if they did not increase.

Antecedents to partition

Eventually, Afrikaner demands and their methods of enforcement drove Kgamanyane out of the Transvaal. In 1869, a year of locusts, Afrikaners, angered at Kgamanyane's refusal to continue to supply labour, had him flogged before his own people and other chiefs brought in to witness the occasion. Soon thereafter, Kgamanyane led his loyal followers, consisting of a majority of the Kgatla, out of the Republic.¹⁵ In 1871, he established a new capital at Mochudi, west of the Marico River, beyond the frontier, and in the country of Sechele's Kwena. Three years later Kgamanyane died, tradition holds, from the effects of the beating sustained five years before at Saulspoort, and was succeeded by his eldest son of the second house, Linchwe (1874–1921), then but eighteen or nineteen years old. Fired more than his father with the ambition to re-establish the Bakgatla under his sole authority, Linchwe struggled during the first twenty-five years of his reign to achieve a measure of independence for his resettled followers in the Kgatleng and regain the allegiance of the Kgatla in the Transvaal.¹⁶

A major obstacle to Linchwe's aspirations was Sechele. The Kwena monarch, whose kingdom stretched from the Kgalagadi desert to the eastern bank of the Marico, had permitted Kgamanyane to occupy the grassy Eastern Kweneng, which was well suited to cattle.¹⁷ At first Kgamanyane rendered up tribute to Sechele in return, but before his death let the annual payments lapse. On his accession, young Linchwe refused to honour Sechele by resuming tribute, and war, started by the Kwena, soon followed. Between 1875 and 1882 Kgatla-Kwena relations were characterised by sporadic attacks and counterattacks, cattle rustling and isolated murders at undefended cattleposts. A stalemate developed. Sechele made life extremely difficult for Linchwe's people, but his Bakwena could neither dislodge the far less numerous Kgatla nor prevent Linchwe's regiment from striking deep into the Kweneng.¹⁸ For Sechele, however, stalemate on a point of allegiance represented defeat. In 1880 Sechele induced the British Transvaal administration to order Linchwe and his people to move east of Mochudi and place themselves under British authority. Linchwe refused to budge. He said he would prefer British rule *and* Mochudi.¹⁹ Linchwe seems to have been as alive to British weakness as the Afrikaners, who began their successful resistance, often called the first Anglo-Boer war, six months later. As Afrikaners fought Britons, the Kgatla-Kwena conflict resumed. In 1883, however, when filibusters* from the newly-independent South African Republic revived old threats of Afrikaner encroachment into the western Tswana kingdoms, Linchwe and Sechele heeded an appeal for a united Tswana front from Montshiwa of the Rolong, and put aside their differences.

---

* Transvaal Afrikaners militarily allied with Tswana opponents of Mankuruane's Tlhaping and Montshiwa's Rolong. Filibusters established south of the Molopo River the short-lived Afrikaner republics of Stellaland (near Mankuruane) and Goshen (near Montshiwa). The Molopo River forms the present boundary between southernmost Botswana and the Northern Cape (including Bophuthatswana).

For more than ten years after that self-imposed truce, Kgatla and Kwena coexisted uneasily.

Regimental battles ended before the declaration of the Bechuanaland Protectorate in 1885, but Linchwe continued to jockey for territory by planting settlements and cattleposts west of Mochudi. In response, Sechele turned to his old allies, the British, for help in restoring his authority over the contested territory. The British, whose Protectorate counted on support from Sechele and other heads of large Tswana groups, regarded the lesser Linchwe as a nuisance. In 1888 H. Goold-Adams of the Bechuanaland Border Police (BBP) tried to settle the Kwena-Kgatla dispute in Sechele's favour, but Linchwe once again rejected Sechele's paramountcy in the same breath as he reiterated acceptance of British rule.[20] Along with other western Tswana leaders, Linchwe hoped that British presence in the area would reduce the Afrikaner threat, but he recognised Britain's inability to impose a pro-Kwena settlement. Protectorate officials lacked the manpower required to deal firmly with Linchwe, because they were attempting to extend and preserve Britain's claim to a vast, still undefined Protectorate that nevertheless held great political and economic importance for British expansion in Southern Africa.[21] Official irritation over Linchwe's intransigence was an indication that they were rationalising the sacrifice of small groups such as the Kgatla to large, imperial goals. Before 1888 they had begun referring to Linchwe as pro-Afrikaner.[22] In 1890, when the South African Republic proposed to the Protectorate the cession of Linchwe's territory to the Transvaal, officials were eager to cooperate. At the encouragement of H.B. Loch, the High Commissioner, the Colonial Office drafted a letter to Pretoria to seal the agreement, and Linchwe was duly informed. Only at the last minute, when Loch discovered that the transfer would result in the loss of the waters of the Marico River and the future Rhodesian railway to the Protectorate, was the acceptance of the offer withdrawn.[23] Thus Linchwe discovered, if he had not confirmed earlier suspicions, that Kgatla security was not coterminous with British protection or the Protectorate boundary.[24]

The diplomacy of Bakgatla unity

For better or worse, however, Linchwe was prepared to accept British rule on condition that the Protectorate accept him as a ruler independent of Sechele and others. And, as the period of the European scramble drew to a close, his persistence eventually paid off. After Lobengula's country was colonised by the British South Africa Company, which in turn lost its influence in the Transvaal and Bechuanaland in the wake of the Jameson Raid, Britain increased its commitment in Bechuanaland to maintain the vital link between the Cape and Rhodesia. While these developments unfolded between 1890 and 1895, Linchwe's jealous protection of his territory and authority continued to irk the British.[25] But after 1895, when Protectorate officials were prepared to recognise the Kgatla independent of the Kwena, Linchwe became a loyal subject. The Kgatla helped to build the railway with a readiness equal to, if not greater than, other Tswana along the line.[26] And in 1899, when hut tax was first levied by the Protectorate, Linchwe's cooperation in collecting it approached the point of excess.[27] Correspondingly, his notoriety disappeared, and praises began appearing in official letters and reports.

Before and after his relations with the Protectorate improved, Linchwe was also seriously occupied restoring the Kgatla of the Transvaal to his authority. While defending his claim to the Kgatleng, Linchwe drew back into the fold the followers of Letsebe and Tshomankane, two uncles whom Kgamanyane had estranged, and established a third breakaway group, under Mantirisi, on the large Holfontein farm in the Transvaal.[28] Tshomankane's grandson, Mokae, tried to set himself up at Moruleng as a chief recognised by Pretoria, but the Transvaal Kgatla remained loyal to Linchwe, who had demonstrated his ability to look after their interests.[29] In 1895, when the Republic's *Plakkers Wek* ('Squatters' Law') forced thousands of Transvaal Africans off their land, Linchwe resettled 2,000 Kgatla in the Kgatleng and, in 1898 and 1899, purchased additional farms adjoining Saulspoort and Holfontein to accommodate many others.[30] Linchwe's farms in the Transvaal relieved Kgatla there from placing themselves in the service of Afrikaner farmers, just as his victory over Sechele provided adequate space west of the Marico for his followers and, just as important, their cattle. Linchwe also permitted several groups of non-Kgatla refugees from neighbouring parts of the Protectorate to settle in Kgatleng.[31] By the time the Protectorate administration demarcated the Kgatla Reserve in 1899, Linchwe had earned the allegiance of all Bakgatla baga Kgafela on both sides of the boundary including fragments lost to the king's authority since the days of Motlotle.

Kgatla unification across the international boundary also afforded Linchwe's people a chance to advance their own economic interests. By securing a reserve boundary within the Protectorate, Linchwe not only created a refuge from Afrikaner ill-treatment for his people in the Transvaal but space to graze and build up their herds. Of the Tswana-speaking peoples not bordering the Kgalagadi, only Linchwe's Kgatla were able, in the early colonial period, to herd cattle on a large scale. The Hurutshe, Fokeng, Tlokwa and many others found themselves without sufficient land and grazing, and faced the necessity of working for wages to supplement their meagre agriculturally-based diet. The rinderpest of 1896-7, which decimated herds in many areas of the Protectorate and the Transvaal, increased the rate of depastoralisation.[32] Only the large Tswana groups — Ngwaketse, Kwena, Ngwato and Tawana — utilised regions large enough to leave pockets of cattle unaffected by the epizootic. The Kgatla herds were hard-hit, but by moving cattle from the Transvaal across the border into the Kgatleng, the national herd was quickly rebuilt and expanded. This good fortune, though accompanied by much personal suffering, was occasioned by Kgatla participation in the South African war (1899-1902).

Linchwe had little choice but to throw his lot in with the British in this 'white man's war' — and allow his people on both sides of the border to pay the price — but the Reserve enabled Linchwe's Kgatla to recover all, if not a surplus, of their losses in land and cattle. In November 1899, British forces used the Kgatla in fighting an Afrikaner commando at Deerdepoort, along the Marico. The Kgatla, who believed the British would help them in battle, realised in the thick of the fight that they had been abandoned instead.[33] Armed with rifles supplied by the British, the Kgatla troops carried the day, but in the weeks that followed, the Afrikaners exacted revenge by attacking Kgatla troops at Sikwane, burning their villages along the Marico and stealing cattle. By then the British regulars had moved well south. For much of the duration of the Anglo-Boer conflict, Linchwe's people were locked in their own undeclared war with the Transvaal Afrikaners. In the Transvaal, Afrikaners took revenge on local Kgatla, and Linchwe's regiments retaliated by striking deep into the Transvaal as far as Pretoria and removing thousands of Afrikaner cattle to the Kgatleng.[34] As the British scorched earth policy and concentration camps emptied much of the Transvaal, some Kgatla began to filter into the Saulspoort area and settle on farms abandoned by the Afrikaners, presumably the very ones vacated after the *Plakkers Wek*.[35]

After the war and until his abdication, Linchwe consolidated his authority over the Kgatla and continued to increase their land and cattle holdings. In 1902 and 1903 Linchwe gained the support of the Protectorate government in his negotiations with the British High Commissioner in Johannesburg to install his junior brother, Ramono, as deputy chief of the Transvaal Kgatla.[36] Between 1908 and 1920 Linchwe purchased thirteen additional farms in the Saulspoort area. These new purchases of over 50,000 more acres in the Transvaal created occupation rights for his people and made it possible for all those still squatting on Afrikaner farms to move on to Kgatla land.[37] There, under Ramono's authority, they cultivated their own plots and built up family herds. In the meantime, Linchwe distributed part of the cattle spoils of the South African war among the men whose regiments had served in the war. Others were retained by Linchwe and loaned for ploughing, and the offspring

Table 1

BAKGATLA FARMS, ca. 1950 (PARTIAL LIST)

No. on Map 2	Name	No.	Year of purchase
1.	Cyerferkuil	372	1913
2.	Rhenosterkop	1,048	1929
3.	Holfontein	593	1877
4.	Witfontein	215	Late 19th cent.
5.	Doornlaagte	161	1929 +
6.	Kraalhoek	516	1931
7.	Application (Isang Pilane's)	984	1925
8.	Schoongezicht	414	1929 +
	Vlakplaats	412	
9.	Elandsfontein	815	1929 +
10.	Vogelstruiskraal	678	1921
11.	Rhenosterkraal	563	1913
12.	Velgeveg	133	1918
13.	Bierkraal	545	1929 +
14.	Wilgespruit	631	1919
15.	Wildebeestkuil	733	1929 +
16.	Middelkuil (Modderkuil)	564	1899 / 1908
17.	Rooderand	299	1916
18.	Zaandfontein	729	1929 +
19.	SAULSPOORT	269	1864
20.	Rhenosterspruit	609	1929 +
21.	Spitskop	298	Pre-1918
22.	Kruidfontein	649	1912 (1918)
23.	Koodoosfontein	818	1919
24.	Doornpoort	251	1919
25.	Legkraal	725	1913
26.	Welgeval	749	1926

were given to individuals to form the core of new family herds.[38] Linchwe banned using cattle as bridewealth as well as selling breeding stock, in order to check the flow of cattle off Kgatla land. He also purchased breeding bulls to improve the weight and hardiness of the existing herd.[39] Cattle were also transferred from Kgatleng back to the Transvaal as newly purchased areas were opened up to grazing and farming. By 1920, when ill-health and senility forced him to hand over to Isang, his eldest surviving son, Linchwe left the seat as the effective leader of all Bakgatla baga Kgafela. His death in 1924 concluded a phase of Kgatla history during which the foundation for future intra-Kgatla relations was laid.

During Linchwe's reign, the international boundary was less a barrier and more a line distinguishing economic and political regions within the area of Kgatla occupation. More often than not, the border was used or ignored by Kgatla to suit their own convenience. By establishing control in the Transvaal and enlarging land holdings through purchases, Linchwe acquired extra land needed to compensate for the restrictions created by the Kgatla Reserve boundary. And just as the Reserve boundary guaranteed claims against the Kwena and Ngwato, the international boundary afforded Linchwe's people vital sanctuary. The appropriation of cattle to the security of the Protectorate also made it possible for Linchwe to enlarge the Kgatleng herd and use it to finance many of the farm purchases in the Transvaal. After Linchwe, moreover, Kgatleng remained 'cattle-rich' and 'people-poor', with the reverse being the case in the Saulspoort area, where Kgatla were densely concentrated and more dependent on agriculture and wage labour.[40] Thus, from the beginning Kgatleng was the Kgatla's cattle centre, and Mochudi was their political capital.

Early colonial policy towards subject people in the Protectorate and the Transvaal allowed the chief in Mochudi to assume political leadership over the Kgatla on both sides of the border. In the Protectorate, a 'dual' or 'parallel' system of authority left the prerogative of law-making and enforcement within the reserves largely in the hands of chiefs, and the latter were under no strict obligation to take legal decisions in consultation with any of their subjects.[41] By and large. Protectorate chiefs who accepted Protectorate policy and collected tax regularly were left to exercise considerable power at the local level. In the Transvaal, the absence of an overall colonial policy before and after the South African war resulted in the carry over into the Union period of a tribal reserve structure under the authority of Native Commissioners.[42] In Johannesburg, the Chief Native Commissioner acted as the 'trustee' for all African-occupied land, purchased or granted, that constituted the reserve. The Native Commissioners in Rustenburg and other districts had direct authority over appointed chiefs, including Ramono and his successors in Saulspoort. Nevertheless, after the 1902 agreement permitting Linchwe to seat his deputy in Saulspoort, the Transvaal Kgatla continued regarding themselves as Linchwe's subjects. Their allegiance is apparent in the levies they paid at the behest of Linchwe and Isang, who used the money for various projects and undertakings, mainly purchasing land in the Transvaal.[43] Moreover, the *kgosi* of Mochudi was apt to demand that certain actions of the Transvaal Government were accountable to him, as in 1917 when Linchwe challenged the right of the Government to settle Ramono's estate without reference to himself and without respect for Tswana laws of inheritance.[44]

Challenge to Linchwe diplomacy: the Isang-Molefi feud

Nor did the Transvaal government refrain from involving itself in the affairs of the Kgatleng. Decisions taken in Mochudi and Johannesburg had a constant ripple effect across the border and back, and not only the Transvaal Kgatla but the Union's Minister of Native Affairs became part of the political arena centred in the Protectorate. A case in point was the intrigue and civil tension that grew out of the feud between Isang Pilane, regent after Linchwe's abdication, and the direct heir to Linchwe's mantle, Molefi Kgafela Linchwe.

The feud was part of a larger conflict that originated in the 1920s between Isang and a number of his discontented subjects. Isang Pilane was an educated, Christianised moderniser whose innovations changed the face of the Kgatleng socio-economy, but whose harshness bred resentment towards the policies and achievements of his reign.[45] Isang's efficiency and resourcefulness nevertheless earned him the respect of many colonial officials on both sides of the border. His approach to modernisation was based on the Afrikaner farming model, and more than any other Kgatla chief before or since he regarded the Dutch Reformed Church as an important instrument of social and economic change among his people. Isang exercised influence among the Transvaal Kgatla through his younger brother, Ofentse, whom in 1922 he appointed as Deputy Chief in the Transvaal.[46] Ofentse ruled at Saulspoort until 1942. Although Isang gave way to Molefi in 1929, he and his royal supporters, including Ofentse, attempted to perpetuate their influence at Molefi's expense. Off and on through the early 1930s, intense quarrels erupted between Isang and his nephew.[47] The bad feeling generated by this royal contest for authority spread throughout Kgatla society and opened wounds that have remained unhealed till this day.

The main bone of contention between both parties was the control of the Transvaal farms. Isang claimed that he and Linchwe had purchased most of the Transvaal property in their own names, and as such it formed part of Linchwe's personal inheritance which was divisible among his sons (Isang being the oldest surviving). Molefi claimed that, despite the way the farms were acquired, they belonged to the *kgosi* on behalf of all Kgatla and as such they, like the cattle on them, were indivisible.[48]

The conflict was deepened by the personalities and ambitions of the leaders of the two camps. Isang regarded Molefi, who was immature, inexperienced and self-indulgent, as unfit to rule. Isang probably hoped that, after a period of constant crises sustained by his own public behaviour and Molefi's incompetence, his nephew would either abdicate out of frustration or be deposed by an exasperated colonial Government. In either case, the Government would be well-disposed to reseat Isang at Mochudi. Shrewd and impatient, Isang left little to chance.

Isang hoped also to establish a personal claim to the chieftaincy in the Transvaal, independent of Molefi. During the inquiry, Isang asserted that before Ofentse was appointed deputy in Saulspoort, Linchwe had asked Isang to succeed Ramono.[49] As Ofentse's senior, Isang was in a position to ask Ofentse to step aside for himself.[50] By sounding the principle of *lapa*, as opposed to chiefly inheritance of Linchwe's property, Isang hoped to acquire outright ownership of sizeable land holdings in the Transvaal and the support of thousands of Kgatla who had no choice but to live on them.[51] Molefi had his own personal interests to protect in the Transvaal, not the least of which was retaining control over the lands and herds needed to subsidise the chief's office. As his penchant for motor cars, travel and smuggled brandy attest, Molefi had expensive tastes, too expensive at any rate for his normal salary.[52] Also since the death of his father, Kgafela, there had been bad blood between Isang and Molefi's mother, Seingwaeng.[53] Molefi's desire to see the Transvaal farms remain intact and out of Isang's control may also account for the fact that Molefi had become fast friends with Tidimane, the eldest son of Ramono, and whose minority in 1922 had enabled Isang to install Ofentse as Saulspoort regent.[54]

While the *kgosi* feuded with the ex-regent, the Union of South Africa's Minister of Native Affairs saw his own opportunity. Since 1924, the Hertzog Government had campaigned to increase direct control over Africans within the Union and to incorporate the Protectorates of Basutoland, Bechuanaland and Swaziland. Piet W. Grobler, Hertzog's Minister of Native Affairs at the time of the Isang-Molefi feud, found in Isang a man who could assist the Union in achieving both aims. For one thing, Grobler wanted a Kgatla chief in the Transvaal who would accept the sole authority of the Ministry of Native Affairs. But more than a loyalist in Saulspoort,

Grobler wanted a friend in Mochudi, i.e. a chief who could claim to speak for Tswana who desired incorporation into South Africa. Sometime in 1934, Grobler and Isang made a deal. Grobler was to inform the Protectorate Government that in the event of Molefi stepping down or being removed, Isang's return to the seat would be quite acceptable to the Ministry of Native Affairs in South Africa. Meanwhile, the Union would cease to acknowledge Molefi's authority in the Transvaal and recognise Ofentse as the chief directly responsible to them.[55] For his part, Isang would use his influence among Protectorate officials and members of the Native Advisory Council, giving the impression that Africans in the Protectorate favoured incorporation.[56]

It is possible that the Isang-Grobler deal, which incensed Protectorate officials, was Isang's attempt to preserve Bakgatla unity in the context of changing times. Protectorate officials, who depended on support from the larger, intensely anti-South African chiefs, interpreted Isang's motives in the crassest of terms.[57] But to Isang winning the chieftaincy in Mochudi, along with the right to individual ownership of the Transvaal farms, would have made possible continued control of the Transvaal Kgatla from Mochudi.

Already by 1930, such radical steps were perhaps the only means possible to preserve the nation that Linchwe had built. After the 1913 Land Act was passed in the Union, a South African 'Native Policy' based on land segregation, restriction of African representation and incorporation of the Protectorate into the Union began to emerge.[58] Hertzog's Government, which gave impetus and form to the policy in the 1920s and '30s, placed the leaders of people straddling the border in an unpleasant dilemma: oppose incorporation and accept the division of your people, or favour incorporation and accept South African rule based on 'northern' (i.e. Afrikaner) principles.

At the time, the momentum of the South African economy during those years of drought, hunger and restrictions on the export of Protectorate cattle to the Union imbued the second option with greater promise for the survival and progress of the Kgatla as a single people.[59] Isang, who had pushed for a revival of Kgatla traditional institutions while pursuing his modernisation schemes, regarded material development and educational progress fitted to traditional beliefs as possible only through association with the Union.[60] In South Africa, it was also assumed at the top, albeit among persons of declining influence, that westernised Africans would play their part in Union affairs.[61] Hertzog had paid lip service to these ideas, and Isang, perhaps the most westernised and articulate African in the Protectorate of the 1920s, and one who had dealt face-to-face with Afrikaner politicians and lawyers on numerous occasions since the turn of the century, might have been justified in feeling that after incorporation he could have as good a chance as any chief in the Union of making his voice heard.[62]

In 1935, a joint Commission of Inquiry into the Linchwe estate involving the Bechuanaland Protectorate and Union Ministry of Native Affairs resulted in a modest victory for Molefi and an end to Isang's ambitions.[63] In May, after taking evidence in Mochudi and Pilansberg, the Commission concluded that the Transvaal properties of Linchwe belonged to the Kgatla as a whole and fell thereby under the trusteeship of the Ministry of Native Affairs, in accordance with the Native Land Act of 1913. Isang retained only a single, though large, farm in the Transvaal: Application 984. Soon after the inquiry, Isang was banished from Mochudi to the northern Kgatleng, where he lived for several years tending his cattle and eventually taking up a position in the Protectorate Government as an educational inspector. He died in 1941. To a degree, his influence in the Transvaal continued during the 1930s through Ofentse, who was Acting Chief in Saulspoort until ill-health forced him to step down in favour of his eldest son, Thari, who sat in the chair from 1942 till 1949. Molefi's troubles with the Administration continued after Isang's banishment, and in 1936 he was suspended by the Government and replaced by his more tractable brother, Mmusi, who held the seat for nine years.

Aside from the instability of the Molefi period, the character of the *kgosi* himself weakened the formal chieftaincy. While in the seat, Molefi was too unsettled to govern Mochudi or make his influence felt in Saulspoort. On both sides of the border, Isang seized all the initiatives. Molefi also turned his back on the traditions of his office. Although many wanted him to be head of the Kgatla, the young man who was installed with the leopard skin did not know how. From childhood, Molefi had learned most things on his own. He played truant from the school of chiefs as much as from Tigerkloof and Trafalgar.[64] He accepted advice and discipline from no one, including his own mother and his father's sister, Kgabjwana, who attempted to perform Kgafela's role of preparing Molefi to succeed Linchwe in the fullest traditional sense. Until the Resident Commissioner suspended Molefi, the affairs of the *kgosi* were governed by personal whim rather than established procedure. By virtue of his birth, Molefi remained the symbol of Kgatla unity, and Kgatla on either side of the Marico regarded him as their true *kgosi*.[65] Only the Protectorate Kgatla, however, organised support for his restoration to the chair. *'Ipelegeng'*, as those who rallied to Molefi's side were known, failed to take hold in Saulspoort mainly because Ofentse opposed it.[66]

The triumph of transborder ethnic unity

Whatever the lapse in leadership from Mochudi, Kgatla on both sides continued to have much in common. Since Kgamanyane's time, the Kgatla intermarried to the extent that few families on one side lacked close relatives on the other.[67] The observance of basic duties within the extended family resulted in constant movement of relatives visiting back and forth. Travel was particularly common among well-to-do royals, who had the advantage of organised ox-wagon transport in the early days and the use of motor-cars thereafter. The introduction of bus services in the 1940s between Rustenburg and Mochudi, however, increased the traffic of commoners, who had previously walked. Thus at weddings, funerals and other occasions, relatives otherwise separated had a few days to spend together, catch up on local news and conduct family business.[68]

Social and legal customary arrangements of the two areas of Kgatla settlement also reinforced the common element. Both Mochudi and the Transvaal Kgatla areas were subdivided into five *dikgoro* (sections), identically named: Kgosing, Mabodisa, Manamakgothe (Matuwana), Morema and Tshukudu. Brother-*dikgoro* (i.e. those on either side with the same name), were legally administered by *dikgosana* descended from the same paternal line, the Mochudi *kgosana* being the senior agnate. The conduct of affairs among relatives, who lived in brother-*dikgoro*, was subject to common law and practice applied by members of a single family, with appeals rendered up directly to the relevant *kgosi*. This system, reflecting one of the mirror images of the two Kgatla societies, has functioned since Kgamanyane's time up to the present.[69]

Kgatla in the *Nederduitse Gereformeerde Kerk* (Dutch Reformed Church) provided another institutional link.[70] The DRC mission began among the Bakgatla before Kgamanyane's trek to Mochudi and, like the *dikgoro*, entered the Kgatleng as a coordinate system. Two congregations, headed by DRC missionaries, were based in Mochudi and Saulspoort, with lesser congregations and attendant schools formed in the outlying villages under the care of African catechists and ministers. For the greater part of a century, the DRC mission enjoyed a royal-sanctioned monopoly, but it gained members also by ministering to non-religious needs. The DRC supported the teaching of Setswana, English and arithmetic in addition to Bible studies, and church activity often extended beyond the strict area of religious observance. Annual meetings of the Kgatla section of the DRC, which took place alternately in Mochudi and Saulspoort, were important social occasions. The DRC evangelistic wing, also, afforded opportunities for Kgatla commoners to rise educationally and socially as part of the mission establishment. This was especially so in Saulspoort, where the DRC was allowed to convert non-royals in Kgamanyane's day. Saulspoort converts, including those of Pedi origin, were conspicuous in the spreading of DRC institutions in the Transvaal and Kgatleng.[71] Popular receptivity to the DRC appeal was greatly influenced, nevertheless, by the attitude of the *kgosi* of the time.

Since Ramono's day, royalty and the DRC have been more closely aligned in Saulspoort than in Mochudi. Ramono's father, Kgamanyane, was no Christian and his brother, Linchwe, though a convert in the 1890s, no catechumen. Kgamanyane sent Ramono and Linchwe's half-brother Segale to Morija in Lesotho; he reserved to the future *kgosi* a Kgatla traditional education.[72] Although he supported DRC work and Western education, Linchwe ruled and died a traditionalist at core.[73] He kept the prerogatives of the *kgosi* quite distinct from mission activity. Ramono and Segale, however, like their nephews Isang and Ofentse, dominated the DRC of their days and ran strict Christian households.[74] In Saulspoort, where Ramono and Ofentse ruled for thirty-five years, the affairs of *kgosi* and DRC were intertwined. In Mochudi, aside from Isang's regency, relations were symbolically maintained but in practice were disconnected. Molefi, like his grandfather, had a chair in the DRC church, but on Sundays he sat elsewhere. During Molefi's first reign, Kgatla in the Protectorate gave support to the brief emergence of the Bakgatla Free Church, led by a breakaway DRC minister from Sikwane, Thomas Phiri, who some Kgatla today are convinced had Molefi's support.[75] After Molefi's suspension, religious independency once more reared its head among his '*Ipelegeng*' members, who broke with the DRC and entered the Zion Christian Church in large numbers.[76] In Kgatleng religious tolerance, reflected more recently in the planting of Roman Catholic and other mission agencies, is characteristic of Linchwe's descendants ruling in Mochudi and represents a policy of subordinating, rather than allying, the pulpit to the *kgosi*'s stool.

The beginnings of divergence

After the 1930s, and within the context of colonial rule in the Protectorate and Union, the roles of the Mochudi and Saulspoort *dikgosi* diverged. In the Protectorate of that time, Indirect Rule theory was applied unsuccessfully in the Kgatleng, leaving the local powers of the *kgosi* more or less where they had previously rested: with the personal interest and energy of the *kgosi* himself. In 1935, the introduction of a District Commissioner system placed a colonial administrator in Mochudi for the first time and increased pressure on the *kgosi* to conform to laws and policies emanating from Protectorate headquarters at Mafeking. But in the Protectorate, chiefs who collected tax and retained popular support had little to fear from the District Commissioner. Conversely, individual Kgatla who ran foul of the *kgosi* were liable to severe treatment.[77] In the Kgatla Reserve, a powerful *kgosi* remained compatible with the public ideal of leadership. In the Union, however, the exercise of chiefly power steadily and increasingly ran the risk of serving the interests of apartheid. In the Transvaal, chiefs were initially part of the rural administrative machinery operated by the Ministry of Native Affairs through the Sub-Commissioner based in Pilansberg.[78] But as heavy rates of urban immigration paralleled white steps to destroy African representation in the Union and to retribalise the African population in Bantustan areas, chiefs were expected to exercise greater powers of control.[79] Much more than in the Protectorate, the Saulspoort *dikgosi* have faced, even before the Nationalist victory in 1948, the risk of being regarded by their own people as tools of the Afrikaner.

For this reason, since 1948 the heightened pain suffered by the Kgatla under apartheid has presented the Mochudi *kgosi* with a

Table 2

DIKGOSI OF THE BAKGATLA BA KGAFELA
SINCE PILANE

Installed	*Saulspoort (Moruleng)*	*Mochudi*	*Installed*
ca. 1825	Pilane		
ca. 1853	Kgamanyane		
(1869)	----------→	Kgamanyane	(1872)
mid-1880s	Mzilikazi (Moruleng)/	Linchwe I	1874
	Ditlhake (Lesetlheng)		
ca. 1892	Mokae		
	(Moruleng)		
1902	Ramono		
1917	Dialwa	Isang	1921
	(*Acting Chief*)	(*Regent*)	
1922	Tlhabane (Ofentse)		
	(*Acting Chief*)		
		Molefi	1929
		Mmusi	1936
		(*Acting*)	
1942	Thari	Molefi	1945
	(*Acting Chief*)		
1949	Tidimane		
		Linchwe II	1963

new role as their symbolic opponent of South Africa. Molefi's ill-health and repeated confrontations with local personalities reduced his value to the Transvaal Kgatla, but his son, Linchwe II, has distinguished himself as an outspoken critic of apartheid. Long before his installation in 1963, Linchwe II wanted to study law, an ambition encouraged by his father. And while studying in England he confided to his friend, the author Naomi Mitchison, that one day he hoped to go before the United Nations and plead for a 'revision of the boundary'.[80] Although his professional hopes never materialised, Linchwe II attempted from the beginning of his reign to resurrect something of his great-grandfather's notion of using the Kgatleng as a haven for Kgatla and other South Africans oppressed by Afrikanerdom. In his installation speech, he welcomed to Kgatleng those Transvaal Kgatla desiring to escape the effects of apartheid, such as Bantu Education.[81]

We of the Bakgatla are willing and prepared to cooperate with all Governments, including that of the Republic of South Africa. But we are not willing to let our people be slaves. In the name of human conscience, we shall always welcome those who have to leave the Republic as refugees and for the sake of their children.[82]

In contrast to the *kgosi*, Kgatla commoners of the Protectorate in the later colonial period viewed political questions involving South Africa in non-ethnic terms. Many Kgatla experienced apartheid while working in the Krugersdorp-Johannesburg area, where they acquired a heightened sense of racial, rather than ethnic, consciousness. More than most Protectorate Africans working in the Union, the Kgatla worked above ground, where they had as much contact with the white man as with his law. In the 1940s and 1950s, many participated in anti-apartheid activities including strikes and boycotts. Some became active members of the African National Congress.[83] Conversely, Kgatla took little interest in bonding themselves together for political or economic interests. Ethnic-based organisations, which characterise urbanisation in other parts of the world, were largely absent in the townships of the Witwatersrand. Kgatla lived in ethnically-mixed neighbourhoods and associated, during and after work, with Africans from all parts. Kgatla came together to receive their visiting *kgosi*, pay tax or collect funeral donations, but leisure activities and job-seeking were individual matters.[84] On the Witwatersrand, Kgatla from the Protectorate came into formal contact with their Saulspoort brethren, and *vice versa*, when they chose to attend the visit to Johannesburg of the respective *kgosi*. These trips, usually connected with tax collection and official newsgiving, were too infrequent and too well supervised by municipal authorities to draw attention to conditions in South Africa.[85]

Similarly, the Saulspoort *kgosi* has attempted to establish himself as a spokesman for an African, as opposed to Kgatla, constituency. Since his installation by Molefi in 1949, *kgosi* Tidimane has become a well-known critic of the homeland policy. He has opposed the establishment of Bophuthatswana and, since its formal creation in 1977, has functioned as the leader of the opposition in parliament against President Lucas Mangope's ruling Bophuthatswana Democratic Party. As the head of the *Seoposengwe* (Unity) party, Tidimane has advocated scrapping the independence formula, granting Bophuthatswana territorial autonomy within South Africa and restoring to its residents South African citizenship.[86] In addition, Tidimane has criticised allowing South African enterprise to generate further underdevelopment in Bophuthatswana. On this count, national attention focused recently on Tidimane when he complained about the effects on his people of 'Sun City', a huge entertainment and gambling complex built by Southern Sun Hotels at Bopitiko, near Saulspoort.

Since 1960 the pressure on Kgatla of either side to adopt national identities has also helped to reduce intra-Kgatla contact. In the Kgatleng, nationalist party politics began in the early 1960s and for the first time enabled Kgatla commoners within the Protectorate to participate in a political arena extending beyond reserve boundaries.[87] Although the *kgosi*'s choice of party was decisive for most Kgatla, the political context in Kgatleng between the radical Bechuanaland People's Party and the conservative Bechuanaland Democratic Party focused attention on coming independence and the Kgatla's role in the future Botswana. This political process, which made outsiders of the Saulspoort Kgatla, culminated in independence in 1966 and in an international boundary reconstituted as a line across which moved national passport holders, not pass-carrying 'tribesmen'. Traffic between Mochudi and South Africa, once casual and frequent, became subject to numerous restrictions imposed by immigration authorities and police.[88]

The survival of Bophuthatswana alongside the movement against white control in South Africa has likewise caused the Saulspoort Kgatla to drift away as part of two distinct political estates, one present, one future. In spite of opposition to its existence, Bophuthatswana forces Tidimane and his Kgatla to function as part of a Tswana state dependent on Pretoria. Kgatla irredentism, used to counter Afrikanerdom since the days of Linchwe I, has become in the age of separate development an obsolete weapon. For Tidimane, it has become as important to be regarded as a *kgosi* in his own right as it has for him to appeal to a wider, non-ethnic constituency. By the same token, the black liberation movement in South Africa accords Tidimane and the Kgatla no role other than as advocates of black rights within the international boundary presently dividing South Africa from independent Black Africa.

Independence for Botswana, therefore, ended any chance for the survival of the Bakgatla baga Kgafela of the Kgatleng and Transvaal as a single people. For the time being, extensive intermarriage across the border among older generations preserves a sense of community, but the present marrying generation is unlikely to continue the pattern. Another cross-border institution, the DRC, is also being redefined as nationally-based. The Kgatla of Botswana, with the support of *kgosi* Linchwe II, are at present leading the campaign to establish the DRC synod of Botswana, free from control of South Africa. Thus, even in the independent state of Botswana, continued need to reduce connections with South Africa in order to contribute to the liberation struggle runs counter to Linchwe I's strategy, which created Kgatla unity in two colonial worlds. Linchwe's perception of strength in ethnic terms no longer applies to the Southern African scene.

BAKGATLA POPULATION: HUMAN AND CATTLE

(*Total Area*: Kgatleng, 2,798 sq. miles [7,247 sq. km,]; Saulspoort, 170.7 sq. miles [442 sq. km.])

DENSITY OF PEOPLE

	Kgatleng	Saulspoort	Kgatleng	Saulspoort
1904	9,450	—	3.4 (1.3)	—
1911	10,706	—	3.8 (1.5)	—
1921	11,604	—	4.1 (1.6)	—
1931	12,004	—	4.3 (1.7)	—
1936	13,915	—	5.0 (1.9)	—
1946	20,874	10,770*	7.2 (2.8)	63.1 (24.4)
1950	22,874	12,000 (est.)	8.2 (3.2)	70.0 (27.2)
1964	32,118	—	11.5 (4.4)	—

DENSITY OF CATTLE

	Kgatleng	Saulspoort	Kgatleng	Saulspoort
1904	16,091	—	5.75 (2.2)	—
1911	36,301	—	13.0 (5)	—
1921	33,231	—	11.9 (4.6)	—
1931	30,000	—	10.7 (4)	—
1936	47,553	—	17.0 (6.7)	—
1946	74,695	—	26.7 (10.3)	—
1950	—	10,145	—	59.4 (23)

* This figure represents Bakgatla residing in the Pilansberg District and roughly half of the Transvaal Bakgatla population. An estimated remaining 8,000–15,000 Bakgatla were residing in the towns and cities of the Rand. Breutz, *Tribes of the Rustenburg and Pilansberg Districts*, p. 247.

The Bakgatla baga Kgafela of Bechuanaland

Map 2
AFRICAN-OWNED FARMS, TRANSVAAL c.1950

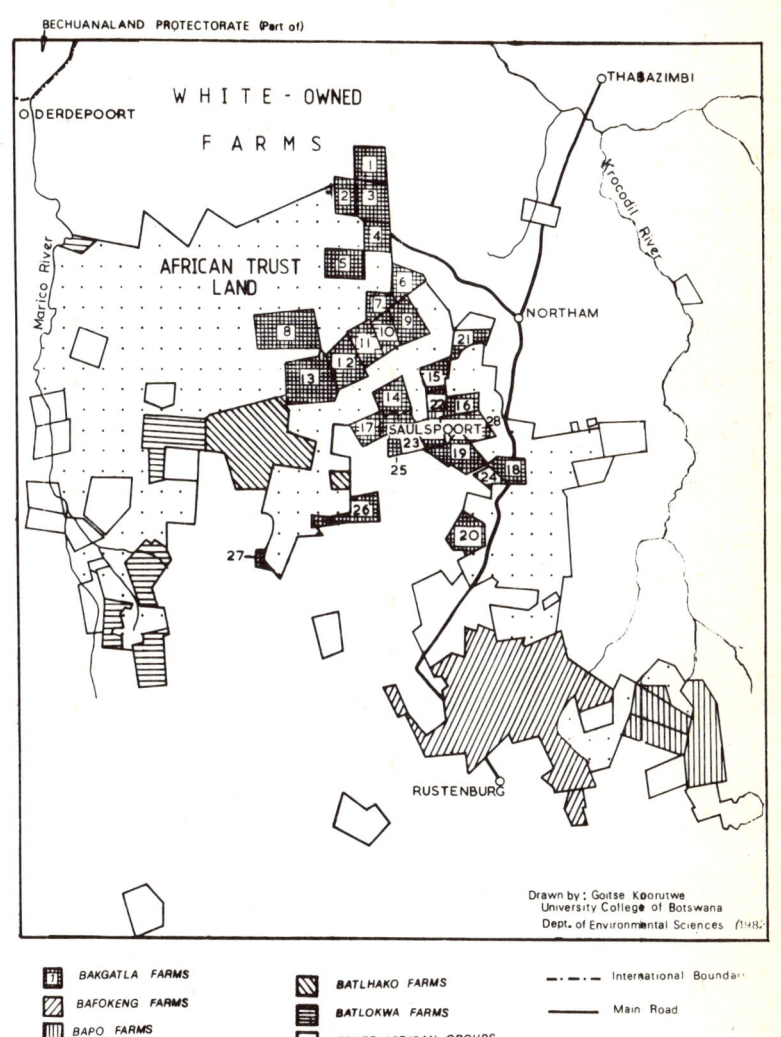

NOTES

Sources: Cattle Censuses, 1904, 1911, S. 295/2, BNA, H.B. Neale to I. Schapera, 15 Aug. 1933, S. 182/1, BNA; Breutz, *Tribes of the Rustenburg and Pilansberg Districts*, pp. 247, 280; Bechuanaland Protectorate, *Bechuanaland Protectorate Government Census 1946* (n.p., n.d.), pp. 4, 66; *idem, Report on the Census of the Bechuanaland Protectorate 1964* (Bulawayo, 1965), p. 19.

1. Research on this topic has been supported generously by a grant from the University of Botswana Research and Publications Committee, to which much gratitude is extended.
2. See Map 1.
3. See Table 1.
4. See Map 2.
5. Properly speaking, Bakgatla baga Kgafela, but used in this study only when distinguishing this from other Kgatla groups. The Kgatla are part of the Kwena cluster of the Eastern branch of the Tswana-speaking peoples of Southern Africa. The Tswana are Bantu-speakers. I. Schapera, with J.L. Comaroff and A. Kuper, *The Tswana* in (London: International African Institute [Ethnographic Survey of Africa], 1979).
6. Royal Kgatla lineages that became independent from one another were, in order of seniority: Mosetlha, Kgafela, Mmanaana, Mmakau, Motshe and Seabe. *Ibid.*, p. 10.
7. I. Schapera, 'Short History of the Bakgatla-baga-Kgafela of Bechuanaland Protectorate', Communications from the School of African Studies, New Series 3 (University of Cape Town, 1942), p. 4.
8. M. Legassick, 'The Sotho-Tswana Peoples before 1800', in L. Thompson (ed.), *African Societies in Southern Africa* (London: Heinemann, 1972), pp. 106–11. For a similar interpretation for the larger region; N. Parsons, *A New History of Southern Africa* (London: Macmillan, 1982), p. 48.
9. See especially I. Schapera (ed.), *Praise Poems of Tswana Chiefs* (Oxford: Clarendon Press, 1965), pp. 45–66.
10. I. Schapera, 'Kinship and Politics in Tswana History', *Journal of the Royal Anthropological Institute*, 93, 2 (1963), pp. 159–73.
11. The sections (*dikgoro*) were: Kgosing (also the name of a ward), Tshukudu, Mabodisa, Morema and Manamakgothe. Based on extracts of traditions recorded in Schapera, *Praise Poems* and Schapera, 'Short History'.
12. In 1820, the traveller John Campbell estimated that the Rolong town of Kuruman consisted of 29 wards and contained approximately 5,000 people. Tswana towns could be larger, as in the case of Kurrichane, of the Hurutshe, which Campbell also visited. He estimated its population at 16,000. Though ward populations certainly varied, the Rolong town structure has shown close resemblance to that of Mochudi in the twentieth century, and it is presumed that a rough correlation exists between average ward sizes. No archaeological investigations have been carried out in the areas settled by the Kgatla in the nineteenth century. R.J. Mason, 'Transvaal and Natal Iron Age Settlements revealed by Aerial Photography and Excavation', *African Studies*, 29, 4 (1968), pp. 167–80; J.D. Seddon, 'An Aerial Survey of Settlement and Living Patterns in the Transvaal Iron Age: Preliminary Report', *ibid.*, pp. 189–94; Seddon, *Iron Age Communities of the Southern Highveld* (Pietermaritzburg: Council of the Natal Museum, 1976), pp. 276–85.
13. The following is based on Schapera, 'Short History', pp. 1–13 and Appendix D; Schapera, *Praise Poems, passim*; P.L. Breutz, *The Tribes of Rustenburg and Pilansberg Districts*. Department of Native Affairs, Ethnological Publications 28

(Pretoria: Govt. Printer, 1953), pp. 251-63; Native Affairs Department. Transvaal, *Short History of the Native Tribes of the Transvaal* (Pretoria: Govt. Printing and Stationery Office, 1905), pp. 27-9.
14. Schapera, 'Short History', 10.
15. *Ibid.*, Appendix D; F. Wilson, 'Farming, 1866-1966', in M. Wilson and L. Thompson (eds), *Oxford History of South Africa*, II (Oxford; Clarendon Press, 1971), p. 115. At the time of Kgamanyane's departure, the Kgatla had already begun to suffer from divisions created by fraternal quarrels in the royal family. Sometime after 1861, Tshomankane, Kgamanyane's brother in the fourth house, withdrew from Kgamanyane's authority and established his followers at Bopitiko, west of Saulspoort. After Kgamanyane's departure, Tshomankane and later his sons assumed authority over the Saulspoort Kgatla until the South African war (1899-1902). Interview with Kgmanyane Pilane and Tidimane Pilane, 5 Jan. 1982, Saulspoort, as recorded in R.F. Morton, 'Interview Notes on Bakgatla History' (typescript, 1982), p. 76. Kgamanyane's brother of the 6th house, Letsebe, also broke away and settled at Molepolole, the capital of the Kwena of Sechele. Schapera, 'Short History', p. 9. And when Kgamanyane departed, Mantirisi, his brother of the 5th house, remained behind in Saulspoort. Interview with Selogwe Dikame Mantirisi Pilane, 30 July 1979, Masiana Ward, Mochudi; Testimony of Isang Pilane, 9 May 1935, S. 343/24, Botswana National Archives, Gaborone (hereafter BNA).
16. Kgatleng (*-eng* is a Iswana locative suffix) refers to the territory to which Kgamanyane moved and, after 1899, to the Kgatla Reserve.
17. In the early nineteenth century, Sechele's father Motswase received support from the Kgatla in the Kwena-Ngwaketse war. Kgatla tradition alleges that in gratitude, Motswasele invited the Kgatla to reside in his territory. Again, when the Afrikaners began to oppress Kgamanyane's people, Sechele invited the Kgatla to live near him in Molepolole. Kgamanyane declined to move too close to Sechele, mindful of past Kwena treachery to Kgatla refugees in the time of Sebetwane and perhaps also because Sechele had already taken under his wing Letsebe, who had seceded from Kgamanyane's rule (see footnote 15). A. Sillery, *Sechele* (Oxford: George Ronald, 1954), 142; Schapera, 'Short History', 11; 'Petition from the Bakgatla "Raad" to the English Government, Gape Town', Nov. 1894, HC. 108, BNA.
18. During the war the Kwena also suffered considerably through loss of cattle and decline in agricultural activity. Sillery, *Sechele*, p. 144; B. Kenosi, 'From Self-Sufficiency to Dependency: The Economic History of Kgatleng, 1871-1930', Dept. of History, BA research essay (Gaborone: University College of Botswana, 1980), p. 4.
19. T. Melville to W.O. Lanyon, n.d. [May 1880] reproduced in Schapera, 'Short History', p. 36.
20. Goold-Adams to OC, BPP, 5 Mar. 1888, as reproduced in Schapera, 'Short History', p. 37. After this incident, Protectorate officials refrained from interfering and accorded Linchwe respect as chief. Moffat to Shippard, 26 Jul. 1888, HC 24/2; Shippard to Loch, 11 Aug. 1888, HC 24/7, and 29 Nov. 1888, HC 24/39, BNA.
21. A. Sillery, *Founding a Protectorate: History of Bechuanaland 1885-1895* (The Hague: Mouton, 1965), pp. 56-68; *idem., Botswana: A Short Political History* (London, Methuen, 1974), pp. 87-8; Q.N. Parsons, 'The Evolution of Modern Botswana: Historical Revisions', Dept. of History Seminar (Gaborone: University College of Botswana, 1981), pp. 5-7.
22. Breutz, *Tribes of Rustenburg and Pilansberg Districts*, p. 267; Schapera, 'Short History', p. 15; see also Resident Commissioner Shippard's admonition to

Linchwe on the dangers of allying with Boers. Shippard to Loch, 11 Aug. 1888, H C. 24/7, BNA.
23. W.L. Leys to H.B. Loch, 11 Sep. 1890 (English transl.); Loch to Lord Knutsford, 23 Sep. 1890; Knutsford to Loch, 27 Oct. 1890; Loch to Knutsford, 3 Dec. 1890, HC. 157/2, BNA; L. Truschel, 'Nation Building and the Kgatla: the Role of the Anglo-Boer War', *Botswana Notes and Records*, 4 (1972), p. 186.
24. As recently as 1884 Britain and the South African Republic in the London Convention revised the boundary of the 1881 Pretoria Convention (which ended the first Anglo-Boer war) at the expense of several Tswana groups in the Western Transvaal. L.D. Thompson, 'The Subjection of the African Chiefdoms, 1870–1898', in Wilson and Thompson (eds), *Oxford History of South Africa*, II, pp. 272–3; S.M. Molema, *Montshiwa, 1815–1896* (Cape Town: Struik, 1966), ch. X.
25. Schapera, 'Short History', pp. 14–15; Loch to Shippard, 20 Sep. 1890, HC. 84/32; C.P. Moyo, 'Linchwe I (1875–1924): Firebrand and Reformer', Dept. of History seminar (Gaborone: University College of Botswana, 1979), pp. 6–7.
26. One surviving tradition holds the British responsible for spreading rinderpest along the rail-line in an effort to punish chiefs who refused to provide labour to build it. Dupleix Pilane, in Morton, 'Interview Notes', 2.
27. Schapera, 'Short History', p. 16; V. Ellenberger, 'Memorandum on the Relations between the Bechuanaland Protectorate Administration and the Bakgatla Tribe from 1885 to 31st December 1927', S. 182/1, BNA; see also Ellenberger's Diary, 23 May 1896, vol. I, EL 1/1/1/1, Zimbabwe National Archives, Harare (ZNA).
28. Schapera, 'Short History', 18; Breutz, *Tribes of Rustenburg and Pilansberg Districts*, pp. 259, 265. Tshomankane died *ca.* 1888 of a bullet wound suffered while fighting on Linchwe's side against the Bakwena. Morton, 'Interview Notes', p. 78.
29. Mokae was the son of Mzilikazi, junior brother of Ditlhake, and leader of Tshomankane's people at Bopitiko (Bopitikwe) and later Lesetlheng. Ditlhake remained loyal to Linchwe. Morton, 'Interview Notes', p. 76.
30. Shippard to Loch, 9 Sep. 1895, HC. 140/6, BNA; Linchwe Estate Commission of Inquiry, pp. 75–79, 83, S. 343/24, BNA; Native Affairs Department, *Short History of the Native Tribes*, p. 27; Linchwe to Ellenberger, 16 Oct. 1902, RC. 8/8, BNA.
31. In 1884 the Tlokwa of Ramonye settled at Mochudi, in 1892 Mokalake's Malete at Modipane, and in 1893, the Kaa under Tshwene left the Kweneng and settled at Tlhagakgama. V.F. Ellenberger, 'History of the Batlokwa of Gaberones (Bechuanaland Protectorate)', *Bantu Studies*, 13 (1939), p. 185; *idem.*, 'History of the Ba-ga-Malete of Ramoutsa', *Transactions of the Royal Society of South Africa*, XXV, 1 (1937), p. 51; I. Schapera, 'Notes on the History of the Kaa', *African Studies*, 4, 3 (Sept. 1945), p. 117.
32. Rinderpest spread south from East Africa into Central and Southern Africa. P. Phoofolo, '*Renepese Lefu La Likhomo: the Rinderpest Epizootic of 1887–1897: a Preliminary Survey*' (Roma, International Conference on Southern African History, 1977).
33. This little episode of British military treachery is detailed in full in the eye-witness account recorded in the Notebook of J. Ellenberger, Gaborone Magistrate, III, ZNA (I am grateful to Q.N. Parsons for a copy of this source). For additional accounts, Schapera, 'Short History', Appendix F (pp. 41–9); J. Ellenberger, 'The Bechuanaland Protectorate and the Boer War, 1899–1902', *Rhodesiana*, 11 (Dec. 1964); Truschel, 'Nation-Building and the Kgatla', pp. 188–9.
34. The Transvaal Kgatla joined Linchwe's men in driving their cattle to Kgatleng. Morton, 'Interview Notes', pp. 69, 78; See also *ibid.*, pp. 30–1; Truschel, 'Nation-Building and the Kgatla', pp. 189–90; Judgement of J. Ellenberger in *Malepa,*

Monnamakgoa and Seboloka vs. *Rakobedi*, 20 June 1901, RC. 4/17, BNA; Resident Commissioner to High Commissioner, 7 Nov. 1901, RC. 8/8, BNA; Linchwe to Ellenberger, 26 Nov. 1901, RC. 6/13, BNA. The British command encouraged Africans to loot the Afrikaners' cattle, which they bought from Linchwe and others at £4 per head, well below the actual value. Lord Methuen to ADT, Mafeking, 30 Oct. 1900; Capt. C.M. Ryan, DAAG to Ag. Resident Commissioner, n.d. (received 29 Nov. 1900), Capt. C.E. Morgan, Senior Officer Transport, to Ryan, 27 Nov. 1900, RC. 4/4, BNA.
35. *Select Committee on Native Affairs* (Cape Town: Cape Times, 1911), pp. 91, 110.
36. Linchwe to J. Ellenberger, 16 Oct. 1902; High Commissioner to S.R. Godfrey Lagden, Nov. 1902; C. Griffith, Native Commissioner Rustenburg, to Secretary for Native Affairs, 6 Feb. 1903, RC. 8/8, BNA.
37. Total acreage of farms purchased by Linchwe after the war as tribal trust land totalled 53,184 acres (25,087 morgen). Together with land acquired before the war, the total was 84,702 acres (39,968 morgen). This represented 78% of the land eventually occupied by the Kgatla of Pilansberg District. Figures compiled from Linchwe Estate Commission of Inquiry, pp. 75–79, S. 343/24, BNA; Breutz, *Tribes of the Rustenburg and Pilansberg Districts*, pp. 244–5.
38. Gabriel Palai, Makophane, Mochudi, 24 Jul. 1979; Selogwe Pilane, Masiana, Mochudi, 30 Jul. and 7 Aug. 1979; Leitsholo Leitsholo, Makopane, Mochudi, 9 Aug. 1979; Ramariba Moremi, Makwadi, Mochudi, 26 Jul. 1979.
39. Selogwe Pilane, Masiana, Mochudi, 30 Jul. 1979.
40. At the time of Linchwe's abdication, the Kgatla Reserve in the Protectorate contained approximately 11,600 people and 33,000 cattle in an area of 8,600 square miles, giving an average population density of little more than 4 persons and 12 cattle per square mile. In the Transvaal, figures comparable in time have not yet been located. In 1946, a total of 10,770 Kgatla lived in an area of 170.7 sq. miles around Saulspoort, to make an average population density of 70 people per sq. mile. In 1950 the cattle population of the Transvaal Kgatla was 10,145 or nearly 60 per sq. mile (see Table 1).
41. Lord Hailey, *An African Survey* (Oxford University Press, 1938), pp. 173–7, 402–13; ibid., revised 1956 (Oxford University Press, 1957), pp. 175–182, 271–5, 498–502; idem., *Native Administration in the British African Territories*, Part V (London: H.M.S.O., 1953), pp. 202–11; Schapera, *Tribal Innovators*, pp. 51–5.
42. E.H. Brookes, *The History of Native Policy in South Africa from 1830 to the Present Day* (Pretoria: J.L. Van Schaik, 1927), pp. 119–47, Breutz, *Tribes of the Rustenburg and Pilansberg Districts*, p. 4.
43. Informants in Saulspoort allege that the Kgatla regarded Ramono as Linchwe's junior placed there to protect them in Linchwe's name. Linchwe installed Ramono in the Saulspoort seat. Morton, 'Interview Notes', pp. 78–9.
44. Linchwe complained of being 'slighted and ignored' by the Transvaal authorities. Williams to Acting Government Secretary, 5 May 1917, RC. 8/8, BNA.
45. This fascinating and extremely complex man awaits a biographer. For Isang's regency, Schapera, *Tribal Innovators, passim*; idem, 'Short History', pp. 22–5, 51–4; R.S. Dikole, 'Isang Pilane and His Modernisation Programme' (B.A. dissertation, History Dept., Univ. Coll. of Botswana, 1977).
46. When Ramono died in 1917, his eldest son Tidimane was too young to take up his father's position. Dialwa, Ramono's brother from the junior *lapa* of Nthweseng (Mmalesage), then served as Acting Chief until 1922, when Isang Pilane replaced him with Isang's younger brother, Tlhabane (Ofentse). Ofentse occupied the Saulspoort chair as Acting Chief until 1942, was succeeded by his son, Thari, and ultimately by Tidimane who was installed by Molefi in 1949. (See Table 2).

47. Within the royal family, Isang received support from his brothers of his mother's *lapa*, and at least two junior Kgamanyane *lapas* (Keiseng and Ngomeng — the 2nd), whose members had earlier supported Isang against the challenge to his regency by Ramorotong of the eldest Kgamanyane *lapa*. Molefi was supported by his mother, Seingwaeng, his brother, Mmusi, and by his uncle, Bakgatla, of the *lapa* of Linchwe's third wife, Lokgwalo.
48. C.F. Rey, Notes, 25 Apr. 1934; R. Reilly, Notes, 26 Apr. 1934, S. 343/24, BNA.
49. Isang's testimony regarding Application Farm, 'Record of Evidence Taken before the Joint Commission of Inquiry', S. 343/24, 111, BNA.
50. Interview with Prof. E.S. Moloto, Gaborone, Univ. Coll. of Botswana, 14 Oct. 1981.
51. In 1934 before the issue of land ownership had been settled by the Joint Commission of Inquiry, Isang had visited the Saulspoort area allegedly telling people that the farms 'are to be divided amongst the chief's sons and the ... people who are found on the farms allotted to me shall become my people.' Statement of Molefi P. Pilane, 12 Nov. 1934, S. 402/10, BNA. See also V.F. Ellenberger to Assistant Resident Commissioner, 13 Sep. 1934, S. 402/4, BNA.
52. Reference to Molefi's high living habits abound in official correspondence. Of note, G.E. Nettleton to R. Reilly, 27 May 1933, in which it is reported that at Molefi's wedding at the DRC Church in Mochudi, the ceremony was heavily attended by Afrikaner 'bootleggers'. S. 329/9, BNA. Those who knew him well attest to his undisciplined behaviour (Morton, 'Interview Notes', pp. 50–1, 60, 73), although it is possible Molefi's defiant attitude toward whites may have led to exaggerated colonial reports (*ibid.*, pp. 65–6,. 85)
53. See the testimony of Molefi's mother and Isang, S. 305/19, BNA.
54. Tidimane spent his holidays from Tigerkloof College in the Northern Cape at Isang's home (Tidimane's sister, Matlhodi, was Isang's wife). Tidimane became Molefi's friend, in 1933 serving at the *kgosi*'s wedding as best man.
55. R. Reilly to S.V. Lawrenson, 1 Apr, 1935, S. 343/22, BNA.
56. H.S. Stanley to Sir E. Hardy, 29 Aug, 1934, Stanley to C.F. Rey, 31 Aug. 1934, and R. Reilly to Rey, 4 Sep. 1934, S. 402/5; Stanley to Harding, 9 Oct. 1934, S. 402/6, BNA.
57. Ibid.,
58. C.M. Tatz, *Shadow and Substance in South Africa: A Study in Land and Franchise Affecting Africans, 1910–1960* (Pietermaritzburg: University of Natal Press, 1962); Brookes, *The History of Native Policy in South Africa*.
59. The theme of economic as well as social isolation formed the basis of Isang's public views favouring incorporation. See I. Pilane 'Native Standpoints: I. In Favour of Transfer', *Race Relations* (Johannesburg), 2 (1935), pp. 149–52.
60. *Ibid.*, p. 150.
61. Tatz, *Shadow and Substance*, pp. 55–73.
62. At the time Isang believed that the Union 'is restoring powers to the ruling chiefs [while] here in the Protectorate they are being continuously curtailed.' Pilane, 'In Favour of Transfer', p. 151.
63. For the 1935 report of the Commission, S. 343/25, BNA.
64. In the 1920s Molefi attended Tigerkloof, in the Northern Cape, and Trafalgar School, near Cape Town. He was expelled from both for misbehaviour. Morton, 'Interview Notes', pp. 60, 73, 85. Molefi, only 20 years old when installed in 1929, was pressured by a large Kgatla majority to take the chair from Isang who had become very unpopular, *Ibid.*, pp. 85, 87; Schapera, 'Short History', p. 24; Schapera, *Rainmaking Rites of Tswana Tribes* (Leiden: Afrika-Studiecentrum, 1971), pp. 20–2.
65. Morton, 'Interview Notes', pp. 57, 60, 81. In Saulspoort, for example, Bakgatla

The Bakgatla baga Kgafela of Bechuanaland 153

    refused to volunteer for service in World War II until Molefi visited Saulspoort and ordered them to join. *Ibid.*
66. *Ibid.*
67. Information on family relationships is drawn from Morton, 'Interview Notes' and interviews with Mochudi residents in August 1979 and June/July 1981.
68. Aside from wives joining their husband's family, however, resettlement across the border has been rare. See Morton, 'Interview Notes', p. 43.
69. *Ibid.*, pp. 21, 42–3, 72, 76, 82.
70. For the history of the DRC among the Kgatla, W.L. Maree, *Uit Duisternis Geroep die Sendingwerk von die Nederduitse Gereformeerde Kerk onder die Bakgatla von Wes-Transvaal en Betsjoenaland* (Johannesburg: N.G. Kerk Boekhandel, 1966); *Botswana, DRC 1877–1977* (Gaborone: Rev. A.T. Barry, 1977); also S. Grant, 'Church and Chief in the Colonial Era', *Botswana Notes and Records*, 3 (1971), pp. 59–63.
71. Morton, 'Interview Notes', pp. 28, 83–4, suppl.; Interview with Selogwe Pilane, Masiana Ward, Mochudi, 12 July 1981.
72. Morton, 'Interview Notes', pp. 2, 83–4.
73. See Schapera's [?] Confidential Report, n.d. [1934], 2, S. 305/19, BNA.
74. These members of the royal family and certain Saulspoort churchmen were tightly intermarried. Ramono's second wife, Martha (Bogadi), for example, was a Moloto and widow of Mabule, a DRC evangelist. Segale's wife, Elisa (Boikanyo) and Ramono's first wife, Mantho, were sisters of a Christian family. Isang married Matlhodi, Ramono's eldest daughter of his second wife, and Tidimane's first wife was the daughter of Segale.
75. Morton, 'Interview Notes', pp. 14–15, suppl.
76. Grant, 'Church and Chief'; Morton, 'Interview Notes', pp. 51, 57.
77. After his reinstatement in 1945, Molefi dealt harshly with individual members of the ZCC, in spite of government efforts to protect their rights in court. One of Molefi's ZCC victims was his own mother, Seingwaeng, whom he banished from the Reserve. On the other occasions, he assulted his aunt, Kgabjwana, as well as Thari, the Acting Chief of Saulspoort, for which he was apparently never brought to book. Personal communications with Amos Kgamanyane; see also Grant, 'Church and Chief'.
78. See page 11 above
79. Tatz, *Shadow and Substance*, pp. 123–6, 150–2, 183–4.
80. E.L. Sykes to S.V. Lawrenson, 23 May 1960, S. 552/4/1, BNA.
81. N. Mitchinson, 'Leopard Skin Symbol. Installation of an African Chief', n.d. p. 3, S. 552/4/1.
82. 'Text of Speech made by Chief Linchwe II at his Installation on 6 April 1963', S. 552/4/1, BNA.
83. Morton, 'Interview Notes', pp. 53, 63.
84. *Ibid.*, pp. 16, 20, 37, 53, 56, 58, 71.
85. Meetings to receive *dikgosi* were held in the Braamfontein hostel compound set aside by the Government for the purpose, and chiefs were housed by the Government in 'Kwa Mzilikazi' in downtown Johannesburg. *Ibid.*, pp. 40, 56, 71.
86. 'National Seoposengwe Party Manifesto', *Mafeking Mail and Botswana Guardian*, 20 Aug. 1982.
87. M.F. Moswela, 'Politics in Kgatleng: Parochialism vs. Nationalism', Dept. of History, BA research essay (Gaborone, Univ. Coll. of Botswana, 1980).
88. Morton, 'Interview Notes', pp. 43, 63, 67, 70.

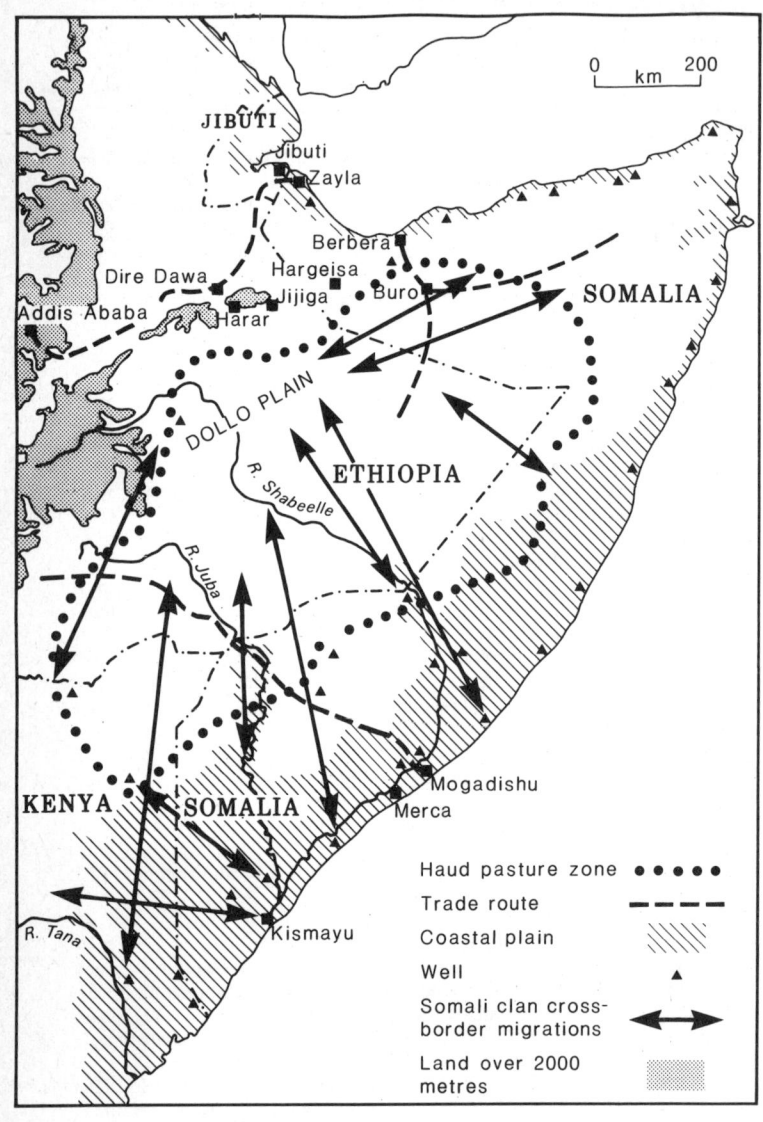

THE HORN OF AFRICA

9
THE SOMALI DILEMMA
NATION IN SEARCH OF A STATE

Said S. Samatar

'Our misfortunes do not stem from the unproductiveness of the soil, nor from a lack of mineral wealth. These limitations on our material well-being were accepted and compensated for by our forefathers from whom we inherited, among other things, a spiritual and cultural prosperity of inestimable value: the teaching of Islam on the one hand and lyric poetry on the other ... No! Our misfortune is that our neighbouring countries, with whom, like the rest of Africa, we seek to promote constructive and harmonious relations, are not our neighbours. Our neighbours are our Somali kinsmen whose citizenship has been falsified by indiscriminate boundary 'arrangements'. They have to move across artificial frontiers to their pasture lands. They occupy the same terrain and pursue the same pastoral economy as ourselves. We speak the same language. We share the same creed, the same culture and the same traditions. How can we regard our brothers as foreigners?'

— quoted in John Drysdale, *The Somali Dispute*[1]

Thus with characteristic simplicity Dr 'Abdirashiid 'Ali Shermaarke, the late President of the Somali Republic, touched on the heart of what the Somali regard as their 'special misfortune,' notably the 'falsification of the citizenship of our kinsmen by indiscriminate "boundary arrangements" '. Dr Shermaarke knew, as do students of African history (or at any rate those contributing to the subject of this book), that the Somali are not the sole victims of Europe's partition of Africa, that the division of kinsmen into bewildering fragments and their lumping together with alien societies through indiscriminate 'boundary arrangements', which had no reason other than to satisfy imperial appetites, had been a grim, continent-wide fact of colonial Africa.

In the face of this continental reality, can a case be made for the claim that the Somali partition represents a 'special misfortune' — which deserves special consideration? It is not the intention of this essay to argue that it can. Rather, it seeks to set forth briefly the way of life and social and environmental peculiarities of the Somali, to present a short narrative of the history of the partition of the Somali peninsula, and to enunciate its impact on Somali life, both in and outside of the Somali state. Setting these matters in perspective will, it is hoped, enable the reader to appreciate the nature of the

'Somali dilemma', especially with respect to the territorial disputes which continue to fester between Somalia and the neighbouring states of Kenya and Ethiopia, threatening to undermine the peace and stability of this part of Africa. The essay ends with a tentative proposal on ways to resolve this seemingly intractable problem.

The Somali peninsula before the imperial partition

Land and people. The Somali inhabit roughly 400,000 sq. miles of what is often described as a savannah grassland in the Horn of Africa. In this land of low population density and high sand dunes, 260,000 sq. miles comprise the Somali Republic and the rest extends to the adjoining countries of Kenya in the south-west, Ethiopia in the north-west, and the newly-independent Republic of Jibuti (Djibouti) in the north-east. To the east and north the Somali Republic is bounded by the Indian Ocean and Gulf of Aden. The Somali population, estimated variously at 4 million and 6 million,[2] occupies continuously, though sparsely, this sizeable chunk of territory. About 3.5 million Somalis live in the Somali Republic, 2 million in Ethiopia's Ogaadeen (Ogaden) and 246,000 in the Northern Province of Kenya. About 150,000 inhabit the Republic of Jibuti.

It is often observed that the dry conditions which define the greater part of Somalia are too arid to give the Somalis opportunities of farming and cultivation. Yet it is not clear at all whether the Somali pastoralists, especially those inhabiting the central Haud region, would opt for farming even if conditions were more favourable to sedentarised life. With their herds of camel and cattle and flocks of goats and sheep, the Somali pastoralists range far and wide in search of the ever-elusive pasture and water; and yet they do not seem at all fazed by the exigencies of a demanding climate and environment. Forbidding though the land is over much of the year, it necessitates personal endurance, courage and above all independence.

Twice a year the rains come and revive man and beast, producing a fresh supply of grass on the land, and for a brief period turning the desert into a blooming garden. Lush vegetation covers the greater part of the land — especially the central grazing plateau where the grass grows several feet tall and sways brilliant green over vast stretches. The thorny acacia bushes — camels' candy — become laced with flowers. The birds return singing and butterflies descend on flower-capped branches and on the humps of dozing, satiated camels. The *Gu* rains begin roughly in April and last till June, and are heavier than those of the *Dayr* (October-December), the other rainy season.

In *Jiilaal*, that is the dry season, the hot north-easterly winds scorch the land, turning vegetation into a shrivelled mass of brown scrub bushes, like the West African Harmattan. Water is exhausted except in a few permanent waterholes and as the grass near these waterholes is depleted, the flocks and herds have to be moved great distances for pasturage, only to be returned for watering. Thus in *Jiilaal* the life of the pastoralist is a life of interminable treks between water and pasture, in which both the nomads and their herds are in danger of death from thirst and starvation. Understandably, the nomad is characteristically mean-tempered during *Jiilaal*, and it is not surprising that a slight provocation can prompt him to violent atrocities. The external demands of climate tend to result in domestic discords and Somali speak of the 'garrulous old wench of the household'.[3] Mostly, however, the nomad is too weak or too preoccupied with the care of his herds in the gruelling heat and hunger of *Jiilaal* to translate his temper into action. *Jiilaal* can also be the season of feud as rival clans compete for the limited supply of water and grass.

On the whole, three zones can be differentiated in Somalia: the coastal plains, the north-eastern mountain ranges and the Haud inter-lands. The northern coastal plains — known as Guban ('burned') from the low rainfall and high temperature — which extend from the lava-strewn deserts of the Republic of Jibuti along the Gulf of Aden shore to Cape Guardafui in the east, are especially barren. Rainfall barely exceeds three inches and in the hot months (June-September) the region is deserted except in the urban centres such as Jibuti (*ca.* 100,000) and Berbera (*ca.* 60,000).

The Ogo and Golis mountains which rise beyond the Guban dominate the topography of Somalia: precipitous but magnificent, the mountain range which joins the Ethiopian escarpment reaches a height of 9,000 ft. at the ancient city of Harar, and 8,000 ft. at some points in the east. From the northern mountains a plateau gradually slopes southwards, keeping an average height of 3,000 ft. The plateau comprises most of Somalia. From Hargeisa in the north-west to Gaalka'ayo in the south-east and from the Ogaadeen Doolo plains in the west to the Nugaal Valley in the east is a region of thornbushes and tall grasses known as the Haud.[4] The Haud forms the bulk of Somali pasturelands, and in the rainy season brings together pastoralist representatives of every major Somali clan. Lack of sufficient permanent water, however, militates against extensive utilisation of the Haud pastures, and herdsmen, especially those with less hardy beasts such as cattle and sheep, are forced away from the Haud as soon as the lush grass turns brown, and to migrate from the Haud grazing areas to the string of wells ringing the coast. Thus the life of Somali pastoralists is a life of migrations — from the coast to the interior during the rainy season and back to the coast during the dry season. Indeed this ecological peculiarity of pasture without water in the Haud and water without pasture by the coast explains not only the historic transhumant migrations of the Somali pastoralists, but also why the imposition of colonial boundaries — which lopped off the grazing areas of the central plateau from water sources in the coast — made life untenable for the pastoralists. The point is illustrated graphically by the accompanying map which shows seasonal migrations of Somali clans in relation to colonially imposed boundaries.

The Somali seem to show marked ethnic and cultural affinities to their neighbours in Kenya, Ethiopia and the Republic of Jibuti, and form a part of what linguists call the 'Eastern Cushites'.[5] Other representatives of the Eastern Cushites include the Oromo (Galla) peoples of Ethiopia and Kenya, the Saho of northern Ethiopia, and the pastoralist 'Afar who straddle the Rift Valley between Ethiopia and Jibuti. Together with the Rendille of Northern Kenya and the coastal Aweera (Boni), the Somali form a Cushitic sub-group called 'Omo-Tana' whose languages are almost mutually intelligible and who, as the name suggests, are found in the region of the Omo and Tana rivers extending from Lake Turkana (Rudolf) to the coast.

The earliest reconstructed history of the Eastern Cushites places their original homeland in the Lake Region of southern Ethiopia. From here the Omo-Tana (or 'Proto-Sam community' as this group is termed by linguists) began to spread southwards, reaching the plains of northern Kenya in the first millennium BC. By the first century AD, Proto-Sam communities moved in a south-easterly direction, and following the Tana River reached the Indian Ocean where they split off, one branch (the Boni) remaining in the Lamu area while another, the Eastern Sam group, spread northwards to occupy southern Somalia. The Samaale (Somali), as the Eastern Sam came to be called, again swept northwards in pursuit of water and pasturelands and occupied the Haud (present day Ogaadeen). They reached the shores of the Gulf of Aden by the middle of the fifth century AD. Thus according to one scholar: 'Within a relatively short period the Samaale or "Somali proper" . . . overflooded and occupied the entire Horn. If there existed any earlier populations on the peninsula they were either driven away or absorbed both culturally and linguistically. By around 1000 AD, if not earlier, the entire Horn including what Arab writers had referred to as the [Berber] coast had been occupied by the Samaale.'[6] Other members of the Eastern Cushitic community, who like the Somali left their homeland in the highlands of southern Ethiopia, included the Saho who ultimately reached northern Ethiopia and the 'Afar who came to forge a new homeland in the bed of the Rift Valley. Thus of twenty-four Eastern Cushitic communities, it is really the Somali, the 'Afar and the Saho who migrated relatively long distances from the areas of their origin, the other twenty-one remaining today essentially in the 'original homeland of Southern Ethiopia-Northern Kenya'.[7]

Having occupied the Horn of Africa, the Somali came in contact with Muslim Arab and Persian traders who acquired footholds along the shores of the Horn by the eighth century. Contact with the Muslims led to the Islamisation of the Somali and to the emergence of 'a new Islamic culture and society'.[8] Settled commercial towns began to emerge — and with them urban communities of traders, artisans and craftsmen, principally in the port towns of Zayla' and Berbera in the north and Mogadishu, Merca and Brava in the south — as well as a series of smaller settlements along the coast. The new interest in upland trade, coupled with the imperative to proselytise, motivated the hybrid urban Muslim communities of the coast to penetrate the pastoral interior, thus setting off the second great Somali migration, this time in a reverse direction from north-east to south-west. This second migration seems to have begun in the thirteenth century and was still in progress when the Europeans arrived at the Horn in force towards the last quarter of the nineteenth century. This second wave of migration has been adequately reconstructed by I.M. Lewis who termed it the 'Somali Conquest of the Horn of Africa', a population movement which, in the light of recent contributions on the subject by such scholars as Bernd Heine, Herbert Lewis and Harold Fleming, may better be termed not so much a conquest as a return.[9] Moreover, this phase of migration seems to have involved mainly northern Somali clans like the Ogaadeen and Mareehaan Daarood, sections of whom reached the eastern bank of the Tana River by 1890, driving groups of Boran Oromo before them. Another cluster of northern Somali clans, principally a confederation of Habar Magadle Isaaq and the Bartire, Geri and Mareehaan Daarood, pushed westwards into the plains of Jigjiga and farther, beyond where they ultimately played an important part in the campaigns of the Muslim Adal state against the highland Christian kingdom of Ethiopia.

An important aspect of these migrations had been the development of trade and trade routes, which appear to have followed the migratory paths and brought about a steady contact between Somali, 'Afar and Oromo countries and Arabia and North Africa. On the whole there emerged three principal routes: one led out of Zayla' and passed through 'Iisa (Issa) and 'Afar countries to the ancient city of Harar, linking this region with the Ethiopian highlands, especially Showa. Traditionally, this had been the most important route, the lifeline that made Zayla' the fabled commercial emporium of medieval writers.[10] The second led out of Berbera, snaked through the Jiirato pass and on reaching the Ogo plateau branched off; one section passed through Milmil and Doollo plains into the Ogaadeen country, and the other turned in a south-easterly direction serving as the main outlet for the Dulbahante, Habar Tol Ja'alo and Majeerteen clans. There were of course other outlets in this region such as the ports of Mait and Mossyllum — the latter now in ruins — in the Warsangali country and a whole series of small ports ringing the eastern Majeerteen coast. The third international trade route led out of the port of Mogadishu, passed through Baardeere into Arsi and other Oromo country as far as Sidaamo.

A variety of goods came to the coast through these caravan routes and found their way ultimately to the Middle East and India. These included ivory, ostrich feathers, civet, furs, hides and skins, frankincense, myrrh, coffee, livestock and — in the case of Zayla' — gold and slaves. Imports included such items as rice, dates, cloth, household utensils and — especially in the last quarter of the nineteenth century — firearms.

Economy and social institutions. Important as the influence of the coastal centres of commerce may have been, the Somali have always remained a nation of herdsmen, having evolved over the years a unique social structure peculiarly suited to their demanding environment. While cattle-, goat- and sheep-keeping play an important part in the economy, the true hero of the Somali desert, as of neighboring Cushitic lands, is the camel. If, to borrow the anthropologists' metaphor, the Maasai[11] and the Nuer[12] are societies with a 'cattle complex', the Somali may be said to have a 'camel complex'. The camel is the basis of the Somali pastoral economy — the 'Mother of Man',[13] in the words of the great pastoral bard Sayyid Mahammad 'Abdille Hasan — that accounts for the survival and welfare of the Somali in their harsh environment, the independence of their character, the range of their activities, their migrations and their frequent wars.

If camel wealth constitutes the mainstay of the economy, lineage segmentation functions as the focus of Somali social and political life. According to a satirical Somali creation myth, God first created the family of the Prophet Muhammad, and was very pleased with the nobility of his handiwork; then he created the rest of mankind and was modestly pleased; then he created the Somali and he laughed! Aside from the sardonic jibe which Somali delight in levelling at themselves, the significance of the tale lies in the implied Somali belief of their being created separately as a people, distinct from others even if they are a laughable sort of creation. The Somali sense of community rests on belief in their common descent from a founding father, the mythical Samaale and, with few exceptions, every Somali is able to trace his/her descent to this common ancestor. The nation is composed of a vast genealogical tree of ever-expanding or dwindling segments — depending on the context — which connect one to all and all to one. The major segments are six clan families, the so-called Dir, Daarood, Isaaq, Hawiye, Digil and Rahanwayn which, as Saadia Touval observed in his fine study of Somali nationalism, correspond to the 'Old Testament version of the tribal segmentation of the Children of Israel'.[14]

Like most nomadic cultures, the Somali are fiercely egalitarian, faction-ridden and prone to schism. They passionately disdain central authority. Yet they view themselves as a community of people who belong together, have a common heritage and a common destiny for the future. So prominent a feature is this sense of community in Somali society that it prompted one scholar to insist that the Somalis 'had been for centuries one nation, professing one religion, speaking one language and pursuing a single pattern of pastoral nomadic culture when the Europeans arrived and carved them up'.[15] Common language, common religion, common traditions, common economy and culture — these are of course some of the potent properties which fire Somali nationalism, making the Somalis, in I.M. Lewis' words, 'a striking anomaly'[16] in the annals of African nationalism. Their sense of community is also the abiding concern which has prompted the Somalis over the last eighty years to brave overwhelming odds repeatedly in an attempt, so far unrewarded, to re-unify what they regard as their 'dismembered nation', and in the process locking themselves into tragic conflicts with their neighbours.

If their genealogy is the basis of their common cultural identity and traditionally their political disunity, their oral poetry is the moulder of the Somalis' national consciousness and solidarity. As we have noted above, the Somalis speak a Cushitic language which shares readily identifiable kinship with the languages of other Cushites, such as the Oromo, the 'Afar and particularly the Rendille and Aweera of Northern Kenya. Somali, virtually an unwritten language until 1972, is commonly spoken throughout the Somali peninsula. It may be of interest to note here that the writing of the

Somali language was delayed for so long because efforts to select a suitable script were repeatedly frustrated and thwarted by becoming enmeshed for seventy years in segmentary politics, as ably recounted by David Laitin.[17]

Despite its late entry into the family of written languages, Somali has been for centuries the vehicle of a vast body of literature, most notably oral poetry. With unfailing regularity, foreign students of Somali language and culture describe the Somali as 'a nation of bards' whose poetry is intimately connected with the vicissitudes of daily life.[18] In 1854 the romantic, eccentric British explorer Sir Richard Burton, somewhat astonished, wrote from the Somali coast of Zayla':

> The country teems with poets . . . every man has his recognized position in literature as accurately defined as though he had been reviewed in a century of magazines — the fine ear of this people causing them to take the greatest pleasure in harmonious sounds and poetical expressions, whereas a false quantity or prosaic phrase excites their violent indignation.[19]

Burton's astonishment that an unwritten language 'should so abound in poetry and eloquence' and that the unlettered Somalis should have a 'fine ear' for literature reflects a widespread if complacent assumption, especially in the West, that literature is to be equated with literary perfection in writing. Yet contemporary students of literature would tell us that the 'connection' between writing and literature is 'actually accidental' and belongs 'only to a secondary phase in the history of literature'.[20]

Burton, however, validly notes the prominent place occupied by poetry among the pastoral Somali, and his observation has been steadily echoed by many students of Somali culture, such as, for example, Kirk, Maino, Laurence, Andrzejewski and Lewis.[21] The Somali for their part regard their oral verse, along with their Islamic religion, as 'two assets of inestimable value'. I have elsewhere given a detailed account of Somali oral poetry, its characteristics, its functions and social significance.[22] For our purposes here, it is only necessary to remark on one aspect of Somali pastoral verse, namely its function as a medium of communication and hence its contribution to Somali national consciousness.

As noted by numerous students of the subject, the criteria of nationhood include not only linguistic, religious, geographic and economic unity but also the ability of the members of the nation to intercommunicate readily and easily on matters of common interest.[23] Until the last thirty years, modern forms of communication such as press and radio, roads and motor transport played no appreciable part in Somali communication. In the absence of these media and given the traditionally low level of literacy among the people, the exchange of information and the flow of ideas from one end of the country to the other (involving distances of roughly 1,400 miles from east to west and 1,000 miles from north to south) might at first glance seem difficult if not impossible. Yet traditionally information travelled with startling rapidity throughout the peninsula and it was not uncommon for events taking place on the north coast to be known in the farthest points of the Somali-inhabited areas in the space of a few weeks. The fact that the great mass of Somali are nomadic pastoralists constantly on the move, sometimes migrating over hundreds of miles within a month, partly explains this phenomenon of rapid communication. The migrations, as we noted, are dictated by the search for water and pasture, and the clans, observing no fixed territoriality or ownership of land, interpenetrate, converging and commingling at water points and well-pastured areas only to disperse again. These constant dispersals and regroupings may have fostered the curious use of oral poetry as a means of communication and as a regulator of the external relations of the clans. Given the constant dispersals and regrouping of the clans, dissemination occurs with amazing speed and a given poetic message is usually known throughout the peninsula within a few weeks or even days of its recital. Amazed by the ease and speed with which poetry travels, Somalis believe it is carried by *jinn* and other supernatural forces.

The poet in Somali pastoral society is, to borrow a phrase, the public relations man of the clan. His craft places him in the mainstream of society and his energies and talents are constantly drawn on for social purposes.[24] His kinsmen expect a pastoral poet to defend their rights, honour and prestige against the attacks of rival poets, to immortalise their fame, and to act on the whole as a spokesman for them. Thus the Gari and Bartire Somali clans of Jigjiga called on their poet/elder, Sheikh 'Aaqip 'Abdullahi Jaama', to define their pasture rights in the face of an encroaching Ethiopian empire. The poet sang:

> I speak the truth: this land is our land
> Hodayo, Wardeer and the plains of Dahare
> and Hananley,[25] beautiful pastures on the other side of the river,[26]
> Also the hills of Harodigeet and Daalooki vales[27]
> And the plains overlooking the corral of Jigjiga . . .
> These are the confines of my land.

As Burton observed, 'Every chief in the country must have a panegyric to be sung by his clan, and the great patronise light literature by keeping a poet.'[28] The pastoral poet's forum is the tribal assembly and from time to time, usually during the rainy seasons, the clans assemble to engage in poetic contests and it is here that each clan presents its best poet(s) to do battle with rival poets of opposing clans, their poetic duelling overseen and evaluated by a hoary panel of elder/arbiters and literary connoisseurs called *heerbeegti*. The clan assembly is therefore a focal point not only for the exchange of ideas but also for an intense inter-clan interaction, hence serving to integrate the nation.

Thus by the time the Europeans arrived towards the end of the nineteenth century, the Somalis had evolved as a fervent cultural community, though politically disunited. Conditioned by the vagaries of an ungenerous and predictable climate, they migrated back and forth over a vast grazing area which had been their homeland for centuries. They maintained an intermittent trade through coastal outlets, fought their factitious wars ('And the Berbers who live in the place [the Somali port town of Berbera] are very unruly',[29] wrote the Greek merchant of the first century AD, author of the *Periplus of the Erythraean Sea*), and assembled periodically to hold their poetic contests.

The imperial partition of the Horn

Rival partitioners. The three decades between 1870 and 1900 were years of fateful events and momentous developments for the history of the Somali. This period saw the partition by treaty — and conquest — of the Somali Horn by Great Britain, France, Italy and, most grave in its consequences, Ethiopia.

Behind the imperial partition of Somalia lay varying motives. The principal concern of Britain was to preserve the northern Somali coast as a supplier of meat and other commodities for her Aden garrison which, given the rising importance of the Red Sea to British plans in the East, was considered vital to the defence of British India.[30] The French, having fallen out with the British over Egypt in the 1880s, wanted a coaling station in the Red Sea to facilitate naval communication with their imperial interests in Indo-China.[31] They were, moreover, challenging British north-south expansion (the vaunted Cairo-Cape Town sphere of influence) by an east-west expansion. The French hoped to connect the Gulf of Aden with their possessions in Equatorial Africa. The attempt to implement these conflicting imperial ambitions was to provoke a major crisis known as the 'Fashoda Incident' between France and Britain when Lord Kitchener's Anglo-Egyptian troops ran into Commandant Marchand's column from the West Coast at Fashoda, Sudan, in 1895.

Recently united and a fledgling nation themselves, the Italians were new to the game of imperial aggrandisement and were interested in staking out a piece of land on the Red Sea and Indian coast wherever they could find one, provided they could do so without incurring the displeasure of either the French or the British. What they, like other Europeans, did not realise then was that the main threat to their imperial designs was not to be a European power but a black power on the rise — Menelik II of Ethiopia.

The advent of the steamship and the opening of the Suez Canal seem to have been the catalysts which drew European attention to the Somali Coast, opposite Aden. But even before the opening of the Canal in 1869, the steamship had demonstrated the importance of the Red Sea for European imperial schemes. In 1829 the *Hugh Lindsay* steamed from Bombay to Suez in about a month. As steamships were small and their consumption of coal was heavy, intermediate coaling-stations were needed. Early unsuccessful attempts were made to construct a coaling station, first at Perim on the Straits of Bab-el Mandeb on the mouth of the Red Sea, then at the island of Socotra further south in the Indian Ocean. But it was Aden that was eventually found 'most attractive... one of Albuquerque's"principal keys" to the Eastern world'.[32] In the following ten years, the British, by diplomacy, guile and force, seized Aden from the Sultan of Lahej and turned it into an important harbour for British shipping.

The conversion of Aden into an important British base from the 1840s was, however, considered incomplete as long as the peoples on the opposite shore had no treaties of protection with Britain. Aden, hot and poor in livestock, was dependent on the Somali coast for its meat supply; thus some sort of rapport with the peoples of the 'Afar and those on the Somali coast was desirable, if only to forestall their passing to a hostile power. Too busy absorbing her recent acquisition of vast dominions elsewhere in Africa, Britain at first seemed somewhat reluctant to annex the Somali coast. But in view of its economic importance to Aden, she was even more reluctant to let it be annexed by another power hostile to British interests. For a while the matter was solved for Britain by the appearance of a new candidate for the possession of the Somali coast. Isma'il Pasha, the ambitious Khedive of Egypt who was vassal first of the Ottoman Turks and then of the British when British influence became preponderant in Egypt from the 1870s, was busy implementing a remarkable project for the extension of Egyptian rule over North-eastern Africa. By the 1870s he had already carried Egyptian influence to the Sudan and even further inland to the lake region of East Africa.[33]

Although at first suspicious of the activities of their sub-imperialist protégé, the British came to regard the Khedive as a convenient proxy through whom to control the coast. Thus they aided and abetted his occupation of Berbera in 1875 and his expedition further inland where the Egyptians overthrew the long-independent Sultanate of Harar and set up an Egyptian administration which was to last a dozen years. But the Khedive's ambitious imperial adventures bankrupted his feeble treasury, wrecked the fragile economy of his country and, worse still, provoked the Sudanese Mahdist revolt which resulted in the collapse of Egyptian authority in Northeastern Africa. In the wake of this Egyptian fiasco, Britain entered into direct dealings with the coastal Somali clans and established itself, by guile and treaty, on the Somali coast by 1884.

From 1886 onwards Britain also began to acquire the extreme south-western edge of the Somali peninsula — an area which became known as Jubaland — as part of her East African sphere of influence. Here the overriding British concern was to safeguard the headwaters of the Nile — Egypt's lifeline — and this called for British control of the East African coast from Kismayu to Zanzibar. Part of Jubaland was later ceded to Italy (1925) and merged with Southern Somalia, but Britain retained a vast interior region of shrublands which later became known as the Northern Frontier District (NFD) of Kenya.[34]

The establishment of British rule coincided with similar French enterprises in the region. In 1862 France acquired Obok, a forlorn port on the Danakil coast, allegedly for the price of 50,000 francs,[35] but exercised little sovereignty over it until 1881 when the Franco-Ethiopian Company was set up there. French interest in the Somali-'Afar coast was fuelled by their seizure of Madagascar and much of Indo-China in the 1870s and, equally important, by the disintegration of the Anglo-French condominium over Egypt by 1884. In order to facilitate naval communication with their Madagascar and Indo-China possessions and to checkmate the formidable British garrison in Aden, the French now sought to establish their own base on the Red Sea. This was all the more desirable from the French point of view, given the humiliating restrictions, such as high duties on French products and bureaucratic harassment, which the British authorities in Aden placed on French shipping in that port. Accordingly, a French Protectorate was proclaimed over the strip of territory which came to be known as French Somaliland (now the Republic of Jibuti) under the governorship of Leonce Lagarde, a flamboyant coloniser who was to play a prominent role in the extension of French influence in North-eastern Africa and Ethiopia.

As the French and the British sought to extend their respective territories on the Somali coast at each other's expense, the two powers were increasingly at loggerheads from 1885 onwards, and for a while they seemed set on a collision course. Despite farcical counter-manoeuvring in the early phases of their imperial rivalries, Britain and France eventually reached an agreement which placed the boundaries of the two protectorates between Zayla' and Jibuti. This treaty was of course drawn in complete disregard of the interests of the Somali, some of whom, like the 'Iise, were torn between the two governments. But this does not seem to have fazed the 'Iise Somali who saw imperial attention as an opportunity to play off the French against the British and crossed the border from one side to the other as the need arose.

Italy, the third European power to participate in the bid for territories in North-eastern Africa in the last quarter of the nineteenth century, was the most ambitious to acquire colonial lands and the least decisive in the methods it adopted to obtain them. The latter fault cost her dearly, as we shall see, at the battle of Adowa when the Italians bungled an ill-fated confrontation with the formidable King Menelik II of Ethiopia and suffered a humiliating defeat. Although Italy ultimately came to possess more territory in the Horn than any other foreign power, this amounted to what one observer wryly dubbed 'Mussolini's collection of African deserts'.[36]

While France and Britain ingorged huge chunks of African real estate and smarted from political indigestion, Italy was distracted by her own national unification which was not finally completed until 1870, and thus, in Jones and Monroe's fitting observation, came late to the 'African feast as a poor relation'.[37] However, by 1885 the Government of Prime Minister Francesco Crispi, at first apprehensive, then increasingly confident, declared a Protectorate over the Eritrean coast from Assab to Massawa. Initially, British officials viewed Italian moves with hostility but eventually came to accept them as less harmful to their interests than French ones would have been. Hence they encouraged the Italians, as a convenient counter-force to the French, to move secretly and occupy Massawa soon after the withdrawal of the Egyptian garrison. Not unnaturally, France took note of the fact and began to do her own bit of intriguing at the expense of the Italians and British with successive Ethiopian rulers, first Emperor John IV and then Menelik whose renunciation of the Treaty of Wuchale (see below, p. 169), which had placed Ethiopia under Italian protection, is attributed at least partially to French intrigue.[38] Meanwhile Italy was also active in Southern Somalia, better known as the Benaadir coast, where she was the main coloniser; and, between 1885 and 1893, the

Italians, somewhat haltingly indeed, extended a Protectorate over the Benaadir coast and the north-eastern sultanates of Obbia and Majeerteen.

Ethiopian participation. An account of the imperial partition of Somali lands in the closing decades of the nineteenth century can scarcely be reconstructed even in bare outline without mention of Ethiopian participation. Indeed the roots of the present turmoil in the Horn of Africa go back to this period when a triumphant Ethiopian prince, Menelik II, taking advantage of a number of propitious events, extended Ethiopian authority over Somali, Oromo, and 'Afar lands. The remarkable story of Menelik's rise to power, his territorial conquests — which resulted in the quadrupling of the Ethiopian empire — and his brilliant triumph over the imperial powers of the day reveal towering qualities of statesmanship and shrewd diplomacy, as well as the character of European imperial rivalry which Menelik consummately exploited.

Judging by the consequences of their interaction, three factors can be seen to have contributed equally to Menelik's rise: (*a*) commerce, especially the trade in arms which shifted the balance of power in the area in Menelik's favour; (*b*) competition among European colonisers, which placed the Ethiopian king in a favourable position to exploit it; and (*c*) Menelik's access to the expert advice of European counsellors who provided him with useful knowledge concerning the motives and methods of European colonisers. These were inter-related factors and amounted to a single position of advantage for Menelik. Trade in arms, for example, gave him a military advantage over his neighbours. This enabled the king not only to defend his Shoan base against northern incursions but to undertake a vast programme of conquest. Conquest, in turn, provided him with the resources, both human and financial, to buy more arms and to monopolise trade more effectively.

As we have seen, by 1884 Britain, France and Italy were established on the Red Sea coast, competing for the trade with the Ethiopian interior. The three main ports on the coast served as outlets to three separate zones in the interior: Shoan trade passed through Zayla' and that of Tigre through Assab, while Berbera shared with Zayla' the trade from the independent city of Harar 'which had become since the Egyptian occupation the greatest trading town of the interior.'[39] France, Britain and Italy sought to gain influence with Ethiopia:

> It was over these ports that the three European powers were to concentrate their gaze, each as fearful and jealous of the other, and it was from the

three western [*sic*] ports that they were to compete for the favours of rival Abyssinian [Ethiopian] kings by trading in modern firearms and ammunition ... with such disastrous consequences.[40]

It would be hard to imagine Menelik's plans of conquest and trade succeeding without the steady support of the Italians throughout the 1870s and 1880s. During this period, Italy provided for Menelik the material and diplomatic means which guaranteed both the Ethiopian's success over his rivals and ultimately the means for undoing Italian interests in the region. After the death of Emperor John IV in 1889, Menelik acceded to the Ethiopian throne, assuming the title of King of Kings, and negotiated the treaty of Wuchale (known in Italian as Ucciale) with Pietro Antonelli, Italy's enterprising representative in Ethiopia. The Italian version of this treaty placed Ethiopia under Italian protection while the Amharic version, the only one Menelik signed, merely gave him the option to use Italy's good offices in the conduct of his foreign affairs. The discrepancy between the two versions was to lead to the Italo-Ethiopian war at Adowa in 1896. The treaty of Wuchale also formally recognised Italy's protectorate over Eritrea.[41]

Meanwhile Menelik used Italian friendship and Anglo-French rivalry to ensure the uninterrupted flow of arms. In 1890, Italy sponsored Ethiopian admission into the Brussels General Act, which permitted her as a Christian state to import arms on an unrestricted scale.[42] Something of the magnitude of the flow of firearms into Menelik's court can be gauged from the fact that in a period of three years (1887–9), Italy alone shipped to Ethiopia some 48,000 rifles, over a million cartridges and at least twenty-eight heavy guns.[43] These weapons ensured, fittingly, Italy's defeat at the battle of Adowa in 1896, a defeat which foiled the ambitious Italian colonisation programme in Ethiopia.

Apart from Italy, other Europeans were involved in the arms trade. French merchants played a leading role in the lucrative business in guns, ammunition, lead and powder which worried some Europeans as having reached alarming proportions. Arthur Rimbaud, the French poet, who resided in Harar as an arms dealer for some seven years, 'estimated that Menelik had received in the last five years more than twenty-four thousand guns of various kinds.'[44] Tsarist Russia, which had considerable ambitions in Ethiopia during the European scramble, probably provided Menelik with the most modern weapons and trained military personnel, the best known of the latter being the notorious mercenary Count Leontiev who conquered for Menelik the Oromo lands of Southern Ethiopia.[45] On one occasion 'eighty thousand repeater rifles arrived as a "personal gift" from Nicholas II to Menelik II,' while on another

Menelik's envoys shopping for arms in Russia 'carried away with them a hundred and thirty-five large boxes of rifles and machine-guns with ammunition and a large consignment of cavalry sabres . . .'[46]

In possession of a formidable arsenal and having consolidated his territorial gains in the south and east through years of Italian favours, Menelik repudiated the treaty of Wuchale in 1893. He now had no more use for Italian protection, and his relations with Italy quickly deteriorated. Italy made several attempts to bring the Shoan king to submission through diplomatic isolation, but Menelik proved too shrewd for her.[47] To show his disdain for the Italians, Menelik entered into cordial relations with the French soon after renouncing the Wuchale treaty, a move which enraged the Italians and provoked them into a war with the Ethiopians which they had cause to regret. Infuriated at Menelik's duplicity, the Italians put their forces in a state of preparedness and began to invade the Ethiopian highlands. Menelik marched north to anticipate them at the head of a combined army of 100,000 well-armed men. He met the Italians at Adowa in Tigre on the morning of 7 March 1896 and scored a thorough victory over them.

The decisive rout of the Italians reverberated in Ethiopian capitals and it was now evident who was the sovereign of Ethiopia. In October the Italian government, admitting defeat, sued for peace; rescinded the Wuchale treaty and recognised full Ethiopian 'sovereignty and independence'. The Europeans who had commercial and territorial designs on the coast now rushed in with delegations to treat with Menelik. In 1897 French and British envoys arrived in quick succession at his newly-built capital of Addis Ababa, seeking to obtain from the victorious king recognition of their colonial boundaries. The two powers made treaties with him which placed the Somali Ogaadeen and the Haud under Ethiopian suzerainty. The settlement also split up such Somali sub-groups as the 'Iise, the Isaaq, and the Godabursi.

The impact of partition and Somali responses

Initial impact and response. By 1898, the year of the inception of the Somali resistance struggle, the main spheres of the three European powers and Ethiopia were tentatively formulated, though their boundaries were ill-defined, especially those between Britain and Ethiopia on the one hand and Italy and Ethiopia on the other.[48] The Somali peninsula, one of Africa's culturally homogeneous regions, was broken up into mini-colonial territories — a British Somaliland, a French Somaliland, an Italian Somaliland, an Ethiopian

Somaliland, and what came to be known as the Northern Frontier District (NFD) of Kenya. The unrealistic and opportunistic character of the partition of the Somali was to prompt Lord Rennell of Rodd, decades later, to observe ruefully:

> If we had been interested enough . . . (and if the world had been sensible enough), all the Somalis . . . might have remained under our administration . . . . But the world was not sensible enough, and we were not interested enough, and so the only part of Africa which is radically homogeneous has . . . been split into such . . . parts as made Caesar's Gaul the problem and cockpit of Europe for the last two thousand years. And Somaliland will probably become a cockpit of East Africa.[49]

Inland herdsmen, the great mass of Somali — who, needless to say, were not consulted in the partition of their pasturelands into mini-imperial spheres — did not come into direct contact with the colonial administrations on the coast. They were therefore ill-disposed either to follow the arcane world of imperial treaties or to appreciate the consequences of such treaties for their country. If the Northern Somali poet, Faarah Nuur, was their spokesman, those who were immediately affected by the partition saw it in apocalyptic terms. He sang in bemused disbelief of what was happening to his country:

> The British, the Ethiopians, and the Italians are squabbling,
> The country is snatched and divided by whosoever is stronger,
> The country is sold piece by piece without our knowledge,
> And for me, all this is the Teeth of the Last Days![50]

The initial impact of European colonialism on the Somali was mild compared to that of Menelik's Ethiopia, an inland power whose livestock raids frequently despoiled the Ogaadeen Somali. The Dervish resistance movement, it will be argued shortly, was largely a Somali response to these raids. It is indeed a remarkable irony that the fledgling British Somaliland administration bungled into a war with the Somali Dervishes, who were primarily formed for self-defence against repeated Ethiopian raids. To say that the Somali suffered more grievously from Ethiopian occupation than they did from that of the Europeans is not to imply that the Ethiopians sought to create particular hardships for the Somalis; or that Ethiopian colonisation was less enlightened or benevolent than the Europeans', as the latter had sanctimoniously claimed. The key difference between European and Ethiopian methods of colonisation seems to have hinged on the difference between their technical and economic resources. Unlike the Europeans, the Ethiopians possessed neither an industrial home base nor a vast accumulation of international monopoly capital to finance their colonial enterprises.

While officials of the three European powers on the Somali coast were often bedevilled by lack of sufficient funds, they nevertheless managed, with the help of their international resources, to set up the rudimentary apparatus of administration. Once this was done, they could levy taxes to obtain the necessary funds to administer the colony or Protectorate. Furthermore, the European efforts were facilitated by their possession of the ports — and, by implication, their monopoly hold on trade — where the assembling of goods in a single spot made taxation a relatively simple task.

The Ethiopians, by contrast, did not have international capital to dip into in extending their influence to the Ogaadeen. Theirs was a subsistence economy and this meant that the army of conquest had to live off the land. In the words of a noted Ethiopianist:

One reason for Menelik's southern conquests was his need to open up fresh lands on which to quarter his growing armies of hungry men who were pressing hardly upon the resources of Shoa. During some of these lean periods in the [eighteen-] nineties, Menelik found the cattle seized from the Galla and Somali herds a very valuable asset for his soldiers and people. It is interesting, too, to read that after the Emperor John had despoiled Gojjam so that its *Negus*, Takla Haimanot, could no longer support his own army there, Menelik proposed to him that he should invade Kaffa in order to provide for his soldiers.[51]

To chance upon the path of a traditional military expedition by the Ethiopians was apparently to undergo a rugged experience for the civilian population. Oromo and Somali informants recall with particular vividness the 'trail of devastation' which Menelik's robber bands left in their wake in 'Aruusa and the Ogaadeen.[52] Margery Perham echoes indigenous assessments as to the harshness involved in the establishment of Ethiopian rule. She observes:

By the sanction of custom, soldiers on the march ruthlessly took all that they could from the inhabitants in order to save their own supplies. Many European travellers, from the earliest to the latest days, have remarked upon the arrogant and extortionate behaviour of the soldiers. Cattle, mules and donkeys trampled down and ate the crops. . . . But woe betide those same soldiers if they returned defeated! For then the people whom they had despoiled would turn on them and take their revenge for the injuries they had suffered. It might almost be said that every large-scale campaign in Ethiopia had some of the features of a civil war.[53]

Beyond the traditional sanctions of the army living off the land, Menelik's hordes under Ras Makonnen seem to have had even more pressing reasons to turn their gaze on the 'vast herds' of the Ogaadeen. As a result of the cataclysmic wars in the 1880s and '90s, the Ethiopian highlands were scourged by a devastating famine in the 1890s. Evidence from the works of Ethiopian specialists such as Richard Pankhurst and Harold Marcus as well as British diplomats of the day would seem to emphasise the importance of this famine as a primary impetus to Menelik's move into the Ogaadeen.[54] At a guess based on indigenous evidence, Ras Makonnen exacted in tribute or seized in raids, between 1890 and 1897, 100,000 head of cattle, 200,000 head of camels and about 600,000 sheep and goats from the Ogaadeen Somali.[55] The Ethiopians appear to have had little use for the camels (whose meat and milk they did not consume) other than as a means to bargain with the Somali who were required to redeem their camels with the payment of cattle and flocks. What the Somali could not redeem, the Amhara gave to their Muslim Oromo followers as a reward for their services. The sedentary clans of the Daarood Geri and Bartire on the plains of Jigjiga and the so-called Reer Baare on the lower Shabeelle basin suffered particular deprivations at the hands of the Ethiopians. They were periodically invested, their villages burned and their crops pillaged. 'The Ethiopians did not seem to come to the Ogaadeen to govern,' says a Western Somali elder from Jigjiga, 'they came to take away livestock.'[56]

There were about twenty Somali religious settlements of both Qaadiriya and Ahmadiya brotherhoods in the Somali interior in the 1890s and many of these were feeling the pressure of Ethiopian expansion. The Italian explorer, Vittorio Bottego, spoke in 1893 of the plight of Somali religious communities whose 'belongings had been looted by the Amhara.'[57] By the time of Bottego's visit, the ancient Tariiqa colony at Qulungul and the tomb of the founding saint of Qaadiriya's northern branch, 'Abd ar-Rahman az-Zeyli'i, lay in ruins 'sacked by the Ethiopians'.[58] Under these circumstances, it was understandable that the Somali shared what a recent student described as 'the fear of many Muslims that their society was threatened' by Christian invaders.[59] It is equally understandable that the Somali religio-nationalist movement provoked by colonial occupation should have been initially directed at the Ethiopians and that its leader belonged to these religious brotherhoods which suffered exceedingly from Ethiopian plunder.

The story of the roving holy man who was to forge out of hitherto decentralised clans a resilient movement which was to lead the Somali nationalist struggle against the combined forces of three colonial powers — Britain, Italy and Ethiopia — first burst on the colonial world in 1899. In April of that year, Britain's representative on the Somali coast, Consul J. Hayes Sadler, anxiously wrote to his government of 'conflicting reports current in Berbera concerning the doings of a Mullah . . . who was collecting arms and men with the ultimate aim [of] head[ing] a religious expedition against Abyssinia'.⁶⁰

The Mullah in question was none other than the Somali Sayyid Mahammad 'Abdille Hasan, poet, mystic and nationalist, who was to be dubbed the 'Mad Mullah' in colonial literature on account of his irreverent refusal to embrace Britain's 'God-given' civilising mission, and his audacity and improbable success in the long Somali struggle against colonial occupation. In 1895, after years of peripatetic religious education, Sayyid Mahammad returned from Mecca at the age of forty as the spiritual envoy of the Meccan Muhammad Salih, the charismatic founder of the new and popular Salihiya order. The Salihiya was a daughter order of the Ahmadiya, the religious brotherhood whose members were being harried by the Ethiopians in the Somali Ogaadeen. Ethnically, Sayyid Mahammad belonged to the Ogaadeen clan-family and thus was doubly bound to the Ogaadeen region — by religion and kinship. Indeed it was the Ogaadeen people who appealed to him 'to deliver us from the Amhaar' (the Somali word for the Amhara, the dominant clan in Ethiopia). And it was in response to this appeal that the Sayyid began to organise a resistance to the Ethiopians, thus prompting Sadler's anxious report concerning 'the doings of a Mullah'.

On learning of the intended expedition on the Ethiopians, the British Somaliland administration instructed the British Resident in Addis Ababa to 'communicate to King Menelik the religious movement on the borders of his empire which the Mullah . . . is conducting.⁶¹ Menelik undertook 'to stifle the movement', and thus began a tradition of cooperation between Menelik's Ethiopia, Britain and, to a less extent, Italy, 'to put down the Mullah'. The stage was thus set for a twenty-year conflict that was to plunge Somaliland into untold misery and to cost, on a conservative estimate, 200,000 Somali lives (or one-third of the population of Northern Somalia).

The history of the Dervish movement (Dervish, from the Arabic Darāwīsh, signifying one who has taken vows of poverty and service to his community, was the name the Sayyid selected for his followers) has been ably recounted,⁶² and does not need to be retold here. We should only note that despite the cooperation of three colonial powers to eliminate them, the Sayyid and his ill-armed Dervishes remained embarrassingly elusive and refractory, mainly because they wisely avoided a head-on confrontation with their better-armed and organised adversaries. Instead, the Dervishes kept up deadly guerrilla skirmishes with their foes on a wild terrain familiar to them but pathless to the enemy.

In 1903, after six years of bloody but inconclusive engagements, the British made peace overtures to the Sayyid, and his answer, because it came to reflect Somali attitudes over the years toward their colonisers, is worth quoting. He wrote in his message to the colonial powers:

> I have no forts, no houses . . . . I have no cultivated fields, no silver or gold for you to take. You gained no benefit by killing my men, and my country is of no good to you . . . . We kill, you kill . . . . If you want peace, go away from my country to your own.[63]

The colonials did not leave, and the struggle tenaciously wore on for seventeen more years of destruction and bloodshed until 1920 when the British delivered a series of devastating aerial bombardments on the movement's headquarters at Taleeh (Northern Somalia), and the 'Dervish Menace' was finally contained.

Elusive boundaries and the struggle over pasture rights. The title of this section is intended to emphasise the two themes which probably stand out most in the history of the Somali under colonial rule. Friction over boundary lines and the struggle for pasture rights remained the central issues in the relations of the three powers — Britain, Italy and Ethiopia — which received the lion's share of the territorial spoil from partitioned Somali lands. The same issues also help to explain the 'marginal life' which the 'border Somali' led under colonialism and which Somali minorities continue to lead under the independent states of Kenya and Ethiopia, as well as the continuously strained relations between these states and Somalia, since the latter became independent in 1960. If the boundary lines separating their respective territories remained murky and ill-defined right up to Somalia's independence, Britain, Italy and Ethiopia can hardly be faulted for not trying to tackle the problem. From the conclusion of their 1897 treaties, the three countries, either bilaterally or trilaterally, tried to demarcate their Somaliland spheres in no fewer than ten official conventions — in 1908, 1924, 1928, 1929, 1934, 1937, 1942, 1946, 1954 and 1955 — all to no avail.[64]

What frustrated their efforts to arrive at a territorial *modus vivendi*? The answer lies in Somali ecology and social organisation which the administering powers failed — either from ignorance or imperial ambition — to take note of. As we have seen, genealogical segmentation — whereby practically every member of a given clan is a relative of everyone else — and migratory movements between pasture and water source characterise Somali pastoral life. In attempting to establish their frontiers, the powers tended to ignore these realities of Somali existence and consequently drew up lines which cut up kinship units into bewildering fragments and cut off entire clans from their traditional sources of water and pasture for their herds. For example, in southern Somalia at the tri-junction point of the three frontiers, the Mareehaan clan was cut by the new frontiers into three parts, one part under the British in the Northern Frontier District of Kenya, another under the Italians in the south, and a third in the south-west under Ethiopia; so were the Bah-Gari and Muhammad Subeer Ogaadeen clans, as were a host of smaller clans. The Mareehaan and Bah-Gari sections who were lopped off to the Italian side of the frontier were lucky enough to have access to water sources in the Shabeelle River, but they lost valuable grazing grounds on the Ethiopian side; on the other hand, their kinsmen in Ethiopia retained the pastures but were cut off from indispensable water sources on the coast. In the north the Dulbahante and Isaaq became British subjects, which enabled them to retain the coastal water points, but they lost the grazing grounds in the Haud (which fell on the Ethiopian side of the frontier) where they traditionally spent six months of the year. The Ogaadeen clans on the Ethiopian side were fortunate to have access to both water and pasture in the Doollo-Harodigeet plains but they were cut off from coastal trade, especially from the port of Berbera (on the British side) through which 90 per cent of their commerce passed.

As can be expected, the splintering of close kinship units, even families, by the new boundary lines created something of an administrative nightmare for the new rulers. In pursuit of the ever-elusive pasture and water, the clans had necessarily to move across frontiers, which made them answerable to competing and conflicting Ethiopian, Italian and British — and later Somali — administrative laws and regulations. They were liable to multiple taxations and multiple legal jurisdictions depending on where they happened to be at a given time in the year. As conflicting imperial claims over migrant Somali increasingly embroiled the powers in perennial friction, they began to resort to their 'peculiar' devices in order to identify their respective 'clans'. The British introduced the system of a 'floating' administration, whereby colonial officers, aided by mounted police and other instruments of government, accompanied the roving pastoralists from pasture to waterhole and to pasture again round the year. The Italians, on the other hand, tried to resolve the problem by issuing an 'identity card' for each wandering nomad whom they regarded as their subject, a measure which not surprisingly prompted them to fall foul of the Ethiopians who 'protected' the same nomad as their citizen when he happened to be on their side of the border for part of the year. (As we will see shortly, a conflict of this sort precipitated the momentous Wal Waal incident which served as Mussolini's pretext for invading Ethiopia in 1935.)

The Somali Dilemma

Soon the question of the nationality of Somali pastoralists came to exercise colonial administrators. Whose citizens were they — Ethiopian, Italian or British? Since a claim over Somali citizenship and loyalities implied a claim over ownership of the lands they inhabited, each administration was eager to claim them as their own. To judge by their largely uncooperative though cunning responses, the Somali answer to the question of whether they were Ethiopian, Italian or British subjects was, in a manner of speaking, 'none'. They tended to reject all three as alien and unacceptable, although in their dealings with the powers this did not prevent them from resorting to the pastoral guile of *kala xad* (lit. to steal one party against another), a term which may be rendered as giving tactical allegiance to one power so as to play it off against another. To cite but one example of 'tactical allegiance', the account of a British administrator of many years' experience in these tempestuous borders is worth relating. It concerns the 'duplicity' of one Ugaaz Doodi, a chief of the Godabursi clan in Northern Somalia, about whom the official reports:

In that year [1921] the town of Borama was established by the British administration close to the western border with Ethiopia because of the ever-growing number of complaints about Ethiopian 'tax collectors' seizing livestock and encroaching on British soil. It was then that the grandson of the Ugaz [*sic*] came from Ethiopia to reside in Borama, professing allegiance to the British Crown. He was given rank and distinction, and spent much of his time energetically establishing, with the assistance of a District Commissioner, the British interpretation of the border line with Ethiopia. Having also learnt that the Protectorate Police were no longer permitted to cross this border, Dodi [*sic*] again transferred his allegiance (and that of his clan) to Ethiopia, confident that his 'tax-collecting' parties could continue ravaging the property of other clansmen on the Ethiopian side of the border without British interference.[65]

Similarly, when they found it convenient to do so, the Somali were prone to ignore the newly imposed international lines and to continue their nomadic business as usual — which on the whole meant the business of pursuing pasture and water for their herds as seasonal changes dictated. Where the new administrations were determined to enforce restrictions on cross-border movements, the Somali resisted the restrictions with equal determination. Understandably, this led to abiding tensions and violent confrontations, not only between governments and subjects but also between the governments themselves who competed for the loyalties of the same pastoral subjects. In 1931, for example, an Anglo-Ethiopian border commission attempted to enforce border restrictions by clearing the bush on either side of the boundary and erecting stone pillars. This stirred an immediate 'outcry' from the clans occupying the grazing areas on either side of the demarcation, and

violence broke out, boundary pillars were destroyed or defaced, and the British authorities promptly introduced a special ordinance declaring this illegal. Serious trouble again broke out at the tri-junction point with French Somaliland. The survey beacons were destroyed and a German assistant commissioner, Herr Emil Beitz, was assassinated by rebellious clansmen.[66]

Somali resistance to demarcation on occasion led to tragic consequences. In 1934, for example, an Ethiopian army of 600 men moved on a cluster of wells called Wal Waal, a watering place for many Somali herdsmen in the Haud. As this area was contested by the Italians, the Ethiopians ran into an Italian force already garrisoned in the area to guard the wells. A provocative face-off followed in which a Somali *askari* (ranker) on the Italian side, named Aadan Low whose Mareehaan clan the Ethiopians had severely pillaged the previous month, fired a revenging bullet at the Ethiopians. The Ethiopians returned the fire and the exchange resulted in the famous Wal Waal incident which precipitated fascist-ruled Italy's invasion of Ethiopia in 1935.[67]

One of the undesirable consequences of Euro-Ethiopian imperial rivalry and the Somali tendency to exploit it was the growth of cross-border hooliganism and outlawry. Given the openly hostile relations of the three powers and the mutual jealousies of their local representatives, they often failed to cooperate on the maintenance of cross-border law and order. They had no treaties of extradition of criminals nor a common policy of prosecuting trans-frontier cases. On the contrary, they tended to destabilise each other's side of the border by encouraging 'their clans' to raid for livestock across the border. Therefore they in effect provided a safe haven for each other's criminals. This was an ideal situation for the likely intriguer who, as a pastoral song put it, 'lived by the bounty of Allah to raid livestock'!

Freed, at least temporarily, from the norms of clan sanctions, and responsible to no authority but their own, persons and groups could (and did) get away with murder — by simply crossing to the other side of the border and giving allegiance to a new government. The situation gave an added incentive to the Somali pastoral propensity for stock theft and inter-clan feuding, and very soon the border developed a reputation as a place of violence and lawlessness. Thus, in the 1950s a pastoral poet was moved to register his impression of the notoriety of border life in these lines.

    Oh! you poor man,
    Who possesses nothing but valour,
    Be brave to build a fortune.

Fly to the border
Where, with the blessing of Allah,
You'll find camels to seize.[68]

There is a note of humour about the comment of one such 'poor man of valour', a Somali elder who flew to the border to build his fortune. Having escaped from a British prison in Kismayu and feeling secure in the Ethiopian zone, the amicable adventurer judged it necessary to write a letter to his 'former captors to say that he had found a change of air absolutely necessary for his health'. 'By-the-bye', the unperturbed elder advised, 'I left a wife and a Koran behind. Don't trouble to return them.'[69]

Indigenous response to the outbreak of cross-border violence and anarchy seems to have involved the intensification of the *heer* institution among the clans. Traditionally, *heer* or common law throughout the Somali peninsula regulated not only the external relations of the clans but also the behaviour of a person among his immediate kin. The most notable aspect, for our purposes, of *heer* concerns the sanction of collective guilt or innocence whereby a perpetrator of crime transmits his guilt to his kinsmen by virtue of his agnatic blood relation to them. Thus, for example, if he was guilty of murder, his kinsmen were seen as accomplices to the crime and were held answerable to the injured party. They were required either to make a satisfactory restitution to the aggrieved or to run the risk of becoming objects of blood vendetta.

The institution of *heer* came into active play with the outbreak of cross-border lawlessness as a control mechanism to maintain order and stability on both sides of the border. Thus potential troublemakers were policed by their own kinsmen who were likely to suffer the consequences of their misdeeds. In 1954, for example, the Habar Yoonis Isaaq clan returned 2,000 head of looted camels to the Reer 'Ali Ogaadeen, and the Reer 'Ali reciprocated by making blood compensation for numerous murdered Isaaq men.

Independence — and disappointment

At the end of World War II, with Italy defeated and Ethiopia liberated by British forces, almost all the Somalilands were placed under temporary British administration. In 1946, the British Foreign Secretary, Ernest Bevin, proposed the re-unification of all the Somalilands — under the British, of course — to his three counterparts on the Four-Power Commission responsible for disposal of the ex-Somalilands. Although, with characteristic British sentimentality, Bevin made a stirring speech concerning the need 'to give those poor nomads a chance to [get] a decent living', his colleagues on the commission remained unimpressed and the Somali were returned to their former colonial status of mini-lands. On 26 June 1960, British Somaliland became independent and four days later, impelled by those powerful emotions of cultural unity and economic interdependence which all Somali share, merged with Italian Somaliland to become the new state of Somalia.

The sudden independence and merger of these two Somalilands became a cause for general rejoicing among the Somali of the three other frontiers, in the confident expectation that they, too, to use the local metaphor of the early 1960s, 'will be let go'. With the departure of two European colonisers and a third (France) under constant verbal barrage by the OAU and the UN, NFD and Ogaadeen Somali felt that good times had come at last. These words of an Ogaadeen poet reflect the euphoria which swept the Ethiopian Somali for a short time:

> Behold our freedom is here at last!
> She soars with the eagle flight of the morning;
> I can hear the flutter of her wings
> and the smell of her foggy mists.
> Our freedom is here at last . . .
> Because the Beloved Emperor of Africa [Haile Selassie] granted it us.[70]

Not to be outdone in the general onset of confident expectation of imminent freedom, the Kenya Somali dashed out blazing lyrics in praise of 'Jomo [Kenyatta], the Champion of African freedom'.[71] Events were to prove, however, that the confidence of the Ethiopian and Kenyan Somali that they too 'will be let go' was premature and that Jomo Kenyatta and Haile Selassie had no intention of letting their Somali subjects go. Indeed the two poems cited above were to be the last Somali praise songs to the leaders of Kenya and Ethiopia; for soon Somali disappointment over being denied by these leaders the right to secede from Kenya and Ethiopia in order to join their brethren across the border in the Somali Republic prompted them to change Haile Selassie's epithet from 'Beloved Emperor' to 'Barbarous Despot of benighted Abyssinia' and Kenyatta's from 'Jomo the Champion' to 'Jomo the Child-killer'.

The NFD flap. In tracing the history of the Somali frontier over the last twenty years, it is necessary, for analytical purposes, to limit the discussion to Ethiopian and Kenyan frontiers, since French Somaliland received her independence in June 1977 (after 115 years of French rule) to become the new Republic of Djibouti. The Kenyan Somali inhabit a region historically known as the Northern

The Somali Dilemma 181

Frontier District (NFD), which is now administratively divided under independent Kenya into two, the provinces of Eastern and North-Eastern. It consists of over 126,000 sq. miles of plateau which gently descend eastward from Lake Turkana. Much of it, like the rest of central Somalia, is semi-arid camel country covered with thorn bushes and acacia trees. According to a Kenya government census of 1969, the population of the North-Eastern province (the Somali part of the old NFD) is 246,000, who are predominantly nomadic herdsmen of cattle and camels.[72].

The NFD was isolated from the rest of Kenya throughout its colonial history by a system of pass laws whereby NFD Somali could enter the rest of Kenya only by special permit. Surprisingly, this law is still in operation, seventeen years after Kenya's independence. That the NFD Somali are required to have a travel document to enter the rest of 'their' country is a telling commentary on the province's status in relation to Kenya. The majority of the Somalis speak no Swahili — the lingua franca of Kenya — and share no cultural ties or traditions with the rest of Kenya. As we have seen, virtually all the Somali who inhabit this region are members of Somali clans on the other side of the border with whom they share the same language, same culture, same religion and — most important of all — the same genealogy and common ancestry. They migrate for half of the year to southern Somalia where the water sources for their herds are located.

In recognition of the NFD's natural affinity with the Somali Republic, the British authorities sent a commission of inquiry in 1962, a year before Kenya's independence, to ascertain the wishes of the inhabitants concerning their future status. Specifically, the commission's task was to enquire whether the Kenyan Somali wished to remain in Kenya or join the Somali Republic. The commission, consisting of an internationally respected Nigerian jurist, G.C.M. Onyiuke, and a Canadian general, found that the Somali population 'almost unanimously' wished to merge with the Somali Republic.[73]

But Kenya's emerging leadership, especially Jomo Kenyatta, soon to be the chief executive of the new sovereign state of Kenya, and his energetic economic minister Tom Mboya, objected vehemently to the transfer of any part of Kenya to Somalia and threatened war to preserve Kenya's territorial integrity. Under pressure from the Kenyan leaders, who had considerable economic leverage over Britain on account of British settler interests in Kenya, and from Emperor Haile Selassie who feared that a secession of the NFD would inspire his Somali subjects to demand similar rights, the British government made a dramatic about-face on the issue of the right to self-determination of the NFD Somali, and ushered Kenya into independence in 1963 without having resolved the NFD problem.

The British decision to force the Somali inhabitants of the NFD to become part of an independent Kenya, and the Kenyan leaders' determination to use force — if necessary — to retain them, resulted in widespread Somali disappointment and frustration. The outcome was that the frustrated Somali resorted to a general armed revolt which continued to rage till 1967, pitting Somali guerrillas against Kenya's security forces. According to an indigenous guess, the three years of warfare took the lives of 5,000 Somali, in addition to severely taxing Kenya's emerging economy. Although no major violence has erupted on Kenya's frontier since 1967, largely due to the operations of an elaborate security service and the garrisoning of substantial contingents of Kenya's military in the region, there is little doubt that this frontier is a ticking time-bomb, likely to explode at the slightest provocation.

Ethiopia's garrison government in the Ogaadeen. The Ethiopian Somali inhabit the country called Eastern Ethiopia (or Hararge Province) by the Ethiopians and Western Somalia by the Somali but which appears in academic literature as the Ogaden (in Somali, Ogaadeen, after one of the Somali clans who live in the region). Inhabited by about 2 million Somali, the Ogaadeen is a vast plateau (roughly 120,000 sq. miles) of scrubland that gradually slopes from the Ethiopian highlands down to Southern Somalia. Although agriculture and cattle-keeping flourish along the Shabeelle River basin, the Ogaadeen is ideal camel country.

A cursory look at the evolution of Somali society under Ethiopian administration reveals two interrelated themes: first, the introduction of what may be termed 'garrison government' as the instrument of Ethiopian rule, and secondly the increasing alienation of the Somali population from Ethiopia as a result of the latter's reliance on this method of government to administer the Somali. As we have seen, the famine of the 1890s which devastated the Ethiopian highlands was a major incentive for Ethiopia's move into the Ogaadeen, with the principal object of recouping her livestock losses from the Somali herds. Motivated by this economic factor as well as by the desire to forestall European occupation, the Ethiopians had established a strong military garrison in the cluster of wells around Jigjiga by the turn of the century. From this forward base, they sallied forth in every direction on their yearly 'tax-collecting' expeditions. In addition to exacting tribute and punishing recalcitrant clans, the armed expeditions represented the Ethiopians'

The Somali Dilemma 183

method of showing the flag. To the Somali, therefore, the Ethiopian administration at first seemed, as one elder put it, 'like another clan of raiders'.[74] While the clans living within a radius of, say, 100 miles from the Ethiopian military garrisons were subject to Ethiopian pressure, the rest of the Ogaadeen from the wells of Dagahbuur in the north to Doolow in the south remained, in the words of a British official, an 'accursed no-man's land' which the Ethiopians 'steadily declined to administer' despite the 'most urgent representations of our government' to do so.[75]

However, the more they became involved in the affairs of the Ogaadeen, the more the Ethiopians learned that running a colony entailed more than just raiding for livestock. As the French and the British timidly but surely impinged on the Ethiopian sphere from the north and the Italians did so from the south, the Ethiopians were forced to compete for the loyalties of the Somali. European competition and the Somali propensity to play it off against Ethiopia triggered a whole set of new relationships between the Somali and Ethiopians. To prove to the Somali the benefits of cooperation, the Ethiopians eased up on the arbitrary seizure of livestock, imposed some discipline on the military, and restrained the rapacious activities of the 'fortune chiefs' whose armed bands of marauders frequently harried the Reer Baare peasant communities on the Shabeelle River. Additionally, the Ethiopians introduced a system of rewards whereby elders and notables of loyal clans received royal titles and offices and became salaried officials of the Ethiopian crown. These *balabats* or chiefly functionaries at first seemed a curiosity to the chiefless Somali and the exotic accoutrements, such as feudal robes and chiefly regalia, which they received from the Ethiopian court did little to diminish the amusement of the egalitarian Somali.

Eventually, however, Ethiopian court appointments and their trappings of material advantage did impress the Somalis, and a small urban élite of Somalis developed in Ogaadeen towns such as Jigjiga, Dagahbuur, Qabridahare and Qallaafo. Indeed the 1950s and '60s witnessed the emergence of important Somali families, such as the Duulane Rafle of Wardeer, the Gareen of Qallaafo and the 'Iise and Godabursi Ugaazes of Jigjiga, whose power and prestige depended on Ethiopian patronage. These vied with each other for Ethiopian favours, especially appointment to the prestigious offices of *Brambaras* and *Dejazmatch*. It was through the instrument of these appointed offices that the Ethiopians attempted to rule the Ogaadeen. Therefore one of the effects of Ethiopian administration in the Ogaadeen was the introduction and growth of hierarchical chiefly institutions.

Yet the backbone of the Ethiopian administration was (and continues to be) the military garrison which extracts loyalty by force where it is not given voluntarily — the latter often being the case. Thus while the military garrisons which dot the country guarantee Ethiopia's hold on the Ogaadeen, they are regarded by the Somalis as an occupation army, and the more Ethiopia relies on military might for her authority in Ogaadeen, the deeper will be the alienation of the local populace.

Cultural assimilation

Nowhere does the alienation of the Ethiopian Somali become more absolute than over the question of cultural assimilation and national integration. Ethiopia, since Menelik II, has been ruled by a minority clan, the dominant Amhara. The survival of Amhara rule depends on the clan's ability to assimilate the vast majority of conquered peoples into the Amhara culture and way of life. It is not far-fetched to observe that just as the French assimilationists tried to mould Frenchmen out of conquered Africans, so Amhara seek to fashion Amhara men out of the Oromo, Gurage, Eritrean, 'Afar, Somali and other defeated peoples. In fairness to the Amhara, however, it is necessary to point out that once a conquered nationality has been absorbed into their culture, they have shown far greater willingness to share the benefits of state with the assimilated people and to treat them as equal citizens than did the French, who excluded assimilated Africans by a rigid racial caste system even while paying lip service to the ideals of liberty, equality and fraternity in an integrated French commonwealth.

The Somali, given their fierce allegiance to a Somali national identity, passionately resist Ethiopian attempts to assimilate them. Symbolic of this resistance is their reluctance to send their children to Ethiopian schools where they are forced to study in Amharic, the official language of Ethiopia. Instead the Somali send their children to Somali government schools across the border, just as Somali nomads send their herds to be watered in Somali-government administered wells. Being fiercely loyal to Somali language and Somali traditions based on an Islamic culture, Ethiopia's Somali find it odious to have to be absorbed into Amhara Christian culture in order to participate in national life. An Ethiopian military officer, Captain Keseteberhan Ghebrehiwet, with long adminstrative experience in Ogaadeen, observed in a moment of rare candour:

The day-to-day lives of the Ogaden Somalis are so attached to Somalia that even if they get primary education in Ethiopia they then go for higher education to Somalia and get jobs there. Some even hold very high government posts. They observe rules and regulations made for the Somali public. They normally cross the border when they need legal help to settle disputes — or else mediators are sent from Somalia. They do not believe themselves Ethiopians, in fact the hatred they have for the Amhara is monumental. During the many operations that Ethiopia conducted to suppress popular revolts in the Ogaden, there was such inhuman treatment of the population that children grow up with a deeply embedded hatred of the Amhara.[76]

A similar sentiment was expressed by an Ogaadeen elder who spoke of a 'two-pronged' resistance in 'our dealings' with Ethiopia:

The first phase is passive resistance and this consists in our giving the Ethiopians a minimum of cooperation so as not to provoke them to slaughter us. The second phase is active resistance composed of armed revolts which we resort to whenever there is a slight chance of success. Thus our history of occupation by Ethiopia has been a history of popular uprisings followed by ruthless suppressions in a pattern very like the succession of dry and rainy seasons.[77]

To say that this succession of uprisings and suppressions has lately made the Horn of Africa one of the world's most unsafe places to live, not only engulfing the region in disastrous conflicts but also endangering the security of Africa by turning a strategic part of it into an arena of superpower rivalry, is to state the obvious.

Wanted: bold initiatives to break the boundary predicament

The splintering of the Somali nation into mini-lands first by colonial boundaries and subsequently by the African successor-states that inherited them, poses — in addition to the usual problems of divided Africans — two grave dilemmas which seem to be almost unique to the Horn. The first is ecological. As we have seen, much of the Somali peninsula is a fragile, modestly endowed environment where the need to survive requires the Somali pastoralists to move constantly across the borders of Somalia, Kenya and Ethiopia in order to have access to essential pastures, water sources, traditional trade routes and markets. As if to mock the absurdity of the new boundary lines, the principal water sources are on the Somali side of the border while the pasture zones are on the Kenyan and Ethiopian sides (see map). When conflicts arise, as they often do in this area, the three countries tend to respond by closing the border so as to control trans-frontier traffic, on the mistaken assumption that this will minimise border friction.

The pastoralists must ignore these restrictions and therefore suffer severe penalties, if caught, for violating a governmental order which is impossible to comply with in the first place. Where they are forced to observe trans-border restrictions, not only do such restrictions humiliate the people's sense of dignity — already aggravated by the partition itself — but they also lead to dangerous overcrowding and overgrazing on either side of the border, resulting in a serious disruption of the fragile ecological balance between forage, plants, animals and people. It would, for example, provide the subject for a fascinating — though grim — study to examine the extent to which the Horn's notorious famines, especially those of 1965, 1967, 1973–4 and 1979, were either caused or exacerbated by the violent confrontations between Somali nationalists and Kenyan and Ethiopian security forces during these periods.

If economic and ecological necessity constitutes the heart of the Somali dilemma, the structure of Somali society tends to exacerbate it. As we have seen, genealogical segmentation whereby all Somali trace their descent to a common ancestor binds their society in a powerful web of kinship ties, making them a community of brothers, cousins and kinsmen. The idea, therefore, of separation, of being completely cut off from all contact with one's kinsmen by an arbitrary boundary line, goes against the Somali's deepest understanding of life and universe. It violates their values, beliefs, ideals and aspirations — their whole world-view. Their sense of loss and calamity as a result of the fracturing of their corporate existence is perhaps well expressed by this lament composed by a pastoral poet shortly after the Ethiopian-Somali war of 1977–8. The poet was denied permission by an Ethiopian garrison near the town of Jigjiga to cross the border to join his family on the other side:

> My brother is there [on the other side of the border],
> I can hear the bells of his camels
> When they graze down in the valley,
> And the leaves of the bushes they browse at
> Have the same sweetness as the bushes near my place
> Because the rain which
> Makes them grow comes from the same sky.
>
> When I pray, he prays,
> And my Allah is his Allah.
> My brother is there
> And he cannot come to me.[78]

Somali, Ethiopian and Kenyan politicians have so far displayed a peculiar insensitivity to this human tragedy of a people whose way of life and understanding of the universe have been shattered by idiotic boundaries in an uneconomic zone of Africa. Ethiopian and Kenyan determination to treat the colonial boundaries as sacrosanct and inviolable is matched by Somali determination to reject the validity of these boundaries. Both sides appeal to different interpretations of statements in the OAU's charter and other official pronouncements.[79] While the leaders stick tenaciously to legalistic abstractions concerning the irreconcilable imperatives of the territorial integrity of Kenya and Ethiopia versus the right of the Somalis to self-determination, the divided kinsmen cry out, 'My brother is there/And he cannot come to me.'

That the Horn of Africa is in the grip of a deadly dilemma may be gauged from the fact that Ethiopia's latest official response to Somali grievances is titled *Somalia: The Problem Child of Africa*, and it amounts to a shrill diatribe in which the Somali are berated, among other things, as 'Hitlerians', 'tough-minded criminals' and 'obsess[ed] freaks'.[80] The alleged author of this sad tract is none other than Mesfin Wolde-Mariam, a man of considerable intelligence and erudition who had put out an earlier monograph on the Ethio-Somali conflict in 1964.[81] Though written from the Ethiopian standpoint at a time when the two countries had fought a nasty little war and were consequently trading mutual abuse and insults through the radio and press, the earlier work nevertheless commends itself for its tone of restraint and even, on occasion, bold and constructive ideas. One therefore wonders what impelled the previously temperate and reasonable Mesfin to produce the ranting hysteria of the later pamphlet. Mesfin's lapse is possibly to be explained by the pamphlet's date and place of publication: 1977 (Addis Ababa). The Addis Ababa of that year was not a place for temperate or cool heads. It was then that a brutal military junta known as the Dergue, in a bid to foist its legitimacy on Ethiopia, unleashed the notorious 'Red Terror' in which, according to Amnesty International, Ethiopians perished by the 'thousands'.[82] Although no section of society was spared during these frenzied massacres, it was the Ethiopian intelligentsia who particularly suffered, subjected as they were to repeated Stalinist-type purges. It is the good fortune of the Horn that Mesfin survived, even if as a price for his survival he may have been forced to put his name to a compromising tract.

Somali government propaganda against Ethiopia is equally shrill,[83] and so long as our leaders can do no better than exchange vitriolic abuse, they are unlikely to represent an African example of statesmen of vision taking the initiative in the resolution of their common problems — boundary or otherwise — and in the worthwhile shaping of the destiny of their long-suffering continent.

The partition of the Somali is a human dilemma undergirded by an ungenerous economic order and exacerbated by the hostile relations of the governments of the region. Its solution — or at least amelioration — requires bold and imaginative leadership that can reason together in a spirit of mutual cooperation and respect in order earnestly to explore ways of resolving the problem. Given the necessary vision and imagination, some sort of compromise solution satisfactory to all parties concerned is possible. Is it not possible, for example, for Ethiopia and Kenya to give internal autonomy to their Somali subjects, a limited self-rule which will give the inhabitants the opportunity to run their internal affairs, allowing them to remove border restrictions and to plan joint economic ventures with their neighbouring kinsmen in the Somali Republic, while remaining parts of Kenya and Ethiopia in external and security matters? Moreover, Kenya and Ethiopia could do much to defuse tension by withdrawing their military garrisons which the Somali regard as occupation armies. In return, the Somali should recognise the emotional, if not the economic, importance of these territories to Ethiopia and Kenya and should therefore desist from all secessionist agitations, especially the guerrilla operations which have tended to sap the economic and manpower resources of the two countries, as well as of Somalia, and which have plunged the whole region into a depth of misery and destruction from which no one can hope to emerge a winner.

Three objections, two by Kenya and Ethiopia and one by Somalia, could possibly be raised to the proposed compromises. The first is that the creation of autonomous entities in parts of Kenya and Ethiopia may inspire other regions of these countries to seek similar arrangements, a prospect that could undermine the strong, centralist principle of government pursued by these two states, and could ultimately destabilise their societies. Admittedly, the giving of self-rule to the Somali may entail risks for Ethiopia and Kenya, though no one can be certain that it would. On the other hand, one can be certain, as the past twenty years have only too painfully shown, that the continuation of the *status quo* (whereby large segments of Kenya and Ethiopia are inhabited by an alienated, hostile population who feel themselves colonially occupied by the very governments which claim to represent them) holds the gravest of risks for the future stability and prosperity of both these states.

The second objection stems from the plausible argument that the affairs of an autonomous NFD and/or Ogaadeen will be so dominated by Somalia — given Somalia's preponderant influence in these regions — that their governing entities are likely to pursue policies which are as inimical to the national interests of Kenya and Ethiopia as they are favourable to those of Somalia. This need not be the case. The example of the Republic of Jibuti is instructive here. Despite the fact that the political and economic life of this tiny nation is dominated by ethnic Somali, their government has managed to steer a strict course of neutrality between Ethiopia and Somalia. Now if, for political and economic reasons, the independent nation of Jibuti finds it prudent to remain neutral, is it not reasonable to argue that an autonomous Ogaadeen and NFD will be induced by the same considerations to avoid the pursuit of policies which will antagonise their parent governments and can therefore only serve to jeopardise their hard-won autonomous positions?

The third objection, and plausibly the most serious, concerns Somalia's likely reluctance to recognise the NFD and Ogaadeen as respectively parts of Kenya and Ethiopia and to abide by the norms of such recognition. Would it not be a bitter pill to swallow for Somalia, one may ask, to have to renounce, once and for all, her historic claim to these territories — over which her citizens have sacrificed so much in an as yet unrewarded attempt to return them to the national fold? What government in Somalia would be bold enough — or strong enough — to face the domestic political fury certain to be unleashed by the disappointed aspirations and disillusioned hopes of Somali nationalism, whose abiding dream has been to re-unify all the Somali under one Somali state?

Admittedly, it will be hard on Somali sensibilities to relinquish the old dream of national re-unification. Yet if in the lives of individuals, as of nations, there are times when it is prudent to question the wisdom of pursuing old dreams, the time may have come for the Somali to do just that, to pause for a moment of self-reflection to determine whether the elusive prize of re-unification is worth the cost of its pursuit. Paradoxically, the interests and welfare of the Somali may ultimately be better served by their repudiation of the abiding issue of re-unification, and by their readiness to enter into larger political and economic compromises with their neighbours which could pave the way for an eventual bringing together of the various nations of the Horn in a federation worthy of the children of the Queen of Sheba.

NOTES

1. London: Pall Mall Press, 1964, p. 8.
2. Reliable census data do not exist for the Somali population. I.M. Lewis estimates the number of Somali within the Somali Republic to be 3.5 million. See *The Modern History of Somaliland: From nation to state* (New York: Praeger, 1965), p. 1; cf. Said S. Samatar, 'Somalia', in Hassan S. Haddad and Basheer K. Nijim (eds), *The Arab World: A Handbook* (Wilmette, Ill.: Medina Press, 1978), p. 157.
3. The pastoralists speak of the Old Wench ('*Ajuuza*') who sows sedition and poisons relations between husbands and their wives.

4. Haud here refers to the central plateau of the Horn as opposed to the more limited area of northern Somalia ceded to Ethiopia by the British in 1948–54 which also carries this name.
5. See, for example, the recent work by Christopher Ehret, *Ethiopians and East Africans* (Nairobi: E.A.P.H., 1974), pp. 32–8. Cf. Bernd Heine, 'Linguistic Evidence on the Early History of the Somali People', in Hussein M. Adam (ed.), *Somalia and the World: Proceedings of the International Symposium* (Mogadishu: National Printing Press, 1979), pp. 23–7.
6. Bernd Heine, p. 29.
7. Herbert S. Lewis, 'The Origins of the Galla and Somali', *Journal of African History*, VII, I (1966), pp. 39–40.
8. Bernd Heine, p. 29.
9. See notes 5 and 7, and Harold Fleming, 'Baiso and Rendille: Somali Outliers', *Rassegna di Studi Etiopici*, XX (1964), pp. 35–96.
10. See, e.g., Shihab ad-Din's *Futuh al-Habash*, the main chronicle of Imam Ahmad Guray's 'The Left-Handed campaigns against Abyssinia in the 16th century', edited and verified by the Egyptian medievalist, Fahim M. Shaltut (Cairo: Hai-a al-Masriya Lilkitab, 1974).
11. D.A. Low, 'The Northern Interior', in Roland Oliver and Gervase Mathew (eds), *History of East Africa*, I (Oxford University Press, 1963), pp. 301–5.
12. E.E. Evans-Pritchard, *The Nuer* (Oxford University Press, 1940), pp. 16–50.
13. From Sayyid Mahammad's poem, 'Haliwaa Rag Hooyadi'. That camel milk is highly nutritious is shown by the fact that nomads who subsist on it almost solely, do not diminish in strength and their durability and resistance to the hard climate is proverbial. For a more detailed note on the role of camels in Somali life, see the present author's *Oral Poetry and Somali Nationalism: The case of Sayyid Mahammad 'Abdille Hasan* (Cambridge University Press, 1982).
14. Saadia Touval, *Somali Nationalism* (Cambridge, Mass.: Harvard University Press, 1963), p. 16.
15. The Earl of Lytton, *The Stolen Desert* (London: MacDonald, 1966), p. 99.
16. I.M. Lewis, 'The Politics of the 1969 Somali Coup', *Journal of Modern African Studies*, X, 3 (1972), p. 384.
17. David Laitin, *Politics, Language and Thought: The Somali Experience* (University of Chicago Press, 1977).
18. Andrzejewski and Lewis, *passim*.
19. Richard Burton, *First Footsteps in East Africa*, I (London: Tylston and Edwards, 1894), p. 82.
20. H. Munro Chadwick and N. Kershaw Chadwick, *The Growth of Literature*, Vol. II (Cambridge University Press, 1936), p. x.
21. J.W. Kirk, *A Grammar of the Somali Language* (Cambridge University Press, 1905); M. Maino, *La Lingua Somala — Strumento d'Insegnamento Professionale* (Alessandria: Ferrari, Occella and Co., 1953); Margaret Laurence, *A Tree For Poverty* (Nairobi: Eagle Press, 1954); Andrzejewski and Lewis, *Somali Poetry*.
22. Said S. Samatar, 'Gabay-Hayir: A Somali Mock Heroic Song', *Research in African Literatures*, XI, 4 (Winter, 1980), pp. 449–76.
23. See, e.g., Saadia Touval, pp. 25–9.
24. This characterisation of Somali poetry draws the people into the mainstream of the rest of Africa, as has been demonstrated in R. Finnegan, *Oral Tradition in Africa*, and A.I. Asiwaju, 'Efe Songs as a Source of Western Yoruba History' in Wande Abimbola (ed.), *Proceedings of the Seminar on Yoruba Oral Tradition, Drama and Music*, University of Ife, 1974.
25. Hodayo, Wardeer, and Dahare are names of water wells in the disputed Ogaadeen region of Ethiopia. Hananley is a grazing plain in the Ogaadeen.

26. Shabeelle River, in Ogaadeen country.
27. Harodigeet and Daalooki are grazing areas in the Ogaadeen.
28. Burton, *op. cit.*, I, p. 82.
29. 'The Periplus of the Erythraean Sea: Travel and Trade by a Merchant of the First Century A.D.', trans. from the Greek by Wilfred H. Schoff and reproduced in *Somaliya: Antologia Culturale*, 4 (Mogadishu: Ministry of Public Instruction, 1967).
30. A good discussion of the connections between Aden, the Somali coast and British India is in A.M. Brockett, 'The British Somaliland Protectorate to 1905', unpubl. diss., Lincoln College, Oxford University, 1969.
31. E. Starkie, *Arthur Rimbaud in Abyssinia* (Oxford: Clarendon Press, 1937), p. 1.
32. R. Coupland, *East Africa and its Invaders* (New York: Russell and Russell, 1965), p. 464.
33. M.S. Kiwanuka, *A History of Buganda* (London: Longman, 1971), pp. 160–6. Cf. R. Hill, *Egypt in the Sudan 1820–81* (Oxford University Press, 1959), *passim*.
34. For the extension of British influence in this region, see *Jubaland and the Northern Province* (Nairobi: n.p., 1917).
35. Foreign Office (Handbook), *French Somaliland* (London: Foreign Office, 1920), p. 19.
36. Robert Hess, *Italian Colonialism in Somalia* (University of Chicago Press, 1966), pp. v–vi.
37. A.H.M. Jones and Elizabeth Monroe, *A History of Abyssinia* (Oxford University Press, 1935), p. 137.
38. Harold Marcus, *The Life and the Times of Menelik II of Ethiopia* (Oxford: Clarendon Press, 1975), pp. 147–50, 152–3.
39. Starkie, p. 3.
40. *The Somali Peninsula*, p. 21.
41. I.M. Lewis, *The Modern History*, p. 50.
42. *Ibid.*, p. 50.
43. *The Somali Peninsula*, pp. 25, 30–1.
44. Starkie, p. 91.
45. For a scholarly discussion of Count Leontiev's career in Ethiopia and for Russia's ambitions in this region, see Czeslaw Jesman, *The Russians in Ethiopia: An essay in futility* (London: Chatto and Windus, 1958).
46. *Ibid.*, pp. 71, 88.
47. Marcus, p. 147.
48. This and the following two paragraphs are taken from my book *Oral Poetry and Somali Nationalism: The case of Mohamad Abdulle Hasan*. I am grateful to Cambridge University Press for permission to re-use them here.
49. Quoted in Sir Gerald Reece, *The British Survey*, Main Series 98 (London, 1952).
50. Quoted in Andrzejewski and Lewis, p. 57.
51. Margery Perham, *The Government of Ethiopia* (Evanston, Ill.: Northwestern University Press, 1969 edn.), p. 161.
52. This note and similar ones below are based on a 9-month field trip (1976–7) in Somalia and Kenya conducted as part of a Ph.D. dissertation research in history at Northwestern University. The project was funded jointly by the Social Science Research Council and Northwestern's Graduate School. The part of these notes (hereafter to be called Fieldnotes) utilised for this essay will be cited as follows: first, the name of the informant, then the nature of the material (identified by the word 'Fieldnotes'), then the place and date of interview. Thus, in the present example, we have: Isahaaq M. Daadi, Fieldnotes, Mogadishu, 24 April 1977. Isahaaq, 79, brother of the late Sultan Nuuh M. Daadi, is currently the hereditary chief of the princely house of the Arsi Oromo in southern

Ethiopia. He is active in the Oromo Liberation Front, at present fighting to gain autonomy from the central Ethiopian Government. For the history of the Ethiopian occupation of the Somali Ogaadeen, a valuable oral source is Sheikh 'Aaqib 'Abdullahi Jaama' of the Bartire Daarood around Jigjiga, Fieldnotes, Mogadishu, 27 April 1977.
53. Perham, p. 163.
54. Richard Pankhurst, 'The Great Ethiopian Famine of 1888–1892: A new assessment', II, *Journal of the History of Medicine and Allied Sciences*, 21, 1966; cf. Marcus, pp. 136–9.
55. Mahammad H. Huseen 'Sheeka-Hariir', 75, is one of two oral sources who provided this information. The other is Sheikh 'Aaquib 'Abdullahi Jaama', 65, mentioned in note 67. Sheeka-Hariir is from the Ogaadeen town of Dagahbuur and is renowned for his knowledge of the history of western Somalia. He claims to have learned the above information from his father who was one of the Ogaadeen elders to work out a *modus vivendi* with the Ethiopian Governor of Harar; Fieldnotes, Mogadishu, 25 March 1977.
56. Sheeka-Hariir, Fieldnotes, Mogadishu, 26 March 1977.
57. *L'Esplorazione del Giuba: Viaggio di Scoperta nel Cuore dell'Africa* (Rome: n.p., 1925), p. 24.
58. This point is also brought out by Robert Hess, 'The Poor Man of God — Muhammad Abdullah Hassan', in Norman R. Bennett (ed.), *Leadership in Eastern Africa: Six Political Biographies* (Boston University Press, 1968), p. 75.
59. B.G. Martin, *Muslim Brotherhoods in 19th Century Africa* (Cambridge University Press, 1979), p. 2.
60. Sadler to Salisbury, *Correspondence Respecting the Rising of the Mullah Muhammad Abd al-Allah Hassan in Somaliland and Consequent Military Operations* (hereafter referred to as *Correspondence*), 1, 21 April 1899, Cmd 597, 1901.
61. Harrington to Cromer, *Correspondence*, 6, 17 July 1899.
62. I.M. Lewis, *Modern History*, pp. 63–91, and Robert Hess, 'The Poor Man of God'.
63. Douglas Jardine, *The Mad Mullah of Somaliland* (London: Herbert Jenkins, 1923), p. 122.
64. These dates and the issues discussed are well documented in Drysdale, pp. 25–99.
65. *Ibid.*, p. 46.
66. *Ibid.*, pp. 48–9.
67. Aadan Low, who allegedly fired the first shot in the Italo-Ethiopian war of 1935, lived to become a cabinet member in the first Somali government in 1960.
68. From the anonymous pastoral poem, 'Ninkii Fakhriyow Xuduudka u Foof'.
69. Quoted in *The Somali Peninsula*, p. 8.
70. From the pastoral poem, 'Xoriyo waa Hubaaloo Xaylaa Nasiiyee' by an Ogaadeen poet, Qallaafo, 1961.
71. Some of these poems were broadcast over Radio Mogadishu as part of the welcoming ceremony for Jomo Kenyatta's visit to Somalia in 1962.
72. Republic of Kenya, *Statistical Abstract* (Nairobi: Ministry of Economic Planning, 1979), p. 13.
73. I.M. Lewis, *Modern History*, p. 191.
74. Sheeka-Hariir, Fieldnotes, Mogadishu, 25 March 1977.
75. Jardine, pp. 285–6.
76. Quoted in Richard Greenfield, 'The Fate of Harar and the Ogaden', *West Africa*, 5 Dec. 1977, p. 2447.
77. Sheeka-Hariir, Fieldnotes, Mogadishu, 25 March 1977.
78. Trans. by John Darton, 'A Barren Ethiopian Desert is Promised Land to Somalis', *New York Times*, 14 Sept. 1978, pp. 1, 7.

79. To support their case, the Somali tend to appeal to the provisions of self-determination in the OAU Charter (i.e. 'the inalienable right of all people to control their own destiny') while Ethiopia and Kenya bolster their case by citing the OAU Cairo resolution of 1964 urging member-states to 'respect the borders existing on their achievement of national independence'.
80. Mesfin Wolde-Mariam, *Somalia: The Problem Child of Africa* (Addis Ababa University Press, 1977), *passim*, esp. pp. 13–37.
81. Mesfin Wolde-Mariam, *The Background of the Ethio-Somali Boundary Dispute* (Addis Ababa: Haile Selassie I University, 1964).
82. Amnesty International, *Human Rights Violations in Ethiopia* (London: Amnesty International, 1978).
83. See, e.g., the belligerently anti-Ethiopian pamphlet, 'The Disastrous Damages of Ethiopian Aggression', put out by the Somali Ministry of Information and National Guidance (Mogadishu, 1978).

10

PARTITIONED CULTURE AREAS AND SMUGGLING
THE HAUSA AND THE GROUNDNUT TRADE ACROSS THE NIGERIA-NIGER BORDER FROM THE MID-1930s TO THE MID-1970s

David Collins

Introduction

As has been demonstrated in the foregoing case studies and more comprehensively in the checklist of partitioned African peoples (Appendix, pp. 253–9), the drawing of international boundaries through coherent culture areas has made it inevitable that peoples of the same race and culture are found in the immediate neighbourhood on both sides of the frontierlines. The particular part of the culture areas immediately affected by the boundary locations are mostly areas of established kinship ties. Thus cross-border social relations are made necessary on the basis not just of the broad fact of identical culture but even more by considerations of parental connections such as prevail almost everywhere in the predominantly rural continent of Africa, where the lineage has continued to count as the most important social unit.

Such situations pose obvious problems to the post-partition African states, based on the model of Europe-type nation-states and characterised by the phenomenon of precise and jealously guarded boundaries. However, the fact of identical culture on both sides of Africa's international boundaries has combined with their conventional character to make the boundaries something other than the barriers they were routinely assumed to be.

The ethnography of African international boundaries poses a permanent challenge to the role of modern state institutions designed to screen the movement of humans and materials into the areas of jurisdiction of the given states. Along most of the international borders, generally characterised by neglect and remarkable absence of governmental efforts to integrate the border-located communities into larger state societies, the local communities often have no choice but to persist in the pre-colonial mode of social relations. This runs counter to the theoretical demands of the new states and provides cover for activities which offend against their border-screening institutions.

In this essay we focus on the phenomenon of smuggling, a universal problem of all territorial states, as an example of anti-state activities that are facilitated, though not necessarily caused, by the fact of identical cultural landscape prevailing on both sides of an international boundary. In this regard, the smuggling of export crops should be seen as part of a wider network of activities featuring not only illegal trade in other goods but all forms of unauthorised movement of persons across state boundaries, including political refugees and even criminals who seek sanctuary from policies or laws operating on the side of the boundaries where they are normally resident. In other words this essay takes the broader view of smuggling as any effort to penetrate the screens instituted by the state to control the flow of persons and goods into its territory.[1]

While the emphasis is on the Hausa, partitioned by the Anglo-French colonial boundary which since 1960 has become the international boundary between the Republics of Nigeria and Niger, the point must be emphasised that the situation is not unique to this particular African locality. Within the Nigerian region, for example, the Hausa case is no more dramatic than that of the Yoruba, especially the Western sub-groups such as the Ketu, the Sabe, the Ifonyin and the Anago, who are split by the Nigeria-Benin boundary, which is also Anglo-French in origin. As studies of the Nigeria-Benin boundary by Alfred Mondjannagni and Robin Mills have shown, there has been much contraband trade there.[2] Indeed, as has been so clearly demonstrated in Ogunsola Igue's more recent published researches on the border, the smuggling of Western Nigerian cocoa into the Benin Republic through the predominantly Yoruba section of the international boundary during and immediately after the Nigerian civil war[3] was on the same scale and had the same policy implications as the clandestine movement of groundnuts back and forth across the Nigeria-Niger boundary by Hausa farmers and traders constantly in search of higher prices for their crops. These Nigerian examples can easily be expanded by the inclusion of several other African parallels including those of the Ewe astride the Ghana-Togo boundary with cocoa and coffee, of the Wolof and the Serer across the Senegal-Gambian boundaries also with groundnuts, with maize and coffee across the Chewa-inhabited section of the Zambia-Mozambique border, and with ivory across the Ethiopian-Sudanese border.[4]

Cultural and historical background

The Hausa whose culture area is under discussion are among the most studied and best known African peoples.[5] Although their communities, especially trading colonies, are known in most parts of West Africa and the Eastern Sudan, their actual homeland is the region occupied by what is referred to in the people's language as Kasar Hausa. The core area is made up of the territories of the traditional Hausa states of Daura, Katsina, Kano, Kebbi, Gobir, Zamfara, Rano, Zaria (Zazzau) and Garun Gabas (Biram). In the words of Mahdi Adamu, 'this was the area in which the majority of the people spoke Hausa as their first and only language and the cultural and social factors often associated with the Hausa people predominated.'[6]

The Nigeria-Niger boundary, which runs through the Hausa culture area, is one of the most conventional. Running mostly through the dry savanna and Sahelian regions, the alignment was initially defined in the Anglo-French Agreements of 1890, ratified by the British government in 1898 and by the French in 1899.[7] With further revisions, final agreements, which gave rise to the boundary more or less as it now is, were concluded only in 1904 and 1906. Demarcation by a succession of Anglo-French boundary commissions proceeded till 1910.

There was a total of 148 markers along the boundary, each of the two responsible European powers being responsible for the maintenance of half of this number. The failure to maintain the boundary markers and the ever-present necessity to give the boundary a consensual character led to further efforts to mark it out more clearly. Thus in 1910 the British, in their determination to demarcate it more precisely in areas of dense population such as Katsina Province, engaged local labour to dig a 208-mile trench along the boundary from Gidan Jibo to Jobi through Makerawa, Dabal, Kalgo, Sarkin Baka, Kulau, Sani, Kongolami, Dubsawa, Zango, Gazabi, Dando, Unguwar, Dashi and Babban Mutun.[8] But within a few years of this laborious effort, the trench, which was in any case disputed by the French, had fallen into disrepair.[9]

The location of the boundary had the characteristic effect of splitting the local culture area into two distinct colonial spheres. Particularly affected were the areas of the more northerly traditional Hausa states of Kebbi, Katsina and Daura. In Kebbi, the boundary placed Birnin Kebbi, the walled capital city of the state, in the British territory while related settlements such as Dagon Duchi, Matankai, and Filingue were located in the French colony of Niger.[10] Similarly in Katsina, the capital (Birnin Katsina) as well as traditional dependencies such as Igara, Yandole, Matazu, Gazaki and Maska were situated in the British territory while Tassawa (Tassoua on French maps) and Maradi were among closely related settlements placed within the French territory.[11]

But perhaps the traditional state which suffered most from the mutilating effects of the Anglo-French colonial boundary was Daura.[12] Though politically less prominent than Kano, Katsina or Zaria, Daura enjoyed the unique status and prestige among the Hausa of the type associated with Ile-Ife among the Yoruba. This was because of the importance attached to it as the first of the dynasties throughout Hausaland, popularly believed to have been created by descendants of Bayajida who, like Abraham of the Israelites, is acclaimed as the legendary ancestor of Hausa rulers. Partly as a result of this historical status and partly as a result of the need to secure the state and surrounding lands against the invasion of hostile neighbours such as the Tuaregs and the state of Zinder, Daura evolved into a confederation the area of which extended at the time of the nineteenth-century Fulani *Jihad* to cover the districts of Kwargwam, Matamaye, Botsotsunwa, Hawan Dawaki and Gabanouri and other places some 80 miles north of the present border. In the east, Daura influence, if not authority, was acknowledged by settlements and communities close to Zinder, including Dan Bartou, Tsatsumburoum, Magaria, Burma and Kance, all placed within the French territory. The remainder of the ancient Hausa state, including the capital Birnin Daura, was then located within the British colony.

Studies of the boundary impact on the Hausa indicate patterns and trends characteristic of most meeting points between French and British colonial administrations in West Africa. The findings in the first of such studies by the geographer Derrick Thom are remarkably similar to the assessment of the same impact elsewhere in West Africa, notably the Yoruba astride the Nigeria-Benin boundary.[13] The similarities include observable differences in the status and prestige of traditional rulers, those on the British side such as the Emirs of Kebbi, Katsina and Daura enjoying demonstrably much higher social status than their counterparts say in Maradi and Zinder in French Niger.[14] Then there was the mutually exclusive attitude of the Western-educated élite in consequence of parallel socialisation into the cultures of the European powers in control and the more general effect of the two socialisation processes on the indigenous culture, especially linguistically.[15]

Finally, there was the same pattern of reaction of the masses who, in their response to the relatively harsher policies of the French, often migrated in their thousands into the adjacent areas on the British side of the border, causing a higher population density there at the expense of the French side of the border. Such cross-border exodus spanned the whole of the colonial period up to the post-World War II reforms in French West African administration. On the Niger-Nigeria border, instances of the cross-border exodus included those of the Tuaregs settling in Northern Sokoto, and Hausa kinsmen, mostly from Mandara and Tessawa, crossing into Nigeria to create new border settlements such as Jibiya and Zandam and swell the size of existing communities such as Katsina, Daura and Kebbi. Through a policy of appointment of head chiefs from original '*Habe*' or Hausa ruling classes, the British succeeded in exaggerating a factor of great local historical significance that produced the desired effects of drawing the Hausa on to their own side of the border.[16] But fascinating as these other effects are, it is on the economic dimension of the boundary impact that we will now concentrate.

The groundnut movement

In considering possible stress arising from colonially created or superimposed international boundaries, Derrick Thom deals mainly with their impact as barriers. However he makes a clear distinction between different types of boundary movements, and furthermore makes no general assumption about the barrier effect of such boundaries. Rather, the extent to which a boundary is or might become a barrier is analysed in terms of four interrelated factors. These are (1) the natural features of the boundary; (2) government policies applied at the boundary itself (attempts, if any, to create a man-made physical barrier); (3) government policies adopted in the borderlands (the impact of the policy if any, in creating an acceptance for the boundary) and, above all, (4) the cohesiveness of the culture group or groups through which the boundary is drawn (the natural consensual basis for the boundary). Thom, who has analysed the Niger-Nigeria boundary in these terms, correctly concludes that this particular boundary has a limited impact as either a physical or consensual barrier.

Along this 1,600 km. boundary there is a notable absence of natural or man-made barriers. People of a common culture and language live on both sides of the border, sharing intimate knowledge of the thousands of bush trails connecting neighbouring markets and villages across the boundary.

At the level of international commerce, especially trade with Europe, the Niger-Nigeria boundary does have a much greater physical reality. The customs stations along major motor roads function to restrict the free movement of goods carried by motor transport. There is also little doubt that the presence of an international boundary 1,000 km. from the sea creates special problems for Niger's foreign trade. The modern economy of Niger is still largely dependent on the sale of its groundnut crop in Europe, and in his analysis of boundary impact Thom gives considerable attention to

Niger's problems in exporting this crop. These problems, however, are primarily a result of poor and costly transport and of lack of control over the allocation and development of transport facilities. Niger has no problems of access *per se*, and is guaranteed free transit through both Nigeria and Benin. By maintaining alternative routes to the sea and generally good relations with its neighbours to the south, Niger has worked hard to ensure that this formal guarantee has a real political base.

Thom sees the potential for stress in colonial and super-imposed boundaries as lying in the possibility that a physical barrier may be created which has little consensual reality. One can agree with Thom that this is not, and is not likely to be, the case for the Niger-Nigeria boundary. The remainder of this paper, however, will disagree with Thom's apparently logical conclusion that this boundary can thus 'be regarded as a stable boundary along which no problems . . . will occur, at least within the foreseeable future.'[17]

Using a source of data on local border movements not available to Thom, we shall attempt to show that an important sector of the modern state economy in Niger faces the possibility of severe disruption as a result of the international boundary with Nigeria. In the discussion which follows we shall have reference to the four categories suggested by Thom, especially the impact of government (economic) policies applied in the borderlands. The conceptual focus of this analysis, however, will be on potential stress resulting from the conduit effect of this boundary, and not its potential as a barrier. Like Thom we shall also be dealing with groundnuts, Niger's major export.[18] Our interest here, however, will not be with the difficulties in exporting this crop. Rather, we shall examine potential problems related to its acquisition.

The pattern of cross-boundary groundnut movements

The Magaria district (Niger) as a case study. Over 90 per cent of Niger's commercial groundnut crop is purchased in the four neighbouring districts of Maradi, Tessaoua (Tesawa), Matameye and Magaria, each of which has a southern border with Nigeria. These four border districts constitute the most productive and most heavily populated agricultural area in Niger. Together they form a narrow band roughly parallel to the northern boundary of present-day Kaduna and Kano States, an important groundnut-growing region in Nigeria. The Magaria district (which until the early 1960s included the smaller district of Matameye) is located to the east and north-east of the historic town of Daura in Nigeria, and to the south of the Zinder region in Niger. Since the mid-1930s, this area alone has annually contributed 35–50 per cent of Niger's total commercial groundnut crop destined for export to Europe. Magaria is typical of Niger's other major groundnut-producing districts in that a large number of its farmers live within walking distance of a groundnut buying station located in Nigeria. In 1970, seven such Nigerian buying stations were operating along Nigeria's 140 km. northern border with Magaria (Matameye). Similarly, nine out of eighteen of Magaria's groundnut markets (buying stations) could be considered border markets, capable of drawing numerous producers from Nigeria.[19]

In the 1969/70 groundnut buying season (November-March), for example, the price paid producers at groundnut markets in Magaria was 20–50 per cent higher than that offered at competing markets across the border in Nigeria. As a result, producers and middlemen buyers from towns up to 50 km. away in Nigeria regularly brought donkey-loads of groundnuts to sell at Magaria's border markets. These sellers from Nigeria would be paid the fixed price of 2,000 CFA francs per 100 kilos of shelled groundnuts, some even getting a cash gift from the buyer in addition. With their newly-acquired franc notes, they would next go to one of the several money changers in the market and buy cheap Nigerian pounds. At this time the local black-market (unofficial) exchange rate was 500 francs or less for one pound. These farmers would then return home to Nigeria having received at least £4 per 100 kilos of groundnuts sold, instead of the £2.7 to £3.3 being offered for an equal weight across the border in Nigeria.[20]

A second form of local cross-border groundnut trade, observed in this same buying season, involved middlemen buyers (*madugai*) from Niger going to Nigeria to buy groundnuts and then returning to sell them at markets at home. Such middlemen were often financed by private groundnut-buying companies operating there, and if this were the case their purchases could be quite large. For example, at the border buying station of Dogo-Dogo in Niger one could frequently observe the arrival of long groundnut caravans consisting of twenty or more camels. Each camel would carry two 80-kilo sacks of shelled groundnuts. These caravans, led by veiled Bouzou camel-drivers, would be returning from the work of a week or so buying groundnuts from farmers in Nigeria for re-sale in Niger.[21]

Estimates on the size and direction of past groundnut movements across Magaria's border with Nigeria are given in Tables 1 and 2 (pp. 213, 214). This information was obtained mainly from annual reports on the groundnut marketing season in Magaria (administrative achives, Magaria). Data on relative price advantage, on the direction of cross-border movements and qualitative estimates on the size of cross-border flows can be considered quite accurate as this is usually general knowledge in the border areas.[22]

Certain clear patterns emerge from these tables. In the early 1940s, as already noted, Magaria lost a large percentage of its groundnut crop to border markets in Nigeria ('large' losses are defined here as 20–40 per cent of Magaria's home-grown potential commercial crop). In the late 1940s and the 1950s there were frequent changes in both the size and direction of these cross-border movements, with the direction of flows occasionally changing even in mid-season. In the 1960s there was a definite pattern of large gains for Magaria (20–40 per cent of actual purchases) as a result of groundnuts from Nigeria being sold in Magaria's markets. Although somewhat diminished in absolute size (because of the drought), this movement of groundnuts from Nigeria into Niger continued through the 1974/5 buying season.

The direction of cross-boundary groundnut movements. The principal factor influencing a farmer's decision to cross the border to sell his groundnuts is the offer of a better price at markets on the other side. Past outflows of groundnuts from Niger also have been attributed to the lure of the *'atmosphère commerciale'* found in Nigeria. The cheaper imported merchandise and larger traditional weekly markets in Nigeria do draw many farmers and merchants from Niger's borderlands. With a price differential favouring groundnut-buying stations in Nigeria, this factor might well contribute to the size of outflows from Niger. However, neither common sense nor observed behaviour supports the view that a groundnut producer from Niger would sacrifice purchasing power simply to be able to sell his groundnuts in Nigeria, which he probably visits anyway twice or three times a month. Such a view would also require one to deny the well-documented existence since the early 1940s of an active local currency market. Price advantage in such cases was thus still determining the direction of cross-border flows.

The proximity of Nigerian buying stations has also been cited as a factor to explain past outflows of groundnuts from Niger.[25] Buying stations in the important Magaria district, however, have always been most heavily concentrated in the border areas. Even before the late 1950s, when the number of groundnut markets in Magaria was increased threefold, few producers would have found a buying station in Nigeria significantly closer. On the other hand, the large number of new groundnut markets in Magaria might well be important in diminishing the size of future groundnut outflows to Nigeria. Our research in Magaria would indicate that a producer living in a town with its own buying station probably requires a relatively greater price incentive to begin transporting groundnuts away from his home market. Such a producer is less likely to own already the donkeys or camels necessary for such transport. He is also more apt to have some strong family, financial or political tie with an individual buyer (weigher) in his local groundnut market.

Such speculation on the importance of more markets must be qualified, however, with the already noted fact that a 20–50 per cent price advantage in 1969/70 brought groundnuts into Magaria's markets from as far away as 50 km. to the south in Nigeria. There is little reason to believe that a similar price differential favouring Nigeria would not have an equal drawing impact on producers from Niger.

The size of cross-boundary groundnut movements. The magnitude of cross-border groundnut flows is generally recognised as being determined by the size of the price differential between competing border markets. Police patrols in a particular area might intimidate some would-be smugglers, but a relatively large difference in price will usually bring relatively large movements of groundnuts across the border. To be more precise than this is difficult, since there are problems in measuring both the price differential and the size of cross-border flows.

While the location of price advantage and the direction of border movements is usually quite clear, the actual size of price advantage may vary both within a single buying season and from one set of competing border markets to another.[26] In the past, higher prices have been fixed in both Niger and Nigeria for buying stations closest to railheads. Sharp competition between buyers may also somewhat raise the general level of prices at a particular buying station. In the early 1970s in Nigeria these seasonal and inter-market price differences still existed, whereas in Niger an effort to enforce a uniform annual producer price, applicable at any market, had been fairly successful.

The problem in measuring cross-border flows is that the only accurate data on groundnut production for Niger and Nigeria are commercial purchase figures. These commercial purchase figures do not include groundnuts consumed locally, sold as oil or cake, or held back for use or sale as seed. There is also a lack of base years (when few cross-border flows occurred) from which the size of border flows could be extrapolated. However, a comparison of the 1956/7 and 1959/60 buying seasons in Magaria does offer one possibility for an independent check on official estimates. In 1956/7 large movements of groundnuts into the Magaria district were reported, and were estimated to be around 8,600 tonnes or about 25 per cent of actual purchases. In the 1959/60 buying season only about 450 tonnes or 2 per cent of Magaria's purchases were estimated to have come from Nigeria. The 1956 groundnut harvest was rated as being 'below average', and that of 1959 as 'poor'. (Actual acreage planted in groundnuts was thought to have increased considerably between 1956 and 1959, a factor which should tend to balance out the better yields per acre reported for 1956.)

Subtracting 1959/60 purchases (22,640 tonnes) from those in 1956/7 (33,187 tonnes), and assuming local use to be constant, it would appear that about 10,500 tonnes or 30 per cent of 1956/7 purchases originated from Nigeria. This rough calculation would indicate that official estimates in 1956/7 on tonnage entering Magaria from Nigeria were probably somewhat conservative. In general, however, this calculation confirms the estimates in official reports where 'large' flows of groundnuts into the district were said to be equal to 20–40 per cent of Magaria's actual purchases, depending on the particular year.

The impact of cross-boundary groundnut movements. Table 3 contrasts actual groundnut purchases in Magaria with what purchases might have been if no cross-border movement had taken place. The record purchase years of the 1960s are especially interesting. Without inflows from Nigeria, purchases in Magaria during the 1960s would probably have been in the range of 35,000–50,000 tonnes. This tonnage would still have represented a large growth in purchases, but would not have been unexpected given estimated increases in acreage and the good groundnut harvests of the early and middle 1960s. In actual fact, however, purchases in Magaria (Matameye) surpassed the 60,000-tonne level in 1963/4, the 70,000-tonne level in 1965/6, and the 80,000-tonne level in 1968/9. Total purchases for Niger generally followed a similar pattern (see Table 4).

In the case of Magaria there is little doubt that an important factor in this surprising increase was the large and consistent inflow of groundnuts from Nigeria. In the period 1962/3–1965/6 it was estimated that a minimum of 20 per cent of Magaria's commercial purchase originated from Nigeria. From 1967/8 to at least 1970/1 these inflows, further stimulated by the weakness of the Nigerian pound and rising producer prices in Niger, increased to an estimated 30–40 per cent of the groundnuts purchased. Local marketing reports for other districts in Niger have not yet been examined. But Niger's price advantage held all along the border and, as noted, the other major groundnut-producing districts of Niger also border on Nigeria. In the 1969/70 buying season, for example, 50.1 per cent of total commercial purchases in Niger were made at buying stations located within 20 km. of the Niger-Nigeria boundary.[28] This fact is indicative both of where a large part of Niger's record tonnage of the 1960s came from, and equally of where it might have gone had price advantage been reversed.

Finally, two important points can be made about the impact of cross-border groundnut flows on purchases in Nigeria during this same period of the 1960s. First, while border movements in either direction are likely to be similar in terms of absolute tonnage, the relative importance of cross-border flows was much less significant for Nigeria. Secondly, although Nigeria was losing groundnuts to Niger throughout the 1960s, it too was enjoying record commercial purchases in this period. The previous Nigerian record of 714,698 long tons in 1957/8 was surpassed five times in the 1960s, with commercial purchases going above 1 million long tons in 1966/7 (see Table 4). In Niger, commercial purchases have never surpassed 191,307 tonnes (188,284 long tons).

Government pricing policy for groundnuts

If price differential is the principal factor determining the size and direction of cross-boundary groundnut movements, what then determines price differential? Since the early 1960s the answer to this question has quite simply been the government of Niger. In 1962 groundnut marketing in Niger was partly nationalised. This involved the establishment of a marketing board arrangement similar to that which had long existed in Nigeria.[29] Annual producer prices were set by government decree, and all buying companies effectively became employees of the Société Nigérienne de Commercialisation de l'Arachide (SONARA) — a para-public groundnut-exporting company responsible for all export and final sales of Niger's groundnuts. In the thirteen buying seasons subsequent to this state intervention in marketing, the Niger government explicitly used its producer-price-setting powers to manipulate the movement of groundnuts across its southern boundary with Nigeria. This policy has been eminently successful as is clear from the Magaria case. Since 1962 there have been no reported clandestine movements of groundnuts out of Niger, and in most years Niger has received large inflows from Nigeria. Turning now to the fourth factor listed by Thom — government policies adopted in the borderlands — this section will ask why, and how, the Niger government has turned its southern boundary into a conduit for Nigerian groundnuts. A probable, and for Niger inauspicious, 'turning of the tables' will be the subject of a concluding section.

Groundnut pricing policy in Niger. The reason why the government of Niger should wish to manipulate cross-border groundnut movements is in part self-evident from Niger's record groundnut purchases in the 1960s. Throughout that decade, groundnuts continually provided 60 per cent or more of Niger's recorded export earning, and much of the growth in the modern sector of the economy was dependent on the steady expansion of the groundnut trade. The increase of groundnut exports in this period, despite an often uncertain world market, was also encouraged by the structure of French foreign aid. Niger received considerable financial support from France in the form of higher-than-world-market prices and a guaranteed market for most of its groundnut exports.[30] To activate this aid, however, Niger had to supply the groundnuts.

Nevertheless, it would be incorrect to portray Niger's price-setting policy in the 1960s as entirely offensive, aimed only at drawing as many groundnuts as possible from Nigeria. A competitive producer price at Niger's border markets would bring groundnuts from Nigeria; however, it would also ensure that groundnuts grown in Niger would be sold in Niger. For the Niger government the necessity of such a defensive pricing policy was clearly shown in 1960/1, and the loss of groundnuts to Nigeria in this first buying season after independence caused great consternation in official reports.[31] This concern was, of course, not shared by producers living in the border areas, nor were the higher prices in Nigeria in 1960/1 viewed with particular disquiet by the private buying companies. Faced that year with an uncertain export market in Europe, many of these companies were not interested in purchasing beyond the tonnage covered by firm contract.[32] This caused the Commandant of Magaria to comment on 'the notorious lack of effort of the local buying companies ... because of an alleged difficulty in placing groundnuts in France'.[33] When, however, SONARA assumed all responsibility for exports in 1962, and these private companies came to be paid on a straight per-ton-purchased basis, they too joined transporters, merchants, processors and central bank and other government officials in the view that groundnuts lost to Nigeria threatened the economic wellbeing of Niger.

This perceived necessity of maintaining a groundnut producer price competitive with Nigeria's was in fact a policy priority which involved considerable frustration for officials in Niger. Niger had massive development needs, and because of impending European Common Market legislation, it was also faced with the imminent loss of the protected French market. Yet any attempt to cut the producer price, so as to raise revenue or lower the cost price of groundnuts involved the threat of a serious drop in commercial purchases. In the early and middle 1960s, rather than being able to lower producer prices, the government often found itself reluctantly being forced to raise prices. The following excerpt from a letter written by the President of Niger is illustrative:

The 1965/66 groundnut buying season will be distinguished by a rise in producer prices resulting from Niger's alignment with similar decisions in this area taken in Nigeria. On [this] point I feel it is necessary to eliminate any ambiguity. The decision taken by authorities of Northern Nigeria leading to a rise in producer price for groundnuts creates significant difficulties in Niger. It is certain that [this] rise in producer price — though always desirable on the social level — will raise difficult problems.[34]

A unique situation arose in the 1969/70 buying season in Niger. Far from the usual attempt to draw groundnuts from Nigeria, there was rather an initial effort to limit inflows. The producer price, which was already above that in Nigeria, was raised in 1969 to offset the devaluation of the CFA and the French franc. Because a bountiful harvest was expected in Niger and inflows from Nigeria increased because of this price rise, it was feared that final purchases would surpass pre-season contract sales already made in Europe. Orders were accordingly given to confiscate groundnuts coming from Nigeria, and close the scales of weighers who purchased Nigerian groundnuts. However, the optimism over purchases, with which the 1969/70 buying season began, quickly faded:

The buying season began with a general feeling of optimism. It was believed we would be marketing about the same quantity of groundnuts as in 1967/68 (181, 823 tons [*sic*]). As a result the authorities judged that it was not necessary to attract groundnuts from Nigeria.

Quickly, however, this optimism came face to face with a less attractive reality. It was apparent that only with difficulty would purchases this year attain the level of last year, that is 163,732 tons. This caused the authorities to do a turn-about on their decision: it was requested that the maximum possible number of groundnuts be let in from Nigeria.[35]

More interesting than *why* Niger would want to manipulate cross-border groundnut movements is the question of *how* this was possible. This is of particular interest in that Nigeria enjoys a natural competitive advantage over Niger because of lower transport costs to the European market.

In part this question has already been answered. In the period 1954–67, as earlier in 1933–7, French price supports for Niger's groundnuts largely off-set Nigeria's lower cost price. Also, the absolute size of commercial purchases in Nigeria meant that Marketing Board officials there usually showed little concern over the impact of cross-border groundnut movements. At times of good harvest and falling world market prices, officials in Nigeria might even have welcomed Niger finding a market for part of their export crop. As noted, this nonchalance over border losses was certainly not shared by marketing officials in Niger. Competition for border area groundnuts in the 1960s was thus often a one-man game, played by Niger alone.

A change in groundnut producer pricing policy by the Northern Nigeria Marketing Board is, however, the key difference between the competitive situation of the 1950s and that of the 1960s. As this change in policy was to lead to a decade of artificially low producer prices in Nigeria, it is also the principal factor in explaining how Niger was able to compete so successful for border area groundnuts.

Groundnut pricing policy in Nigeria. In 1962, the Northern Nigeria Regional Government relieved the Marketing Board of its task of subsidising producer price in years when the world market was poor. The price-setting powers of the Board were henceforth to be used primarily to mobilise funds for 'development' and not to support the producer price in lean years.[36] Potential producer profit, already lowered by produce and export tax, was now to be further diminished by the Marketing Board also taking its cut.

This had definitely not been the case in the 1950s. Indeed, the accounts of the Northern Nigeria Marketing Board from its creation in 1954 through 1961/2 show that it actually transferred to groundnut producers about 8.4 million *naira* (£4.2 million) more than it earned from sales of their crop (see Table 5).[37] Throughout most of the next decade, however, the Board followed just such a policy of artificially lowering the producer price. This policy was followed despite the continued existence of large financial reserves accumulated in the pre-1954 period.[38]

From 1962/3 through 1965/6, the producer price was fixed so that each year the Board showed a profit in its groundnut trading operations. In 1966/7 the need to maintain political support following the change in regime and at the outbreak of the civil war, protected producers from the full impact of a fall in world prices. From 1968/9 through 1971/2, however, the Board returned to a policy of low producer prices. Despite a steadily rising world market price for groundnuts, the producer price in Nigeria remained below the 1967/8 level of 70 *naira* per long ton. The overall result of this policy, shown in Table 5, was a surplus for the Board of 27.89 million *naira* from groundnut trading in the decade following the 1961/2 buying season.

The very low producer prices offered in the late 1960s and early 1970s in Nigeria and the continued weakness of the Nigerian pound relative to the CFA franc combined to produce a situation where Niger enjoyed the best of all worlds: a competitive producer price in the border areas, a 'socially desirable' rise in the producer price, and the accumulation of large surpluses from its groundnut trading operations. In 1967/8 SONARA had had to draw on its reserve fund to pay even the low (but competitive) producer price of 18,200 francs per tonne. In 1968/9 and the succeeding three years, the producer price not only rose to a level of 23,000 francs, but there were also transfers of respectively .47 billion francs, 1.06 billion francs, 1.67 billion francs and 1.35 billion francs to Niger's development and stabilisation fund.

A probable reversal of the conduit impact

Since the early 1960s the government of Niger has been able to manipulate successfully the movement of groundnuts across its long and porous southern boundary with Nigeria. The success of this policy has been based on three factors discussed above: direct French support for Niger's groundnut exports, a relative indifference to cross-border groundnut movements on the part of Marketing Board officials in Nigeria, and the maintenance of artificially low producer prices in Nigeria. At present, however, this favourable conjunction of factors is in the final stages of dissolution. French support for Niger's groundnut exports was replaced by far less protective European Common Market (EEC) aid. Direct external support now depends on the level of world market prices and the profitability of Niger's groundnut sales. The Common Market did provide subsidy payments of around 460 million CFA francs in 1967/8, the first year that all Niger's groundnuts were sold at world market prices. In the late 1960s and early 1970s, however, no further direct price support was forthcoming because of the sharp improvement in world market prices.

Of more immediate concern for Niger was the fact that by 1972 in Nigeria government officials, the Marketing Board and the press had begun to show considerable agitation over the smuggling of groundnuts into Niger. This concern was definitely something new although, as Table 2 indicates, the flow of groundnuts into Niger was not new. The new agitation in Nigeria might not have been unconnected with a general heightening of sensitivity about state security stimulated by the civil war. This sensitivity was especially high in view of the need to increase foreign exchange earnings so as to be able to prosecute the war successfully.[46]

Anxiety in Nigeria over clandestine cross-border sales corresponded, not surprisingly, with a period of rapidly rising prices on the world market and a severe falling-off in Marketing Board purchases (see Tables 4 and 5). In 1969/70 commercial purchases in Nigeria hit a nine-year low, and the 1970/1 and 1971/2 buying seasons were the worst for purchases since 1950/1.

Claims from Nigeria in 1971/2 that it had lost up to 100,000 long tons to Niger were clearly exaggerated. Total purchases for Niger in this buying season were only 143,000 long tons. Nevertheless, in 1972/3 there was a concerted effort in Nigeria to stop these outflows of groundnuts. This was done by heavy police patrols along the border, an increase in the producer price, and apparent direct negotiations with Niger to establish a uniform producer price. In 1972/3, for the first time in ten years, producer prices were raised in Nigeria: from 67.60 to 80.60 *naira* per long ton. This would have brought prices at Nigeria's border markets in line with the 24,000 francs per tonne paid to producers in Niger, if Niger had not secretly raised prices in mid-season to 26,000 francs at certain border markets — and only at border markets.[47]

The threat to Niger's competitive price advantage is, however, much more serious than that implied by Nigeria's simply showing a new interest in what had formerly been a one-man game. The decline in Marketing Board purchases in the early 1970s was recognised by most observers as only partly a result of produce smuggling and poor weather. As a result of the relatively low Marketing Board prices of the late 1960s and early '70s, many groundnut producers were thought to have switched to other more profitable crops, or to be withholding groundnuts from the Marketing Board and selling them on the now competitive indigenous market. This in any case was the judgment of the Federal Government. In early 1973, the First Progress Report on Nigeria's 1970–4 Development Plan announced that a review of the marketing board system was in progress, and further stated:

The indications show that the system as presently operated discourages increased efforts and production by the farmers. The stagnation in the output and export of some cash crops is attributed to the marketing board system.[48]

This harsh criticism was soon followed by action. By the 1974/5 buying season the Federal government had taken over the power to fix the producer price, formerly the prerogative of the regionally based marketing boards; eliminated all export and produce tax on marketing board crops; and, in the specific case of groundnuts, raised the producer price 105 per cent over its level in 1972/3.

The impact of these reforms on groundnut purchases has so far been blunted by the effects and aftermath of drought. The 1973 groundnut harvest failed completely in many areas of Nigeria and Niger. Through 1974/5, commercial purchases remained abnormally low in both countries. In Nigeria (less so in Niger) growing urban demand, inflation, and shortfalls in production continue to present farmers with viable alternatives either to growing groundnuts or to selling them to the Marketing Board.

The drought-related West African groundnut shortages have also kept world market prices high. These high prices, plus the renewed strength of the CFA franc in border currency markets, enabled Niger to meet and even beat the producer price increases in Nigeria.[49] The future is bleak, however, for the para-public groundnut marketing system in Niger.

If Nigeria were simply attempting to stop smuggling or to regain the purchase levels of the 1960s, producer price rises might possibly be limited by some consideration for Niger, for instance through a joint agreement to harmonise groundnut prices in the border areas.[50] The objective of the Nigerian government in maintaining high producer prices, however, has evolved far beyond this. Oil-rich Nigeria, at the height of its oil boom, launched a 30 billion *naira* Third Development Plan for the 1975–80 period, in which 'priority will be given to those programmes and projects directly benefiting the rural population, particularly projects to increase the income of small-holder farmers....'[51] The Federal government's producer price-fixing power was seen as a major tool for accomplishing this objective. As stated in the Development Plan,

The overall strategy of the Plan is simple. Due to development in the oil sector substantial resources are becoming available to Nigeria. Since oil is a wasting asset, it is the development strategy of the government to utilize the resources from oil to develop the productive capacity of the economy and thus permanently improve the standard of living of the poeple. (Third Plan, p. 30)

To facilitate income re-distribution and increased agricultural production, the operation of the new marketing board system will be geared to the payment of reasonably high prices to farmers. (Third Plan p. 34)

Although the [previous] Second National Development Plan identifies wages and salaries as the most sensitive aspect of income policy, events which have occurred since 1969 have demonstrated that drastic falls in rural incomes can be equally explosive. For this and other reasons, government has taken policy measures to increase producer prices in respect of agriculture exports. As indicated ... this policy will be carried much further during the Third Plan Period (Third Plan, p. 35).

In Nigeria earnings derived from groundnuts are viewed as a very minor element in the country's export economy.[52] Marketing board policies can quite painlessly be shaped with social equity and long-term goals in mind. For Niger, however, the picture is different. The country is still very poor, and dependent on agricultural exports, especially groundnuts. Yet in the future it will be faced with the choice either of subsidising the groundnut producer price or of seeing Nigerian markets dominate the competition for 'border area groundnuts', a category which in the late 1960s easily included up to 50 per cent of Niger's commercial purchases. Soon after the presentation of the Third Development Plan early in 1975 a further 54 per cent increase in the producer price for groundnuts was announced, and the Marketing Board was offering farmers the previously unthinkable price of 254 *naira* per long ton.[53]

Conclusion

An international boundary which is largely unpatrolled and unpatrollable, which has little consensual or physical reality at the local level, where its existence is more or less completely blurred by the prevalence of an identical culture area, is probably best conceived of not as a barrier but as an inter-state pathway, a conduit, an incentive to movement not only of persons but also of trade goods. Many of the colonially created boundaries of Africa are as porous at the local level as that which separates Niger and Nigeria. Yet this characteristic has seldom been emphasised. Equally neglected is the impact of resultant border movements on the national economy, or on inter-state relations.

Cross-boundary movements which are undocumented, usually extra-legal, and sometimes the result of an explicit policy of 'beggar my neighbour' do pose special research and policy problems. This neglect might also be partly explained by the implicit assumption of a stand-off or balancing effect acting to minimise the final importance of such movements. One might well hypothesise that, where the economies of neighbouring states are of similar importance or where there is a definite mutual dependence in their relations, there is likely to be a natural limit on the total loss or gain from such boundary movements. Significant gains for one state would be more immediately felt as a significant loss for a neighbour. Retaliation would also be both possible and probable.

In an unequal relationship, however, there is a real possibility that for certain sectors of trade such a porous boundary could become a one-way conduit for the movement of goods and people. Resources which a poor state siphons off the borderlands of a richer neighbour may go unnoticed or be considered insignificant.[54] Alternatively, a weak state may find that policies adopted in the borderlands of a more powerful neighbour have harmful but uncontrollable repercussions on the pattern of local border movements.

To disregard either of these possibilities or to think of boundaries only as barriers, in the Niger case at least, is to neglect both the actual benefits and the potential danger bequeathed to Niger through the legacy of its colonially created boundaries. The obvious challenge to policy implied by this case study can be met only by the arrangement, assumed in the protocols setting up regional organisations like the Economic Community of West African States (ECOWAS), which would encourage if not compel affected member-states to harmonise their economic policies, including their prices.

Table 1

PRICE ADVANTAGE, DIRECTION OF GROUNDNUT MOVEMENTS, BETWEEN COMPETING BORDER MARKETS IN NIGERIA AND THE MAGARIA DISTRICT, NIGER

Buying seasons	Price advantage[a]	Direction border flows
1935/6–1936/7	Magaria district	n.a.
1937/8	Nigeria	n.a.
1938/9–1945/6	Nigeria	To Nigeria
1946/7	Prices equal	n.a.
1947/8	Magaria	To Magaria, then Nigeria[b]
1948/9–1949/50	Magaria	To Nigeria, then Magaria[c]
1950/1	Magaria	To Nigeria, then Magaria
1951/2–1952/3	Nigeria	n.a.
1953/4	Prices equal	To Nigeria[c]
1954/5	Nigeria, then Magaria	To Nigeria, then Magaria
1955/6–1956/7	Magaria	To Magaria
1957/8–1958/9	Nigeria	To Nigeria
1959/60	Magaria	To Magaria
1960/1	Nigeria	To Nigeria
1961/2	not available[d]	n.a.
1962/3–1965/6	Magaria	To Magaria
1966/67	First equal, then Magaria	n.a.
1967/8–1971/2	Magaria	To Magaria
1972/3	First equal, then Magaria	To Magaria
1973/4	Prices equal	Few flows
1974/5	Magaria	To Magaria

Sources: 1935/6–1969/70, Annual *Rapport sur la traite des arachides*, Administrative Archives, Magaria; 1970/1–1974/5, interviews, Niger and Nigeria.
(a) Niger and Nigerian market prices compared on the basis of local border CFA franc/pound exchange rates at the time.
(b) Normal market operations disrupted in Magaria.
(c) Flows to Nigeria took place before Magaria's markets had opened.
(d) Prices equal, if not higher, in Magaria's markets.

Table 2
MAGARIA (MATAMÈYE) DISTRICT, NIGER: ESTIMATED SIZE OF CROSS-BOUNDARY GROUNDNUT MOVEMENTS

Buying season	Magaria's losses to Nigeria[a]	Magaria's gains from Nigeria[b]
1935/6	n.a.	n.a.
1936/7	n.a.	n.a.
1937/8	n.a.	n.a.
1938/9	medium	none
1939/40	large (5,500 tons)	none
1940/1	very large	none
1941/2	large	none
1942/3	n.a.	none
1943/4	large	none
1944/5	n.a.	none
1945/6	large	none
1946/7	n.a.	n.a.
1947/8	large	large
1948/9	medium-large (5,000 t.)	small (400 tons)
1949/50	medium (750 t.)	small (70 t.)
1950/1	n.a.	n.a.
1951/2	large (8,000 t.)	none
1952/3	large (750 t.)	none
1953/4	small-medium	none
1954/5	small (500 t.)	large (6,500 t.)
1955/6	none	large (10,000 t.)
1956/7	none	large (8,600 t.)
1957/8	medium (3,000 t.)	none
1958/9	small-medium (2,000 t.)	none
1959/60	none	small (450 t.)
1960/1	medium-large (5,000 t.)	none
1961/2	none	n.a.
1962/3	none	large
1963/4	none	large
1964/5	none	large (10,000 t.)
1965/6	none	large
1966/7	n.a.	n.a.
1967/8	none	large (21,000 t.)
1968/9	none	large (33,000 t.)
1969/70	none	large

Source: Annual *Rapport sur la traite des arachides*, Administrative Archives, Magaria.

(a) Large losses equal 20–40% of Magaria's home-grown potential commercial crop; medium equal about 10%; small equal less than 5%.

(b) Large gains equal 20–40% of Magaria's actual purchases; medium *c.* 10%; small less than 5%.

Table 3
MAGARIA GROUNDNUT PURCHASES CONTROLLED FOR CROSS-BOUNDARY MOVEMENTS

Buying season	Actual purchases[a]	Adjusted purchase[b]	Usual harvest (if noted)
1935/6	16,596	n.a.	
1936/7	23,260	n.a.	'excellent'
1937/8	17,000	n.a.	
1938/9	16,400	n.a.	
1939/40	10.900	16,400	
1940/1	400	n.a.	
1941/2	7,300	n.a.	
1942/3	n.a.	n.a.	
1943/4	2,293	n.a.	
1944/5	5,472	n.a.	
1945/6	3,900	n.a.	
1946/7	10,200	n.a.	
1947/8	20,370	20,400	
1948/9	22,415	27,000	'very good'
1949/50	6,783	7,500	'very poor'
1950/1	n.a.	n.a.	
1951/2	18,680	26,700	'very good'
1952/3	19,250	26,800	
1953/4	26,162	n.a.	
1954/5	30,690	24,700	
1955/6	41,114	31,100	
1956/7	33,187	24,600	
1957/8	37,154	40,200	'excellent'
1958/9	29,460	31,500	
1959/60	22,610	22,200	'poor'
1960/1	29,121	34,100	
1961/2	28,321	n.a.	
1962/3	47,514	n.a.	
1963/4	66,033	n.a.	
1964/5	50,354	40,400	
1965/6	70,328	n.a.	
1966/7	78,265	n.a.	'very good'
1967/8	69,536	48,500	
1968/9	83,406	50,400	
1969/70	76,142	n.a.	

(a) Magaria-Matamèye district, tonnes, shelled, *Source:* Annual *Rapport sur la traite* . . . . , Magaria.
(b) To the nearest 100 tonnes. Compiled from quantitative estimates in Table 2: Adjusted purchases = Actual purchases *plus* Border losses *minus* Border gains.

Table 4

GROUNDNUT PURCHASES, NIGER AND NIGERIA
(Note: 1 tonne = 0.98 long ton).

Buying season	Purchases Niger (tonnes, shelled)[a]	Purchases Nigeria (long tons, shelled)[b]
1954/5	61,000	372,776
1955/6	97,800	530,215
1956/7	79,100	357,932
1957/8	100,200	714,698
1958/9	83,920	533,354
1959/60	57,556	445,441
1960/1	75,000[c]	619,051
1961/2	62,500	687,986
1962/3	91,848	817,518
1963/4	114,13	785,859
1964/5	106,361	675,884
1965/6	156,081	937,999
1966/7	191,307	1,026,822
1967/8	182,675	687,439
1968/9	163,731	770,917
1969/70	164,867	645,381
1970/1	130,136	281,322
1971/2	145,249	301,755
1972/3	109,674	545,226
1973/4	25,553	42,202
1974/5	89,734	157,780

(a) *Source:* Société nigérienne de commercialisation de l'arachide (1974/5, as of 4 April 1975).

(b) *Source:* 1954/5 to 1968/9. Annual Report of the Marketing Board; 1969/70 to 1973/4. Research Unit, Northern States Marketing Board, Kaduna, 1974/5. *New Nigerian*, 11 July 1975, p. 16.

(c) 1954/5 and 1960/1, Niger, approximate figures only.

Table 5
NORTHERN STATES MARKETING BOARD (NIGERIA), PRICES AND RESULTS

Buying season	Producer price (Naira/long ton)[a]	Export price (Naira/long ton)[b]	Trading surplus (million Naira)
1954/5	71.18	115.79	−2.37
1955/6	70.83	122.94	+2.15
1956/7	64.83	135.72	+6.06
1957/8	74.83	105.30	−7.95
1958/9	67.83	110.22	−3.91
1959/60	72.83	124.70	+1.66
1960/1	74.83	119.80	−1.78
1961/2	67/33	113.57	−2.26
1962/3	60.68	108.24	+0.25
1963/4	60.78	114.60	+4.46
1964/5	65.33	134.48	+5.97
1965/6	68.43	126.61	+6.99
1966/7	65.40	—[c]	−0.58
1967/8	70.30	105.50	−15.66
1968/9	52.00	122.18	−1.14
1969/70	59.80	131.95	+15.8
1970/1	67/60	149.21	+9.2
1971/2	67.60	156.59	+2.6
1972/3	80.60	227.68	'large surplus'[e]
1973/4	94.25	—[d]	
1974/5	165.00	220.00[e]	
1975/6	254.03		

Source: 1954/5-1968/9, Annual Report of the Marketing Board; 1969/70-1975/6, Research Unit, Northern States Marketing Board, Kaduna.

(a) Not produce tax, 1954/5, price, standard grade, Kano area: 1955/6 — 1967/8, 'guaranteed net price', Kano buying station (standard grade 1955/6 and 1956/7, special grade thereafter): 1968/9-1975/6, minimum net producer price for all gazetted buying stations.
(b) Average export price (f.o.b.) received by Marketing Board.
(c) Not clear. Board withdrew from market when prices declined.
(d) Because of drought, few purchases and no sales. Purchases distributed as seed.
(e) Estimate only (NSMB).

NOTES

This essay, the only one in the book not written expressly for it, is the adapted and updated version of a journal article by the author, entitled 'The Clandestine Movement of Groundnuts Across the Niger-Nigeria Boundary', published in the *Canadian Journal of African Studies*, X, 2, 1976, pp. 259–76. The notes under 'Introduction' and 'Cultural and Historical Backgrounds' are the editor's while the rest of the chapter is as in the original article. We are grateful to the *Canadian Journal of African Studies* for permission to adapt this article for inclusion in this book.

1. This definition has benefited from the discussion of the phenomena of smuggling and border screen in J.A. Price, *Tijuana: Urbanization in a Border Culture* (University of Notre Dame Press, Indiana, 1973), pp. 163–72.
2. A. Mondjannagni, 'Quleques Aspects Historiques, Economiques at Politiques de la Frontière Nigéria-Dahomey', *Etudes Dahoméennes*, 1, 1963–64, pp. 17–59, and R. L. Mills, 'The Development of a Frontier Zone and Border Landscape along the Dahomey-Nigeria Boundary', *Journal of Tropical Geography*, 36, pp. 42–9.
3. O.J.P. Igué, 'Un Aspect des changes entre le Dahomey et le Nigeria: le commerce du cacao', *Bulletin de L'I.F.A.N.*, Dakar, série B, 3, 3, 1976, pp. 636–69; and his 'Evolution du commerce clandestine entre le Dahomey et le Nigéria depuis la Guerre de Biafra', *Canadian Journal of African Studies*, X, 2, 1976, pp. 235–57.
4. See the case-studies by S.H. Phiri and F.A. Renner. Also Z. Bahru (1976) and A. Akakpo (1974) in the Select Bibliography.
5. Studies of the Hausa include M. Adamu, *The Hausa Factor in West African History* (Zaria: Ahmadu Bello University Press and Oxford University Press, Nigeria, 1978); Y.B. Usman, *The Transformation of Katsina, 1400–1883* (Zaria: Ahmadu Bello University Press, 1981) and M.G. Smith, *The Affairs of Daura* (University of California Press, 1978). Each of these contains an excellent detailed bibliography.
6. Adamu, *op. cit.*, p. 1.
7. For a detailed history of the boundary, see Anene, *op. cit.*, ch. 7
8. G.A. Ma'adua, 'The Impact of the Border on Daura', B.A. essay, Bayero University, Kano, Dept. of History, June 1982, p. 23.
9. *Ibid.*
10. Adamu, *op. cit.*, map facing p. 1.
11. Usman, *op. cit.*, p. 248.
12. See Ma'adua, *op. cit.*, p. 17.
13. The first of these efforts is D.J. Thom, 'The Niger-Nigeria Borderlands: A politico-geographical analysis of boundary influence upon the Hausa' (unpubl. Ph.D. thesis, Michigan State University, 1970). The findings are remarkably similar to those in respect of the Yoruba astride Nigeria-Benin boundary as contained in Asiwaju, *Western Yorubaland . . .* , *op. cit.* (The one other major study is J.D. Collins, 'Government and Groundnut Marketing in Rural Hausa Niger: The 1930s to the 1970s in Nigeria', Ph.D. thesis, SAIS, Johns Hopkins University, 1974.
14. See, e.g., M. Crowder, 'Indirect Rule: The French and British Style', *Africa*, XXXIV, 1964, pp. 197–205.
15. The Scientific Committee directing the UNESCO *General History of Africa* (a series to be translated into Hausa) has faced the problem of the choice to be made between the Nigerian and *Nigérien* Hausa, the one heavily influenced by English and the other by French.

16. The Hausa states concerned were among the most resistant to the nineteenth century Fulani *Jihad*. Like the Sarkin Zazzau who led the exodus of his people to found Abuja further south, in protest against the Fulani conquest of Zaria, the Sarkin Katsina left for Maradi and his Daura counterpart for Yekuma; and the people then launched a permanent war against the new Fulani rulers of their original ancestral territories. It was this Hausa-Fulani hegemonic conflict which the British exploited in their pro-Hausa policy in the border region.
17. Thom, *op. cit.*, esp. pp. 24–6; and D.J. Thom, *The Niger-Nigeria Boundary 1890–1906: A study of ethnic frontiers and colonial boundaries* (Africa Series, no. 23, Athens, Ohio, University Center for International Studies, 1975), pp. 38–9.
18. The border area was not always so heavily populated. According to Thom, the present superimposed or artificial appearance of this boundary in Hausaland is the result of migration during the early colonial period. The area through which the present boundary is drawn was formerly a relatively sparsely-populated political frontier between the unconquered Hausa-speaking states to the north and the Fulani-dominated ones to the south. Thus, even in an historical sense Thom would question the term 'artificial' when applied to the present Niger-Nigeria boundary. Prescott and Anene both agree that the final Anglo-French boundary settlement of 1904 and 1906 gave heavy weight to this former political frontier. Anene, however, stresses 'how completely the peoples of the Central Sudan divorced trade from politics' (p. 263). See D. Thom, *A Study of Ethnic Frontiers*, pp. 34–41; J.R.V. Prescott, *The Evolution of Nigeria's International and Regional Boundaries, 1961–1971* (Vancouver: Tantalus Research, 1971) ch. 4: and J.C. Anene, *The International Boundaries of Nigeria* (London: Longman, 1970), chs. 7 and 8.
19. Thom, 'A Politico-Geographical Analysis', p. 232.
20. *Ibid.*, p. 232; and p. 242. Also his related 'A Study of Ethnic City . . . .'
21. Throughout the 1960s groundnuts and groundnut products consistently provided 60 per cent or more of Niger's recorded earnings from exports. This percentage fell somewhat in the 1970s with drought-related shortfalls in the groundnut crop, and increased exports of uranium — equal to 17.2 per cent by value of total exports in 1972.
22. Farmers may sell their groundnuts to a middleman buyer, but highest prices are obtained when groundnuts are sold directly to a buying company at an officially designated groundnut purchase and stockage station (market).
23. For example, the Niger border markets of Dan Tchiao and Dogo-Dogo received many groundnuts from Albasu, Garki, Dan Ladi and Dan Zomo in Kano State.
24. The gazetted minimum producer price in Nigeria in 1969/70 was £19 18s. 0d. long ton. Producers in the border regions of Nigeria were actually paid at a rate which varied from £27 5s. 0d, to a high of £34/long ton (from £26.82 to £33.46 per tonne).
25. In the 1970s in Nigeria there were allegations about two other forms of 'smuggling' not dealt with in this paper: groundnuts entering Niger from Nigeria by truck with the collusion of border guards, and groundnuts which never leave Nigeria, but which are given certificate of origin papers from Niger (see for example, *New Nigerian*, 3 March 1972, p. 4, and 11 Feb. 1975, p. 1; W. Okefie Uzoaga, 'Nigeria's Illegal Trade: Implications for Nigerian Revenue and Foreign Exchange Reserves', *Genève Afrique*, XIII, 1, 1974, pp. 46–8; and M.N. Ogbonna, 'Tax E Evasions in Nigeria', *Today*, 22, 1, 1975, pp. 57–9).
26. The small size of these inflows in the 1948/9 and 1949/50 buying seasons (see Table 2) was explained at the time by the very late opening of Niger's markets. The small inflows in 1959/60 were accounted for by the relatively small price advantage held by Niger's border markets.

27. Since 1954 the opening date for Niger's groundnut markets has been carefully aligned with that in Nigeria.
28. Yves Pehaut, *L'arachide au Niger* (Paris: A. Pedone, 1970).
29. Thus in late December 1960 there was a price differential (favouring Nigeria) of 16% between the competing border markets of Sasoumbouroum (Niger) and Zango-Daura (Nigeria); 20% between the competing border markets of Magaria town (Niger) and Babura (Nigeria); and 33% between the competing border markets of Dungass (Niger) and Maigatari (Nigeria). Letter no. 17/11C, from the Chef du Sous-Secteur Agricole, Magaria, December 1960, Administrative Archives, Magaria.)
30. Agriculture Service estimates show that the area planted in groundnuts in Magaria (Matameye) increased from 82,000 ha. in 1958 to 110,000 ha. in 1961, and to 146,000 ha. in 1966. This increase in acreage planted can be attributed primarily to a rapidly growing population, estimated to have increased from around 160,000 inhabitants in 1958 to 347,500 in 1968, in part as a result of immigration into the region.
31. Purchase figures for 1969/70 by market, supplied by SONARA.
32. State groundnut marketing began in Nigeria in late 1939 (see P.T. Bauer, *West African Trade*, London: Routledge and Kegan Paul, 1953 and 1964). In 1949 the Nigerian Groundnut Marketing Board was created out of the West African Produce Control Board. In 1954 groundnut marketing became the responsibility of the newly-created Northern Regional Marketing Board, which became the Northern Nigeria Marketing Board in 1961, and the Northern States Marketing Board in 1967.
33. On French (and later Common Market) support for groundnut exports, see I.M.F., 'Niger', *Surveys of African Economies*, 3 (Washington, DC, 1970); and Teresa Hayter, *French Aid* (London: ODI, 1966).
34. For example: 'This buying season ought to serve as a lesson to our government which in the future must make adequate measures to prevent the ruin of our national economy, which could bring a halt to the internal peace and tranquility in our young nation,' (letter no. 4/CF to the Président du Conseil des Ministres, Niamey, from the Commandant de Magaria, Djibrilla Maiga, 17 Jan. 1961, Administrative Archives, Magaria). A year-by-year analysis of Nigerian documents on groundnut prices and pricing policy is found in J.D. Collins, *Government and Groundnut Marketing*, ch. 4.
35. Letter no. 1874 MAE/AE/L, from the Minister of Economic Affairs, A. Mayaki, 6 Dec. 1960, Administrative Archives, Magaria.
36. Letter no. 4/CF, from the Commandant of Magaria, 17 Jan. 1961, Administrative Archives, Magaria.
37. Letter no. 72, to the Chefs de Circonscription, from Diori Hamani, 8 Nov. 1965, Administrative Archives, Magaria.
38. Niger, UNCC, *Rapport d'Activité: Les Commercialisations de Campagne 1969/ 1970*, by Y. Glorieux, Aug. 1970, 2, p. 4.
39. Gerald K. Helleiner, *Peasant Agriculture, Government, and Economic Growth in Nigeria* (Homewood, Ill.: Richard D. Irwin, 1966), pp. 172, 165–71.
40. H.V. Kriesel's adjusted figures show an even larger groundnut trading deficit for 1954/5–1961/2 (H.C. Kriesel, *Marketing of Groundnut in Nigeria* (CSNRD-19, Michigan State University, and Ibadan: NISER, 1968), pp. 14, 17, 21; see also Helleiner, pp. 163–6. *Note*: 1 Nigerian *naira* was then worth ten shillings.
41. In 1961, the Northern Nigeria Marketing Board's total earnings surplus (1947–61) was still an impressive £31.9 million (63.8 million *naira*) (G.K. Helleiner, p. 166).

The Hausa and the Nigeria-Niger boundary 221

42. SONARA, *Bulletin de liaison et d'information*, Niamey, numero special, 1973, pp. 6-9.
43. I.M.F., *Surveys of African Economies*, vol. 3, pp. 10 and 410-16.
44. As a signatory of the 1975 Lomé Convention between the EEC and forty-seven African, Caribbean and Pacific countries (ACP), Nigeria should also be eligible for participation in the 'Stabex' scheme which will compensate ACP countries for shortfalls in earnings from certain commodities exported to the EEC. However, as Nigeria has indicated that it will not draw on the much more important EEC European Development Fund, it is unlikely that it will be interested in 'Stabex' payments (see *West Africa*, 24 Nov. 1975, p. 1398).
45. E.g. 'NSMB Warning on Produce Smuggling', *New Nigerian*, 6 Oct. 1972, p. 1; 'The Truth about Produce Smuggling in Nigeria', *New Nigerian*, 3 Aug. 1972, p. 4: and 'Yahaya Gusau speaks on produce smuggling', *New Nigerian*, 17 Aug. 1972.
46. A similar agitation influenced the Nigerian Federal Military Government's stiff control measures to stop the new cocoa smuggling into the Benin Republic at the same time.
47. Producers selling at these border markets in Niger were led to believe that buyers had suddenly become extra-generous with their gifts. These 'gifts', however, had been officially authorised (confidential interviews, Zinder and Magaria, Dec. 1972).
48. Federal Republic of Nigeria, Second National Development Plan 1970-74: First Progress Report (Lagos: Central Planning Office, 1972), p. 66.
49. The local value of the *naira*, worth over 300 CFA francs in late 1972 and 1973, had fallen to a value of only 250 CFA by April 1975. The *naira* officially floats with the dollar, and the CFA franc is tied to the French franc. The weakness of the *naira* on local currency markets is explained primarily by currency restrictions imposed during the civil war and maintained by Nigeria despite a petroleum-financed post-war economic boom.
50. A commitment to harmonise the producer price for major export crops might also be achieved through the auspices of some wider economic union such as the Economic Community of West African States (ECOWAS), established in 1975, and largely fostered by Nigeria. Such a future commitment, however, is conspicuously absent from the ECOWAS treaty (see *West Africa*, 16 June 1975, pp. 678-9).
51. Federal Republic of Nigeria, Third National Development Plan 1975-80, 1 (Lagos: Central Planning Office, 1975), p. 30.
52. Of the 46 billion *naira* total export earnings projected for the Third Plan period (1975-80), 44 billion were to be from oil exports, and only about 4 billion, or less than 1% of projected earnings, from groundnut and groundnut product exports. (Third Plan, pp. 59, 47.)
53. Niger's official groundnut producer price was not announced until the opening of the 1975/6 buying season, and it remained unchanged from the previous year. For purchasers in both Niger and Nigeria, however, these official prices had little meaning, Groundnuts were in extremely short supply as a result of pest attacks and an epidemic of rosette groundnut virus.
54. Such was the case with the smuggling of cocoa from Nigeria into Dahomey from 1969 to 1975. Although the impact was seriously felt by Nigeria, it would obviously have been worse for Dahomey (present-day Benin Republic) were she to be in the position of Nigeria at the time (see Igue, 'Un Aspect...', op. cit.).

Part III

11
PARTITIONED GROUPS AND INTER-STATE RELATIONS

Saadia Touval

The subject of this chapter is the reactions of the independent African states to the problems raised by the partitioning of cultural groups by international boundaries. To limit the discussion to manageable proportions, we confine ourselves to the policies of the central governments and omit the many important problems with which the local authorities along the frontiers are concerned.

The partitioning of cultural areas and groups has confronted the independent African states with two major problems: (1) whether to accept the partition and the boundaries inherited from the colonial period or to demand their revision; and (2) what attitude to adopt when the solidarity within a partitioned group leads to the involvement of those who live in one country in civil strife in the neighbouring state.

Support for the status quo

It is noteworthy that after their emergence to independence only four African states rejected the boundaries inherited from the colonial period, and sought to have them drastically altered. Three of these — Somalia, Togo, and Ghana — justified their policies on the grounds that the boundary cut across ethnic groups which had the right to be united and incorporated within one state. The fourth, Morocco, demanded boundary revisions on historical grounds, and thus will not concern us here.

That so few states sought to rectify the boundaries indicates that only a few of the innumerable partitioned groups openly sought to unite with their brethren in a single state. The rarity of such demands can be attributed largely to two main factors: (1) the ethnic and cultural structures of the states, and (2) the regime along the partition boundary.

Most African states are multi-ethnic and include groups that have been partitioned by the international border. Where the state as a whole is multi-ethnic, partitioned groups usually do not feel themselves threatened as an alien minority in a state ruled by a single dominant group. Rather, *all* the ethnic groups in the state are 'minorities'. They do not have equal influence, but the pluralistic structure of the state generally makes it possible for a disadvantaged group to increase its share of power by skillful management of its political alliances with other groups. Moreover, the element of cultural oppression which is known to stimulate group consciousness was absent in many African states, though not in all. When minority groups are pressed to abandon their identities and either to assimilate in a dominant group or to adopt its language, customs, values or symbols, such pressure often stimulates self-assertion and separation. In most African states, the realities of ethnic heterogeneity have precluded attempts to impose the language or culture of any single ethnic group upon the rest of the population.[1]

The pluralistic character of most African states has led to the development of mechanisms of adjustment enabling the accommodation of the interests and needs of the diverse ethnic groups. Most have developed norms and procedures enabling the maintenance of an ethnic balance within the political and administrative institutions. Thus, most groups have not felt alien within the state's pluralistic structure as they would have done had states been more homogenous, and had their situation as a minority group thus been exceptional.

In addition, the fact that members of the same ethnic group lived under separate colonial administrations, sometimes subject to the rule of different colonial powers, led to divergent economic, social, cultural and political development. Groups became integrated into the economic life of the territory in which they lived. Some of their members were educated, learned the language of the European colonial government, were formed within different educational and cultural systems, and developed links with educated members of other ethnic groups in the same territory. Many came to participate in political movements along with members of other groups. Thus, élites gradually became integrated in the economic, cultural and political-administrative life of their territory, and had little or almost no contact with members of the same traditional group across the international boundary.[2] Thus their interests favoured continued membership within the state that emerged with the withdrawal of colonial rule. Political unification with kinsmen across the international border could have meant risking loss of status or some other disadvantage.

Furthermore, the partitioning of some groups failed to cause serious resentment because it was only a partition on paper, having little practical significance. Some borders were not enforced during the colonial period, and the peoples living on either side did not experience major inconveniences or disabilities because of the line. Moreover, many colonial boundary agreements created regimes which made some allowance for the interests of frontier populations, enabling them to pursue their everyday economic and social activities as if the international border had not existed.[3] The permeability of borders did not necessarily reduce conflict between frontier groups; but it created circumstances which did not encourage the development of interest in border revisions.

Although the non-enforcement of boundaries or the existence of a liberal and permeable boundary regime was usually inherited from colonial times, there is also an element of deliberate policy implied in such situations. To be sure, boundaries were often left unenforced, or boundary regimes existing in colonial times were left unaltered, because governments accorded higher priority to other issues. Or perhaps they were not stimulated, or were challenged into formulating their own policy on boundary problems or on groups partitioned by them. But permitting a *status quo* to continue by refraining from action is as much a deliberate policy choice as is the taking of steps to change it. Furthermore, in recent years a few African states have concluded new agreements updating the boundary regimes established in colonial times.[4] Since the partitioned groups did not clamour for unification, the governments of independent states were seldom inclined to demand boundary revisions.

Quite to the contrary — governments were usually interested in maintaining the territorial *status quo*. The heterogeneous social and cultural composition of states had an important influence in shaping governmental attitudes and policies on boundaries. Boundaries may be likened to the external shell of the state. Since the majority of African states did not possess internal cohesion, it was in their interest to preserve this shell intact. In many cases, maintenance of the *status quo* came to be associated with the self-preservation of the state. It was feared that to grant any group or region the right to secede would stimulate secessionist demands from others, and thus be conductive to disintegration of the state.

Grounds for such apprehensions were provided by the secessionist movements that have sprung up in several states. The Congo (now Zaire) saw strong secessionist sentiment among the Bakongo in the 1950s. After coming to independence in 1960, it had to contend with Katanga's attempt to secede. Ethiopia has been troubled by the secessionist stance among its Somali population in the south, and among the Eritrean population in the north-east. In Ghana, the Ewe claimed the right to secede and join their brethren in Togo. In the Ivory Coast, the Sanwis rose in 1959 and claimed the right to secede. On the eve of independence in Kenya, sentiment in the coastal province favoured separation and union with Zanzibar, and in addition a strong secessionist movement existed among the Somali in Northern Kenya. In Mali, the Touareg rose in revolt in 1963 and refused to recognise the government's authority. The Sudan was torn by civil war between 1955 and 1972 because the non-Arabised black population in the south claimed the right to secede. Uganda's unity was threatened both before and after independence by separatist sentiment among the important Baganda people who, until 1966, possessed a measure of autonomy in their Buganda kingdom. In Nigeria the Igbo people tried to secede and establish the abortive 'Republic of Biafra'.

The interest of states in preserving the *status quo* is reflected also in the qualms that many of them have shown over annexing regions or peoples from neighbouring states. In Europe separatism and secession were often encouraged by nation-states, which acted as poles of attraction. In Africa, with few exceptions there are no nation-states to act as poles of attraction or to engender irredentism aiming at national unification. Ethnic groups may develop grievances against the government, but neighbouring states usually do not claim them as long-lost brothers. Certain ethnic groups may lack a feeling of loyalty toward the state in which they live, but they have no loyalty to any other state. A number of ethnic groups have sought to redraw the boundaries to permit reunion with kinsmen, but in most instances these attempts foundered as the kinsmen were content to accept the territorial-political *status quo*, and the irredentist group failed to enlist the resources of a state to back its aspirations.

African governments have not normally aimed at unifying peoples divided by a border, partly because they feared that support for the aspirations of any ethnic group would open the government to charges of ethnic favouritism. Moreover, the addition of any population to the state would alter the delicate political balance between ethnic groups and for that reason would be opposed by all other groups. Thus, for example, internal political considerations were an important factor behind the Nigerian government's opposition in the early 1950s to suggestions by some politicians belonging to the Action Group (at that time the main political party in the Western Region, dominated by the Yoruba), concerning the annexation of the Yoruba-populated area of Dahomey.

Advocacy of the right of self-determination could have led to the rejection of colonial borders. It is significant then, as Rupert Emerson has pointed out, that most African interpretations of the right of self-determination, and in particular of who is entitled to it, chose to interpret this right as applicable to the colonial territory as a whole, within the inherited boundaries. No section of the population, however defined, was considered entitled to this right.[5]

Because African states had to define themselves according to colonial boundaries, the majority realised that they had a mutual interest in establishing respect for the *status quo*. Since most states are vulnerable to external incitement to secession, reciprocal respect for boundaries and abstinence from irredentism were clearly to their mutual advantage. One method by which the territorial *status quo* could be legitimised was through a proclamation by the Organisation of African Unity. An overwhelming majority of African states thus supported the adoption of a resolution to this effect at the 1964 OAU summit conference in Cairo at which member-states pledged themselves to respect the borders existing on their achievement of national independence.

Irredentism

Only rarely did partitioned groups wield so much influence within a state that the state identified with their ethos, thus becoming virtually a nation-state. When such a situation prevailed, and when in addition some vital interests of the group were affected by the partition, the group harnessed the state to pursue an irredentist policy.

The most striking example is Somalia's irredentism *vis-à-vis* Ethiopia, Kenya and Jibuti. It stems in part from an underlying sentiment of cultural and religious solidarity among the Somali, stimulated among the Ethiopian and Kenyan Somali by their subjection to culturally alien peoples. It has also been stimulated by the hardships generated by attempts to enforce an international border, and thus interfere with the seasonal migrations of the nomads who depend for their livelihood on access to grazing and watering areas which are often located across the border.[6]

Another example is the Togo unification movement, which seeks to detach the former British Togoland from Ghana and join it to the Republic of Togo. This movement originated among the Ewe people who had been divided between British and French jurisdictions after World War I. The demand to be reunited stemmed largely from a feeling of ethnic solidarity, stimulated by the disadvantages caused by the partition: the disruption of traditional trading activities across the international border, and a relative loss of influence on the part of the Ewe of British Togoland on their incorporation into Ghana. Although Togo is not a nation-state as

Somalia is, the prominent part played by the Ewe in Togolese affairs enabled them to influence foreign policy to the extent of imparting to it from time to time a distinct irredentist tone.[7]

Ethnic irredentism may be developing in the south of the continent too (both Lesotho and Botswana have raised territorial claims against South Africa), but it is too early even to guess how these sentiments and claims may develop.

In both the Somali and Ewe cases, states have become the principal actors in the drama. Somalia and Togo pursued irredentist policies seeking to annex parts of their neighbours' territories, while Ethiopia, Kenya, and Ghana sought to defend the integrity of the territories within which they established their independence.

Somalia pursued irredentism by both diplomatic and military means. It sought to enlist international support for its goal, capitalising on its cultural and religious affinity with the Arab world, the Sudan's conflicts with neighbouring Ethiopia, and the strategic interests of the Soviet Union. However, the principle of preserving the borders existing on the achievement of national independence, as legitimised by the OAU in 1964, became so widely accepted that Somalia was unable to enlist overt diplomatic support for its irredentist cause. Military means were also ineffective; Somali sponsorship of and assistance to various guerrilla groups failed to advance its goal, and the invasion of Ethiopia by regular Somali forces in 1977 was repulsed after Ethiopia obtained Soviet and Cuban support.

Togolese support for Ewe unification, much more circumspect than Somalia's irredentism, was expressed principally by diplomatic and propaganda pronouncements. However, Togo did grant asylum to Ghanaian Ewe who sought separation from Ghana, and allows them to use Togo as a base for their activities. There may even have been some truth in the Ghanaian allegations in the early 1960s that Togo was supporting groups seeking to overthrow the Nkrumah regime in Ghana by force.

The contrast between the vehemence of Somalia's irredentism and Togo's circumspection probably stems from two factors: the extent to which the border affected the livelihood and way of life of the partitioned group; and the fact that the Ewe, although an influential group, were unable to harness the multi-ethnic Togolese state to the irredentist cause, while the Somali Republic is virtually a Somali nation-state.

Faced by the challenge of an irredentist claim by a neighbouring state and separatist demands by parts of their own population, Ethiopia, Kenya, and Ghana responded politically and militarily, both at the domestic and international levels. Yet, despite the similarity of the challenge with which they were confronted, their diplomatic-international responses differed. In view of Somalia's effort to win support for its policy by reference to the principle of self-determination, Ethiopia and Kenya bolstered their defences by promoting the acceptance of the norm that the boundaries inherited from the colonial period must be respected, and that the principle of self-determination does not apply to groups living within the boundaries of newly-independent states. (Before Somalia's independence, Ethiopia had responded by promoting a counter-claim, mainly on historical grounds, for the incorporation of all Somali territories within the Ethiopian state. But, as a large number of African countries gained independence, it became obvious that Ethiopia could counter the Somali challenge more effectively by promoting the norm of respect for existing borders rather than by counter-irredentism.)

Ghana's response was different. Kwame Nkrumah, propelled by his vision of Pan-Africanism, placed emphasis on political unification and on the abolition of colonial barriers dividing African peoples. Through the early 1960s Ghana's response was irredentism in reverse, justified by the Pan-African principle.

Both similarities and differences in the responses can be discerned at the domestic level. The similarity lies in the measures taken to suppress separatist sentiment: leaders of separatist groups were arrested and their organisations suppressed. In addition, each of the three threatened states closed its borders against its irredentist neighbour. This had a double effect: it impeded the introduction of men, material, propaganda and other means to facilitate separatist activity, and was punitive to the groups concerned, whose interest lay in unimpeded trans-border contacts, trade and migration. Although the border could not be sealed hermetically, the threat of punishment was largely effective. It contributed to the temporary decline of irredentist pressure, and to the desire of both Somalia and Togo to normalise their relations with their adversaries.

Domestically, both Ethiopia and Ghana sought to win over members of the disaffected divided groups and to encourage their attachment to the state in which they lived. Ethiopia hoped to achieve this by offering Somali clans cooperating with the authorities preferential access to water and grazing, educational opportunities, and the promise of employment to those who acquired an Amharic education. This policy was ineffective for two main reasons: the dominant Amhara tended to keep power within their own hands, distrusting the various minority ethnic groups, especially Muslim ones; and from the Somali standpoint, identification with the Ethiopian state would have meant identification with a

Christian culture, which most of them found unacceptable.

Ghana was relatively successful; some sections of the Ewe population identified themselves with the Ghanaian state and rejected their Togoland identity. This difference can be attributed in part to historical divisions among the Ewe, some of whom regarded cooperation with other Ghanaian groups as more attractive than attachment to rival Ewe-speaking groups within a greater-Togolese state. But, in part it was also due to the differences in the ethnic-cultural-political structures of Ghana and Ethiopia. Ghana's structure is pluralistic, in the sense of associating members of different ethnic groups in the ruling political élite, while Ethiopia is dominated by a single group — the Amhara. Thus, Ghana's ruling political and economic élite has usually been open to the Ewe, whereas Ethiopia's was closed to the Somali.

Not being faced by a military threat from Togo, there was little if any military response on Ghana's part. But the Somali military effort stimulated military measures on the part of Ethiopia and Kenya. These two states entered into a political-military alliance in 1964, and coordinated their anti-guerrilla activity. Significantly, since the build-up of Somali forces between 1963 and 1967 was assisted mainly by the Soviet Union, Ethiopia and Kenya sought and received military aid from the United States and other Western countries. This was used effectively in the 1960s in the suppression of guerrilla activity in the frontier regions. It was only after the great weakening of Ethiopia's armed forces following that country's revolutionary upheavals that Somali guerrilla pressure was seriously resumed, followed in 1977 by the invasion of Ethiopia by Somalia's regular army. The reversal of political and military alliances which occurred at this stage probably did not stem from any change in Soviet views of Somali national goals, but rather from a belief that the Ethiopian revolution opened the way to more valuable opportunities than did continued identification with Somalia. It was only through massive Soviet and Cuban support that Ethiopia was able to repulse the Somali invasion and preserve its territorial integrity.

At the time of writing, the military alignments in this conflict do not correspond as neatly as before to an East-West division. Ethiopia, heavily supported by the Soviet bloc, continues to maintain its political-military alliance with Kenya, which receives its military supplies and assistance from the West. And Kenya's military effort continues to be stimulated by the fear of Somalia, which receives its military assistance from the same source.

The spillover of civil strife

Besides the usual problems of maintaining law and order in frontier regions and preventing smuggling — problems aggravated by the existence of ties between the populations on both sides of the boundary — states sometimes face a more serious challenge in the spillover of civil strife from a neighbour.

In some cases members of partitioned groups opposed their government and worked for its overthrow. This was quite different from irredentism/separatism because the goal was not to secede from one state and join another, but to replace the existing government; it was not directed against the structure of the state, but against a particular group of leaders. Furthermore, it was not the fact that they were partitioned that set them apart from other opposition groups. The difference between such groups and other opposition groups lay in their ability to profit from ethnic links on the other side of the international border and utilise them for obtaining a sanctuary, a base of operations, and sometimes even active support. To be sure, opposition groups from one state often obtain such facilities in a neighbouring state even without ethnic or cultural links on which to build, but the existence of such links makes assistance much more likely. The ubiquity of partitioned groups astride African international boundaries therefore greatly facilitates the spillover of domestic strife across boundaries, tending to complicate domestic conflict by the addition of an international dimension. It also contributes to the readiness of people to flee from their home and become refugees in neighbouring states. In many African states this creates serious social and economic problems.

The most dramatic example of ethnic links drawing a neighbouring state into a domestic conflict has been the strife between the Tutsi and the Hutu in Rwanda and Burundi. Whereas the Tutsi dominate Burundi, the Hutu are in power in Rwanda. Periodic strife between the two groups in one state sends streams of refugees across the border to where their kinsmen are in power. The popular and governmental support that they elicit there creates severe tension between the two states. Other examples include the support of the Sudan to Eritrean secessionists in Ethiopia, the support the Southern Sudanese have received in Ethiopia, Uganda and Zaire, and the periodic tensions between Angola and Zaire. When faced by such a situation, governments have usually reacted by following the same policy in reverse: supporting some group in the neighbouring state seeking to secede or to overthrow the government there. Relations between the Sudan and Ethiopia, and Angola and Zaire, illustrate patterns of this sort.

Although in all these cases support was rendered to a group

across the border because of numerous and complex considerations, the relationship with kinsmen across the border made the transformation of the domestic conflict into an international one almost inevitable.

Conclusion

The potential for inter-state conflict in Africa appears to be high. Additional groups among the hundreds divided by boundaries may seek to reunify, demanding boundary revisions and harnessing government support for their aspirations. The social and economic transformations which African states are undergoing is certain to create domestic strife; as we have seen, this may easily spill over the border and lead to international conflict.

But, as the foregoing discussion suggests, it is not the partition of groups which is the direct cause of conflict, but rather the union of disparate groups — the enclosure of partitioned groups within a single state with others with whom their interests conflict. The obvious remedies that could reduce strife are the fostering of liberal, pluralistic political systems within states, and the liberalisation of boundary regimes so as to minimise the hindrance to contact between groups living on opposite sides of the line. Such measures could reduce the incidence of disaffection and alienation of groups within states, and thus also reduce the frequency of irredentism, separatism and inter-state conflict.

NOTES

1. Cf. Dov Ronen, 'Alternative Patterns of Integration in African States', *Journal of Modern African Studies*, 14, 4 (Dec. 1976), pp. 577–96.
2. For an illustration of this process see A.I. Asiwaju, *Western Yorubaland under European Rule 1889–1945* (London: Longman, 1976).
3. For examples of boundary agreements making allowance for the needs of the frontier populations see Ian Brownlie, *African Boundaries* (London: C. Hurst, 1979), pp. 171 (Benin-Nigeria), 246 (Ghana-Ivory Coast), 401 (Liberia-Sierra Leone), 1051–61 (Angola-Zambia).
4. E.g. the 1970 Ethiopian-Kenyan agreement. See Brownlie, pp. 791–5, 821–2.
5. Rupert Emerson, *Self-Determination Revisited in the Era of Decolonization* (Cambridge, Mass.: Harvard University, Center for International Affairs, Occasional Papers in International Affairs, 9, Dec. 1964).
6. See my *Somali Nationalism* (Cambridge, Mass.: Harvard University Press, 1963) and *The Boundary Politics of Independent Africa* (Harvard University Press, 1972). For recent developments in this conflict see Tom J. Farer, *War Clouds on the Horn of Africa*, 2nd edn revised (New York: Carnegie Endowment for International Peace, 1979).
7. For a detailed discussion see *The Boundary Politics of Independent Africa* cited above. Subsequent developments are reported in Colin Legum (ed.), *Africa Contemporary Record*, published annually.

12
THE GLOBAL PERSPECTIVE AND BORDER MANAGEMENT POLICY OPTIONS

A.I. Asiwaju

This concluding chapter is designed not merely to achieve a discussion of the policy implications of the data and analyses in the studies presented. Equally important, it seeks to place the studies within the context of the wider world of borderland peoples and their culture areas and, by so doing, to secure a more solid base for resultant policy considerations. Discussions of the global perspective is particularly demanded by the need to avoid the parochial stance, so much the feature of local studies, which tends to claim uniqueness for experiences that are shared by other peoples and places elsewhere in the world. Such a global perspective allows for generalisations to be made and solutions to be suggested, which may not be irrelevant to the many parts of the world where the African situation that we examine in this book is replicated.

The global perspective

It may therefore be as well to begin by stating the elementary, though seldom articulated, truth that Aftica was not the only or even the first continent to be partitioned; and Africans were not the first or the only partitioned peoples. Indeed, political partition is among the commonest of human experiences irrespective of the part of the world where one lives. The European partition of Africa in the last quarter of the nineteenth century was essentially an extension of a process by which the same powers who partitioned Africa had partitioned and were continuing to partition their own continent and peoples among themselves. Indeed, the Europeans' partition of their own continent proved to be a much more protracted process than their partition of Africa, America and Asia. The partition and repartition of Central, Eastern and South-eastern Europe and the related territorial adjustments of a good number of West European international boundaries, all following the wars of 1914–18 and 1939–45, were still going on long after most of the colonially imposed boundaries of Africa had been regarded as diplomatically settled.[1]

Those who see a fundamental difference between metropolitan Europe and colonial Africa because of the racial similarity between the dominant and the muted groups in the one and the racial distinction between the two groups in the other[2] miss a more vital point, namely the essential sameness of the experience of the dominated. This latter point has been borne out by studies of reactions to colonialism, whether internally or externally imposed.[3] A comparison of the history of international boundary arrangements in Europe and Africa demonstrates the semantic essence in the distinction often drawn between expansionist nationalism and imperialism. Partition is essentially an exercise in power politics; and the strains and stresses on the politically mutilated units are more or less the same irrespective of the racial identity of the group exercising dominance.

The history of African partition and its impact on partitioned culture areas is so closely linked to contemporary European history that any effort to place the African experience within its global context must begin with a discussion of the European precedent and contemporary parallels. In terms of both politics and international law, the connection with Europe is too obvious to warrant any elaborate discussion, even if such a discussion came within our specific terms of reference. At least we know that the original agreements, treaties, protocols and exchange of notes between the partitioning European powers are still the legal instruments which provide the bases for both the diplomatic and legal resolution of disputes concerning any of the 103 international boundaries on the African continent. Accordingly, the institutions for the management of the boundaries are still part and parcel of the same European legal traditions and usages. The rulers and administrators of independent Africa inherited the boundaries created by Europeans; and, in doing so, they necessarily took over the European instruments and mechanisms for the management of the boundaries. In terms of the increasing literature on neo-colonialism in Africa, it may even be argued that the leaders of independent Africa have been inheritors of the imperialistic intentions and considerations which determined the attitude of the original partitioning European powers.

In the case of partitioned culture areas, the situation in Africa is replicated not only on the European continent but also in the wider world of European imperialist influence and impact. In Europe the problem of partitioned culture areas has resulted from the creation of the individual nation-states and the eventual conflicts and clashes among them. France is ethnically one of the most pluralistic of all West European nations, but despite several centuries of application of the nation-state ideology, the ethnic structure of the state is not essentially different from the structure of the more recent nation-states that have grown out of her former colonies in Africa. Peter McPhee has written the following of the partitioned culture areas and internal multi-ethnic structure of the French state:

> The territorial map of France does not correspond to an ethnocultural map, either within the hexagon or along its borders. To the northeast the borders slices into the Flemish ethnic entity [the rest of which is located in the adjacent area of Belgium]. In the south, the border cuts through two Iberian lands: the Basque country (Euskadi) and Catalonia [each shared with Spain]. Corsicans speak Italian dialects. Lower Brittany has a million people using the Celtic language [historically related to such other Celtic culture areas as Wales, Scotland and Ireland, the latter split between Great Britain and the Irish Republic]. There are at least ten or twelve million people who know something of Occitan [add to this list the French-speaking Germans in Alsace-Lorraine]. Inversely, the territorial map of France does not include the French-speakers of Belgium and the Bernois Jurà... Franco-Provençal is spoken between St.-Etienne and Fribourg, Grenoble and Lons-le-Saunier, even in the Val d'Aosta.[4]

While the other West European nations are less ethnically divided, they all share in the problem especially as it relates to the question of mutilated frontier communities. Thus, the German, French and Italian nationalities or ethnic groups in Switzerland are culturally and historically related to kinsfolk in adjacent communities across the boundaries with the neighbouring states.[5] Similarly, the boundaries of the German Democratic Republic and the Federal Republic of Germany were drawn specifically to prevent the future resurgence of the united German state which had so troubled the peace of Europe and, by implication, of the world dominated by Europe. However, the boundaries have also functioned to split the people as an ethnic unit. The German culture area is further fragmented by the demarcation of the boundaries of Austria, the Low Countries and Italy (South Tirol).[6] In Britain the problem of the 'Celtic fringes' still leaves a major question mark on the national integration efforts of the English and the anglicised British.[7] Thus, the pre-Union boundary between the English and Scottish kingdoms is still regarded as 'the Border' by the generality of the Scots;[8] the Welsh are far from being completely quiescent; and the Celtic Irish, split by the boundary between the Irish Republic and the British-controlled North, continue to challenge the legitimacy of the boundary as a line of demarcation between the two Irelands.[9]

When the cultural or ethnic structures of modern African and European states and their boundaries are compared, the similarity is seen to be far more dramatic in Eastern and South-eastern Europe.

Here the local nationalist struggles of the Slav and related populations combined with the expansionist ambitions of the established nation-states such as Italy, Germany and Russia to achieve the disintegration of the Austro-Hungarian empire and the resultant creation, at the end of the 1914–1918 war, of new nation-states manifesting multi-ethnic internal structures and cross-border ethnic configurations of the type known in Africa since the era of the European partition. It is the spectacular character of the political partition in this part of Europe, and especially the Balkans, which led to the adoption of the term 'balkanisation' in the political vocabulary of French and English to refer to situations of imposed multiple political divisions.[10]

Yugoslavia, for example, is as multi-ethnic as Nigeria, and its federal constitution is even more explicit in its recognition and acceptance of the autonomy of the constituent 'nations' and 'nationalities'. While the term 'nation' is a reference to major ethnic groups (referred to as 'national majorities' up to 1960) more or less completely contained within the borders of the state, 'nationalities' are those minor ethnic groups (formerly referred to as 'national minorities') with communities in adjacent localities across the boundaries of geographically contiguous states in which such communities enjoy a predominant status.[11] Yugoslav 'nationalities' include Albanians and Turks in Kosovo, the first of the two 'autonomous regions' recognised by the Yugoslav Constitution; and the Hungarians, Rumanians, Ruthenians and Slovaks in Vojvodina, the second of the autonomous regions.

Yugoslavia also shares some of its dominant Slav populations or 'nations' with neighbouring countries, especially with Italy which, at the end of the 1914–18 war, exploited its diplomatic advantage over Yugoslavia when fixing the Italo-Yugoslav boundary in the Giulia region.[12] In consequence, not only did Italy succeed in retaining a Slovene territory of over 500,000 indigenes sharing the same culture with the bulk of the Slovene sub-group of Slavs concentrated in the adjacent area of the present-day Slovene republic in Yugoslavia; but the Italian politicians also succeeded in retaining control over the Adriatic seaport of Fiume with a considerable Slovene community.[13] The irritation caused by the 'balkanisation' of the Slovenes along the Italo-Yugoslav boundary and the retention of Fiume outside Yugoslav control combined to sow the seeds of conflicts which have since characterised Italo-Yugoslav relations across the common boundary in the Giulia region.

Further east around what might be termed the Eurasian border the drawing of international boundaries at the end of the 1914–18 War also caused the mutilation of the Kurds with the result that an estimated 2 million were placed in Iraq, 4 million in Turkey, 2.5 million in Iran, about 600,000 in Syria and 100,000 in the Soviet Union.[14] Although the Kurds lack any record of political unity and were indeed often organised into small rival political and dialectal groups, there is no question that an essentially coherent culture existed before partition. Quite apart from the fact of a common basic language which was and is still the major feature of the group distinction, there is also the fact of adherence to religious doctrines which distinguish them from their more immediate neighbours.

Although the Kurds are Muslims like the Turks, Arabs and Iranians, the adherence of most of them to Shaffii Sunni rites contrasts them with the predominantly Hanafi Sunni Turks and Arabs and Shiite Iranians and Arabs.[15] The Kurds, on this score, bear a striking resemblance to the Berbers of North Africa who, as an expression of their indomitable spirit of independence, generally embraced off-beat doctrines of the religion that was accepted by others in their neighbourhood. For example, the Berber Christians embraced the Coptic monophysite doctrine when Roman North Africa as a whole embraced Roman Catholicism. As Muslims, they were Shiites in contrast to the Sunnism of the region's later Arab settlers and rulers. As with the Berbers also, the mountainous terrain of the Kurdish homeland has allowed for centuries, if not millennia, of isolation from the external world; and while they did not evolve a common political organisation, Kurds are united in their common folk memories and traditions.

The fact of the Kurds as a coherent culture area, even if not a political unit, brings them in line with most of the African groups treated in this book. Not surprisingly, the Kurdish attitude to the new international boundaries of Turkey, Iran, Iraq, Syria and the Soviet Union which break up their culture area very much resembles the general attitude of partitioned Africans. George Harris has well summed up the Kurdish position: 'Except in unusual circumstance, when frontiers were sealed, customary tribal movement continued with little impediment. And in times of crisis, the border areas could provide embattled tribes sanctuaries from their enemies.'[16] It is this sense of community which has led to the situation in which developments among the Kurdish people in any of the new nation-states into which the culture area has been fragmented automatically became a matter of interest, if not concern, for all the neighbouring states. This is especially true of Turkey, Iran and Iraq where the Kurds are found in many millions. Harris has presented a fascinating account of the ripple effects in Turkey and Iran of the Kurdish secessionist movement in Iraq, leading to the short-lived Mahabad Republic under Mulla Mustafa Barzarin, which collapsed in 1946.[17]

The trauma suffered since the 1890s by the ancient Christian nation of Armenia, whose homeland is divided between the Soviet Union and Turkey, is relevant to our discussion, but raises issues which are beyond its scope.

The universal character of the partitioned Africans' experience is further illustrated by parallel cases in other parts of Europe and Asia as well as in the two Americas. In Europe, the ethnic character of the international boundaries in the east and the south-east is replicated in the far north of the continent where the nomadic Lapps, to mention the most significant example, were split by the boundaries between Norway, Sweden and Finland in much the same way and with the same consequences as with the Cattle Fulani astride the several West African international frontierlines drawn across this well-known Sudanic culture area.[18]

In Asia, there is perhaps no more similar case to that of Africa than the impact of the Sino-Soviet boundary in Central Asia, described by June Dreyer as 'an artificial boundary that divides several minority groups, including such closely related ethnic and sub-ethnic units as the nomadic and semi-nomadic Kazakh, the Kirghiz, the Karakalpak, the Kazan Tatar and relatively sedentary communities like the Uzbek, the Uighur and the Tajik.[19] It is difficult not to agree with Dreyer that, in this range of partitioned Central Asians, the Kazakh are the most typical because of their situation close to the boundary on both sides and their constant movement across it on account of their nomadic mode of life.[20] The Kazakh are also representative of most other Central Asians found in both China and the Soviet Union in their general Turco-Muslim culture and ancestry and the more specific cultural traits of language, folk arts and memories.[21]

There are an estimated 700,000 Kazakh in China, mostly in Ili Kazakh autonomous community or 'Chou' in the Sinkiang Province, and a similarly estimated total of 5.3 million in the adjacent Soviet Republic of Kazakhstan.[22] The central position of the Kazakh among the ethnic components of Sino-Soviet boundary relations has been studied; and it has been sufficiently demonstrated that the factor of partitioned frontier communities, especially this particular one, has been an extremely important moderating influence on Sino-Soviet border relations. It conditioned the situation under which the two relating states were compelled to name the common boundary a "Friendly Border" and promote its development as such.[23] Conversely, it was also an important factor for the subsequent strains between the two nations.[24]

As for the two American continents, the appropriate parallels include not only the various indigenous 'Indian' populations split by the frontiers of the United States with Canada and Mexico respectively but also the original English-speaking colonists (today's Americans and Canadians) who, as Mason Wade has observed, were also products of the partition generated by the American Revolution and formally sanctioned by the Treaty of Paris of 1783, which contained the original provisions for the definition of the US-Canadian boundary.[25] A more dramatic instance of fragmentation of a pre-established European colonist culture area was the case of the Hispanics or the Spanish area split by the US-Mexico border following the expansionist war waged by the United States in 1846-8 and the imposed definition and demarcation of the present international boundary. It is in consequence of this division that the culturally Spanish south-western US states of California, Arizona, Texas, New Mexico and Colorado have been created in close proximity to such adjacent northern Mexican states as Baja California, Sonora, Chihuahua, Coahula, Nuevo Leon and Tamaulipas.[26]

This dual locational arrangement, especially manifest in the geopolitical positions of California and Baja California states, is typical of the general boundary settlement pattern; and it is replicated strikingly in the several cases of dual settlements all along this border area.[27] These include such dual cities as San Luis (Arizona, USA) and San Luis Rio Colorado (Sonora, Mexico); El Paso (Texas, USA) and Ciudad Juarez, originally called El Paso (Chihuahua, Mexico); San Ysidro, formerly Tijuana (immediately south of San Diego in California, USA), and Tijuana (Baja California, Mexico); and Nogales (Arizona, USA) and Nogales (Sonora, Mexico). The others are Calexico (USA) and Mexicali (Mexico); Laredo (USA) and Nuevo Laredo (Mexico); and Brownsville (USA) and Matamoros (Mexico). While the network of relations between the dual cities has been extensively researched, as indeed has that between the communities on both sides of the border generally,[28] adequate note is still to be taken of the policy potential of the informal linkages and the existence of identical cultures on both sides of the international boundary.[29]

Modes of responses of frontier communities

Boundaries between sovereign states mark the sharp edge of the territorial limits within which the states exercise their distinct jurisdictions. They are, therefore, the lines of contact, more often for conflict than for harmony, between rival systems of governmental control. The parallel political socialisation processes that normally accompany such rival controls pose the main policy questions regarding split frontier communities or culture areas. There is more often than not a contradiction between tendencies of indivisibility or inviolability of the unity of borderlands culture, as manifested by the local peoples on the one hand and, on the other, the divisive functions of modern state boundaries. Since the problem of partitioned culture is more or less the same in and outside Africa, it is useful and relevant to our search for policy recommendations on the Africian situation to examine the main manifestations of this problem and the strategies adopted for its management in the other and often older parts of the wider world of partitioned peoples.

In general, there appear three main phases in the development of the frontier community's attitude to the presence of the political boundary in its midst. The initial stage is usually one of indifference based largely on inadequate education as to the intention of the partitioning powers. Secondly there is irritation generated by the growth and development of awareness of the truth. Finally there is the rejection of the boundaries as lines of division. The expression of this third category may vary from the militant irredentist agitation to the more routine human and material movement across the borders and against the barriers instituted by the states. More often than not such movements are labelled as clandestine in the context of the laws of the new states exercising jurisdiction on the different sides of the frontier. In all these, fragmented frontier communities are generally viewed with suspicion by state officials, and border areas often become victims either of a strategic neglect or strict control for reasons generally related to state security.

In Europe, as in Africa, national boundaries were normally negotiated with little or no reference to the local communities whose patterns of life were to be immediately affected by them. For example, in his arguments for a more westerly location of the present Italo-Yugoslav boundary, arguments more or less repeating those advanced by the Sabe sub-group of the Western Yoruba, also for a westerly shift in the present Nigeria-Benin (Dahomey) boundary,[30] the Slovene historian Dr Milko Kos seemed to express the sentiments of all mutilated ethnic groups when stating the case of his own people:

Il résulte de ces faits que des puissances étrangères forment et tracent les limites sans tenir compte du peuple indigène, sans avoir égard à la frontière nationale [i.e. ethnic frontier]. Mais malgré toutes les révolutions politiques, malgré tous les traités relatifs aux frontières, des limites linguistiques n'ont pas éprouvé de dommage. Dans la province de l'Isonzo, la langue slovène disparaît à la frontière naturelle, marquée par la limite extrême entre la contrée montagneuse d'une part et la plaine de l'autre, la òu cette plaine rejoint le Carse, les Coteaux (Coglio) et les crêtes de la Slovénie venétienne.

The Global Perspective; Border Management 241

C'est là notre frontière géographique et naturelle, elle existe depuis treize siècles, depuis le temps òu cette partie occidentale de la nation yougoslave, en marche vers l' ouest et vers le sud, s'est arrêtée à la porte de l'Italie entre les hautes Alpes at la mer. Cette nation y est restée jusqu'à aujourd'hui.[31]

This lamentation about the disruptive effects of an arbitrary boundary on the Slovene cultural unity merely re-echoed the opinions, noted earlier in this work, of an Alaketu of Ketu and a Maasai warrior, who also believed that the Anglo-French (present-day Nigeria-Benin) and Anglo-German (present-day Kenya-Tanzania) frontierlines could only divide the British and the French in the one case and the British and the Germans in the other, and not the Yoruba or the Maasai.[32]

In situations that approximate to that of the Slovenes, where international boundaries have been located and are allowed to remain fixed against the current of an obvious cultural or ethnic unity, partitioned peoples usually have no choice but to continue and indeed expand the pre-partition networks of intra-group relations in spite of the boundary. The mutual exchange of populations across the Franco-Belgian boundary, which René Sevrin has significantly described as presenting 'le caractère de frontière artificielle typique',[33] becomes a characteristic feature of human activities in the border areas. As with many a west African borderlands people migrating from one side of intercolonial boundaries to another, usually in protest against policies of the regimes operating on the abandoned side,[34] cross-border migrations in identical culture areas in Europe are facilitated, as Sevrin has found in respect of his Franco-Belgian case study, by the fact that 'la communauté de langue et la similitude de genres de vie favorisent une assimilation rapide des étrangers dans leur nouvelle résidence'.[35]

Facilitated by the prevalence of an identical language and similarity of culture generally, the cross-border migrations and resultant frontier settlements of the type studied by Sevrin help to boost other types of trans-frontier communications. Frontier communities, and groups and individuals who use them as camouflage, are known everywhere in the world to have taken advantage of international boundaries drawn through the specific culture areas usually on a short-term basis but to their great economic and political profit. Economically, there is the universal phenomenon of cross-border contraband trade or smuggling; and to this must be added the advantages of the proximity or contiguity of two sovereign states, which allows affected citizens to seek and find prompt and safe asylum or sanctuary from the laws, regulations and obligations in force in one state or the other.

Policy implications

The similarities in the attitudes and types of response of frontier communities to their situations as partitioned peoples have also prompted widespread similarities in the instruments of control that are applied for the management of the resultant political, economic and social problems. The demonstrable limits to the effectiveness of many of the existing strategies call for bolder and more imaginative policy options for Africa as a priority region of the partitioned world. Since frontier communities are administratively indistinguishable from the boundaries themselves within the wider context of relations between the nations or states that they separate, the management of the communities forms part of the broader issue of boundary management in particular and international relations in general.

There are in existence two broad categories of control measures which, for convenience, may be described simply as the negative and the positive. We should begin with a review of the negative or restrictive measures, since they are more dominant and better known. These options cover all regulatory mechanisms, including legislative and judicial processes as well as the use of the executive instruments of governments. They involve the application of formally enacted laws and regulations to screen cross-border flows of unauthorised persons and materials. The police and police-related forces are used to apprehend and punish offenders, and by definition restrictive control measures exist all over the world in situations where the official policy is in support of strict boundary maintenance. Essentially, they are short-term, expensive, prone to corruption, inhumane, and generally ineffective. The question of ineffectiveness is especially prominent in relation to frontier communities. For quite apart from the difficulty of identifying those who offend against rules regulating border crossings where there is an identical cultural landscape on both sides of borders, there is the fact that no boundary can ever be completely patrolled. The considerable distances between control posts and the difficulty of the terrain generally present formidable obstacles.

Certain aspects of the regulatory system are motivated by the awareness of the stark realities of the human situation in frontier zones. These cover inclusion of special provisions in the various legal instruments such as the treaties, protocols and other diplomatic exchanges between the original partitioning powers, which recognise the need and the right of partitioned frontier communities to move, engage in economic activities and transport products within specified limits of the frontier zones. These provisions, so commonly found in the legal instruments which determined most of the boundary alignments in Africa, have their precedents and parallels in Europe.[36] In Africa, however, these provisions were ultimately disregarded in the face of the more overt restrictions and control measures that were subsequently mounted along the borders of the rival colonial governments. By contrast in Europe the provisions were more or less faithfully observed so that they formed a solid legal basis for cross-border movement of men and material within the specified limits.[37] These provisions suggest the link between the strictly restrictive, negative and essentially unrealistic control strategies, on the one hand, and the positive, harmonising, development-oriented policy alternative, on the other.

Positive policy options

The chief distinguishing feature here is the acceptance of the principle of 'simplification of the boundary function', as stated by Whittemore Boggs.[38] This position argues that, in view of the enormous political difficulties involved in asking for boundaries to be shifted or completely nullified, the boundaries should be retained but their functions as lines of division should be reduced to allow them to assume more welcome functions as lines of positive and productive contact. Boggs concluded his discussion of the European boundaries by suggesting that the solution to border problems rested in the 'simplification of the boundary function'. His words, used of Europe in 1940, are extremely relevant to Africa today:

The boundary problems ... can therefore never be solved to any considerable degree by shifting boundaries. ... The solution of many of the perplexing poblems may be found in progressive and far-reaching simplification of the boundary function. ... Where all the furies that can be unleashed have failed to induce nations to lower the barriers, the warmth of feelings that would develop in common recognition of present mutual needs and interest might prove effective. ...[39]

Since Boggs' book was published there have been developments which indicate an acceptance of the need to experiment with the idea of 'progressive and far-reaching simplification of the boundary function'. The fundamental problem is that so clearly stated in J.W. House's criticism, namely that attention is greater on 'the broad effects ... upon the economies of the states concerned ... than localized results on the economy and social life of frontier communities.'[40] There are three broad categories of boundary policy which have tended to reduce the function of international boundaries as lines of division. These are (1) development programmes with specific reference to border areas; (2) border areas within the wider context of bilateral relations and co-operation between the states concerned; and (3) border areas in the still wider context of functional international organisations aimed at regional grouping or integration of the several states in geographically contiguous areas.

We may cite a few examples to illustrate the main character of each of the three categories. The first includes Mexican governmental programmes aimed at the national integration of the northern states along the border with the United States. In this bid, the Mexican government inaugurated the *Programa Nacional Fronterizo* (PRONAF) in 1961, replaced in 1967 by the Border Industrial Programme (BIP). The latest in this succession of border programmes of the Mexican government was the Interministerial Commission for the Economic Development of the Northern Border Zone and Free Zones.[41] All the schemes have the common characteristic of being national or unilateral, rather than joint or binational governmental efforts. Although private American capital was involved in the establishment of the few border industries which resulted from the BIP, the US government was not directly involved. There is also the common failure of the projects, especially PRONAF and BIP, as deterrents to Mexican emigration into the United States. For rather than discourage such emigration, the modern transportation network of roads and railways built under the auspices of PRONAF were used more as improved routes from Mexico into the United States than as reorientation for Northern Mexico towards the rest of the republic.[42]

Of a similar unilateral character, though enjoying the tacit support of the other concerned state, was the Soviet-dominated programme for the development of the Sino-Soviet 'Friendly Border'. Unlike PRONAF, which aimed at national integration of Mexico's northern border areas, the Soviet programme for the Sino-Soviet border, inaugurated in 1951, was explicitly aimed at the development of the Kazakh area of the common boundary as a major bridgehead for the development of a Sino-Soviet link and collaboration. However, the Soviet Union bore the financial cost and supplied the technicians for the development of the vital cross-border communication network that grew out of the programme.[43]

As in the case of PRONAF, which worked less to integrate northern Mexico with the rest of the nation than to endorse the more powerful pull of the United States, initial Chinese acquiescence in the Soviet Union's cross-border integration efforts (including a systematic cultural assimilation attempt) ultimately resulted in pulling Chinese minorities, such as the Kazakh, towards kinsmen on the Soviet side of the border even to the extent of revived secessionist expressions.[44] A wedge was consequently driven into the initial

Sino-Soviet border in an attempt at co-operation and the related development of the 'Friendly Border'. These two examples demonstrate the problems inherent in one-sided initiatives and efforts. The rural development programme of the Zambian Government, discussed in Dr Phiri's contribution to this book, may be considered an African parallel.

The second and third categories of positive action, though with only indirect reference to the frontier zones and communities, are the familiar bilateral and multinational functional arrangements. The former may be illustrated by the effect on their common border of the series of bilateral agreements and functional institutional links between the United States and Canada, regarded today as model friendly neighbours. Such agreements and arrangements cover many shared water resources like the Great Lakes and both Atlantic and Pacific oceans; common defence agreements; shared mineral resources such as oil; and the repatriation of capital and profit in respect of businesses which citizens of the one country carry on in the territory of the other. This North American example may be compared with African cases such as the Lake Chad Commission created and run by Nigeria, Chad, Niger and Cameroon as states with obvious vested interests in this all-important inland water; the Mano River Union between Sierra Leone and Liberia; and the Niger River Basin Commission connecting Nigeria, Benin, Niger, Mali and Guinea (Conakry). On the other hand, the European Economic Community (EEC) and the Economic Community of West African States (ECOWAS) are examples of functional regional integration efforts with indirect effects on the border areas of the member-states.

Policy recommendations for Africa

In view of the special emphasis which we have sought to place on the human factor in political partition and resultant boundary politics, we suggest a significant re-direction that would allow frontier communities to become a major policy goal. Because of the tremendous cultural pull across the boundaries drawn through ethnic homelands, so strongly emphasised in the African case studies, restrictive measures need to be cut down and measures for positive development, aiming directly at frontier communities as distinct policy goals, need to be maximised. The studies show conclusively that the cultural foundations of African unity are immensely stronger and firmer than the political ones, and that the policy potential of these foundations has continued to be ignored rather than explored. Partitioned Africans, like all similarly split frontier communities, should be regarded as providing the basis for extremely valuable ethnological, social and cultural links on which to build surer traditions of international relations in the continent. This point is important in view of the greater value that is still accorded human feelings and kinship affinities in Africa than in the more mechanised and industrialised societies of Europe and North America.

The failure to take adequate cognisance of the human factor has combined with an obsession for the use of externally derived legal concepts to create difficulties and even crisis. For example, there is the obvious difficulty in applying the legal definitions of 'citizens' and 'aliens' as contained in the largely Western-oriented constitutions of most modern African states. This is because such definitions always refer to the same state boundaries, so well known as 'artificial' lines. In Nigeria, for example, the court case generated by the politically motivated deportation of Alhaji Abdulrahman Shugaba, the Majority Leader of the Borno State House of Assembly, on the orders of the Federal Minister of Internal Affairs in 1980 elicited so much public interest in Africa's most populous nation-state precisely because of its implications for millions of other Nigerians with historical and cultural background similar to that of Shugaba. He is a Nigerian Kanuri with established kinship relations across the border with Chad, to which he was deported.[45]

The interest shown in the case by the Awolowo-led and predominantly Yoruba Unity Party of Nigeria (UPN) derived immediately from an existing alliance with the Great Nigerian People's Party (GNPP) a predominantly Kanuri political grouping led by Ibrahim Waziri. The GNPP controlled the membership of the Borno State House of Assembly where Shugaba was the majority leader (both the UPN and GNPP were in alliance against the National Party of Nigeria [NPN], the party in power at the federal level). However, a very important undercurrent was the awareness of the implications for several other Nigerian peoples who, like Shugaba's Kanuri, are also bisected by the other Nigerian national boundaries. These include the Yoruba, particularly the Western sub-groups in Lagos, Ogun and Oyo States of Nigeria, whose homelands stretch across the boundary with the Benin Republic; the Bariba of Borgu split between the Kwara State and the adjacent area of Benin; the Hausa of Sokoto, Kaduna, Kano and Gongola States, whose culture area straddles the Nigerian boundaries with the north-eastern part of Benin, southern Niger and north-western Cameroon; and the Efik in Nigeria's Cross River State and south-western Cameroon. The African case studies included in this book are sufficiently indicative of Africa-wide potential sympathy for Shugaba's kind of situation.

The inadequacy of foreign legal concepts when used to describe the realities of local situations is further demonstrated by the application or misapplication of the European definition of 'refugees'. The difficulties which arise in respect of fragmented frontier communities have been noted in the essay covering the Mozambican Ngoni and Chewa who, when they crossed over into Zambia in large numbers during the Mozambican national liberation war, refused to stay in the special refugee camps made available by the Zambian government but preferred rather to live among Zambian kinsmen, who readily accommodated them. Of greater dramatic importance is the plight of Somali 'refugees' in the Ogaadeen region of Ethiopia, traditionally regarded as part and parcel of the Somali homeland or culture area.[46] These situations lead once again to the question of whether or not 'refugees' like those constantly crossing over from neighbouring states into the Sudan and settling in parts of that Republic to which they claim historical and cultural links, should be regarded as 'returnees' or 'immigrants'.[47] All these instances suggest the existence of potential for cultivating traditions of healthy neighbourliness across international boundaries. However, as the Shugaba case demonstrates, there is always the possibility of making negative use of an otherwise positive situation.

More specifically, the African case studies, especially those on the Somali, the Chewa and the Ngoni, the Mandara, and the Bakgatla baga Kgafela, point to the need for a special arrangement that will allow local governments in close proximity to borders to be used as additional instruments for the management of international relations in border regions. Such an arrangement would involve a significant increase in the powers and resources of border-located local governments.

Objections may be raised against this suggestion: conservative individuals inside and outside government might, for example, see the outmoded European notion of sovereignty in danger while the nationalistic youth may see it as unpatriotic.[48] The point, of course, is in the logic of the position of frontier communities as distinct local communities, not any less so than parallel communities situated away from the borders. But in placing frontier communities under local governments with a greater measure of independence, the trans-frontier orientation of the communities must justify the giving of additional power to the frontier local governments to cope with problems arising from their peculiar position along international boundaries. Our studies, especially of the Chewa and Ngoni, also emphasise the need for bi-national co-operation and joint developmental programmes within the boundary localities. The concern here is not different from that which has propelled borderlands scholars in Europe and the United States to present 'frontier zones' as distinct planning regions.[49] In Europe, concrete organisations of borderlands have been created within the general framework of the Council of Europe and the European Economic Community.[59]

The concentration on the human factor, which distinguishes the studies of *Partitioned Africans* from the more usual type of diplomatic studies of boundaries, further emphasises the need to recognise the general features of mutilated ethnic groups as national minorities. It is not by accident that nearly half of the studies so far conducted by the Minority Rights Group in Britain have focussed on divided culture areas.[51] In Africa, and elsewhere, mutilated ethnic groups are located in inaccessible fringes of their states, and almost always form the most neglected parts of the generally neglected rural landscapes of the various states. Because of this special feature of neglect, frontier communities must surely qualify for automatic inclusion in the 'Affirmative Action' programmes[52] of all the states where the fragments of partitioned peoples are located.

The policy suggestions for Africa have the advantage of marrying nationalistic aspirations, understandably insistent on keeping the boundaries, with the realities of ethnic or cultural relations across the national boundaries. The proposals favour the retention of the boundaries, but seek to convert them from hostility-oriented functions as lines of exclusion to more productive, more harmonious and, from the viewpoint of traditional African history, more defensible roles as lines of mutual contact and inclusion.

NOTES

1. It is not always appreciated that the current national boundaries of such European countries as the two Germanies, Austria, Hungary, Poland, Czechoslovakia, Yugoslavia, Bulgaria, Rumania, Greece, Italy in relation to Austria and Yugoslavia, and Finland are more recent than the boundaries of most African countries including those of Nigeria. Senegal, Zaire, Angola, Mozambique and Libya, to mention only a few. The Italo-French and Danish-German borders changed drastically in the nineteenth century.
2. The traditional African nationalist definition of colonialism stresses race as the major delineating feature. It is so, for example, in the definition offered by Frantz Fanon; and for a recent study, see L.A. Jinadu, *Fanon: In search of the African Revolution* (Enugu: Fourth Dimension Publishers, 1980), chs. 2–4. A similar stress tends to be placed by some German intellectuals who cannot see any affinity between the African experience of political partition and their own. Thea Buttner, Direction of the Institute of African and Asian Studies in Leipzig, GDR, expressed this view at a seminar in the History Department, University of Lagos, in 1981.
3. For relevant studies of internal colonialism see Michael Hechter, *Internal Colonialism: The Celtic Fringe in British National Development, 1536–1966* (University of California Press, 1975); Peter McPhee, 'A Case Study of Internal Colonization: The Francisation of Northern Catalonia', *Review*, III, 3, Winter 1980, pp. 399–428; and M.B. Akpan, 'Black Imperialism: Americo-Liberian Rule over

the African Peoples of Liberia, 1841–1964', *Canadian Journal of African Studies*, 7, 2, 1973, pp. 217–71; and compare these with reactions to external colonialism in studies such as Thomas Hodgkin, *Nationalism in Colonial Africa*; E. Kedourie, *Nationalism in Asia and Africa* (New York, 1970); Prem Narain, *Press and Politics in India*, and Fred Omu, *Press and Politics in Nigeria* (Longman, 1978), and J.S. Coleman, *Nigeria: Background to nationalism* (University of California Press, 1959).
4. McPhee, *op. cit.*, pp. 400–1.
5. A historical assessment of the impact of the Franco-Swiss border is contained in S. Daveau, *Les Regions Frontalières de la Montagne Jurassienne* (Paris, 1959), as cited in J.R.V. Prescott, *The Geography of Frontiers and Boundaries* (London, 1965), ch. 4.
6. For a study of the impact of the German-Dutch boundary, see R.S. Platt, *A Geographical Study of the Dutch-German Border*, Münster, 1958, also cited in Prescott, *op. cit.*
7. Hechter, *op. cit.*
8. This information derives from personal correspondence with Prof. J.D. Hargreaves of the University of Aberdeen. For a study of the evolution of the Anglo-Scottish border from an international to an internal boundary see S.J. Watts, *From Border to Middle Shire: Northumberland, 1586–1625* (Leicester University Press, 1975). Of a more specifically economic historical perspective is C. Gulvin, 'The Union and the Scottish Woollen Industry, 1707–1760', *Scottish Historical Review*, Oct. 1971, pp. 131–7.
9. For studies of the Irish partition, see T.G. Caroll, 'Northern Ireland' in Suhrke and Noble (eds), *op. cit.*, pp. 21–42; and R.N. Lebow, 'Ireland', in Henderson, Lebow and Stoessinger (eds), *op. cit.*, pp. 197–266.
10. In English 'balkanise' and 'balkanisation'; in French '*balkaniser*' and '*balkanisation*'.
11. See a recent discussion of the ethnic composition of the Yugoslav population in Trivo Indjic, 'Affirmative Action: The Yugoslav Case', paper presented at the International Conference on Affirmative Action, Bellagio Conference Centre, Italy, 16–20 Aug. 1982.
12. For a special study, see A.E. Moodie, *The Italo-Yugoslav Boundary: A study in political geography* (London, 1945).
13. *Ibid.*, pp. 145–8.
14. G.S. Harris, 'The Kurdish Conflict in Iraq', in Suhrke and Noble (eds), *op. cit.*, p. 69.
15. *Ibid.*
16. *Ibid.*
17. *Ibid.*
18. For notes on the impact of partition on the Lapps see S.W. Boggs, *International Boundaries: A study of boundary functions and problems* (New York: Columbia University Press, 1940), pp. 96–101.
19. J.T. Dreyer, 'The Kazakhs in China' in Suhrke and Noble (eds), *op. cit.*, p. 142.
20. *Ibid.*, p. 148.
21. *Ibid.*
22. *Ibid.*, p. 146.
23. *Ibid.*, p. 156.
24. *Ibid.*, pp. 159 ff.
25. M. Wade, 'Partition in North America', *Journal of International Affairs*, XVIII, 2, 1964 (special issue on 'The Politics of Partition'), pp. 234–40.
26. This border has been focussed in several studies which are included in Ellwyn Stoddard, Richard Nostrand and Jonathan West (eds), *Borderlands Sourcebook* (University of Oklahoma Press, 1982). Leading titles include R.A. Fernandez,

The United States-Mexico Border: A politico-economic profile (University of Notre Dame Press, 1977), J.A. Price, *Tijuana: Urbanization in a border culture* (University of Notre Dame Press, 1973), and Oscar J. Martinez, *Border Boom Town: Ciudad Juarez since 1848* (Austin, Texas, 1978).

27. Price, *op. cit.*, pp. 14 and 19.
28. *Ibid.*; also W.V. d'Antonio and William H. Form, *Influentials in Two Border Cities* (Notre Dame University Press, 1965).
29. For a special study of this neglect see Ellwyn Stoddard, 'Local and Regional Incongruities in Bi-national Diplomacy: Policy for the US Mexico Border', *Policy Perspectives Journal*, 2, 1, pp. 111–36.
30. Asiwaju, *Western Yorubaland, op. cit.*, pp. 61–2.
31. M. Kos, *La formation historique des limites italo-slaviennes* (Ljubljana, 1919), p. 10, as quoted in Moodie, *op. cit.*, p. 158.
32. The persistence of this view among Yoruba traditional rulers was dramatised in the visit, which took place on 9–10 January 1983, of the Oni of Ife and four other Nigerian Yoruba Obas to Ketu in the Republic of Benin (see A.I. Asiwaju, 'Visit of the Black Pope', *Sunday Tribune*, Ibadan, 30 Jan. 1983, and *West Africa*, 28 Feb. 1983, for reports on the visit).
33. R. Sevrin, 'Les échanges de populations à la frontière entre la France et le Tournaisis', *Annales de Géographie*, LVIII, 1949, pp. 237–44.
34. For an appropriate study, see Asiwaju, 'Migrations as Revolt . . .', *op. cit.*
35. Sevrin, *op. cit.*, p. 244.
36. Boggs, *op. cit.*, p. 132.
37. *Ibid.*, pp. 132–3.
38. *Ibid.*
39. *Ibid.*
40. J.W. House, 'The Franco-Italian Boundary in the Alpes Maritimes', *Transactions of the Institute of British Geographers*, 26, 1959, p. 107.
41. For detailed discussion of the US-Mexico border development programmes, see Fernandez, *op. cit.*, esp. chs 2 (pp. 128–30) and 3, and Price, *op. cit.*, chs VIII and X.
42. *Ibid.*, especially Fernandez.
43. Dreyer, *op. cit.*, p. 157.
44. An opinion poll conducted by Chinese Communist Party agents among the Chinese Kazakh in 1956 is reported to have led to the discovery of strong expressions of preferences for the Soviet Union and a nostalgia for the aborted East Turkestan Republic which resulted from the Soviet-backed secessionist movement of the period immediately after World War II by which the Chinese Kazakh attempted to set up an independent state of their own close to Soviet Kazakhstan.
45. For details, see *Suit No. BOM/13M/80 Judgement: Shugaba Abdulrahman Darman (Applicant) and (i) the Federal Minister of Internal Affairs, (ii) M. Mofio, (iii) His Excellency Alhaji Shehu Shagari President of the Federal Republic of Nigeria sued in his Capacity as the President of the Federal Republic of Nigeria, (iv) The Hon. Mr Justice P.C. Akpambo (Respondents) in the High Court of Borno Judicial Division holden in Maiduguri before the Hon. Mr Justice Oye Adefila, Judge*, 1981, 129 pp.
46. Interviews and discussions with officials at the O.A.U. Secretariat in Addis Ababa during visits in 1981.
47. Interview with Dr El-Gaali, Director of the International Boundaries Division, Sudan Ministry of the Interior, Khartoum, 1980.
48. This view has had the benefit of being expressed at a recent national Seminar; and I express my appreciation to participants whose comments and criticisms have further sharpened my conviction. See A.I. Asiwaju, 'Border populations

as a neglected dimension in studies of African boundary problems: The Nigeria-Benin frontier case', paper presented at the Conference on Nigeria's International Boundaries, Nigerian Institute of International Affairs, Lagos, 5–7 April 1982.

49. For the United States see Stoddard, 'Local and Regional Incongruities in Binational Diplomacy...', *op. cit.*, and N. Hansen, *The border Economy: Regional development in the South West* (Austin, Texas, 1981). The European case is covered in Hans J. Briner, 'Co-ordination of Regional Planning Across National Frontiers: Test Case Switzerland France Germany.' *Regio Basiliensis*, Basel, 1981.
50. Hansen, *op. cit.*, ch. 2 and his 'International Co-operation in Border Regions: An overview and research agenda', Austin, Texas, 1982.
51. The concern for minorities is the motivation for studies conducted by the Minority Rights Group in England. Significantly such studies have concentrated on quite a number of politically fragmented units including *Mexican Americans* (Monograph 39); *The Sahrawis of Western Sahara* (40); *The Two Irelands* (2); *Eritrea and Southern Sudan* (5), the *Crimean Tatars, Volga Germans and Meskhetians: Soviet Treatment of some National Minorities* (6), *The Basques and Catalans* (9), *The Burundi* (20), *The Kurds* (23), and *Cyprus* (30).
52. 'Affirmative Action' is synonymous with the concept of 'Positive Discrimination', used in reference to measures deliberately adopted to right wrongs imposed by history. It is often used to describe programmes designed to assist minorities which have been left behind in the course of the development of a society.

PARTITIONED CULTURE AREAS: A CHECKLIST

A.I. Asiwaju

Introduction

The purpose of this tabulated checklist is to demonstrate the continental extent of the situation discussed in the selected case studies. While there is an attempt to be comprehensive, the list does not pretend to be exhaustive. To avoid unnecessary duplications, the distinct culture areas are listed in relation to each of the 103 separate international boundaries on the continent.

The present compilation of the boundaries themselves has depended especially on Professor Ian Brownlie's *African Boundaries: A legal and diplomatic encyclopaedia* (London: C. Hurst, 1979). Readers interested in more detail, especially relating to the description of the alignments and histories of the various boundaries, should refer to this magistral and authoritative volume. The other titles that have proved similarly useful, though covering more restricted areas, include J.C. Anene's *The International Boundaries of Nigeria, 1885–1960* (London: Longman, 1970), A.C. McEwen's *International Boundaries of East Africa* (Oxford University Press, 1971) and the much older and more global S.W. Boggs' *International Boundaries* (New York: Columbia University Press, 1940).

There is not equally copious source material on the partitioned African culture areas. Despite the admittedly large and still increasing body of ethnographical and anthropological literature on Africa, surprisingly little attention has been paid to the impact of inter-colonial or international boundaries where these were drawn through the culture areas concerned. This omission is especially surprising in researches within the specialised field of culture contact for which border situations offer a special attraction. A similar neglect has been observed in the area of African linguistics (cf. D. Dalby, *Language Map of Africa and the Adjacent Islands*, London: International African Institute, 1975). In fact, rather than helping, scholars of the African language situation, especially the ever-expanding legion of foreign experts from Europe, the United States and the Soviet Union, have complicated the problem even of identifying African cultural and linguistic landscapes including those that were partitioned at the turn of the last century. They have done this largely through the uncontrolled creation and use of numerous artificial cover-names for language units which are, in many cases, identifiable essentially as dialects of the same basic language. This practice has had the effect of exaggerating the picture of cultural diversity in the continent. The seriousness of this situation has led David Dalby in his *Language Map* to suggest a moratorium on the practice.

Of similar effect has been the influence of the diverse orthographical traditions of the partitioning European powers and the peculiar accents of their own national tongues which they imposed as official languages for their respective colonies. The practical results of these features of colonial partition, in the development of separate types of administration and political culture in divided culture areas and ethnic groups, have been sufficiently discussed elsewhere in relation to West Africa, the sub-region where balkanisation by European powers is most in evidence.[1] Attention has also been drawn in the introductory chapter to the widespread practice whereby different categories or names have been imposed on the different fractions of the same ethnic group by the respective colonial authorities operating on the different sides of the new international boundaries.[2]

There is particular fascination in the multiplication of ethnonyms resulting apparently from the auditory idiosyncracies of individual expatriate colonial officials or researchers who were responsible for the compilation of most, if not all, of the ethnographical data on particular colonial territories. The phenomenon of diversity of forms for particular ethnonyms, resulting largely from the different impressions of the same sounds received by different recorders and by the same recorder at different times, has been found to be especially characteristic of areas that fell under overtly assimilationist colonial powers like France and Portugal which firmly discouraged the use of indigenised orthography. In a few instances, the problem has been created by researchers who work on different parts of the same culture area and assume that the peculiarities of the parts reflect the general characteristics of the whole. This, for example, has been an important explanation for the varieties of categories found in studies of the Maasai.

While some French West African examples have been documented in English,[3] the continent-wide character of the occurrence can be seen from the experience in other parts of Africa. The situation in Central Africa is particularly instructive in view of the ethnographical revisions being carried out by Theophile Obenga, who has been rightly concerned with the need to discover the real or indigenous forms, sounds and meanings of ethnic categories.[4] Among the groups split by boundaries of the various Central African states, the cases can be cited of the Tshokwe, the Lunda and the Baholo across the Zaire/Angola/Zambia boundaries; the Tabwa, a sub-group of the Bemba, astride the Zaire/Zambia frontier; and the Yombe split by the Zaire/Congo/Angola (Cabinda) frontiers.

The case of the Tchokwe is easily the most spectacular. The category known generally in modern ethnographical literature as the Tshokwe or Cokwe refers to a people who recognise themselves in singular form as Katshokwe and in plural form as Tutshokwe or Ifutshokwe. However, the same group has been recorded in French and Belgian ethnographic literature, both of the colonial and post-colonial periods, in an almost infinite variety of forms, *inter alia* Chokwe, Ahioko, Atsokwe, Bachoko, Badjok, Badjoko, Babioko, Butchokwe, Batchioko, Batchiokwe, Bashoko, Katsokwe, Khioko, Kioke, Kioko, Kioque, Makioko, Matchioko, Quioco, Shioko, Tschiokwe, Tsiboko, Tsibokwe, Tsivokwe, Tsokwe, Tutschchokwe, Utsihiokwe, Vichioko and Watschokwe.[5]

Similarly, the Lunda, whose self-identification has now been recorded as the Karuund for singular form and the Arund for the plural, have been recorded variously as Alunda, Arunda, Balondo, Balounda, Baloundou, Bamlunda, Kalunda, Lounda, Mahundo and Valunda.[6] In the same way, the Baholo, whose traditional sovereign capital was located on the Angolan side of the Zaire-Angola boundary while the bulk of the affiliated lands and people lay on the Zairean side, were variously known as Holoholo, Baholoholo, Bahorohoro, Wahorohoro and Wahoroholo.[7] With respect to the Yombe, known to themselves in singular form as the Muyombe or simply Muyomb' or Bayombe, the varieties in the existing literature are Majombe, Iomba, Majumbe, Mayombu, Majumbo and Mayumbe.[8]

A final limitation to the usefulness of the existing literature is illustrated by the errors of mistaken identity contained in the otherwise important pioneering ethnographic survey by George Murdock and the fascinating essay by K.M. Barbour based on that survey: see George Murdock, *Africa: Its People and Culture History* (New York, 1959) and K.M. Barbour, 'A Geographical Analysis of Boundaries in Inter-Tropical Aftica' in K.M. Barbour and R.M. Protheroe (eds), *Essays on African Population* (London, 1961). The error of mistaken identity has invariably led Murdock and a dependent generation of armchair researchers, making little or no effort at field investigation, to list as separate and different, ethnic groups who speak basically the same language and share the same set of other cultural symbols, institutions and value systems. Murdock's list is, for example, grossly inaccurate where the Yoruba, the Ijebu, the Egba, the Ife, the Egbado and the Awori are enumerated separately, set against their belonging to the same Yoruba-speaking culture. A similar error is in evidence in respect of Bakongo who, in Murdock's survey, are listed as separate from the Vili, the Kamba, the Yombe, and other sub-groups of the Bakongo who are given distinct and independent cultural identities in the survey.

The situation is not always helped by cartographers, especially those who produce national atlases such as those published in a series by *Jeune Afrique*. In these atlases, maps showing ethnic distribution are dressed in conventional sharp-edged lineal frameworks suggested by the national boundaries. In this form, maps conceal the reality of the continuous nature of ethnic distribution and the extensions of lands and peoples into neighbouring states, and thus lose most of their serious educational value. The one important exception known to the present writer is the *National Geographic and Ethnographic Map of the Peoples of Africa,* published in 1971 by the US National Geographic Society, Washington, DC. Even so, the question about the use of truly indigenous ethnonyms has not been resolved, and some of the errors of mistaken identity in Murdock's older map are still being made.

To fill these gaps in the existing source-material extensive research trips have had to be undertaken to various parts of the continent. The direct investigations have yielded some information and improved the present writer's insight into the problem as it relates to the frontier communities. The experience has demonstrated the immensity of the work remaining to be done, work that it behoves Africans themselves to undertake. It is clear, for example, that Africa still awaits a definitive ethnographical survey, detailed enough to justify the studies undertaken by African scholars over a period exceeding twenty-five years. To this end, the first step has to be in the form of a detailed survey of each of the constituent countries on the model of Theophile Obenga's ethnography of the People's Republic of the Congo and, to a smaller extent, of the Democratic Republic of Zaire. The task demands a multidisciplinary effort by historians, geographers and ethnographers. The defects that will be apparent in the checklist that now follows are the measure of the urgency of this task.

Partitioned Culture Areas: A Checklist

Boundaries	Partitioned ethnic groups
1. Algeria-Libya	Arabs, Berbers, Tuaregs
2. Algeria-Mali	Berbers, Tuaregs
3. Algeria-Mauritania	Arabs, Berbers
4. Algeria-Morocco	Arabs, Berbers
5. Algeria-Niger	Tuaregs, Berbers, Hausa
6. Algeria-Tunisia	Arabs, Berbers
7. Algeria-Western Sahara	Reguibat, Berbers, Arabs
8. Angola (Cabinda)-Congo	Villi and Bayombe Sub-groups of Bakongo
9. Angola-Namibia	Ovambo
10. Angola-Zambia	Lunda and Mbemba
11. Angola-Zaire	Bakongo Sub-groups including the Villi, Bawoyo, Yombe, Mbata, Bankanu, Songs; Baholo; Bapende, Bapindi, Bakwese and Ambundu
12. Benin-Niger	Hausa, Fulani, Gourmantche
13. Benin-Nigeria	Adja (Gun/Egun), Yoruba (Anago, Ketu, Sabe), Borgu (Bariba/Borgawa), Hausa, Fulani
14. Benin-Togo	Aja (mostly Ewe), and Yoruba
15. Benin-Upper Volta	Gourmantche
16. Botswana-Namibia	Ova Herero, Khoisan Basarwa (so-called Bushmen), Bayei, Hambukush/Hambusushu, Tonga, Subiya
17. Botswana-Zambia	Tonga, Subiya
18. Botswana-Zimbabwe	Va-Kalanga, Ba-Birwa
19. Botswana-South Africa	Ba-Tswana
20. Burundi-Rwanda	Rwanda, Burundi, Hema, Lindu
21. Burundi-Tanzania	Burundi
22. Burundi-Zaire	Bahavu, Nyaga
23. Cameroon-Central Africa Republic (CAR)	Gbaya, Baka, Kaka, Maka-Nyem, Pande, Ikenga
24. Cameroon-Chad	Kanembu, Shuwa Arabs
25. Cameroon-Congo	Bakwele, Njem
26. Cameroon-Gabon	Bakwele, Njem, Fang
27. Cameroon-Equatorial Guinea	Fang
28. Cameroon-Nigeria	Kanembu, Shuwa Arabs, Mandara, Wakura, Matakam, Gude, Veve, Adamawa, Chamba, Jibu, Ekoi, Ododop, Efik
29. CAR-Chad	Azande
30. CAR-Congo	Azande
31. CAR-Sudan	Azande, Fertit, Kriesh, Banda

Partitioned Culture Areas: A Checklist

Boundaries	Partitioned ethnic groups
32. CAR-Zaire	Azande; Mundzombo; Ngbandi, Sango, Yakoma, Ngbako, Manja, Gbaya; Bandain
33. Chad-Libya	Tubu, Tuaregs, Berbers, Arabs
34. Chad-Niger	Tubu, Tuaregs, Kanembu, Fulani
35. Chad-Nigeria	Kanembu/Kanuri, Shuwa Arabs
36. Chad-Sudan	Tubu, Bidiyat, Kriesh, Fur, Banda, Massalit
37. Congo-Gabon	Maka (Njem), Echira, Teke, Kota
38. Congo-Zaire	Bakongo
39. Djibouti-Somalia	'Afar, 'Iise (Issa), Somali
40. Djibouti-Ethiopia	'Afar, 'Iise
41. Egypt-Libya	Arabs, Berbers
42. Egypt-Sudan	Nubians
43. Ethiopia-Kenya	Somali
44. Ethiopia-Somalia	Somali
45. Ethiopia-Sudan	Beni Amir, Annak, Dinka
46. Equatorial Guinea-Gabon	Fang
47. The Gambia-Senegal	Wolof, Serrer
48. Ghana-Ivory Coast	Sanwi, Afema, Lobi
49. Ghana-Togo	Ewe, Akposso, Konkomba, Ahufo, Moba
50. Ghana-Upper Volta	Mossi, Dangara Kusasi, Dyula (Dioula), Sissala, Birifor, Padon, Mankana, Bissa, Aculo
51. Guinea(Bissau)-Guinea (Conakry)	Bambaraca (Baydyaranke in Guinea-Conakry)
52. Guinea(B)-Senegal	Dyula
53. Guinea(C)-Ivory Coast	Mandinka, Tchien
54. Guinea(C)-Liberia	Guerze or Kissi (called the Kpelle in Liberia), Mende, Peul (Fulani), Mano, Kra, Tchien
55. Guinea(C)-Mali	Bambara
56. Guinea(C)-Senegal	Tukulor (Toucouleur), Dioula, Manjak
57. Guinea(C)-Sierra Leone	Mende, Susu, Baga
58. Ivory Coast-Liberia	Mende
59. Ivory Coast-Mali	Peul (Fulani)
60. Ivory Coast-Upper Volta	Fulse, Nabe, Guin, Lobi
61. Kenya-Somalia	Somali
62. Kenya-Sudan	Turkana, Danyiro
63. Kenya-Tanzania	Maasai, Luo, Kuria
64. Kenya-Uganda	Luyia, Teso, Luo, Karopakot, Turkana, Marukwet, Samia, Hesu, Seuei, Bagisu
65. Lesotho-South Africa	Sotho
66. Liberia-Sierra Leone	Vai, Gbande, Kissi, Mende
67. Libya-Niger	Tubu, Tuaregs

Partitioned Culture Areas: A Checklist

Boundaries	Partitioned ethnic groups
68. Libya-Sudan	Berbers, Arabs
69. Libya-Tunisia	Berbers, Arabs
70. Malawi-Mozambique	Yao, Sena, Nyanja, Chewa, Ngoni
71. Malawi-Tanzania	Ngonde
72. Malawi-Zambia	Chewa, Ngoni, Tombuka, Ngonde
73. Mali-Mauritania	Soninke, Toucouleur (Tukulor)
74. Mali-Niger	Tuaregs, Mandinka
75. Mali-Senegal	Mandinka, Soninke
76. Mali-Upper Volta	Peuls (Fulani), Bobo, Samo, Bolon, Senoufo, Bwaba, Pona, Maka
77. Mauritania-Morocco	Moors
78. Mauritania-Senegal	Tukulor, Soninke
79. Mauritania-Western Sahara	Moors, Reguibat
80. Morocco-Western Sahara	Tekna, Arabs, Berbers
81. Mozambique-South Africa	Swazi
82. Mozambique-Swaziland	Swazi
83. Mozambique-Tanzania	Makonde, Yao, Ngoni, Matengo
84. Mozambique-Zambia	Chewa, Ngoni, Nsenga
85. Mozambique-Zimbabwe	Barwe, Ndau, Manyika
86. Namibia-South Africa	Nama
87. Namibia-Zambia	Subiya
88. Niger-Nigeria	Hausa, Fulani
89. Niger-Upper Volta	Peul (Fulani), Gurmantche
90. Rwanda-Tanzania	Ha, Haya, Zinza, Hangaza
91. Rwanda-Uganda	Banyarwanda (Kigesi), Bujumbira
92. Rwanda-Zaire	Rwanda
93. South Africa-Swaziland	Swazi
94. South Africa-Zimbabwe	Tonga, Venda
95. Sudan-Uganda	Acoli, Kakwa, Jiya, Lango, Dongatona
96. Sudan-Zaire	Lugbara, Alur
97. Tanzania-Uganda	Haya
98. Tanzania-Zaire	Boyo
99. Tanzania-Zambia	Mambwe, Inamwanga
100. Togo-Upper Volta	Bissa, Kusasi
101. Uganda-Zaire	Alur, Batoro
102. Zaire-Zambia	Lunda, Unga, Lungu
103. Zambia-Zimbabwe	Balocalough

NOTES

1. See 'Notes on Names' in Asiwaju, *Western Yorubaland, op. cit.*, pp. xiii–xiv.
2. See chapter 1
3. Asiwaju (as in Note 1 above) and 'Appendix on Place Names' in I.A. Akinjogbin, *Dahomey and its Neighbours*, Cambridge University Press, 1967.
4. T. Obenga, *Introduction à la Connaissance du Peuple de la République Populaire du Congo*, Brazzaville, 1973, and T. Obenga, *Le Zaire: civilisation traditionnelle et culture moderne*, Paris, 1977.
5. Obenga, *Le Zaire*, p. 91
6. *Ibid.*, p. 144.
7. *Ibid.*, p. 162.
8. *Ibid.*, p. 202.

SELECT BIBLIOGRAPHY

Introduction

The following does not, needless to say, pretend to be a critical or an exhaustive bibliography. However, the items have been listed to provide a clear perception of the range of available relevant material. The listed items are arranged under headings intended to denote the main categories. The disciplinary bias of each unit demonstrates both the distinctions and, more important, the essential inter-relationships which at times make it almost impossible to draw the line between, e.g., history and geography or political science and law. There is a renewed emphasis on the need for collaboration between the disciplines in the humanities, social sciences and law for a more purposeful study of man in society.

Each heading of the bibliography embraces both published and unpublished works of scholarship. Primary data of an archival nature are not included; but all the works listed, especially the higher degree dissertations and publications in both book and journal-article form, based on original research, include such sources.

The fact is sufficiently demonstrated that frontier communities in Africa, as elsewhere, are affairs of peripheries of states. Characteristically, studies dealing with them have not hitherto commanded the priority attention of bibliographers. There exists at the time of writing only one specialised bibliography known to the present writer, which touches on the subject; namely D.H. Zidouemba's *Les sources de l'histoire des frontières de l'Ouest Africain* (Dakar: Nouvelles Editions Africaines, 1979). While this bibliography covers the West African sub-region specifically, the introduction lists works which treat frontiers generally and African frontiers in particular. The author is a national of Upper Volta which, in terms of its experience of partition, has been described rather aptly as 'the Poland of West Africa'.

Mr Zidouemba's research is limited to the material in the main documentation centres in Dakar: IFAN (L'Institut Fondamental [formerly 'Français'] d'Afrique Noire), the University of Dakar, the Dakar University Library and the National Archives of Senegal, most of which is made up of the archives of former French West Africa. Not surprisingly, therefore, this otherwise useful bibliography is dominated by the works of French authors and understandably biased in favour of the francophone area of West Africa. But despite this limitation, the bibliography must be regarded as hitherto the only one of its kind. It is obviously an indispensable instrument of research in its own area of interest and has been one of the sources used for the compilation of this select bibliography.

We have included a list of the leading anthropological and ethnographical works which have yielded useful information on African border communities. Only items dealing with major regions and providing helpful theoretical information are listed. Here, as with the entries dealing directly with the boundaries and their impact, the balance must be sought in the notes and references at the end of chapters.

Select Bibliography

Works on basic concepts, theories and the global perspective

Boggs, S.W., *International Boundaries: A study of boundary functions and problems* (New York: Columbia University Press, 1940).
D'Antonio, W.W., and W.H. Form, *Influentials in the Two Border Cities: A study in community decision-making*.
Daveau, S., *Les régions frontaliers de la montagne jurassienne* (Paris, 1959).
De Lapradelle, P., *La frontière* (Paris: Les Editions Internationales, 1928).
Fernandez, R.A., *The United States-Mexico Border: A Politico-economic profile* (University of Notre Dame Press, 1977).
Goody, J., *Inheritance, Social Change and the Boundary Problems* (The Hague: Mouton).
Gottmann, J., *La politique des états et leur géographie* (Paris: A. Colin, 1952).
Hartsborne, R., 'Geographic and Political Boundaries in Upper Silesia', *Annals of the American Geographers*, XXIII, 4, 1933, pp. 195–213.
Henderson, G., R. Lebrow and J. Stoessinger (eds), *Divided Nations in a Divided World* (New York: McKay, 1974).
House, J.W., 'The Franco-Italian Boundary in the Alpes Maritimes', *Transactions and Papers, Institute of British Geographers*, 26, 1959, pp. 107–31.
Johnson, R.E., *The Politics of Division, Partition and Unification* (New York: Praeger, 1976).
Jones, S.B., *Boundary Making: A handbook for statesmen, treaty editors and boundary commissioners* (Washington DC: Carnegie Endowment, 1945).
Journal of International Affairs, XVIII, 3, 1964, special issue on 'The Politics of Partition'.
Moodie, A.E. *The Italo-Yugoslav Boundary: A study in political geography* (London: Hutchinson, 1945).
Platt, S. (with P. Bucking-Spitta), *A Geographical Study of the Dutch-German Border*, Münster, 1958.
Prescott, J.R.V., *The Geography of Frontiers and Boundaries* (London: Hutchinson University Library, 1965).
Price, J.A. *Tijuana: Urbanisation in a Border Culture* (Notre Dame, Ind.: University of Notre Dame Press, 1973).
Samora, J., *Los Mojados: The Wetback story* (University of Notre Dame Press, 1971).
Sevrin, R., 'Les échanges de populations à la frontière entre la France et la Tournaisis', *Annales de Géographie*, 58, 1949, pp. 237–44.
Whittlesey, D., 'Trans-Pyrenean Spain: The Val d'Aran' *The Scottish Geographical Magazine*, XLIX, 1933, pp. 217–28.
Wilkinson, H.R., 'Jugoslav Kosmet: The evolution of a frontier province and its landscape', *Transactions and Papers, Institute of British Geographers*, 21, 1955, pp. 171–93.

Studies of African international boundaries: history and historical/political geography

Akakpo, A., 'La Délimitation des Frontières Togolaises' in *Symposium Frobenius, Perspectives des Etudes Africaines Contemporaines* (Cologne and Munich, 1974), pp. 92–100.

Anene, J.C., *The International Boundaries of Nigeria, 1885–1960: The Framework of an Emergent African State* (London: Longman, 1970).

Barbour, K.M., 'A Geographical Analysis of Boundaries in Inter-Tropical Africa' in K.M. Barbour and R.M. Prothero (eds), *African Populations*, London: 1961, pp. 303–23.

Cornevin, R., 'Ethnies, frontières et stabilité en Afrique', *Marchés Tropicaux*, 1071, 1966, pp. 1465–7.

Covu, J., 'Etudes des échanges interfrontaliers Rosso-Mauritanie, Rosso-Sénégal' (Dakar, Faculté des Lettres, Département de Géographie [Maitrise de Géographie], 1971).

Diallo, I., 'Border Migrations: a survey of the Senegambian rural areas (1970–1971)', United Nations African Institute for Economic Development and Planning, Dakar, Monograph IDEP/ET/R/2428/Rev. 1, Oct. 1972., 140 pp.

Hargreaves, J.D., *Prelude to the Partition of West Africa* (London: Macmillan, 1963).

———, *West Africa Partitioned*, vol. 1 (London: Macmillan, 1974).

Husson, P., *La question des frontières terrestres du Maroc*, Paris, 1960.

Obichere, B.I., *West African States and European Expansion: The Dahomey-Niger Hinterland, 1885–1898* (New Haven: Yale University Press, 1971).

Person, Y., 'L'Afrique noire et ses frontières', *Revue Française d'Etudes Politiques Africaines,* Aug. 1972, 80, pp. 18–42.

Prescott, J.R.V., *The Evolution of Nigeria's International and Regional Boundaries, 1861–1971*, Vancouver: Tantalus Research, 1971.

Studies of African international boundaries: emphasis on law

Boutros-Ghali, B., *Les conflits des frontières en Afrique (études et documents)*, Paris, 1973.

Brownlie, I., *African Boundaries: A legal and diplomatic encyclopaedia* (London: C. Hurst, 1979).

El-Gaali, B.A. 'Boundaries in Africa: a case study of the diplomatic evolution and legal aspects of the international boundaries of the Sudan, with special emphasis on the boundary with Egypt' (unpubl. Ph.D. thesis, Faculty of Law, University of London, 1975).

Gonidec, P-F., 'Les conflits de frontières en Mauritanie et dans la Corne orientale de l'Afrique', Paper for UNESCO Seminar, Ouagadougou, May 1979.

Hertslet, Sir E., *The Map of Africa by Treaty*, 3 Vols (London, 1909).

Jouve, E., 'L'Afrique à l'épreuve de ses frontières', paper for UNESCO Seminar on the methodology of African contemporary history, Ouagadougou, May 1979. (Contains a detailed bibliography of works on the subject in the French language.)
McEwen, A.C., *International Boundaries of East Africa* (Oxford University Press, 1971).
Queneudec, J.P., 'Remarques sur le règlement des conflits frontalières en Afrique', *Revue General de Droit International Public*, LXXIV, 1970, pp. 69-77.
Yakeintchouk, R., 'Les frontières africaines', *Revue Géneral de Droit International Public*, 3e Série, LXXIV, 1970, pp. 27-68.

Studies of African international boundaries: political science

Ayela, Neguse, 'The Politics of the Somalia-Ethiopia Boundary Problems, 1960-1967', (unpubl. Ph.D. thesis, University of California, Los Angeles, 1969).
Bouvier, P., 'Une problème de sociologie politique: Les frontières des états africains', *Revue de l'Institut de Sociologie*, 4, 1972, pp. 686-720.
Boyd, Jr. J.B., 'African Boundary Conflict: An empirical study', *The African Studies Review*, XXII, 3, 1979, pp. 1-15.
Hamilton, D.N., 'Ethiopia's Frontiers: The boundary agreements and their demarcations, 1896-1956' (unpubl. Ph.D. thesis, Oxford University, 1974).
Rezette, R., *Le Sahara occidental et les frontières Marocaines* (Paris: Nouvelles Editions Latines, 1975).
Touval, S., *The Boundary Politics of Independent Africa* (Cambridge, Mass.: Harvard University Press, 1972).
―――, 'The Organisation of African Unity and African Borders', *International Organisation*, XXI, 1, 1967.
―――, 'Africa's Frontiers: Reactions to a Colonial Legacy', *International Affairs*, 4, 1966, pp. 641-51.
―――, 'Treaties, Borders and the Partition of Africa', *Journal of African History*, VII, 1966, pp. 279-93.
Widstrand, C.G. (ed.), *African Boundary Problems* (Uppsala: Nordiska Afrikainstitutet, 1969).
Zartman, I.W., 'The Politics of Boundaries in North and West Africa', *Journal of Modern African Studies*. III, 2, 1965, pp. 155-73.

African international boundaries: studies of local frontier economies and societies

Abir, Mordechai, 'The Origins of the Ethiopian-Egyptian Border Problem in the Nineteenth Century', *Journal of African History*, VIII, 3, 1967.

Al-Nur, T.H., 'The Sudan-Ethiopia Boundary: A study in political geography' (unpubl. Ph.D. thesis, University of Durham, 1971).
Amenumey, D.E.K., 'The Ewe People and the Coming of European Rule, 1850–1914' (unpubl. MA thesis, University of London, 1964); 'A Political History of the Ewe Unification Problem' (unpubl. Ph.D. thesis, University of Manchester, 1972).
Asıwaju, A.I., *Western Yorubaland under European Rule, 1889–1945: A comparative analysis of French and British colonialism* (London: Longman, 1976).
———, 'Migrations as Revolt: The example of the Ivory Coast and the Upper Volta before 1945', *Journal of African History*, XVII, 4, 1976, pp. 577–94.
———, 'Migration as an Expression of Revolt: The example of French West Africa up to 1945', *Tarikh*, 5, 3, 1977.
———, 'The socio-economic integration of the West African sub-region in the historical context: Focus on the colonial period', *Bulletin de l'IFAN*, Dakar, Série B, 40, 1, 1978, pp. 160–78.
———, 'The Aja-speaking peoples in Nigeria: A note on their origin, settlement and cultural adaptation up to 1946', *Africa*, 49, 1, 1979, pp. 15–28.
———, 'Towards an Ethnohistory of African State Boundaries' (paper for UNESCO Seminar on Methodology of Contemporary History of Africa, Ouagadougou, May 1979).
———, 'The Alaketu of Ketu and the Onimeku of Meko: The changing status of two Yoruba rulers under French and British rule', in M. Crowder and O. Ikume (eds), *West African Chiefs: Their changing status under colonial rule and independence,* (Ile-Ife Nigeria: University of Ife Press, 1970).
———, 'Trade and Politics Across Nigeria's Borders' in O. Ikime (ed.), *Trade and Politics in Africa* (Essays in Honour of Kenneth O. Dike), forthcoming.
———, 'The Concept of Frontier in the Setting of State in Pre-Colonial Africa', *Présence Africaine*, special nos 32/34 on 'The Problematic of State in Africa' (Paris, 1983).
Bahru, Z., 'Relations Between Ethiopia and the Sudan on Western Ethiopian Frontier, 1898–1935' (unpubl. Ph.D. thesis, University of London, 1976).
Beyrani, C., 'A Comparison of the Impact of Colonial Partition and Administration on Barotseland and Ukraine' (unpubl. MA dissertation, University of Zambia, Lusaka, 1982).
Collins, J.D., 'Government and Groundnut Marketing in Rural Hausa Niger: The 1930s to the 1970s in Magaria' (unpubl. Ph.D. thesis, School of Advanced International Studies, Johns Hopkins University, 1974).
———, 'The clandestine movement of groundnuts across the Niger-Nigeria Boundary', *Canadian Journal of African Studies*, X, 2, 1976, pp. 259–76.
Fanso, V.G., 'Transfrontier Relations and Resistance to Cameroun-Nigeria

Colonial Boundaries, 1916-1945', Doctorat d'Etat, University of Yaounde, Cameroon, 1983.

Igué, O.J., 'Evolution du commerce clandestin entre le Dahomey et le Nigéria depuis la Guerre du "Biafra"', *Canadian Journal of African Studies*, X, 2, 1976, pp. 235-57.

———, 'Un aspect des échanges entre le Dahomey et le Nigéria: Le commerce du cacao', Bulletin de l'IFAN, Dakar, Série B, 1976, pp. 636-69.

———, *Le commerce de contrebande et les problèmes monétaires en Afrique Occidentale* (Université Nationale du Bénin, Centre de Formation Administrative et de Perfectionnement, Cotonou, Feb. 1977).

Mills, R.L., 'The Development of a Frontier Zone and Border Landscape Along the Dahomey-Nigeria Boundary', *Journal of Tropical Geography*, 36, June 1973, pp. 42-9.

Mondjannagni, A., 'Quelques aspects historiques, économiques, et politiques de la Frontière Nigéria-Dahomey', *Etudes Dahoméennes* (Nouvelle Série) 1, 1963-4, pp. 17-59.

Musambachime, M.L., 'The Development and Growth of the Fishing Industry in Mweru-Luapula' (unpubl. Ph.D. thesis, University of Wisconsin, 1981).

Phiri, S.H., 'Some Aspects of Spatial Interaction and Reaction to Government Policies in a Border Area: A study in the historical and political geography of rural development in the Zambia/Malawi and Zambia/Mozambique frontier zone (1870-1979)' (unpubl. Ph.D., University of Liverpool, 1980).

Smith, M.G., *The Affairs of Daura* (Los Angeles: University of California Press, 1978).

Thom, D.J., 'The Niger-Nigeria Borderlands: A politico-geographical analysis of boundary influence upon the Hausa' (unpubl. Ph.D. thesis, Michigan State University, 1970).

———, 'The Niger-Nigeria Boundary, 1890-1906: A study of ethnic frontiers and a colonial boundary', Africa Series, 23, Athens, Ohio University Centre for International Studies, 1975.

Waller, R., 'The Maasai and the British, 1895-1905: The origin of an alliance', *Journal of African History*, XVII, 4, 1976, pp. 529-33.

Relevant anthropological and ethnographic studies

African National Atlases, especially the *Jeune Afrique* series.

Barth, F. (ed.), *Ethnic Groups and Boundaries* (Bergen, Oslo: Universitetsforlaget, 1969).

Baxter, P.T.W., and A. Butt, *The Azande and Related Peoples of the Anglo-Egyptian Sudan and the Belgian Congo* (London: IAI, 1953).

Chapelle, J., *Nomades Noirs du Sahara*, Paris: Plon, 1957.

Forde, D., *The Yoruba-speaking Peoples of South-Western Nigeria* (London: International Africa Institute [Ethnographic Survey of Africa], 1951, repr. 1969).

Geertz, Clifford, *The Interpretation of Cultures* (New York: Basic Books, 1973).

———, 'The Integrative Revolution: Primordial Sentiments and Civil Politics in the New States', in C. Geertz (ed.), *Old Societies and New States* (New York: Free Press, 1963).

Hechter, M., *Internal Colonialism: The Celtic Fringe in British National Development, 1536–1966* (Los Angeles: University of California Press, 1975).

Holloman, R.E., and S. Arutiunov (eds), *Perspectives on Ethnicity* (Paris: Mouton, 1978).

IFAN, Dakar, *Cartes Ethno-Démographiques de l'Afrique Occidentale*, nos 2, 3, 4, 1963.

———, *Haute Volta: Groupes ethniques d'Après la carte Ligel inspirée des Travaux de Moal.*

Jacobs, Alan, 'The Pastoral Maasai of Kenya: A report of anthropological field research' (mimeo, Nairobi, 1963).

Lebeuf, A.M.-D., *Les populations du Tchad* (Paris, IAI, 1959).

Lembezat, B., *Les populations daiennes du Nord du Caméroun et de l'Adamoua* (Paris: IAI, 1962).

Le Rouvreur, A., *Sahariens et Sahéliens du Tchad* (Paris: Editions Berger-Levrault, 1962).

Levine, D.N., *Greater Ethiopia: The evolution of a multi-ethnic society* (University of Chicago Press, 1974).

McPhee, P., 'A Case Study of Internal Colonisation: The francisation of Northern Catalonia', *Review*, III, 3, 1980, pp. 399–428.

Murdock, G., *Africa: Its peoples and culture history* (New York: McGraw-Hill, 1959).

Naroll, R., 'On Ethnic Unit Classification', *Current Anthropology*, 5., 1964, pp. 283–312.

Obenga, T., *Introduction à la connaissance du peuple de la République Populaire du Congo* (Brazzaville: Librairie Populaire, 1973).

———, *Le Zaire: civilisations traditionnelles et culture moderne* (Paris: Présence Africaine, 1977).

Santandrea, S., *A Tribal History of the Western Bahr El Ghazal* (Bologna: Nigrizia, 1964).

Smith, M.G., *The Plural Society in the British West Indies* (University of California Press, 1965).

Urvey, Yves, *Histoire des populations du Soudan Central (Colonie du Niger)* (Paris, 1936).

Vansina, Jan, *Introduction à l'ethnographie du Congo* (Kinshasa: Edition Universitaire du Congo, 1965).

Wallerstein, I., 'Ethnicity and National Integration in West Africa', *Cahiers d'Etudes Africaines*, 3, October 1960, pp. 129–39.

Young, Crawford, *Politics of Cultural Pluralism* (Madison: University of Wisconsin Press, 1976).

INDEX

'Aaqip 'Abdullaahi Jaama 163
Abyssinia *see* Ethiopia
Acoli 51, 87, 90–2
Adamawa 29, 31–4, 37–8
Adamu, Mahdi 197
Adoko, Akena 63
Adowa, battle of 167, 170
'Afars 158–9, 161, 168
African National Congress 144
Aja 2
Ajayi, J.F. Ade. 8
Akans 4, 23
Alan, W. 111
Al Hajj 'Umar 19, 73
Alur: colonial period 93–8; partition 58, 90–100; pre-colonial history 87–93
Amin, Idi 58, 60–7, 97–8
Amnesty International 187
Amula 95
Anago 196
Andrzewski, S. 162
Anene, J.C. 8, 9, 253
Angola 11, 231
Antonelli, Pietro 169
Anya-Nya guerrillas in Sudan 59–67
Appolonians 23
Atyak 92
Austria 6, 235
Aweera (Boni) 158, 161
Awolowo 246
Azande 2, 51

Babira 88, 91
Baganda 97, 99, 226
Baker, Samuel 54, 90
Bakgatla baga Kgafela: 247; *dikgosi* (table) 143; farms (table) 135; population (table) 146; pre-partition situation 128–30; unification movements 77, 145–6; *see also* Kgatla
Bakgatla Free Church 142
Bakongo 2, 225

Bambaraca 3
Banda, President 118–20
Bantu 51, 58, 88
Banyali 88, 91
Barbour, K.M. 225
Bari 52
Bariba of Borgu 246
Barnes, J.A. 110
Barth, Heinrich 32–3
Bartire 159, 173
Batswana 2
Baydyaranke 3
Bechuanaland *see* Botswana
Beitz, Emil 178
Belgium 6, 58, 92–7, 241
Bell, Hesketh 55
Benin (formerly Dahomey) 9, 240, 245
Berbers 237
Berlin Conference (1884–5) 1, 20
Bevin, Ernest 179–80
Biafra 226
Blyden, E.W. 22
Boggs, S.W. 7, 243, 253
Boran Oromo 159
Borno 29–31, 33, 38–9
Botswana: frontier 127–8, 131n., 132, 136, 145–6; independence 127, 146; territorial claims against South Africa 228
Bottego, Vittorio 173
Boyd, J.B., Jr 12
Britain: 235; Anglo-Egyptian Condominium over Sudan 54, 59, 93; Anglo-French Condominium over Egypt 166; colonial policy: Cameroon 29, 33–4, 37–46; East Africa 113–17, 164–82; Gambia 22, 75–80; Gold Coast (Ghana) 21; Nigeria 22, 29, 40–6, 197–9; Northern Rhodesia (Zambia) 107, 110, 113–17; Nyasaland (Malawi) 107, 110, 113–17; Southern Africa 131–6, 140;

267

Uganda 54-8, 90-7; and the South African war 131-2, 134
British Central African Protectorate see Malawi
Bromley, V. 7
Brownlie, Ian 253
Brunschwig, Henri 20
Bukar Afadi 35, 41
Burton, Richard 162-3
Burundi 231

Cameroon: colonial period: British and French rule 29, 33-4, 37-46; German rule 33-7; frontiers 38-9, 43, 44; League of Nations Mandates 29, 37; partitions 29, 33-9, 45; pre-partition history 30-3; referendum on boundary adjustments 1-2, 45; Trusteeship Territories 29
Cameroon, Republic of 46, 245
Canada 238-9, 245
Cardew, Colonel 24
Chad 11, 245
Chewa: colonial period 113-17; independence 117-24, 196, 247; partition 107, 110, 113-17, 196; pre-partition history 106-9
China 238, 244-5
Cipeta 107, 109
Collin, Jean 80
Collins, J.D. 12
Colo (Shilluk) 87
Congo see Zaire
Council of Europe 248
Crailsheim, Hauptmann von 36-7
Creoles 22
Crispi, Francesco 167
Cuba 228
Cushites, Eastern 158

Daarood Geri 173
Dahomey see Benin
Dalby, David 253-4
Denham, Dixon 31-2
Denoon, J.D. 66
Dervish movement 174-5
Diagne, Blaise 77

Diallo, Ibrahima 79
Digo 58
Diop, Bara 71
Diouf, Abdou 82
Djibouti, 115, 156, 166-7, 180, 188-9
Djimi 3, 38
Dongatona 51
Donyiro 51
Doodi, Ugaaz, 177
Dreyer, June 238
Drysdale, John 155
Dulbahante 160, 176

East African Community 102
Economic Community of West African States (ECOWAS) 82, 213, 245
Efik 246
Egypt 53-4, 93, 165-6
Emerson, Rupert 226
Emin Pasha 54, 89, 90, 93
Ethiopia: frontiers 11; occupation of Somali lands 164-5, 168-73, 182-8; support from Soviet bloc 228, 230; territorial dispute with Somalia 156, 175
Europe: partitioned culture areas 6-8, 25, 233-6
European Economic Community (EEC) 206, 209, 245, 248
Ewe 45, 77, 196, 225-30

Faarah Nuur 171
Fallers, J.J. 56
Fashoda Incident 164
Finland 238
Fisher, H.A.L. 19
Flegel, Robert 32
Fleming, Harold 159
Fokeng 134
Fombina 31-2
Forster, Sir Samuel 77
France: 6, 235, 241; Anglo-French Condominium over Egypt 166; colonial policy: Cameroon 29, 33-4, 37-46; Dahomey 115; East Africa 164-80; Senegal 75-80;

Index

West Africa 197-9;
Front for the Liberation of Mozambique (Frelimo) 117-19
Fulani 3, 100; Cattle Fulani 238
Fulbe 72
Fye, Bishop J.C. 77

Galla 100
Gambia *see* Senegambia
Gann, L. 110
Geertz, Clifford 6
Geri 159
Germany 6, 29, 32-7, 110, 115, 235
Ghana, 1, 23-4, 45, 223, 225, 228, 230
Ghebrehiwet, Keseteberhan 184-5
Godabursi 170
Gold Coast *see* Ghana
Gomani 110
Goold-Adams, H. 132
Goranes 3
Gordon, General 93
Gordon, Richard 54
Goshe 35
Gourmantché 2
Grobler, Piet W. 138-9
groundnuts: Nigeria-Niger boundary 199-213, (tables) 213-17; Senegambia 79-80
Gude 3, 38
Guinea 21, 24, 100, 245
Gueye, Lamin 77
Gungu 92

Haile Selassie 181
Hanna, A.J. 110
Harris, George 237
Haud 170
Hausa 99, 100, 116, 196-9, 246
Heine, Bernd 159
Henderson, Gregory 5
Higis 3, 38
House, J.W. 243
Hungary 235
Hurutshe 129, 134
Hutu 231

Ifonyin 196

Igbo 99, 226
Igue, Ogunsola 196
'Iise (Issa) 167, 170
Ile-Ife 198
Iran 237
Ireland 235
Isaac, Harold 6
Isaacman, A.F. 109
Isaaq, Habar Magadle 159-60, 170, 176
Isang 136-40
Isma'il Pasha 54, 165-6
Israel, 61-6
Italy 164-70, 236, 240
Ivory Coast 225-6

Jaden, Aggrey 61
Jalaure 95
Jalusiga 98
Jameson raid 133
Jato, Yerima 40
Jawara, Sir Dawda 82
Jibuti *see* Djibouti
Jieng 87
John IV of Tigre 167, 169, 172
Johnston, Harris 114
Johnston, R.E. 5
Jolas 72
Jones, A.H.M. 167
Junam 90-2

Kabarega 89, 96
Kakwa: colonial period 56-60; partition 55-8, 67; pre-partition situation 51-4; Sudanese civil war 59-67; Water of Yakan 53, 57
Kali, Abdallah 60
Kalonga 109
Kanuri 246
Kapsiki 3, 38
Karakalpak 238
Karimu 24
Katanga 225
Kawaza 111
Kazakh 238, 244
Kazan Tatars 238
Kenny, Captain 24
Kenya: frontiers 167; independence

182; revolt of Somalis 182; territorial disputes with Somalia 156, 175, 181
Kenyatta, Jomo 180–1
Keta 94–5
Ketu 196
Kgabjwana 140
Kgamanyane 130–1, 133
Kgatla: administration by South Africa 130–46; Afrikaner demands for labour 130, 133; antecedents to partition 128–32; Isang-Molefi feud 137–41; transborder unity 132–7, 141–2; see also Bakgatla baga Kgafela
Kgafela 138
Khoisan Basarwa 2
Kikuyu 99
Kirghiz 238
Kirk, J.W. 162
Kitchener, Lord 164
Kola Adama 41
Kos, Milko 240–1
Kpelle 3
Kuka 52
Kurds 6–7, 236–7
Kwena 129, 131–4, 136

Lagarde, Leonce 166
Lagu, General 60, 62
Laitin, David 162
Laka 130
Lake Chad Commission 245
Langworthy, J.W. 109
Lapps 238
Laurence, Margaret 162
League of Nations Mandates for Cameroon 29, 37
Lebron, Richard 5
Legassick, M. 128–9
Lendu 88, 91–2, 98
Leontiev, Count 169
Lesotho 228
Letsebe 133
Lewis, Herbert 159
Lewis, I.M. 159, 161
Liberia 25, 245
Limbas 21

Linchwe 131–7
Linchwe II 144, 146
Lobengula 132
Loch, H.B. 132
Loma 3
Lotuko 52
Low, Aadan 178
Luawa 24–5
Lugard, Lord 33
Lugbara 91, 98
Lunda 2
Luo 87, 99
Lwo 87–8, 91–2, 94

Maasai 2, 9, 58, 160, 241
McCall, Storrs 59
McEwen, A.C. 8, 9–10, 58, 253
McPhee, Peter 235
Madagali 35
Madi 52, 88, 91–2, 98
Magaria district (Niger): groundnut trade 200–6; tables 213–17
Mahdist revolt 54, 59, 93, 166
Mahgoub 60
Mahin 115
Maino, M. 162
Majerteen 160
Makonde 58, 100
Makua 100
Malawi 107, 110, 113–22
Mali 226, 245
Mambisa 88, 91, 92
Mandara: before partition 30–3; colonial period 33–45; early European travellers and colonial scramble 31–3; independence 46, 247; partitions 29, 33–9, 45
Mandingo 100
Mandinka 72
Mangope, President 145
Mano River Union 245
Mantirisi 133
Marchand, Commandant 164
Marcus, Harold 173
Mareehaan Daarood 159, 176
Maroua 35
Martin, David 62
Matakam 3, 38

Index

Mazrui, Ali 58
Mbo 107, 109
Mboya, Tom 181
Menelik II of Ethiopia 165, 167-70, 172, 174
Mesfin Wolde Mariam 187
Mexico 238-9, 244
Mg'anja 107, 109
Mills, Robin 196
Mitchison, Naomi 144
Mkanda 111
Mlolo 111
Mmusi 140
Mokae 133
Molefi Kgafela Linchwe 127, 137-40, 144-5
Mondjannagni, Alfred 196
Monroe, Elizabeth 167
Morocco 2, 223
Moru 51
Motlotle 130
Mounteney-Jephson, A.J. 90
Mozambique: 247; colonial period 113-17; frontiers 100, 107, 110, 113-14; independence 119-24; struggle for independence 117-19; territorial claims of Malawi 118
Mpezeni 110, 114
Msoni, Mizeke 112-13
Mudenda, Elijah 120
Muhammad Ali 53-4
Muhammad Salih 174
Murdock, George 255-6
Mwale, Skeva 111
Mwambera 110
Mwangala 111

Nago 3
Nath 87
Ndebele 130
Ngombe, Dr Francis 67
Ngoni: colonial period 113-17; independence 117-24, 247; partition 107, 110, 113-17; pre-partition history 106-7, 109-13
Ngwaktse 134
Ngwato 134, 136

Niger: 245; frontier 196-9; groundnut trade 199-213; tables 213-17
Niger River Basin Commission 245
Nigeria: 245; civil war 196, 209; colonial period 22, 29, 40-6, 197-9; frontiers 11, 35, 39, 196-9; groundnut trade 199-213; tables 213-17; referendum on boundary adjustments 1-2
Nilo-Hamites 51-2, 58
Nilotes 51, 58
Nimeiry, General 62-3, 65
Nkrumah, Kwame, 228-9
Noble, Lela Garner 6-7
Northern Ireland 235
Northern Rhodesia see Zambia
Norway 238
Nsenga 107, 109, 113
Nubians 2
Nuer 160
Nyanja 107, 109
Nyasaland see Malawi

Obenga, Theophile 254, 256
Obote, Apolo Milton 59-67
Ofentse 137-8, 140
Ogaadeen 159, 170, 174, 180, 182
Okebo 88, 91-2, 98
Omar Ceesay 79
Omar Faye 77
Omdurman, battle of 54
Omer-Cooper, J.D. 110
Omo-Tana 158
Onama, Felix 64
Ong'wech 94, 96
Onyiuke, G.C.M. 181
Organisation of African Unity (OAU): boundary policy 2, 99, 101, 227-8; Somalia 180, 187
Oromo (Galla) 158, 160-1
Ova Hereo 2
Owiny 94, 96

Palwo 56, 92
Pankhurst, Richard 173
Pedi 129
Pembanoyo 111
Perham, Margery 172

Peuls 3
Phiri, Thomas 142
Pilane 130
Poland 6, 25
Portugal, 20, 107, 109, 113–16
Pound, N.J.G. 5
Prescott, J.R.V. 8–9
Protheroe, R.M. 255

Rabeh b. Fadlallah 31, 34
Ramono 134–5, 138
Ras Makonnen 172–3
Rau, W.E. 110
Read, Margaret 110, 114
Red Sea 164–6, 168
Reer Baare 173, 183
Rendille 158, 161
Rennell of Rodd, Lord 171
Rimbaud, Arthur 169
Rolong 129
Russell, Peter 59
Russia, 169
Rwanda 58, 231

Sabe 196, 240
Sadler, J. Hayes, 173
Saharawi 14
Saho 158–9
Said, Khedive 54
Samia 100
Samu 24
Sanwis 225–6
Sayyid Mahammad 'Abdille Hasan 160, 173–5
Scandinavian Institute of African Studies 7–8
Sebetwane Fokeng 130
Sechele 131–2
Segale 142
Seingwaeng 138
Senegal *see* Senegambia
Senegambia: colonial period 22, 75–80; frontiers 24, 75, 80–1; independence 80–3; partition 75–81; pre-colonial history 72–5
Senegambia Federation 71–2, 82–3
Senghor, Leopold 77, 82
Serers 2, 72, 196

Sevrin, René 241
Shermaarke, 'Abdirashiid 155
Shetima Hamidu 41
Shugaba, Abdalrahman 246
Shulis 90
Sierra Leone 21, 24, 245
sleeping sickness in Middle Nile Valley region 56
Somalia: independence 99–100, 179–80; irredentism 227–9; sought boundary revision 2, 223; territorial dispute with Ethiopia 156, 175; territorial dispute with Kenya 156, 175, 181
Somaliland, British *see* Somalia
Somaliland, French *see* Djibouti
Somalis: 247; before partition 156–64; colonial rule 175–80; elusive boundaries and pasture rights 175–9, 185–9; partition 2–3, 13, 155, 164–70, 175–6; revolt in Kenya 182; rule by Ethiopia 164–5, 168–73, 182–8; unification movements 77, 225–6
Soninke 2
Sotho, 129, 130
South Africa: administration of Kgatla lands 130–46; apartheid 127, 136, 139–40, 143–5; frontiers 128, 131n., 132, 136, 145–6; territorial claims of Lesotho and Botswana 228; war with Britain 131–2, 134
Soviet Union 228, 230, 237–8, 244–5
Stanley, H.M. 55, 90
Steiber, Resident 35
Steiner, Rolf 63
Stoessinger, John 5
Sudan: Anglo-Egyptian Condominium 54, 59, 93; civil war 59–67, 226; assistance to South from Uganda 60–7; frontiers 11, 54, 56–8; Mahdist revolt 54, 59, 93, 166; occupation by Egypt 54, 165–6
Suez Canal 165
Suhrke, A. 6–7
Susus 21

Sweden 238
Switzerland 6, 235
Syria 237

Tajik 238
Takla Haimanot 172
Tanganyika *see* Tanzania
Tanzania: frontiers 110, 113; merger of Tanzania and Zanzibar 2, 226; territorial claims of Malawi 118; Uganda power struggle 66
Tawana 134
Temnes 21
Thari 140
Thom, Derrick 198-200, 205
Tidimane 138, 145
Tligrea Mustapha 41
Tlikire Limani 41
Tlokwa 134
Togo 1, 223, 227-9
Tol Ja'alo 160
Toposa 51
Touval, Saadia 8-10, 161
Tuaregs 198-9, 226
Tubu 2-3
Tukulor 2, 72
Turkana 51
Turkey 237
Tutsi 231

Ucibu, 92
Uganda: colonial period 54-8, 90-7; frontiers 54-8, 90, 92-4; independence 58, 97-100; power struggle 59, 63-7, 97; Sudanese civil war 60-7
Uighur 238
Ujuru 94-5
Umar, Sultan 35, 41

Undi Phiri 109
United Nations: referenda on boundaries in Togo and Cameroon 1-2, 45; Trusteeship Territories of the Cameroons 29
United States 230, 238-9, 244-5
Upper Volta 100
Uzbek 238

Versailles conference (1919) 37

Wade, Mason 239
Wal Wal incident 176, 178
Wandala *see* Mandara
Watch Tower Bible and Tract Society 117-18, 120
Waziri, Ibrahim 246
Wolof 2, 72, 196
World Council of Churches 65
Wula 3, 38

Yao 58, 100
Yoruba 2-4, 9, 20, 116, 196, 227
Yugoslavia 236, 240

Zaire 11, 92-4, 97-100
Zambia: colonial period 107, 110, 113-17; frontiers 107, 113-14; independence 117-24; rural development programme 105-6, 121-4, 245; territorial claims of Malawi 118
Zamir, General 63
Zande 2
Zanzibar *see* Tanzania
Zimba 107, 109
Zimbabwe 119
Zubairu, Emir 34
Zulus 106

NOTE ON THE CONTRIBUTORS

A.I. Asiwaju A Nigerian Ketu-Yoruba with a homeland partitioned by the Nigeria-Benin international boundary. Professor of History, University of Lagos. Author of several comparative studies of governmental policy and localised impact of borders, including *Western Yorubaland Under European Rule, 1889–1945: A Comparative Analysis of French and British Colonialism* (London: Longman, 1976) and *Borderlands Research: A Comparative Perspective*, Border Perspectives Monograph Series, Centre for Inter-American and Border Studies, University of Texas at El Paso, 1983.

Ade. Adefuye Associate Professor, Department of History, University of Lagos. His acquaintance with East African history derives from the research for his Ph. D. thesis for the University of Ibadan, 1973, 'Pre-Colonial History of the Palwo of Uganda', currently being produced as a book by Nok Publishers, Enugu.

Bawuro M. Barkindo Senior Lecturer, Department of History, Bayero University, Kano, Nigeria. Author of 'Origins and History of the Sultanate of Mandara to 1902' (unpublished Ph. D. thesis, Bayero University, Kano, 1980).

David Collins Formerly Lecturer, Department of Government, Ahmadu Bello University, Zaria. Author of 'Government and Groundnut Marketing in Rural Hausa Niger: The 1930s and 1970s in Magaria' (unpublished Ph. D. thesis, SAIS, Johns Hopkins University, 1974).

J.D. Hargreaves Burnett-Fletcher Professor of History, University of Aberdeen, Scotland. Author of several books including *Prelude to the Partition of West Africa* (Macmillan, 1963) and *West Africa Partitioned* (1974).

R.F. Morton Lecturer in History, University of Botswana, Gaborone. His case study in this volume derives from a larger study provisionally titled 'Of King and Royals: A political history of the Bakgatla ba Kgafela of the Bechuanaland Protectorate and the Transvaal, 1872–1945'.

S.H. Phiri Lecturer in Geography, University of Zambia, Lusaka. Author of 'Some Aspects of Spatial Interaction and Reaction to Governmental Policies in the Border Area: A study in the historical and political geography of rural development in the Zambia-Malawi and Zambia-Mozambique frontier zones (1870–1979)' (Unpublished Ph. D. thesis, University of Liverpool, 1980).

F.E. Renner Gambian Research Fellow at the Institute of African Studies, University of Ibadan, she is author of 'Inter-Group Relations and British Imperialism in Combo (Gambia), 1850–1902' (unpublished Ph. D. Thesis in History, University of Ibadan, 1983).

Said S. Samatar A Somali of the Ogaadeen region. Assistant Professor of History, Rutgers University, New Jersey, USA. Author of *Oral Poetry and Somali Nationalism: The Case of Sayid Mohammed Abdella Hassan* (Cambridge University Press, 1982).

Aidan Southall Professor of Anthropology, University of Wisconsin, USA. Author of several works on the Alur, including *Alur Society* (Cambridge and Oxford University Presses, 1956 and 1969).

Saadia Touval Professor of Political Science, University of Tel Aviv, Israel. Author of books including *The Boundary Politics of Independent Africa* (Harvard University Press, 1972).